Essentials of
Chemical
Dependency
Counseling

Essentials of
Chemical Dependency Counseling

Fourth Edition

Gary W. Lawson

Ann W. Lawson

Erik E. Schoen

pro·ed
An International Publisher
800-897-3202 Fax 800-397-7633
www.proedinc.com

© 2016, 2001 by PRO-ED, Inc.
1301 W. 25th St., Suite 300
Austin, TX 78705-4248
800-897-3202 Fax 800-397-7633

Library of Congress Cataloging-in-Publication Data

Lawson, Gary.
  Essentials of chemical dependency counseling/Gary W. Lawson, Ann W. Lawson,
Erik E. Schoen.—Fourth edition.
  pages cm
  Includes index.
  ISBN 978-1-4164-0691-4 (textbook)   ISBN 978-1-4164-0692-1 (e-book PDF)
    1. Drug abuse counseling—United States. 2. Alcoholism counseling—United States.
    I. Lawson, Ann W. II. Schoen, Erik E. III. Title.
HV5825.L38 2016
362.29'186—dc23

2014050328

Art Director: Jason Crosier
Designer: Tom de Lorenzo
This book is designed in Adobe Caslon and Myriad Pro.

Printed in the United States of America

3 4 5 6 7 8 9 10 11 12   31 30 29 28 27 26 25 24 23 22

Contents

Chapter 7
Family Counseling: Seeing the Family as the Client 175

Chapter 8
Dealing With Diversity 229

Introduction

We hope that those utilizing this textbook—whether students, instructors, or professionals—are as excited about studying and working in the field of chemical dependency as are we. Perhaps never before in the history of the field have we had so many technologies converging that both (a) support the understanding that substance abuse is something that must be treated and (b) give us an amazing toolbox filled with more proven and promising options for helping those who need it. Although there is still much to learn to be optimally effective in treating addictions, we are further now than when the last edition of our textbook came out nearly 15 years ago.

We have done our best with this new edition to keep the reader abreast of new developments. We've extensively updated our research and included new material and three new chapters to provide even more context for readers. It has been our intention to provide a textbook that is both comprehensive in its scope and detailed in its discussion of important concepts. If we have, at the same time, infused these pages with the optimistic regard that we have for the field of chemical dependency, then we have done what we set out to do.

All the best,

Gary W. Lawson

Ann W. Lawson

Erik E. Schoen

Acknowledgments

A book is never written by just the authors; it is a figment of our imagination that we think it so. With respect to the new edition of this textbook, I am indebted to many. First and foremost, to my wife, who never doubted and loved me through every word written. To Gary and Ann, for taking a chance and believing that I could contribute something meaningful. To Dr. Meri Shadley, at the University of Nevada, Reno, who saw something I hadn't recognized in myself and breathed life into it. To Bob Reid, whose perspective and gentle support led to this book's inception. To Shaun Griffin, whose words of encouragement to write a simple story many years ago marked the beginning of my putting pen to paper. To the professors of the Masters of Counseling program at Arizona State University, for a wonderful experience, wonderful memories, and most importantly, instilling the belief that the sacredness of the counseling space is worth protecting. To Dr. Catherine Hale, at the University of Puget Sound, for insisting I get on with the world. And lastly, to Doctors Scott Hendrickson and Lance McDonald—your examples of loving and caring therapy continue to live on.

Erik E. Schoen

CHAPTER 1

Becoming a Chemical Dependency Counselor

CHAPTER OBJECTIVES

* Learn the qualities and characteristics of good counselors
* Examine the qualities and characteristics of good chemical dependency counselors
* Examine the role of values in counseling
* Identify common issues faced by chemical dependency counselors
* Encourage the reader to examine his or her reasons for wanting to become a chemical dependency counselor and to identify potential areas of conflict or difficulty
* Give examples of how chemical dependency counselors can avoid burnout and stay healthy while helping others
* Understand the helpfulness of using person-first language

The first step for a person who wants to become a chemical dependency counselor to take is to thoroughly evaluate why he or she wants to enter the field. It is not a field with high earning potential. It is a difficult and demanding job. It is often hard to judge success, and appreciation and rewards are often few. It is a field in which failure can come as suddenly as the death of a client and in which counselor burnout is a frequent occurrence.

The outcome of this initial evaluation, for many people, is that they have a desire to help others and to do something meaningful in their work. Some people enter the field after making money in other professions that they found lacking in meaning. Others want to give back what they received in their own treatment and recovery. Many people who enter the field of chemical dependency counseling have some personal history with substance abuse or addiction. They may be recovering from their own personal struggles with chemical dependency or from the effects of living with someone with an addiction.

As the field has grown, it has accepted the idea that others (rather than just those with alcohol or drug problems) are affected by substance abuse, and that these affected others have a stake in the addictive process and its treatment. As a result, spouses, children, parents, other relatives, and even friends of persons with chemical dependency issues have become chemical dependency counselors. Individuals without personal histories of substance abuse also can have genuine commitments to helping others and can be particularly interested in chemical dependency. Some are mental health professionals, such as social workers, psychiatrists, nurses, psychologists, family therapists, and mental health counselors who are interested in specializing in chemical dependency treatment. Still others are people with no previous mental health training. American society, in general, has become more interested in alcohol and other drug abuse and is more aware now of the problems it poses for individuals and society as a whole. The drug wars, anti–drinking-and-driving campaigns, programs for the prevention of fetal alcohol syndrome, and drug prevention programs for children have all drawn attention to the problems. Hopefully, increased awareness will not lead to increased stigma for those with problems. Celebrities with addictions have attempted to remove some of this stigma of alcoholism treatment with public statements about their own alcoholism and drug abuse treatment. The debate still continues as to whether addiction should be punished (as with drunk driving) or treated, but at least the problem is reaching a wider audience and more people are being drawn into the field.

Counselors who have personal experience with their own recovery have advantages and disadvantages over counselors without this experience. Their own experience with addiction and with the recovery process enables them to empathize with their clients and to speak from experience. The disadvantages occur in the "blind spots" they developed in the process. Substance abuse is a multigenerational problem. It is very probable that a chemical dependency counselor has one or more family members with substance abuse problems or with problems that resulted from living with someone who had an addiction. He or she not only may have unresolved issues with these family members and/or spouses but also may have untreated interpersonal characteristics that can lead to projection of these dynamics onto their clients or excessive countertransference with some clients. For instance, if a counselor's mother was dependent upon alcohol, then he or she may be particularly harsh with women who have similar issues with alcohol because they share similar attitudes or behaviors with the counselor's mother. The counselor may be unaware of this if he or she has not addressed it in some way, such as through personal therapy. This can lead to a vicious rescue–revenge cycle. Counselors who believe that they entered the field to help others who are suffering but have not resolved their own pain around their personal experiences with those with addiction issues can easily get caught in this trap.

Family members try for years to get loved ones to stop drinking and using, often with little success. This can leave them angry and frustrated and feeling like failures. It is easy for a counselor to get caught up in the attempt to get his or her clients sober and thus take on too much responsibility for another person's sobriety. When this happens, the counselor is on the *rescue* side of the circle, with thoughts like, "I didn't save my mother, but I'll save this woman (i.e., substitute mother)." If she fails at treatment or relapses, the circle shifts to the *revenge* side, with all of the anger, hurt, and disappointment of the original failure. With some self-evaluation, however, people who have personal experiences with chemical dependency can become excellent counselors.

There is some debate in the field as to whether recovering or non-recovering counselors are better able to treat chemical dependency. One counselor shared the following:

> We had staff who were in recovery and staff that were not in recovery and that was talked about a lot. Well, it got to the point where the management decided that we were no longer allowed to disclose our recovery status because they felt it was almost becoming a distraction. . . . And it is a good mix to have people who are in recovery and have that perspective, but also people who know how to live without substances. . . . So they ended up just not even allowing staff to share anymore whether or not they were in recovery. (Oser, Biebel, Pullen, & Harp, 2011, p. 397)

There is some evidence, at least initially, that clients with chemical dependency issues see recovering counselors as having a more unconditional acceptance and level of regard—or possibly imagine that they do. When patients were asked to rate their counselors after the third counseling session, they rated recovering and generally older counselors higher than non-recovering and younger counselors (Lawson, 1982). Counselors, too, believe that it may be more important for a client early in recovery to have a counselor who has had his or her own experience with recovery (Oser et al., 2011).

The Characteristics of Good Counselors

There are three major areas of consideration for becoming a chemical dependency counselor: *knowledge and skills, experience,* and *knowledge of self.* This introductory chapter will consider the last area: the self as used in counseling. Although knowledge, skills, and experience are important for becoming a good counselor, people who are aware of their own values, belief systems, philosophies of life, strengths, weaknesses, and how they, as human beings, impact others will have valuable tools for the art of counseling. Self-knowledge is also helpful for preventing burnout.

For the last 60 years, the field of counseling has tried to identify the personal characteristics of counselors that make them successful. The earliest list of characteristics of good counselors included the following: being interested in people, patience, sensitivity to others, emotional stability, objectivity, respectfulness of facts, trustworthiness, and personal maturity (National Vocational Guidance Association, 1949). Later, the following characteristics were considered: belief in each individual, commitment to individual human values, alertness to the world, open-mindedness, understanding of self, and professional commitment (Association for Counselor Education and Supervision, 1964).

In trying to distinguish between effective and ineffective counselors, Combs (1986) summarized studies involving five different helping professions. He found that the differences involved what these helpers believed about empathy, self, human nature, and their own purposes. Effective counselors had positive beliefs about people and saw them as generally trustworthy, capable, dependable, and friendly. They also had a positive view of themselves and self-confidence in their ability as helpers.

Experience is another variable that distinguished effective and ineffective counselors. Regardless of the therapists' orientation, the therapeutic relationship created by experts in one school of therapy more closely resembled experts in other schools than non-experts in their own school (Fiedler, 1950). In many outcome studies comparing the effectiveness of treatment models, this has been true. Experience was more predictive of a good outcome in counseling than was the model of treatment used. Carl Rogers (1962) found that counselors with more experience showed more congruence, empathy, and unconditional positive regard than did less-experienced counselors, and more-experienced counselors were better able to communicate these conditions to their clients.

Other studies have looked at the relationship between counselor effectiveness and the personality of the counselor. Effective counselors were different from ineffective counselors in regard to self-concept, motivation, values, feelings about others, and perceptual organization. Further, effectiveness was associated with tolerance for ambiguity, understanding of the client, maturity, ability to maintain an appropriate emotional distance from the client, and ability to establish good social relationships with people who were not clients (Shertzer & Stone, 1980). In a study by Wicas and Mahan (1966), highly rated counselors were anxious, sensitive to the expectations of others and society, patient and non-aggressive in interpersonal relationships, and concerned about social progress, but always with appropriate self-control.

Corey (2012) created a list of 14 personal characteristics for counselors to strive for in becoming therapeutic persons and models of awareness and growth for their clients. Corey stated that counselors should see these characteristics as on a continuum, rather than all-or-nothing characteristics.

1. Effective counselors have an identity—They have a solid sense of self, values, life direction, and principles by which they live. They set goals and achieve them. They possess a certain sense of their own individuation and separateness but are also willing to evaluate their ideas, beliefs, and values.

2. Effective counselors respect and appreciate themselves—They have good self-esteem, can give and receive love, and feel a connectedness to others.

3. Effective counselors are open to change—They are willing to risk new behaviors for the potential of learning or experiencing something new that could make them a better person.

4. Effective counselors make choices that shape their lives—They learn from mistakes and make good choices based on continual self-evaluation.

5. Effective counselors are authentic, sincere, and honest—They do not play roles or hide behind masks. Their communication is straightforward and non-defensive.

6. Effective counselors have a sense of humor—They can laugh at themselves and their mistakes. This is extremely important in treating substance-abusing individuals and their families, who have often forgotten, or never knew, how to laugh and play with one another. This is also the best antidote for burnout.

7. Effective counselors make mistakes and are willing to admit them—In a field where attempts at perfectionism abound, being able to admit and learn from mistakes is important. They also become excellent role models for clients who hide their mistakes because of feelings of extreme guilt.

8. Effective counselors generally live in the present—Counselors who can live in the present are more available to their clients. Although the past may be interesting and useful in understanding their clients, they do not dwell on their own past or worry about the future.

9. Effective counselors appreciate the influence of culture—Counselors need to be aware of how their own cultures have affected them, and should also understand how culture, race, and gender create different experiences for others.

10. Effective counselors have a sincere interest in the welfare of others— Their work is based on a genuine respect for, and desire to help, others.

11. Effective counselors have well-developed interpersonal skills—They can clearly distinguish between the clients' issues and their own, and work within a collaborative relationship.

12. Effective counselors become deeply involved in their work and derive meaning from it—These counselors enjoy the process of helping others and look forward to going to work. They recognize the ego needs that are met by helping others, yet they know how to balance their lives and are not workaholics.

13. Effective counselors feel alive, and their choices are life oriented—They radiate a sense of possibility.

14. Effective counselors maintain healthy boundaries—Though there is a recognition and capacity for being fully present for clients, they are able to leave their clients' issues "at the office" and not have them intrude into their personal lives. They are able to say "no" when needed so that they can approach life from a place of balance.

The Characteristics of Good (Chemical Dependency) Counselors

Unlike counseling in general, there is not a 75-year body of research in the area of characteristics of good chemical dependency counselors. One study surveyed residents in an addictions treatment program (Roher, Thomas, & Yasenchak, 1992). The first group of residents was asked to list traits that they felt were the most positive and negative in a counselor. These traits were then compiled into a list of 62 positive and 55 negative traits and given to a second group of residents, who rated the top 10 positive and top 10 negative counselor traits. This second group of residents abused both alcohol (37) and other drugs (40). The most frequent drug abused was cocaine (36). The subjects ranged in age from 18 to over 43; they all had a history of previous treatment and legal involvement. The residents used colorful, profane, and imprecise language in their lists, and no attempt was made to define or change their words, in order to maintain the residents' true feelings.

The following are the ranked positive and negative addiction counselor traits (Roher et al., 1992, p. 728). The list of positive traits contains 11 items because there was a tie for 10th place.

Positive Traits	Negative Traits
1. understanding	1. asshole
2. concerned	2. can't relate
3. caring	3. dishonest
4. experienced	4. treat like children
5. honest	5. uneducated
6. certified	6. bullshitter
7. good listener	7. rude
8. streetwise	8. foul mouth
9. easy to talk to	9. show favorites
10. direct	10. unfair
11. open minded	

Another study interviewed 71 different clients to explore their experiences of helping relationships while in psychiatric care (Denhov & Topor, 2011). Not only were many of the positive traits identified above mentioned by many of the clients as being important but aslo three main categories and two core themes emerged as important components of a therapeutic relationship. The first category, "interpersonal continuity," referred to the benefit conferred in an established helping relationship through the process of developing trust and familiarity. "Emotional climate," the second category, referred to the quality of the therapeutic relationship—whether it felt safe and whether clients felt they were treated with respect. "Social interaction," the third category, referred to the importance of having someone whom the clients could talk to, someone who would listen and demonstrate a genuine interest in who they were and what they were facing.

Two themes emerged clearly across these three categories. The first was the importance to the therapeutic relationship of professionals having non-stigmatizing attitudes toward the clients with whom they worked: "The professionals behaved 'as if' their relationship with the [client] was one of equality, resembling more of a person-person than patient-professional relationship." The second was the perception that professionals were willing to do something extra, to go "above and beyond," to help their clients. This was reflected in an active interest in, a desire to help, and an interest in spending time with their clients.

It appears that clients want a well-balanced counselor who is able to be empathetic, genuinely caring, and non-judgmental. This is interesting in light of what were once the traditional confrontational addiction treatment approaches used to break down denial. A typical addiction counselor using the Synanon approach—which was developed for therapeutic communities that treated those with drug addictions—was attacking, aggressive, and intolerant. The research cited previously, however, raised the question of whether the type of counselor the residents preferred would be the best counselor for those with alcohol and drug issues.

A second study examined the characteristics of counselors who were successful in their treatment of clients in a methadone maintenance program (McLellan, Woody, Luborsky, & Goehl, 1988). Two counselors left the program at the same time, and their clients were randomly assigned to four program counselors with at least 8 years of experience each. The counselors' performance was measured by their clients' urinalysis results, methadone dosage, prescriptions for psychotropic medications, employment, and arrest rates. Two counselors were more successful than the other two. The most successful counselor significantly reduced the average methadone dose, number of medications, positive urine tests, and unemployment of his clients. In contrast, the least successful counselor significantly increased the average methadone dose, positive urine tests, and unemployment of her clients.

More training was associated with better counselor performance. The most successful counselors' charts reflected clearly formulated plans of rehabilitation that had been worked out in consultation with a treatment team and with the patients. Their charts were thorough and accurate and indicated that initial plans were generally followed and that progress was documented. Their patients followed program rules and were seen more frequently. These patients were also more frequently referred to program resources such as physicians, nurses, and employment counselors. They were also given help with day-to-day problems through letters to legal authorities and public assistance agencies, encouragement, support, and basic, sensible advice. The less successful counselors kept charts that were less organized in their treatment plans and contained far less detail in the treatment notes. They were less likely to enforce program rules and use referrals to program resources.

The most successful counselor's notes indicated an approach of "*anticipating problems* in the patient and *discussing strategies* to deal with the anticipated situations" (McLellan et al., p. 429). The rehabilitation thus focused on new behaviors and new ways of thinking. This approach is consistent with other studies of successful professional psychotherapists. McLellan et al. concluded the following:

> The consistent and professional patient management practices shown by better drug counselors . . . enabled the patients to stabilize their lives and to use the other social/medical services available to address their problems. These patient management techniques appear to be the hallmark of the effective, professional counselor and may be the minimal conditions necessary for continued patient improvement, even with the powerful effects of methadone. (p. 429)

The addition of psychotherapy techniques to these skills was the most effective approach to help patients reduce their need for mood-stabilizing medications, including methadone, psychotropic medications, and street drugs.

Several other studies (e.g., Campbell et al., 2013; Duryea & Calleja, 2013; Warren, Cisler, Weatherford, & Zakaria, 2013) have referenced the importance of advanced training and education for ensuring an openness to new treatments, having good counseling skills, keeping up with the increasing complexity and breadth of addiction, and managing increasingly complex interventions. Such training should be sure to include substance-abuse–specific education.

An attempt in April 1995 to describe effective chemical dependency counselors involved a meeting of the Task Force on the Characteristics of Effective Addictions Counselors, sponsored by the Center for Substance Abuse Treatment (CSAT) in Washington, DC. The purpose of this task force was to generate ideas concerning (a) characteristics of addictions counselors who work successfully with clients and (b) methods for assessing these counselor characteristics. The task force—made up of a diverse group of experts with experience in clinical practice, training, and research—came to consensus on the following requisite counselor characteristics:

- Good mental health and personal adjustment
- Investment in personal and professional growth
- Ability to create the core conditions of a therapeutic relationship, including empathy, respect, genuineness, and concreteness
- Therapeutic optimism
- Ability to be well organized
- Ability to recognize and maintain appropriate boundaries and balance between client and counselor needs
- Experience with recovery, personal growth, and change
- Understanding of professional and personal ethics and values
- Sense of humor
- Openness and a willingness to celebrate diversity

The task force was also asked to address the differences between generalist and addiction-specialized counselors. Task force members agreed on the changes generalist counselors should make to become addiction-specialized counselors:

- Develop appropriate conceptualizations of addiction.
- Examine the effects of alcohol and other drugs in their own lives and the lives of their families.
- Be prepared to deal with challenges around personal boundaries.
- View themselves as role models.
- Become familiar with 12-step work.
- Conceptualize the meaning of "powerlessness."
- Understand the effects of group processes on recovery.
- Learn to be direct if needed.

The task force suggested that addiction-specialized counselors working with broader issues would need to recognize the psychosocial context of addictions and learn to accept the use of medications when appropriate for specific clients. Also, they would need training in broader areas before moving beyond the counselor's scope of practice.

These characteristics are, of course, speculation based on task force members' experiences in the field. The next step is to study these counselor traits in order to answer several research questions: (1) Which characteristics predict positive outcomes in addicted patients? (2) Are there universally desirable counselor characteristics, or does the set of characteristics vary based on treatment setting (e.g., inpatient vs. outpatient), patient characteristics (e.g., mandated treatment vs. voluntary; alcohol abuse vs. other drug abuse), stage of patient's recovery (early, middle, late), or modality (e.g., group vs. individual treatment)? (3) Can these counselor characteristics be taught? (4) To what extent do counselor characteristics vs. knowledge and skill predict the outcome of treatment? (5) To what extent do counselor characteristics vs. counselor backgrounds (such as recovery or non-recovery status, level of training, experience level, professional vs. nonprofessional, addictions specialist vs. non-specialist) predict treatment outcome?

In a report to Congress on the nation's substance abuse and mental health workforce issues (Substance Abuse and Mental Health Services Administration [SAMHSA], 2013), examples of eight specific workforce objectives were provided in regard to what those in behavioral health fields should know:

1. **Prevention of substance abuse and mental illness**—This includes education about successful interventions—such as screening, brief intervention, and referral to treatment (SBIRT)—as well as about suicide prevention and prescription drug abuse.

2. **Trauma**—Practitioners will ideally be trained in trauma and trauma-related work.

3. **Military families**—Behavioral health practitioners who work with the military should understand its culture, as well as special risks that affect this population, including post-traumatic stress disorder (PTSD) and traumatic brain injury (TBI).

4. **Recovery support**—Practitioners should have an understanding of recovery-oriented practices and how to include peers in the current workforce for peer-run services.

5. **Health reform**—Practitioners will need to stay abreast of changes in health care delivery systems.

6. **Health information technology**—Practitioners will need to develop skills for working with electronic health records and for using health information technology.

7. **Data, outcomes, and quality**—Practitioners will need to develop an understanding of and ability to deliver evidence-based practices.

8. **Public awareness and support**—Practitioners will need ongoing access to the information needed to provide successful prevention, treatment, and recovery services.

Although there are no absolute answers about which personal characteristics are important for chemical dependency counselors, there are many commonalities in the lists of characteristics generated from various sources. The more counselors are aware of their personal strengths, personality characteristics, and value and belief systems, the more valuable they will be in the counseling process.

The Role of Values in Counseling

Part of the search of self in which counselors should engage is to examine their values and to see how these values are likely to affect their work as counselors. Since it is impossible to keep values and beliefs out of the counseling process, counselors need to be completely aware of their own biases and beliefs. They need to recognize when their clients have values and beliefs that have caused them harm or are self-destructive, and challenge them.

It would be difficult for a counselor to set goals and move in a positive direction if he or she had no values concerning what a mentally healthy individual, marriage, or family might be. A national survey of mental health professionals discovered that there is a set of values that is used by therapists to guide their work (Jensen & Bergin, 1988). Ten values were listed by these professionals as contributing to a positive, mentally healthy lifestyle. (Note how many overlap with the previous lists of what makes for an effective counselor and the characteristics of good counselors.)

1. Competent perception and expression of feelings
2. A sense of being a free and responsible agent
3. Management of stress
4. Self-awareness and growth
5. Commitment to marriage, family, and other relationships
6. Self-maintenance and physical fitness
7. Have orienting goals and meaningful purpose
8. Forgiveness
9. Regulated sexual fulfillment
10. Spirituality/religiosity

It is important to allow clients to come to their own decisions about whether they want to pursue these same goals. It is not ethically responsible for counselors to make decisions for their clients. It may be clear to a counselor that his or her client should leave her husband who has been abusive to her, but the client needs to come to that decision herself. More than 20 years ago, Corey (1991) listed areas that frequently cause dilemmas for counselors whose values clash with the beliefs, choices, and behaviors of their clients. These continue to be relevant today:

- **Religion**—Experience with religion helps form an important part of a person's value system. There are many possibilities for client–therapist disagreements in religious belief. The therapist may have strong fundamental Christian beliefs. This may cause difficulty in working with clients from other religions or other Christian denominations, or with clients with no religious belief. Therapists who are atheists may also have difficulty with clients whose lives are strongly connected with their religion and church. A third problem arises when the therapist is unfamiliar with a client's religion and how it impacts the client's life. The client's goals may be driven by his or her religious beliefs and be contrary to the therapist's values of mental health (e.g., self-sacrifice vs. independence).

- **Abortion**—Perhaps no other issue is as emotionally charged as abortion. People tend to become polarized and are unable to hear the opposite perspective. Counselors working with women, especially young women, will inevitably confront this issue in counseling. It may be difficult for a counselor who is strictly against abortion to be supportive of a woman who has chosen to end a pregnancy. It may be equally difficult for a counselor who emotionally supports women's rights to support a 14-year-old girl's decision to give birth to her second child when she has abandoned the first one. Counselors with strong opinions on this issue need to decide if they can help their clients struggle with difficult abortion decisions or if they need to refer these clients to someone else.

- **Alternative lifestyles**—Persons who are gay, lesbian, bisexual, queer, or transgendered are at high risk for chemical dependency. Counselors in this field may be treating individuals with substance use disorders who are gay or lesbian, and they need to be clear with themselves about their feelings and beliefs concerning these less mainstream and frequently marginalized sexual orientations. Counselors should examine whether they can support these clients' goals. Counselors with a high level of homophobia should deal with this issue in supervision and, if it is in the client's best interest, should consider referring their clients who are gay and lesbian to other counselors.

- **Extramarital sex**—A number of myths surround the issue of infidelity. Couples have varying contracts concerning what constitutes an affair—from flirting with someone of the opposite sex to agreeing that men can have affairs but women cannot. This is a significant issue in the treatment of chemical dependency. Extramarital sex is an area deserving attention and treatment in the recovery process, and counselors need to understand the damage that infidelity can inflict.

  There is a high posttreatment divorce rate among clients undergoing chemical dependency treatment. Many of these divorces could be avoided if infidelity were directly confronted in the recovery process. Counselors need to examine their values concerning extramarital sex and not be quick to blame these affairs on the disease process. It might be useful for a person with an addiction to be absolved of guilt for having an affair while using or drinking, but the spouse can still be left feeling hurt and angry.

- **Divergence of cultural values**—It would put clients in a dilemma if they had been raised to respect and follow their parents' wishes, but the counselor encourages them to make their own decisions and be independent because the counselor believes this is healthier. Counselors need to listen to clients who are from other cultures and ethnic backgrounds to learn what values they bring with them. It will be more productive to work with their values than against them, even if they are not values held by the counselor.

- **Drugs**—This may seem like an issue that would not be a problem for a chemical dependency counselor. However, certain counselors are willing to help those with alcohol problems but balk at treating users of illegal drugs because they are breaking the law. Another area of conflict may come when counselors take a dogmatic stance against any drug or alcohol use. How will these counselors treat family members who use these substances in a non-harmful way? And yet another potential area of conflict is the increasing legalization and medicalization of marijuana. The field of chemical dependency treatment is filled with high emotion around the use of alcohol and other drugs. Counselors should be careful that their emotions do not lead to value judgments that are harmful to their clients.

- **Right to die**—In the field of chemical dependency counseling, it is possible for counselors to have clients in advanced stages of AIDS or other terminal diseases, and/or who suffer from interminable excruciating pain. These clients may want to evaluate suicide as an option to prolonged suffering and expense. Counselors may have very strong convictions against any type of suicide or against needless suffering. There are also legal issues that should be considered in this situation.

- **Difficult/abrasive clients**—Counselors also have an ethical obligation to not treat clients for whom they have disdain. Clients may evince certain qualities or characteristics that counselors cannot get beyond, and certain problems they bring to counseling that make it difficult to work with them in a helpful way. Counselors should be aware of problems they are unable to work with or that cause difficulty for them personally. When this occurs, counselors should refer these clients to other counselors who can be more helpful.

Common Issues Faced by Chemical Dependency Counselors

Corey (2012) discussed issues he believes are areas of difficulty for beginning therapists. Many of these issues are the same problems or concerns that chemical dependency counselors have. This section will briefly address these issues in the context of chemical dependency counseling.

Dealing With Anxieties

Most beginning counselors and some experienced counselors experience anxiety about what to do in a counseling session. They have fears that their clients will not like them, they will look foolish, or their clients' problems will be too overwhelming. These anxieties are normal and even desired. They indicate a genuine concern to do well. Wicas and Mahan (1966) identified anxiety as a characteristic of an effective counselor. However, too much anxiety can paralyze counselors and leave them unable to access their knowledge, resources, and strengths. A good way to deal with these anxieties is in supervision.

Being Genuine and Using Self-Disclosure Appropriately

The use of self-disclosure in therapy is extremely powerful. "Therapy is a deeply intimate and vulnerable experience, requiring sensitivity to one's own state of being as well as to that of the other. It is the meeting of the deepest self of the therapist with the deepest self of the patient or client" (Satir, 1987, p. 17).

Beginning counselors may be concerned about what they should do or act like in a counseling session. This can lead to wearing masks or hiding behind a front of insincere caring. If counselors rely too much on what they read about theories of counseling or focus too much on technique, they will miss the human connection and intuitions created by being in the here and now. When counselors can trust that they have integrated their learning, and that it will come to them when they need it, they will be more available to their clients. Being genuine does not mean always being warm and caring. It means acknowledging what the counselor is really feeling at the time. Counselors' reactions to clients are probably similar to other people's reactions, and this is good information for clients. If a counselor is being bored or irritated by a client, that information may provide the client with good feedback about how he or she may be boring or irritating others.

Self-disclosure is a common concern with chemical dependency counselors who feel that they are role models for their clients. It can be very helpful for a client who is struggling with chemical dependency to know that his or her counselor has been through this same struggle and is doing well. The problem comes when self-disclosure is used too frequently or inappropriately. If the therapy session is dominated by the counselor's recovery story, it may be more therapeutic for the counselor than for the client. A good question for counselors to ask themselves in deciding whether self-disclosure would be appropriate is, "Who will benefit from this self-disclosure?" If the answer is anything other than "the client," then it is probably inappropriate. Issues that arise for the counselor during counseling sessions are best processed in supervision or in the counselor's own therapy.

Avoiding Perfectionism

It is easy for counselors to believe that they must be perfect: say the right thing, have the right feeling, know the right answer. These counselors have an exaggerated fear that making a mistake will ruin their clients' lives. These irrational thoughts will stifle the creative and intuitive process of counseling. In all honesty, it is often the mistakes that help counselors learn and grow. Just as it is true when learning to snow ski that the skier who never falls is neither learning nor improving, so it is with counseling. Taking risks in the therapy process can lead to greater changes for both the client and the counselor. Additionally, clients are rarely damaged by incorrect assumptions, statements, or reflections on the counselor's part. They will usually just correct the counselor and go on.

Counselors who are overly concerned with being perfect usually take too much responsibility for solving their clients' problems. This can be particularly problematic in the field of chemical dependency. Those with alcohol and drug issues are more than willing for someone else to take responsibility for their problems. The more difficult but more therapeutic process is to get those with alcohol and drug issues to take responsibility for their problems. Counselors who believe that they have the power to change anyone other than themselves will be repeatedly disappointed.

Being Honest About Limitations

Counselors who believe that they can handle any problems that their clients bring to therapy may be actually doing their clients a disservice. It is important for counselors to know their limitations and not practice beyond their competencies. This ethical issue is addressed in full in Chapter 2. Counselors should not enter into areas that they are not trained for, such as legal advice, medical advice, financial planning, or other areas where their clients might be having trouble. The clients should be referred to the proper professionals.

It is especially important for chemical dependency counselors who are working with clients who have a multitude of life problems that coexist with their chemical dependency—including mental illness, marital problems, parenting problems, and family dysfunction—to refer them to other professionals.

All of these problems do not need to be addressed by one counselor. A treatment team approach may be more helpful to these clients with multiple problems.

There are also issues that clients bring to therapy that may cause counselors to be uncomfortable or that challenge their values and beliefs. Counselors who can recognize their limitations and refer clients to other specialists will be seen by their clients as more honest, trustworthy, and competent than counselors who try to fake it in areas either that they are unfamiliar with or that cause them difficulties.

Avoiding Blurred Boundaries Between Counselor and Client

A problem similar to taking too much responsibility for client change is blurred boundaries. Counselors who lose themselves in the therapy process become overwhelmed with their clients' problems. They ruminate over their cases and even lose sleep worrying about their clients. They become overly empathetic with their clients and lose their ability to help them. Counselors are responsible for being completely present with their clients in the process of counseling, but they need to let clients take what they want from the interaction, and to make mistakes. Counselors who cannot forget about a client once therapy has been terminated are especially vulnerable to becoming lost in the helping process. They need to be able to allow their clients to take charge of their own lives so that the counselors can be completely present for their new clients.

Countertransference, or what occurs when a counselor's own needs or past unresolved personal issues and conflicts arise in the therapy process and become entangled with the client's issues, can lead to the blurring of boundaries. Countertransference is often unrecognized at the time by the counselor, but over-involvement with a client should be brought to supervision so the counselor can sort out what his or her personal issue might be that is contributing to the loss of self.

Chemical dependency counselors who are recovering also need to make a clear distinction between their professional clients and the 12-step group members that they sponsor. There are different expectations for a sponsor than for a professional counselor. Chapter 2 elaborates on this issue.

Developing a Sense of Humor

Counseling is a serious commitment to helping others, but counselors who take themselves too seriously are missing the healing tool of genuine laughter. Laughter can be used to avoid confronting painful issues or to cover up insecurities, but when a counselor can distinguish between humor that is distracting and humor that is helpful, he or she will have a powerful tool for genuine connection with others and an antidote for burnout.

Humor and fun are often sadly lacking in individuals and families in recovery. Families who associate the use of alcohol or other drugs with parties, celebrations, and having fun may believe that fun and laughter must be given up with the drugs. It is vitally important to help individuals and family members learn how to play, laugh, and have fun without abusing substances. Often these families have never experienced playing together, and they need help in discovering how to do this. Counselors should be good role models for how to laugh and play appropriately.

Establishing Realistic Goals

In working with chemical dependency recovery, counselors need to be realistic about what can be accomplished in the time they are often given by external sources, such as insurance companies, managed care organizations, program guidelines, and financial limitations. It is also unrealistic to set goals such as re-establishing intimacy with a spouse early in recovery, when neither the pain and disappointment of the spouse nor more practical issues of how the recovering person will be integrated back into the daily running of the home and parenting have been addressed. Counselors who can see therapy and personal recovery as a long-term process are able to see that their encounter with the client is just one small part of this journey. They are not responsible for fixing all of the problems that they might see with their clients. In setting goals with their clients, it may be useful to contract for short-term goals and discuss how these will lead to long-term goals.

Declining to Give Advice

It is very tempting for counselors to give advice to their clients. This may even seem necessary in chemical dependency counseling, where education and role modeling are part of the process. Education and advice-giving, however, are two different things. Education involves giving out information to clients in a way that allows them to use whatever is useful to them (e.g., teaching the 12 steps of Alcoholics Anonymous [A.A.], recommending books to read). Advice-giving is a no-win proposition for a counselor. If a counselor advises his or her client to do something and it turns out to be poor advice, the client loses respect for the counselor. If it is useful advice, the client does not get to experience the rewards because he or she did not think of it, or feels inadequate for not thinking of it. This erodes the client's self-confidence.

There may be times when advice-giving is necessary (e.g., if the client is a danger to himself or herself or is in a state of confusion), but it should not be overused. The counselor's job is to empower clients to discover their own solutions and not to deprive them of the freedom to choose their own paths. This is also liberating for the counselor.

Avoiding Burnout

Burnout is common in chemical dependency counseling, but it is not inevitable. Counselors with a good burnout-prevention program can be free of this problem throughout their careers. Burnout is caused by a combination of personal, interpersonal, and organizational dynamics. These can include monotonous work with little reward, work that is not meaningful and does not provide a sense of accomplishment, too much pressure and too many deadlines, non-supportive supervisors, a lack of supportive colleagues, too many work hours, difficult clients who drop out of therapy or have been mandated to therapy, a lack of opportunities for learning and growth, poor boundaries between self and clients, unrealistic expectations of self and clients, rigid family roles and unhealthy family dynamics replayed in the workplace, ensnarement in the rescue–revenge cycle, and personal and family problems that spill over into work.

Therapists play an important role in their own burnout when they attribute the stress of their job and the problems they are having entirely to outside sources. They believe that they are victims, with no responsibility for their burnout and no control over it. The first step that they need to take in combating burnout is to take responsibility for what they can control: their behavior; their thoughts; and their feelings concerning their work, the work environment, and their co-workers, administrators, and supervisors. The second step is that they need to take action and change what they can.

The best way to battle burnout is to follow a burnout-prevention plan that might include the following:

- Continually evaluate whether you are learning and growing.
- Take regular vacations and do not take work along.
- Compartmentalize—be present in the activity you are doing. Don't worry about your client while you are on a date.
- Take mental health days off from work.
- Do not give your home phone number to your clients except in special circumstances.
- Turn off your cell phone when possible.
- Regularly attend workshops and trainings to update your skills and get new energy.
- Take coffee and lunch breaks, but have juice instead of coffee.
- Follow an exercise program.
- Practice good nutrition.
- Read new books and journals in your field.
- Read novels and go to movies, concerts, and art museums.

- Learn to say "no" when you have reached your limits.
- Find a group of colleagues whom you admire and begin a supervision group if you are not getting regular supervision.
- Balance your time between personal growth, recovery and development, intimate or marital relationships, family connections, recreation, and work.
- Travel.
- Develop hobbies.
- Take a break from email and texting.
- Relax.
- Sleep.
- Find time for spiritual growth.
- Support your professional organizations.
- Volunteer.
- Seek professional help for your problems.
- Keep a journal.
- Be open to new experiences and the potential for learning about others.
- Find ways to be creative in all areas of your life, including your job.
- Save all of the thank-you notes and special messages that you receive from clients and co-workers and read them regularly.
- Buy flowers for your office.

This is by no means an exhaustive list. What is important is for counselors to create a plan that works for them.

Becoming a chemical dependency counselor is a process. It is a process that requires continual self-examination and self-care. The field of chemical dependency can be addictive itself, and it holds great rewards and personal satisfaction for those who pursue it.

A Note on Terminology Used Throughout This Book

The words *addict* and *alcoholic* are used to refer generally to individuals who have difficulties with drugs and alcohol, respectively. These are imprecise terms that mean different things to different people. For some, they are an important tool for sobriety, as in the tradition of 12-step programs, where participants admit their powerlessness over their substances of choice (i.e., "My name is Chuck and I'm an alcoholic"). For others, they are used as a pejorative because of the negative connotations with which they are associated (i.e., "You are nothing but a no-good addict").

It is important that clinicians not unconsciously "label" their clients as alcoholics, addicts, junkies, and so forth. Labels can become self-fulfilling prophecies and increase the likelihood that a clinician will see a "disease" before seeing the person. Which of the following descriptions better maintains a client's dignity and helps the counselor to conceptualize the client?

"Ralph is an alcoholic."

OR

"Ralph is a 50-year-old unemployed truck driver
who is struggling with alcohol dependency."

Person-first language evolved from the disability movement and is an empowering way of acknowledging the person first and the disability second. Instead of "Amy is autistic," person-first language would propose "Amy has autism." Thus, it is better to say that counselors assist people with substance use disorders than to say they assist alcoholics and addicts. (For more information on person-first language, see the Disability Is Natural website: http://www .disabilityisnatural.com/explore/people-first-language.)

This is neither an idle exercise nor political correctness run amok. Kelly and Westerhoff (2010) found that treatment professionals were more likely to assign blame and be punitive when person-first language was not used. Language shapes perception, and counselors' perceptions will profoundly affect their work with their clients. Therefore, this edition of *Essentials of Chemical Dependency Counseling* has included the use of person-first language.

When working with certain clients, though, a counselor would best be served by asking the clients how they would prefer to refer to themselves. Some will reject the negative cultural baggage associated with such terms and readily identify as "alcoholics" and "addicts" as a way of empowering both themselves and their sobriety. A good counselor will use whatever terminology clients are most comfortable with.

Finally, from a purely diagnostic perspective, the terms *alcoholic* and *addict* are undefined and unhelpful. The closest one will come to finding such terms in the *Diagnostic and Statistical Manual of Mental Disorders—Fifth Edition* (DSM-5; American Psychiatric Association, 2013) is the rather clinical-sounding term *substance use disorder*. The DSM is the go-to diagnostic tool for chemical dependency counselors. Whether clients meet the criteria listed in that manual will determine whether and where they will be eligible to receive needed services. This will be addressed in more depth in Chapter 5.

Suggested Reading

Baldwin, M. (Ed.). (2013). *The use of self in therapy* (3rd ed.). New York: Taylor and Francis.

Bugental, J. F. T. (1987). *The art of the psychotherapist.* New York: Norton.

Center for Substance Abuse Treatment. (1995, April). *Task force on the characteristics of effective addictions counselors.* Washington, DC: Author.

Corey, G., & Corey, M. (2010). *I never knew I had a choice* (3rd ed.). Pacific Grove, CA: Brooks/Cole.

Corey, G., & Corey, M. (2011). *Becoming a helper* (6th ed.). Pacific Grove, CA: Brooks/Cole.

Kilburg, R. R., Nathan, P. E., & Thoreson, R. W. (Eds.). (1986). *Professionals in distress: Issues, syndromes, and solutions in psychology.* Washington, DC: American Psychological Association.

Kottler, J. A. (2010). *On becoming a therapist* (4th ed.). San Francisco: Jossey-Bass.

Kottler, J. A., & Blau, D. (1989). *The imperfect therapist: Learning from failure in therapeutic practice.* San Francisco: Jossey-Bass.

References

American Psychiatric Association. (2013). *Diagnostic and statistical manual of mental disorders* (5th ed.). Arlington, VA: Author.

Association for Counselor Education and Supervision. (1964). The counselor: Professional preparation and role. *Personnel and Guidance Journal, 42,* 536–541.

Campbell, B. K., Buti, A., Fussell, H. E., Srikanth, P., McCarty, D., & Guydish, J. R. (2013). Therapist predictors of treatment delivery fidelity in a community-based trial of 12-step facilitation. *American Journal of Drug and Alcohol Abuse, 39*(5), 304–311.

Combs, A. W. (1986). What makes a good helper? A person-centered approach. *Person-Centered Review, 1,* 51–61.

Corey, G. (1991). *Theory and practice of counseling and psychotherapy* (4th ed.). Pacific Grove, CA: Brooks/Cole.

Corey, G. (2012). *Theory and practice of counseling and psychotherapy* (9th ed.). Pacific Grove, CA: Brooks/Cole.

Denhov, A., & Topor, A. (2011). The components of helping relationships with professionals in psychiatry: Users' perspective. *International Journal of Social Psychiatry, 58*(14), 417–424.

Duryea, D. G., & Calleja, N. G. (2013). Current expectations and existing deficits among addiction specialists. *Alcoholism Treatment Quarterly, 31*(2), 254–269.

Fiedler, F. E. (1950). A comparison of therapeutic relationships in psychoanalytical, nondirective and adlerian therapy. *Journal of Consulting Psychology, 14,* 436–445.

Jensen, J. P., & Bergin, A. E. (1988). Mental health values of professional therapists: A national interdisciplinary survey. *Professional Psychology: Research and Practice, 14,* 290–297.

Kelly, J. F., & Westerhoff, C. M. (2010). Does it matter how we refer to individuals with substance-related conditions? A randomized study of two commonly used terms. *International Journal of Drug Policy, 21*(3), 202–207.

Lawson, G. (1982). Relation of counselor traits to evaluation of the counseling relationship of alcoholics. *Journal of Studies on Alcohol, 43*(7), 834–838.

McLellan, A. T., Woody, G. W., Luborsky, L., & Goehl, L. (1988). Is the counselor an "active ingredient" in substance abuse rehabilitation? An examination of treatment success among four counselors. *The Journal of Nervous and Mental Disease, 176*(7), 423–430.

National Vocational Guidance Association. (1949). *Counselor preparation.* Washington, DC: Author.

Oser, C. B. , Biebel, E. P., Pullen, E. L., & Harp, K. L. H. (2011). The influence of rural and urban substance abuse treatment counselor characteristics on client outcomes. *Journal of Social Service Research, 37*(4), 390–402.

Ridley, C., Mollen, D., & Kelly, S. (2011). Counseling competence application and implications of a model. *The Counseling Psychologist, 39*(6), 865–886.

Rogers, C. (1962). The interpersonal relationship: The core of guidance. *Harvard Educational Review, 32,* 416–429.

Roher, G. E., Thomas, M., & Yasenchak, M. S. (1992). Client perception of the ideal addictions counselor. *The International Journal of Addictions, 27*(6), 727–733.

Satir, V. (1987). The therapist story. In M. Baldwin (Ed.), *The use of self in therapy* (3rd ed., pp. 19–25). New York: Taylor and Francis.

Shertzer, B., & Stone, S. (1980). *Fundamentals of counseling* (3rd ed.). Boston: Houghton Mifflin.

Substance Abuse and Mental Health Services Administration. (2013). *Report to Congress on the nation's substance abuse and mental health workforce issues.* Retrieved from http://store.samhsa.gov/shin/content//PEP13-RTC-BHWORK/PEP13-RTC-BHWORK.pdf

Warren, J., Cisler, A., Weatherford, J., & Zakaria, N. S. (2013). Assessing the impact of addictions education on attitudes of students: A preliminary investigation. *Journal of Alcohol & Drug Education, 57*(3), 18.

Wicas, E. A., & Mahan, T. W. (1966). Characteristics of counselors rated effective by supervisors and peers. *Counselor Education and Supervision, 6,* 50–56.

CHAPTER 2

Ethical and Legal Issues in Chemical Dependency Counseling

CHAPTER OBJECTIVES

- Examine ethical issues in chemical dependency counseling
- Provide a model of ethical decision making
- Examine laws governing the practice of chemical dependency counseling
- Provide examples of difficult ethical and legal questions for discussion and evaluation

As the field of chemical dependency counseling becomes recognized as a professional discipline, self-regulation in the area of the ethical behavior of counselors is imperative. It appears that substance abuse counselors have the highest number of ethical violations, more than tripling that of other human services providers in social work, professional counseling, and marriage and family therapy. Even more alarming is the rate of ethical violations, with one study finding that 1 out of every 200 licensed chemical dependency counselors committed an ethical violation, which is a rate five times higher than that of the next closest human services provider (Gallagher, 2009).

One insurer that provided liability coverage to several counseling disciplines, including drug and alcohol counselors, found that over the course of 10 years most frequent allegation was of inappropriate sexual/romantic relationships with the client, the client's spouse, or another family member, accounting for 39.7% of all closed claims (Health Providers Service Organization [HPSO], 2014). Issues related to counselors failing to practice within their scopes of competence were the second most frequent, accounting for 15.8% of all closed claims. The third-most-frequent (12.7%) were those involving the "sharing of confidential/private client information without appropriate authorization" (HPSO, 2014). Other claims included "counseling plan failed to provide reasonable likelihood of success," "improper acceptance/requesting of fees from clients," "failure to provide client with pre-termination counseling referral recommendations," and "use of inaccurate, lapsed or deceptive license or certifications" (HPSO, 2014). Similar findings for ranking of ethical transgressions have found issues regarding improper dual relationships, including sexual relationships; lack of competence; misrepresentation; and breaches of confidentiality to be the top-rated complaints to state licensing boards (Neukrug, Millikin, & Walden, 2001).

Such statistics may explain why a panel of counseling-ethics professionals identified the top current issue facing counselors to be ensuring that such counselors practice ethically (Herlihy & Dufrene, 2011). Indeed, there was concern expressed that the profession "is not doing a good job of helping counselors understand ethical behavior and demonstrate it in practice and that most violations are not addressed by licensing boards, professional associations, or colleagues" (Herlihy & Dufrene, 2011, p. 18).

This chapter addresses ethical and legal concerns and dilemmas that arise in the field. There will not be absolute answers, which may be troubling to the reader. "An ethical dilemma is a situation in which a person is faced with one or more ethical obligations that cannot be fulfilled at the same time" (Geppert & Roberts, 2008, p. 12). Ethics often deal with principles that "ought to" govern human behavior in gray areas. Ethical principles are guidelines for professionals that are designed to protect consumers and the profession.

These principles are usually developed by professional organizations that certify the professionals who belong to them. Currently, many state and national organizations have taken on the task of certifying chemical dependency counselors. The certification process tests counselors on their knowledge of the law and ethics that govern chemical dependency counseling, in order to safeguard patients and to let the public know that this is a profession that will scrutinize its members and take a self-regulatory stance. Certification also lets the consumer know that the clinician has basic competence in the field of chemical dependency treatment. These codes of ethics also provide some protection if the counselor is sued for malpractice (Corey, Corey, & Haynes, 2015; HPSO, 2014).

This chapter is divided into two parts: ethical issues in chemical dependency counseling and legal issues. Some issues, such as confidentiality, will fall into both ethical and legal categories and are addressed in codes of ethics, as well as being governed by federal law in the treatment of chemical dependency.

Ethical Considerations in Chemical Dependency Counseling

The field of chemical dependency counseling is unique in that it is multi-disciplinary. Treatment is provided by physicians, psychiatrists, psychologists, social workers, clergy, family therapists, and chemical dependency counselors, often working as a team. Each of these disciplines has one or more professional organizations and a code of ethics that set guidelines for providing services and treatment. Professionals in each of these areas need to be familiar with their professional code of ethics. This chapter will not attempt to cover all of these guidelines but will address the special issues that arise in the treatment of substance abuse. Probably the most recent code of ethics to be adopted is by the National Association of Alcoholism and Drug Abuse Counselors (NAADAC) in 2011. While this is not the only national organization attempting to certify chemical dependency counselors, its code of ethics does address issues that are important for any professional who treats chemical dependency. It is not the intent of this chapter to promote NAADAC as the only professional organization for chemical dependency counselors nor to support its positions; but they have a code of ethics that addresses issues pertinent to chemical dependency counseling. Their code is used as an example. Other organizations may have different codes, but they will probably address similar ethical issues.

NAADAC established a code of ethical standards for alcoholism and drug abuse counselors that is divided into 10 major areas. Astute readers will note that though the 10 major headings appear to be independent areas of focus, there is considerable overlap and reiteration of major points and themes throughout. In the interest of brevity, we will not elaborate on all of the major areas of ethical considerations detailed below. Instead, certain elements are amplified and explored in the interest of furthering understanding and critical thought. It is recommended that readers read this chapter with a copy of NAADAC's code of ethics available for consultation and comparison. It is available to download free from NAADAC's website at http://www.naadac.org/code-of-ethics.

The following is included in NAADAC's (2011) introduction to its ethical code:

> NAADAC recognizes that its members and certified counselors live and work in many diverse communities. NAADAC has established a set of ethical best practices that apply to universal ethical deliberation. Further, NAADAC recognizes and encourages the notion that personal and professional ethics cannot be dealt with as separate domains. NAADAC members, addiction professionals and/or licensed/certified treatment providers (subsequently referred to as addiction professionals) recognize that the ability to do well is based on an underlying concern for the well-being of others. This concern emerges from recognition that we are all stakeholders in each other's lives—the well-being of each is intimately bound to the well-being of all; that when the happiness of some is purchased by the unhappiness of others, the stage is set for the misery of all. Addiction professionals must act in such a way that they would have no embarrassment if their behavior became a matter of public knowledge and would have no difficulty defending their actions before any competent authority.

Major Heading I: The Counseling Relationship

The first major heading speaks to the importance of the counseling relationship and exhorts addiction professionals to "safeguard the integrity of the counseling relationship and to ensure that the client is provided with services that are most beneficial" (NAADAC, 2011). What is notable about this first major heading is that, most likely for its focus on dual relationships, it was responsible for the highest percentage—at 58.7%—of closed claims of all the major heading areas for legal settlements related to ethical violations (HPSO, 2014). While the code of ethics used for analysis in this retrospective study was the American Counseling Association's, the ACA's major heading "The Counseling Relationship" contains many of the same elements of NAADAC's first major heading (American Counseling Association, 2014).

There are five specific standards contained under this major heading.

Standard #1: Client Welfare

The first standard clearly states that the client's welfare must come first. Treatment decisions, termination of treatment, referrals, and so forth must all be made in the client's best interest. On the one hand, this may seem like common sense and may seem to be easy to follow, but it may not seem so clear when terminating or referring a client means lost income, especially if the program is struggling to keep its doors open. On the other hand, one must recognize that premature termination can be just as damaging. If a counselor cannot work with a particular client due to value conflicts, personality conflicts, or excessive countertransference, he or she must refer the client to someone who *can* work with him or her. This also brings up the issue of currently using or relapsing clients. Is it in the best interest of clients to refuse to work with them if they are not sober or have had a relapse? Should those who've relapsed be kicked out of treatment programs when they are being treated for an illness that has loss of control as part of its definition? These clients are certainly in need of treatment, but are counselors enabling them to continue using if they continue to see them or refer them to someone who will work with them? If the use or relapse is confronted, it can be helpful in focusing on the main goal of therapy. Counselors need to examine their own belief systems concerning this treatment dilemma while keeping the principle of client welfare in mind.

This guideline for protecting client welfare can be useful to the counselor in making difficult decisions. At times, however, it can be difficult to determine who the client is. For example, a supervisor who discovers that a counselor has been unethical during a supervision session may have a conflict between reporting this behavior to the program director and/or certification board and believing that the counselor revealed this to the supervisor in confidence. This confusion can be eliminated if the counselor who is in supervision understands from the beginning that the supervisor is being paid by the program director to make certain that good and ethical treatment is being provided to program clients and that confidentiality will not be guaranteed to the supervisees. The first standard (taken from NAADAC, 2011) specifically highlights the following four elements in regard to client welfare:

1. The addiction professional understands and supports actions that will assist clients to a better quality of life, greater freedom, and true independence.

2. The addiction professional will support clients in accomplishing what they can readily do for themselves. Likewise, the addiction professional will not insist on pursuing treatment goals without incorporating what the client perceives as good and necessary.

3. The addiction professional understands that suffering is unique to a specific individual and not of some generalized or abstract suffering, such as might be found in the understanding of the disorder. On that basis, the action taken to relieve suffering must be uniquely suited to the suffering individual and not simply some universal prescription.

4. Services will be provided without regard to the compensation provided by the client or by a third party and shall render equally appropriate services to individuals whether they are paying a reduced fee or a full fee or are waived from fees.

Standard #2: Client Self-Determination

This standard is one of the lengthiest in NAADAC's (2011) code of ethics. In a nutshell, it is concerned with ensuring that counselors respect "the fundamental human right of all individuals to self-determination and to make decisions that they consider in their own best interest." The first 4 elements (of 10) directly address the importance of what is known as "informed consent." This involves informing clients, or guardians of minor clients, about the potential impact of their participation in therapy that is recorded, observed, or used for demonstrations and how this information will be used. In working with minors, the parents or legal guardians have the legal right to privileged communication and can request information about the therapy of a minor. Usually, it is in the best interests of the minor client for the parents or guardians to agree to the confidentiality of the therapy content. The remaining six elements of client self-determination further discuss client welfare while underlining best practices in which counselors are expected to engage.

Standard #3: Dual Relationships

The third standard ensures that addiction professionals will provide services only in a professional setting and that the goal of treatment "is to nurture and support the development of a relationship of equals of individuals to ensure protection and fairness of all parties." It spends considerable amount of space describing factors that would interfere with the counselor–client relationship or compromise the client or the therapy process. These problems have been referred to as "dual relationships" and are discouraged because of the erosion that takes place in the therapy process, as well as the potential harm to the client. Dual relationships exist whenever a counselor has any other relationship with a person who is a client, and such relationships become unethical if there is any harm or potential for harm to the client or benefit to the counselor (Corey, 2012).

Dual-relationship dilemmas are very common, particularly in the treatment of chemical dependency, and include sexual exploitation of clients, which is considered to be one of the most harmful, yet most common, violations (Herlihy & Dufresne, 2011; HPSO, 2014; Neukrug et al., 2001). Sexual contact with clients and former clients is not only strongly discouraged by ethical codes but also a felony in some states, punishable by prison terms, considerable fines, and multimillion-dollar settlements (Corey, 1991; HPSO, 2014). Professional liability insurance has limited coverage pertaining to sexual intimacies or has eliminated the coverage altogether.

So why is sexual contact still so prevalent? The potential for sexual exploitation has several roots. First, whether counselors believe it or not, clients see them as being in a powerful position. Clients have come for help and have surrendered to the counselor, which puts them in a humble one-down position. The power of the helping relationship also comes from the transference that occurs when clients work out their past issues with others through the counselor. Clients are often confused about strong feelings that occur in this process. Countertransference on the part of counselors may also cloud the picture; they may be flattered by the client's adoration. The counseling process is a very intimate encounter between two people that may remind both parties of sexually intimate relationships they have had. Counselors may hold the false belief that the way to show total acceptance of their clients is to validate them through sexual behavior, and they delude themselves that this would somehow be therapeutic.

Another problem is counselors who need to be validated by their clients in order to boost their self-esteem. In addition, women who suffer from substance abuse frequently have a history of sexual molestation, rape, and/or promiscuous sexual behavior coupled with a false belief that they can only get love or acceptance through sex. Counselors who are having sexual thoughts about their clients should seek help through supervision and consultation with other counselors and/or refer the clients to another therapist.

Yet another complicating factor lies with the number of counselors in recovery from alcohol and drug problems who are employed in the treatment field. One study found that as many as 70% of one state's licensed chemical dependency counselors self-identified as recovering (Gallagher, 2010). While this makes sense clinically, it sets up unique circumstances that encourage dual relationships. Often these counselors come from families with alcohol and drug issues where personal boundaries were not recognized, and they may have problems setting appropriate professional boundaries with their clients. Alcoholics Anonymous and other self-help group attendance can also present some difficult situations. Recovering counselors may find themselves sharing group attendance with their current or former clients (Gallagher, 2010). This leads to the dilemma of whether to be in the counselor role, which may block their own self-disclosure, or the A.A. member role, which puts them in a peer relationship that may feel awkward for the counselor and the client. If members of the meeting go for coffee afterward, this could create another uncomfortable situation. Differentiating the role of sponsor and counselor can be very difficult, as well. It seems important to keep these two roles separated since a counselor usually has firmer boundaries concerning client contact and accessibility. Counselors who try to be both counselor and sponsor to their clients may find themselves with very little time for the rest of their life and family, which is not good role modeling. Treatment programs that encourage counselors to sponsor their clients should reconsider this policy. Bissell and Royce (1987) offer two measures to avoid some of these traps: (1) Schedule no appointments with former patients (although it may be awkward to try to avoid casual contact) and (2) avoid situations in which the counselor would be alone with former patients, particularly those of the opposite sex. Some additional advice and common sense in differentiating between being a chemical dependency professional and an A.A. member can be found in the *A.A. Guidelines for Members Employed in the Alcoholism Field* (Alcoholics Anonymous World Services, 2013).

In a field where hugging is viewed as a therapeutic tool, problems surface when counselors become confused about when touching in therapy is appropriate and when it might be construed as erotic or sexual contact. Some clients may even *expect* to be hugged by their therapists. This can be a tricky issue, especially between opposite-sex clients and counselors. It is possible that non-erotic contact in therapy can be beneficial in some circumstances. There is agreement about what elements should be present in order for touch to be viewed as therapeutic: (1) The decision to touch a client should have a strong and defensible rationale; (2) the decision to touch should be for the benefit of the client, not the counselor; (3) use of touch should be considered from a larger theoretical framework, and its use should be carefully considered; (4) the counselor should clearly ask for permission from the client before touching him or her, and let the client know that it is acceptable to decline; (5) a strong therapeutic alliance should already be in place for anything more than a handshake; and (6) the counselor should consider and monitor the client's reactions to being touched (Bonitz, 2008). Other things should be considered, such as age differences, gender differences, the client's history, transference and countertransference issues, and the meaning of physical contact to the client (Bonitz, 2008). For instance, clients with a history of incest or sexual molestation may be frightened by the contact, and clients with certain cultural backgrounds may be uncomfortable with physical closeness. Counselors also need to evaluate their part in the interchange. If it is not genuine or authentic, the client will become suspicious or not trust the sincerity of the contact or the counselor. Timing is also important. Clients need to be allowed to experience and struggle with their pain, not be rescued from it by touch that serves a counselor's need over that of the client. A good test of when to touch is to evaluate whose needs are really being met by the touching. A second question should be, "What meaning will this have for the client?" (Bonitz, 2008).

A further caution in the third standard is against treating family members, close associates, or intimate friends. Doing so is a certain formula for failure. Family members and friends have a certain image of the counselor that blocks their ability to see him or her in the counseling role. They will also be more guarded and less able to share difficult issues with someone with whom they will be interacting in other situations. Usually counselors cannot counsel members of their own families because they are too close to them, and their own needs interlock with the other family members' problems (Corey, 1991). A good solution is to go with family members to another therapist.

The question of whether counselors can accept gifts from clients or other treatment organizations is also addressed. It may seem that one could avoid any situation that could be interpreted as a conflict of interest by adopting a policy that no gifts can be accepted, but what about the client who is just learning pro-social behaviors and brings an appropriate gift with which to demonstrate her appreciation? Refusing such a gift could possibly irreparably harm the client, which the code of ethics specifically prohibits. On the other hand, surely a counselor could accept something as simple as a soda from a client without any ramifications? This, too, depends on the therapeutic context. If the soda was offered while the client was in group counseling, could the client's gesture be perceived by other group members as an attempt to curry favor? If the counselor in this context accepted the drink, would the group members wonder if the counselor was "going easy" on the client?

Chemical dependency counselors in training sometimes have difficulty in knowing how to distinguish between training and therapy. Teachers of these students need to be careful not to get themselves into dual relationships with their students by allowing didactic training to become personal therapy. Teachers need to keep themselves in the role of trainer and must not slide into the role of therapist to their students. Students will often identify themselves as in recovery and may use their own experiences in class discussions. Although this is appropriate, it can easily slide over into therapy when it becomes evident that there are unresolved problems and the students are fishing for advice or treatment. Role-playing in class is also a potential problem area if the students are not really role-playing but are using their own current problems. It would be appropriate for teachers who are faced with these situations to discreetly refer these students for personal therapy.

As well, the third standard is concerned with the exploitation of patients newly in the recovery process. It may be tempting for public relations departments and hospital administrators to solicit newly released patients for donations or to entice them to go public with their substance abuse treatment. For patients new to recovery, this can be an exploitation of their mental state for the profit of the treatment program. Although it is true that celebrities and famous people who speak openly about their addictions and recovery help reduce social stigma and encourage others to seek help, if this disclosure is done prematurely without proper thought to all of its ramifications for the client's family and career, it may constitute exploitation of the client to benefit the treatment center (Bissell & Royce, 1987). This can be avoided by allowing plenty of time, even two years after discharge from the program, for the client to be clear about his or her desire to donate money to the program or be a public figure that promotes it.

With the advent of social media sites on the internet, there are additional questions to consider, such as whether to "friend" a client on Facebook. Doing so may erode the distinction between "professional" and "friend." Furthermore, a client may be able to learn details about a counselor's life, including those that may be unsavory or untherapeutic. Because new and evolving technology will continue to present unforeseen complications and ethical quandaries, it is advised that counselors proceed cautiously. Be careful, for example, of what is shared online since even text messages and email can be reposted and forwarded to unintended recipients. Better, perhaps, to have a policy informing clients that they will not be "friended" by counselors as way to preserve a healthy therapeutic alliance. Assume that information shared online is unencrypted, and never share confidential information unless absolutely certain that proper safeguards are in place (Shallcross, 2011).

Counselors, too, are advised to strongly consider not Googling their clients online for the boundary-blurring that may result between the personal and professional (Meyers, 2014). It is advisable that in order to limit confusion and liability, counselors explicitly inform clients that they will not utilize social media in communications. To not do so may open a counselor to legal liability in the case of a client who tweets, for example, that he or she is feeling suicidal, because timely intervention would be unlikely unless the counselor is checking social media networks every 5 to 10 minutes (Meyers, 2014).

Standard #4: Group Standards

Since so much of the counseling that clients with substance use disorders receive is in the context of group counseling, the fourth standard under the Counseling Relationship heading pertains to making sure that such services are provided in ways that ensure the "physical, emotional, spiritual, and psychological health and safety" of their clients. Specifically:

1. Confidentiality standards are established for each counseling group by involving the addiction professional and the clients in setting confidentiality guidelines.

2. To the extent possible, addiction professionals will match clients to a group in which other clients have similar needs and goals.

The first element speaks to the importance of clients having an active role in co-creating the confidentiality guidelines that pertain to their particular counseling group(s). This is important not only to help clients develop a sense of responsibility and buy-in for the group process by giving them shared ownership, but also for ensuring that clients understand fully the limits of such confidentiality. The counselor, for example, cannot guarantee absolute confidentiality in a group counseling setting as it is possible that while the counselor will maintain confidentiality, group members may intentionally or unintentionally break confidentiality. A good counselor will discuss with a group how all of its members can ensure the highest standard of confidentiality.

As well, the second element reminds counselors to make sure that clients are only placed in groups that are appropriate to their needs and goals. As but one example, a woman with a history of sexual abuse and a distrust of men might better be served by being placed in a group of other women with similar needs and goals.

Standard #5: Preventing Harm

This standard speaks to the words first penned by Hippocrates: "First, do no harm." This means that addictions professionals will refrain from utilizing any counseling techniques or interactions that have the potential to produce any sort of harm, whether "physical, psychological, financial, legal, or spiritual." It goes on to indicate that counselors will readily admit and seek to repair or ameliorate any harm they may have caused, except where doing so might cause greater harm. Addiction professionals should, at all times, strive to honor the humanity of their clients and seek to work collaboratively with them.

Major Heading II: Evaluation, Assessment, and Interpretation of Client Data

There are 12 specific standards contained in the second major NAADAC heading. Since so many addictions professionals utilize assessment instruments as part of the counseling process, these 12 standards ensure, in a nutshell, that the assessment process "promotes the well-being of individuals clients or groups" and utilizes only those assessment instruments verified by research and for which they have received education and training. Clinicians who utilize assessment instruments remember that the information from such tools is to be considered in the larger context of the clients' clinical presentation. Addictions professionals also understand the limitations of such instruments and recognize and mitigate, when possible, the harmful effects of social stigmatization related to many diagnoses.

Major Heading III: Confidentiality/ Privileged Communication and Privacy

The third major NAADAC heading concerns the ethical principle of confidentiality. In the field of chemical dependency counseling, this is also covered by a federal law, which will be reviewed in the next section of this chapter. Confidentiality is extremely important in providing any type of counseling or mental health treatment. It is linked to the concept of trust and sets the counseling session apart from a talk with a good friend. Confidentiality is simply defined as the guarantee that a counselor gives a client that what is said in a counseling session will be held in confidence and the client's privacy will be protected by the counselor. People need to believe that they will not be discriminated against or suffer from social stigma associated with therapy and addiction and that harm will not come to them from the act of seeking treatment. Otherwise, they will resist pursuing the help they need. Confidentiality protects the client from unauthorized disclosures without their consent. There are, however, certain exceptions to confidentiality that will be discussed in the legal section regarding exceptions to privileged communications—the legal version of confidentiality. At 17.5% of all closed claims regarding allegations of unethical behavior, this major heading accounted for the third highest percentage (HPSO, 2014).

The ethical principle of confidentiality is presented by NAADAC in the following way:

> Addiction professionals shall provide information to clients regarding confidentiality and any reasons for releasing information in adherence with confidentiality laws. When providing services to families, couples or groups, the limits and exceptions to confidentiality must be reviewed and a written document describing confidentiality must be provided to each person. Once private information is obtained by the addiction professional, standards of confidentiality apply. Confidential information is disclosed when appropriate with valid consent from a client or

guardian. Every effort is made to protect the confidentiality of client information, except in very specific cases or situations.

This guideline gives some practical ways that the principle of confidentiality is applied in clinical work. For instance, counselors must get permission to video- or audiotape a counseling session or to allow others to observe the session. Records are also covered by confidentiality and, therefore, should not be left on a desk or even in an unlocked file cabinet. A temptation for counselors who are working in a treatment program that requires many forms and unending recording and paperwork is to take the records home with them to complete. Since this allows the records to be accessed by others not working for the treatment program or sets up the possibility of the loss of records, this practice can lead to unauthorized disclosures and cause great concern for program administrators and licensing boards.

Major Heading IV: Professional Responsibility

After the first major heading regarding the importance of the counseling relationship, the fourth major heading is the lengthiest and most involved because of the breadth of each of its standards. It essentially outlines a variety of best practices that an addiction professional should utilize in order to maintain the highest standards of the services provided. More than 20%, the second-highest total, of one insurer's closed claims were due to cases falling into this major heading (HPSO, 2014).

Standard #1: Counselor Attributes

One of the primary themes that this NAADAC standard is addressing is competence. Competence is difficult to define, but it is an important issue in the treatment of chemical dependency counseling. The counselor can err in both directions: assuming too much or too little. When chemical dependency treatment specialists assume that they can provide everything their clients need to achieve recovery from addiction, they are taking on an enormous task and doing their clients a disservice by isolating them from professionals with unique skills that can aid in their client's recovery and treatment. Addiction is usually clustered with a number of other problems such as legal difficulties, financial problems, lack of job skills, medical problems, sexual dysfunction, marital problems, parenting problems, lack of transportation, educational deficits, inadequate social skills, and general living difficulties. The more of these problems that are attacked in the course of treatment, the better the potential for success. Rarely is one counselor trained to deal with this myriad of problems. What often interferes with professional cross-referral and networking treatment is the concept of patient ownership. The attitude "My client is fragile, and I am the only one who understands and my client might relapse in having to deal with these problems" perpetuates this notion of ownership. Not only does this give clients a perception that they are weak but it also is a false assumption because these are the very problems, if left unsolved, that may set up a relapse. When therapists make the assumption that addiction is the only problem, we run the risk of not meeting our clients' needs (Berton, 2014). Removing the drug from the client or the family system does not relieve all the other associated problems. Working with other professionals also gives the chemical dependency counselor an opportunity to teach them about the treatment of addiction and get them interested in the field. In fact, Alcoholics Anonymous (A.A.) has a strong tradition of cooperation without affiliation with professionals (Alcoholics Anonymous World Services, 1986).

The issue of competency becomes even more of a problem if the chemical dependency counselor decides to set up a private practice. This is a very different situation than working as part of a treatment team in a hospital or treatment clinic. Private practice requires far more competence and professional training. Counselors working on their own may find themselves adequately trained in the early part of treatment, where stabilization of sobriety is the goal. Different skills are required, however, as treatment moves into the related problems, for instance, sexual dysfunction, marital instability, and intergenerational family dysfunction. Although substance abuse is seen as a family problem, simply knowing the problems it causes to families and the "role behaviors" that family members play in the systems maintenance of the problem does not give the counselor the skills to treat these problems. Family therapy is a unique field of training with its own professional organizations and licensure processes. Too often the family members have been used by untrained counselors to confront patients about their behavior, while the therapeutic needs of the family as a whole and the problems of the individual members have been sacrificed. Counselors with an interest in treating families should get training and supervision in family systems therapy. The combination of chemical dependency counseling skills and family therapy training can be a very powerful tool in treating substance abuse, which is often an intergenerational family problem affecting many members (Lawson & Lawson, 2004).

Equally problematic is the giving of medical and/or legal advice by a counselor struggling with these co-existing problems of their clients. "As an addictions counselor, you are not qualified to diagnose your clients nor to prescribe them medications" (Berton, 2014, p. 21). The advice to discontinue prescriptions is often supported by the notion that "a drug is a drug is a drug." Certainly there are prescription drugs that are abused by those with addictions, including amphetamines, barbiturates, opiates, and benzodiazepines (e.g., Valium, Xanax), and that abuse needs to be addressed in treatment. There are, however, prescription drugs that are needed to treat medical problems like heart conditions, diabetes, seizure disorders, and mental illnesses (e.g., manic-depression) that are not mood altering in the sense of the psychotropic medications that are abused. In the past, the interest in patients with co-occurring disorders was often fueled by insurance practices of refusing hospital admission for substance abuse diagnoses and approving admission for a mental health diagnosis, such as depression. This practice led some counselors to question whether patients with dual diagnoses were not just exhibiting symptoms caused by their alcohol and drug use. Again, this is an area of diagnosis that should be reserved for a medical professional. Psychotropic medications such as antidepressants and lithium can be lifesaving for properly diagnosed patients with co-existing mental illnesses. All non-medical therapists working in the substance abuse field should develop a referral relationship with a psychiatrist, a pharmacologist, or an addictionologist who has special training in the field and is aware of the dangers of certain medications for alcoholics and drug addicts, yet can prescribe and monitor medications that may make recovery more successful and improve the quality of life for the patients.

As the legal system becomes more involved in incarcerating and treating prisoners who have committed drug-related crimes, employment opportunities are opening for chemical dependency counselors both in prison settings and in outpatient clinics. Many drug-addicted clients are on probation, which necessitates interfacing with the probation officers, writing reports, and doing urinalyses. The counselor's ignorance of the legal implications of certain actions and court procedures can be of harm to the client and can reflect poorly on the profession. Special training and consultation may be necessary to operate effectively with these legal agencies. It may be very tempting to spare a client a return to prison because of a relapse that the counselor believes is part of the recovery process, while probation sees it as a violation of parole. Collaboration with probation officers and close monitoring of the consequences of alcohol and other drug use can be very effective in the counseling process. The counselor who works with clients who have committed crimes while intoxicated or under the influence of drugs needs to reconcile society's need for protection from offenders with his or her own belief system concerning the disease process of addiction. If counselors believe that one's breaking the law under the influence is part of the disease process, they will be more vulnerable to enabling their clients or protecting their clients from the consequences of their behavior.

One of the main ways of avoiding practicing beyond competence is the recognition of the need for ongoing training and learning. Counselors who recognize their deficiencies are much less likely to make poor ethical decisions than counselors who assume that once certified, they know all there is to know. Continuing education requirements are a part of many certification processes.

Standard #2: Legal and Ethical Standards

This standard is concerned with protecting the consumer and the association. A chief reason for certification is to let consumers of chemical dependency treatment know that this counselor has certain basic skills in the treatment of chemical dependency. Counselors who claim to be psychologists, family therapists, social workers, marriage counselors, or sex therapists but do not have the appropriate training and certification or license are misrepresenting their qualifications to the public. Similarly, if members of NAADAC make claims about their certification that go beyond what the certification means, they are not being truthful to the public.

This standard also addresses the inflated or false claims of treatment success made by treatment programs to entice clients to enter their programs. Success rates are difficult to measure. Programs that eliminate people who do not finish the program, for any reason, from their statistics and that measure success at the end of an inpatient stay are not being honest with the public about the lifelong nature of recovery or about their treatment failures. This kind of advertising of inflated success rates or quick cures also misleads the public about the nature and treatment of addictions.

Another section of the standard deals with services, products, or books that are sold by chemical dependency counselors. With the significant amount of pain and suffering that addiction causes to millions of people in this society, the opportunity to make money at their expense is always present. People looking for quick fixes and miracle cures can be easy targets for those who are more interested in making money than in helping people. Not only do these unprofessional practices mislead the public, but also they tarnish the field of chemical dependency treatment.

Other sections of the standard discuss the importance of not practicing while impaired and seeking the necessary support for oneself or for a colleague if needed, maintaining a support system outside of work to ensure continued professional growth and an ability to work as a professional if in recovery, and making sure to have the necessary liability and other insurance policies in place to protect both the counselor and the agency.

Standard #3: Records and Data
Not much elaboration is needed in regard to the third standard, which is a collection of best practices as they relate to the maintenance and handling of client records. They are important because a higher quality of treatment delivery is associated with utilizing these practices, and confidentiality is better protected.

Standard #4: Interprofessional Relationships
Professional therapists need to respect other professions and cooperate with them in the provision of services. It is not useful to the client or the profession of chemical dependency counseling to discredit another therapist or type of therapy. It may be tempting for chemical dependency counselors to believe their clients when they tell stories of their previous therapists' incompetence,

and it may make them feel more competent themselves. However, counselors need to remember that they will soon be these clients' previous counselors, and may have stories told about them to the next therapist. Clients may do this for several reasons: (1) They may truly have had a bad experience; (2) they may be trying to flatter the counselor to gain a more powerful position in therapy, or they may be trying to triangulate in a third person to reduce the intensity of the dyadic interaction; or (3) they are warning their counselor that the previous therapist made them uncomfortable and they do not want that to happen again. Unfortunately, the previous therapist may have been right on target and the client was not ready to change. The best policy is to obtain a signed release of information from the client to talk directly to any previous therapists. Client reports are often clouded by subjectivity. A special area of concern, however, is when a client reports that he or she was sexually exploited by a previous therapist. Counselors cannot report this information to certification boards, licensing boards, or the authorities without a signed consent from the client, who should be informed of the consequences of this disclosure for the previous therapist, as well as the possibility of an investigation. Another way to handle this information is to have the client make the report to the proper professional agencies and authorities.

This standard also discourages counselors from treating clients who are already in treatment with another professional. When clients are in therapy with more than one person, they can become very confused if they are working on different, and sometimes even conflicting, goals. Another danger arises when the client believes that just attending therapy sessions is sufficient. This idea leads to "therapist-hopping," triangulating one therapist against the other, and generally not taking responsibility for change.

Major Heading V: Working in a Culturally Diverse World

The fifth major heading is really one of non-discrimination and states that alcoholism and drug abuse counselors "do not discriminate either in their professional or personal lives against other persons with respect to race, ethnicity, national origin, color, gender, sexual orientation, veteran status, gender identity or expression, age, marital status, political beliefs, religion, immigration status and mental or physical challenges." Although this seems fairly straightforward, it brings up questions about how to avoid discrimination in making decisions of who will receive service when there is a waiting list. Should a program assess people on the waiting list to see who would benefit most from services or who needs treatment the most? Should they take paying clients before those who cannot pay? Where should limited resources go? Does non-discrimination mean that treatment programs must be able to serve all populations equally well when these populations have unique needs and often speak different languages? Is it equally unethical for treatment programs designed for heterosexual adults to advertise to and treat those who are gay, lesbian, queer, or transgendered without making modifications to their treatment design? What about the hiring practices of treatment centers that will only hire people who are recovering from their own addiction? Although non-discrimination is a good principle to guide decisions, it can be difficult to implement in all situations.

As well, the code of ethics reminds addictions professionals that "accommodations are made as needed for clients who are physically, mentally, educationally challenged or are experiencing emotional difficulties or speak a different language than the clinician." This would include adapting treatment for those who have what the code of ethics refers to as "invisible disabilities," such as a hearing impairment, learning disability, brain injury, chronic illness, and so forth.

Major Heading VI: Workplace Standards

The sixth major heading addresses the issue of competence and the need for ongoing education and training. The issue of competence means not only having competence in the treatment of chemical dependency but also not treating problems outside of this competence, nor allowing others without this competence to treat alcohol and other drug abuse. This may be quite difficult, however, if the chemical dependency counselor is working with a treatment team and the hierarchy of command or politics of the situation makes it difficult to confront a person in an authority position. The other problem is knowing what constitutes a qualified person and who should make this determination. The NAADAC code of ethics indicates in the first major heading regarding the counseling relationship that incompetence should be reported to the appropriate certifying authority, who would then investigate whether the therapist is practicing beyond his or her training and qualifications. This does imply that there is a body of knowledge that is unique to the treatment of chemical dependency, and therapists who are qualified to treat other types of problems may not be qualified simply by virtue of their training in psychology, mental health, or social work to provide chemical dependency treatment.

This sixth major heading also requires counselors to seek help for themselves and their colleagues if they become impaired in any way. This is especially important for the substance abuse field, in which the possibility of relapse is a reality. This presents a dilemma for the treatment center that believes that relapses are to be expected in the recovery process, yet denies credibility as a role model to the chemical dependency counselor who relapses. Should the counselor be fired? What will happen to his or her patients, and what will they be told? Is it fair to keep the counselor employed and treating patients with more sobriety than he or she has? Must this counselor achieve the required number of years (usually two or three) of sobriety before he or she can counsel others? Even more of a problem is the chemical dependency counselor with no previous addiction who develops a problem while working in the field. Even non-recovering counselors with no problems with alcohol have created concern in others when they have been seen drinking alcoholic beverages in public. Should non-recovering chemical dependency counselors drink any alcohol in public? These are questions that need to be considered by treatment programs in making personnel policy, and chemical dependency counselors need to be made aware of such policies concerning impaired therapists before they begin their jobs. Although this will not lead to easy solutions, it is a place to begin.

Finally, the sixth major heading provides guidance as it relates to maintaining a confidential and safe working/therapeutic environment.

Major Heading VII: Supervision and Consultation

The focus of the seventh major heading is to provide direction and guidance for both those providing supervision and those seeking supervision. In one study of over 200 clinical supervisors, researchers concluded that "many supervisors come to their role through promotions that occur because of seniority." Furthermore,

> on the basis of our findings, it is important to consider how beginning supervisors, especially those new in recovery, can receive a significant level of supervision training to offset any deficits that may be present of how they came to their supervisory position. (Culbreth & Cooper, 2008)

In large part because the quality of supervision in the chemical dependency field has primarily been poor and unstructured, the guidelines contained in the seventh major heading are provided so that both supervisors and supervisees have a structure and aspirational definition of what good supervision looks like:

> Addiction professionals who supervise others accept the obligation to facilitate further professional development of these individuals by providing accurate and current information, timely evaluations and constructive consultation. Counseling supervisors are aware of the power differential in their relationships with supervisees and take precautions to maintain ethical standards. In relationships with students, employees and supervisees he/she strives to develop full creative potential and mature independent functioning.

The standard then lists specific element of good supervision, including training and education specific to supervision; maintenance of ethical standards in relating to supervisees and a prohibition against romantic or sexual relationships between supervisors and supervisees; informed consent; and regularly scheduled supervision meetings that are subsequently documented.

Major Heading VIII: Resolving Ethical Issues

The eighth major heading provides very specific and concrete directions to addiction professionals in regard to resolving their ethical responsibilities:

> The addiction professional shall behave in accordance with legal, ethical and moral standards for his or her work. To this end, professionals will attempt to resolve ethical dilemmas with direct and open communication among all parties involved and seek supervision and/or consultation as appropriate.

Major Heading IX: Communication and Published Works

The ninth major heading concerns giving credit to authors and contributors to published materials, such as books, articles, and pamphlets. It is not an acceptable practice to plagiarize another person's writings or to present another person's theories, techniques, or work as the author's original ideas. Written credit must be given to the originator of the work.

Major Heading X: Policy and Political Involvement

This heading describes the social obligations the chemical dependency counselor. Alcoholism and other drug abuse is not just a medical and psychological problem; it is very much a social concern. The public atmosphere concerning this problem has shifted over the course of U.S. history. Alcoholism has been seen as a moral weakness, something to be attacked through prohibition; an untreatable problem; a disease; an illness; a psychiatric disorder; a family problem; and a social menace when it involves drunk driving. When alcoholism is coupled with other drugs of abuse, it is also seen as criminal behavior. Public hysteria over illegal drug abuse puts an additional stigma on drug addicts, but also allows for public and institutional denial of the huge problems that legal drugs cause society, the tremendous health care costs associated with them, and the lack of treatment and prevention programs. Public policy is often determined by society's view of the problem at the time, and money is shifted from one attempted solution to another. There is usually the debate between treating the person with the disease versus incarcerating the lawbreaker. This major heading summarizes the need for the alcoholism and drug abuse counselor to have a wider view of chemical dependency treatment that also takes in his or her responsibility to social policy as such:

> The addiction professional is strongly encouraged, to the best of his/her ability, to actively engage the legislative processes,

educational institutions and the general public to change public policy and legislation to make possible opportunities and choice of service for all human beings of any ethnic or social background whose lives are impaired by alcoholism and drug abuse.

Ethical Decision Making

Although the above principles can be used as guidelines in making difficult ethical decisions, a process for weighing both sides of ethical dilemmas to arrive at the best possible response is useful. Corey, Corey, Corey, and Callanan (2014) proposed eight steps to apply when working through an ethical dilemma.

1. Identify the problem or dilemma—Is a problem an ethical problem; a problem of a legal, moral, professional, or clinical nature; or some blend of these? "Because most ethical dilemmas are complex, it is useful to look at the problem from many perspectives" (Corey et al., 2014). In each of these steps, it is important to think about how to include the client.

2. Identify the potential issues involved—In this step, it is important to decide which issues are critical and which may be discarded. The critical issues then need to be evaluated in light of the rights, responsibilities, and welfare of all involved, especially the client. Cultural considerations are important to assess. Again, it is important to think about how best to involve the client, if possible.

3. Review the relevant ethics codes—Consult all that could apply in a given situation; for example, a social worker working in the schools who is also licensed as a substance abuse counselor may have at least three different codes to consult. It is important to document this process in this step (as well as all of the others) and to note divergence from particular standards and why. It may be helpful to seek guidance from national professional organizations, which often provide telephonic support on ethical and legal issues to members.

4. Know the applicable laws and regulations—Just as it is important to know the relevant ethical codes, one must also stay current with workplace rules and regulations, as well as relevant state and federal laws. This can be particularly helpful in circumstances concerning whether to violate confidentiality as it relates to abuse of vulnerable populations (e.g., child and elder abuse), threat of harm to self or others, rights of parents, documentation, and more.

5. Obtain consultation—Consulting with others helps a person to consider his or her situation objectively. This can involve consulting with one's supervisor(s) and trusted colleagues, who will help to consider all angles. It may be necessary and advisable to seek legal counsel. The question trying to be answered is, What would a "reasonable person" would do in this situation? In other words, what are the accepted professional standards of care for resolving the dilemma?

6. Consider possible and probable courses of action—This will involve generating a wide variety of possible options for resolving the situation, as well as the ethical and legal implications for each possible solution. Again, think about how best to involve your client when possible, as well as continue consulting with other professionals. As always, document, document, document.

7. Enumerate the consequences of various decisions—For each possible strategy for resolving the ethical dilemma, consider the ramifications not only for the client but also for family members and colleagues who may be affected, as well as for you as the counselor. Weigh all the pros and cons, including emotional, psychological, social, material, and more. Consider, too, that there will likely be multiple outcomes, as opposed to one, in resolving any ethical dilemma. Continue to brainstorm, to consult with colleagues and supervisors, and to involve the client.

8. Choose what appears to be the best course of action—After carefully considering all of the information acquired from the previous steps, make the best decision you can. Consider how your solution fits with the relevant codes of ethics, as well as the client's values and experiences. Keep in mind that adjustments may be necessary as circumstances develop. Keep the client involved in the process, and thoroughly document this and all previous steps taken to adequately reach resolution.

The Laws Governing the Practice of Chemical Dependency Counseling

The laws that govern the practice of chemical dependency counseling can be federal, state, county, or city laws. Because of the overlap between counseling and law enforcement in the field of addictions, due to the illegality of some drug use and the criminal behavior associated with addiction, it is important for chemical dependency counselors to be aware of the laws concerning treatment and the rights of their clients. It is also important in protecting themselves against malpractice suits. It will be helpful for counselors to be familiar with the different types of laws, five of which are provided below:

1. Common Law—This is the fundamental law of the United States. Common Law is derived from the tradition and usage of English Common Law. Many of our laws and practices are based in beliefs and attitudes of our

English ancestors. Many of these ideas, however, have been modified by current legislation.

2. Statutory Law—These laws are passed by a state legislature or Congress and signed into law. These statutes are binding only in the jurisdiction where they are passed. For example, a law passed in California cannot be applied in Oregon, but federal laws are in effect in all 50 states.

3. Administrative or Regulatory Law—These are laws made by agencies that have areas of specialized knowledge. Congress or state governments can determine areas that are beyond the scope of the average legislator and delegate rule-making authority to agencies that can then regulate specific areas.

4. Case Law or Court Decisions—These are a body of legal decisions and interpretations of laws. Courts consider statutes and legislative history and decide what the legislators meant when they wrote the law. These decisions are based on federal as well as state laws and determine which law has precedence over the other if they are in conflict. Many legal decisions are taken collectively to make rules for deciding other cases. There are various levels of courts that make these decisions. Trial courts determine the facts and make decisions. The losing party in the trial may appeal to an appellate court that decides whether the law was properly applied. A higher court is usually available for further appeals.

5. Criminal vs. Civil Law—Civil law pertains to offenses to individuals, while criminal law applies to offenses to society. Criminal violations result in punishment to the perpetrator, and civil violations result in compensation to the victim.

Confidentiality—A Federal Law

The field of chemical dependency counseling is unique in that it is governed by a federal regulation concerning the confidentiality of alcohol and drug abuse patient records. The two relevant statutes are the Comprehensive Alcohol Abuse and Alcoholism Prevention, Treatment and Rehabilitation Act of 1970 (42 U.S.C. 290 dd-3) and the Drug Abuse Office and Treatment Act of 1972 (21 U.S.C. 290 ee-3). These statutes require that records of alcohol and drug abuse patients be kept confidential, except in certain limited circumstances. Additional regulations are in the Code of Federal Regulations (42 C.F.R. Part 2).

The purpose of these statutes and regulations was to increase the likelihood that people with alcohol and other drug addictions would seek treatment because their privacy would be protected. These regulations apply only to programs that specialize in alcohol or drug abuse diagnosis, treatment, or referral and that are provided with any direct or indirect federal assistance in the form of federal grants, contracts, revenue-sharing funds, or state block grants. These programs must give patients written notice of these confidentiality regulations upon admission or as soon as they exhibit rational communication. Although the regulations use the term *records,* they refer to any information, whether it is recorded or not, that relates to a patient that was received or acquired in connection with alcohol or drug abuse treatment or prevention. These records can include general medical records if the patient is identified as an alcohol or drug abuser, pretreatment records, records of former patients in aftercare or follow-up treatment, and oral records.

As per 42 C.F.R. Part 2, this information may be disclosed only with patient consent in certain circumstances and without patient consent in even more limited circumstances. Some disclosures can be made that do not come under this regulation. These are communications that do not identify the patient, like reporting statistics to a central registry; communications within a treatment program among counselors, supervisors, administrators, and other personnel; and communications between a program and a qualified service organization with whom the program has an agreement to share information. It is generally accepted that disclosures concerning clients' treatments are permitted between treatment team members who fall under the umbrella of the treatment program. There are also occasions where patients have been released by the criminal justice system and granted probation or parole on the condition that they enter a treatment program. The patient, in this circumstance, may consent to unrestricted communication between the program and the court and between the parole board and probation officers. This does not include communication to the police.

As noted, disclosures of information other than the above exceptions can only be made with the patient's consent, with a court order and subpoena, or in other limited situations as defined in 42 C.F.R. Part 2 as described below. If the disclosure is made with the patient's consent, it must be written consent that includes the following nine discrete items of information:

1. Name of the program or person that is to make the disclosure
2. Name of the program or person to which the disclosure is to be made
3. Name of the patient
4. Purpose or need for the disclosure
5. Extent and nature of the information
6. Signature of the patient and signature of a parent or guardian or other authorized person in the case of a minor, incompetent, or deceased person
7. Date signed

8. Statement to the effect that consent can be revoked at any time

9. Date, event, or condition when the consent will expire

Disclosures can be made without patient consent in the case of medical emergencies; for research, audit, or evaluation purposes; when authorized by court order and accompanying subpoena; or when the patient poses a threat to a third party or has committed an extremely serious crime, including causing serious bodily harm, child abuse, or neglect. In medical emergency cases, the information about the patient must be conveyed directly to medical personnel and not the police or others. Although the regulations permit disclosures for conducting scientific research, management audits, financial audits, or program evaluations, programs must ensure that an independent group of three or more individuals has reviewed the research protocol and determined that the patients' rights would be protected and that the benefits of the research would outweigh any possible risk to the patients' confidentiality.

Clients should be warned through the informed consent process that all insurance companies, and especially managed care and health maintenance organizations (HMOs), require a great deal of information from the providers to process claims. Frequently, confidential materials are handled by non-professional personnel who are not bound by ethics codes. This information includes history, diagnosis, treatment plans, progress toward goals, and information they request to determine "medical necessity." Counselors are often caught in a bind between overestimating the seriousness of the problems so insurance will pay for treatment and underreporting the seriousness to protect the client from unauthorized use of the materials.

The federal regulations were revised in 1987 to allow for additional situations for disclosure without obtaining a court order. One change allowed information to be provided to law enforcement officers without restriction regarding the individual's name, address, and patient status, and the last known whereabouts of patients who had committed crimes on program premises or against program personnel. Another important change concerned the reporting of child abuse. Because of the narrow limitations of disclosures without consent, this federal regulation was in conflict with state mandatory child abuse reporting laws. The statute has been changed to exempt child abuse and neglect reporting from the confidentiality requirements. The confidentiality protection, however, still applies if the state authorities attempt to gain the original records for related civil or criminal prosecution.

A further change in the regulation allows patients to access their own records. The regulation does not grant patients a right of access, but it states that the regulation will not interfere with any right of access to records that patients may have under state laws or court decisions.

It is important, too, to consider how the Health Insurance Portability and Accountability Act (HIPAA), passed in 1996, impacts a counselor's obligation in regard to confidentiality. HIPAA set strict guidelines for when "protected health information" can and cannot be shared and advises limiting uses and disclosures only to the "minimum necessary." Because the standards around confidentiality are somewhat looser, in that HIPAA allows for "protected health information" to be shared without the patient's written consent (which 42 C.F.R Part 2 would not allow), it is important for counselors to be clear on which standard applies. When both standards are applicable, the counselor is legally required to follow that which is more restrictive.

This discussion of the statutes and regulations governing patient confidentiality is a brief summary and is not a legal interpretation. Counselors should be familiar with the details of these regulations and responsible for staying abreast of the inevitable changes and interpretations of these statutes and regulations. They also need to inform their clients of their rights under the law and the exceptions to these rights prior to treatment.

Other Legal and Ethical Issues in Chemical Dependency Treatment

Duty to Warn

One of the most difficult decisions to make in counseling is whether to maintain a client's confidentiality or break confidentiality to warn a potential victim. In 1976, the California Supreme Court handed down a decision in *Tarasoff v. Board of Regents of the University of California* that set a precedent for protection of the public's safety over the right of the client's confidentiality in psychotherapy. This case involved a client who threatened during therapy to kill his girlfriend and proceeded to follow through with the threat two months later. The court found that if a therapist has a "special relationship" with a person whose conduct needs to be controlled and can "reasonably" predict that he or she poses a threat to a third party who is a "foreseeable victim," the therapist must warn the third party and the police. These legal terms can be difficult to determine at times, and this is not a clear mandate to warn, in contrast to mandated child abuse reporting laws.

Counselors should have a process for determining if they should break confidentiality and warn intended victims. First, they should decide if this is a vague threat or a clear threat. If it is a clear threat, does it pose serious danger or marginal danger? If the counselor does not have enough information to identify and warn the victim, he or she should attempt to get a name and phone number. Next, the counselor should determine if there is imminent danger that requires action, or if there is no real immediate danger. If the counselor suspects that there is imminent danger to a family member, he or she may be able to deal with the problem if the client is amenable to family therapy. If the client is not amenable to family therapy, the counselor needs to consider initiating involuntary commitment, warning the police, and warning the victim. All of these decisions in this process should be done in conjunction with a supervisor, program director, and other colleagues and should be documented completely in treatment records. In these difficult situations, it is also advisable to consult an attorney for advice.

Confidentiality in Treating Clients With HIV/AIDS

Duty to warn becomes an even more difficult issue in treating clients with HIV/AIDS. HIV/AIDS is a problem that chemical dependency counselors cannot deny because the same groups that are at high risk for HIV/AIDS are also at high risk for substance abuse: sexually active homosexual or bisexual men and present or past intravenous drug users. Professional literature, ethics codes, and the legal system have not clearly defined the limits of confidentiality raised by the life-threatening activities of clients who have HIV/AIDS and who continue to be sexually active without telling their partners (Corey et al., 2014). The dilemma lies with protecting the confidentiality of the client versus protecting the safety of the unsuspecting partner. This could be a sex partner or someone with whom the client shares needles. Does this constitute a duty to warn? Is this imminent danger? What damage could result from the disclosure?

DiMarco and Zoline (2004) recommend six main areas of consideration for therapists to assist them in resolving the question of whether to disclose:

1. **HIV Knowledge and Sexual History Taking**—Clinicians should be knowledgeable about those behaviors that increase HIV-risk, such as, sharing needles and using drugs or alcohol. They should also be comfortable asking questions about a variety of sexual behaviors.

2. **Assessment of Danger**—Clinicians should assess whether malicious intent exists to infect others, thoroughly assess risky behaviors, determine to what degree underlying emotional and psychological factors may be compromising judgment, and ascertain to what degree a client can change his or her behavior.

3. **Objectivity/Professional Judgment**—Clinicians should consult with peers in order to ensure objectivity and examine their own feelings about HIV and those populations most likely to encounter HIV. As well, clinicians should utilize the steps of an ethical model (such as those provided earlier in this chapter) to provide additional clarity.

4. **Legal Issues**—Because state laws vary, it is important for clinicians to fully inform themselves about laws pertaining to confidentiality regarding HIV and AIDS in their specific states. Seek legal help as needed.

5. **Identifiability of the Potential Victims**—This involves ascertaining whether there are specifically identifiable partners or victims.

6. Proper Documentation—This documentation should include the clinician's rationale for the clinical steps taken, consultation with other providers, consultation with ethics boards and professional associations, and consultation with legal professionals.

Chemical dependency counselors need to take this responsibility seriously. Each case should be carefully considered and decisions to break confidentiality should be made only after consultation with supervisors, colleagues, and legal advisors. At some point in the future, case law may provide better guidelines with regard to warning potential victims of clients with HIV/AIDS. Until that time, counselors can best resolve this dilemma by using the therapeutic relationship to help the client act in a responsible way for the safety of others.

Child Abuse Reporting

Since child abuse is not a federal crime, federal law only makes money available to the states that meet the reporting guidelines and agree to set reporting standards. In order for states to be eligible for federal funds granted by the Child Abuse and Treatment Act of 1974 (reauthorized in 2010), they must agree to grant immunity to reporters, acting in good faith, from civil and criminal suits. All of the states have complied with these requests and have adopted definitions of child abuse that vary from state to state. None of the states require that a reporter be certain of the abuse. Usually the wording of the state laws is that the reporter has "reason to believe" or a "reasonable suspicion" of the abuse or neglect. Laws do vary from state to state with regard to the definition of child abuse and what types of child abuse must be reported. The types of abuse that are usually reportable include physical injury, mental or emotional injury, and sexual molestation or exploitation. Neglect is often included in the reporting laws, but it is more difficult to prove. Counselors are mandated to report their suspicions to the proper authorities—usually a child protective agency or the police. The authority in charge of investigating child abuse makes the determination and decides on a course of action. Reports are often made by telephone immediately and followed up with a written report. Since physical abuse, sexual abuse, and incest are co-existing problems in many substance-abusing families, it is quite likely that substance abuse counselors will encounter these problems. Thus, chemical dependency counselors should be familiar with the child abuse reporting laws of their states. It is also a good idea to consult with supervisors and colleagues before breaking confidentiality and reporting child abuse. The changes in the federal regulation that exempt child abuse and neglect reporting from the confidentiality requirements make it clear that chemical dependency counselors are bound by their state laws and may be breaking the law by not reporting suspected child abuse. Failure to report is a misdemeanor in most states and could carry a jail sentence and a fine, although this is rare. This may put the counselor in an ethical dilemma of deciding between the welfare of the client or the safety of a child. The state laws usually make it quite clear that this is not a choice the counselor can make; he or she *must* report the child abuse.

A related area that affects chemical dependency counselors is the use and abuse of drugs by a pregnant woman. There is certainly evidence that drinking and using other drugs during pregnancy can create fetal alcohol syndrome or drug addiction in these women's babies. However, there are no absolute data concerning the amount and frequency of use that create these problems for children. It is hard to define what could be considered abuse. The other issue for counselors who are fairly certain that a pregnant woman is abusing enough drugs to create problems is whether the fetus is protected by child abuse laws. There is concern, too, that criminally sanctioning such women may provide a disincentive for women to seek needed treatment for both themselves and their unborn children (Lambert, Scheiner, & Campbell, 2010). This is a difficult area that requires legal advice and a knowledge of the state definition of child abuse. Cases in the courts may add clarity to this issue in the future.

Danger to Self—Suicide Threats

Alcoholics and drug abusers have a high risk for suicide, and within that population, adolescents and the elderly have an even higher risk (Lawson & Lawson, 1989). One of the more difficult situations for chemical dependency counselors is the treatment of suicidal patients. The stakes are high in making the decision whether or not to break confidentiality to potentially save a patient's life. The decision must be based on the counselor's assessment of the seriousness of the threat. However, if there is any indication that the patient is depressed, has a history of suicide attempts, or a family history of suicide attempts, the counselor should do a suicide-potential evaluation immediately, using direct questioning. It is a myth that asking about suicidal thoughts will put the idea into a person's head. It may be a relief for someone to talk about these thoughts and associated fears. In determining the level of danger to self, the counselor should ask questions such as: "Are you thinking about hurting yourself?" "Have you been feeling suicidal?" "For how long have you been feeling that way?" Next the counselor should assess the patient's impulsivity. Can the patient guarantee that for a period of time or until the next counseling session, he or she will not attempt suicide? An assessment of the plan and the means to carry out suicide is important. The more specific the plan for the suicide attempt, the more the danger. Patients who just wish that they were not alive are in less immediate danger than those who have a loaded gun at home and live by themselves. Other factors that increase the risk of suicide are a history of destructive or self-destructive behavior, a family history of suicide, and current alcohol and other drug use. Factors that decrease the risk are a strong relationship with the therapist and a current strong level of support from family, friends, and the community. Other areas for assessment are the person's affective state, stress level, and level of reality testing. A person who is very depressed might not have the energy to commit suicide. Risk, however, increases as a person's energy level begins increasing. A shift from a crisis state to becoming at peace also may indicate that a person has made a decision to take his or her own life.

Management of a suicide threat should begin with the least restrictive alternative. The first level of intervention should be negotiating a contract between the counselor and the patient that has clear guidelines regarding contacting the counselor if the suicidal idea becomes stronger, asking for extra sessions, and being in situations where hospitalization might be necessary. It would also be helpful for the counselor to ask the patient for written consent to alert family members of the suicide risk and to have them remove lethal weapons from the house. If there is a more immediate need for intervention, the patient should be evaluated by a psychiatrist for medication or hospitalization. If the patient is not willing to voluntarily enter the hospital, the psychiatrist or other health professional can have the patient held on an involuntary commitment, usually for 72 hours, for further evaluation. If the suicide threat arrives over the phone, the counselor can have the line traced and ask the police or a mental health crisis team to pick that person up and take him or her to an emergency room.

Sometimes these interventions do not work or work only temporarily. Counselors need to realize that they can only do so much to prevent suicide. If they lose a patient to suicide, they may need to process this with a supervisor or colleague so they can go on with their work and help others.

Professional Liability—Malpractice Suits

Therapists have not only an ethical obligation but also a legal responsibility to give their clients an honest representation of their skills, methods, conditions of treatment, fees, and appointment schedules, and the client's informed consent should always be obtained (Huber & Baruth, 1987). This understanding and agreement constitute a contract between the counselor and the client, and each party has a responsibility to abide by the agreement. Counselors' legal liability involves civil liability, including contract law, unintentional torts or malpractice, and intentional torts (Schultz, 1982). If the counselor's practice is a fee-for-service arrangement, it has implied contractual elements and legal responsibility that make the counselor liable through contract law (Huber & Baruth, 1987). Tort liability, however, is a civil wrong that is not part of contractual liability. A tort is a harm done to an individual in a manner that allows the law to order the person who inflicts the harm to pay damages to the injured party, whether the harm was intentional or unintentional (Huber & Baruth, 1987).

Unintentional torts are referred to as "malpractice," wherein a counselor caused injury to a client (through ignorance or negligence) by not providing an acceptable standard of care. Intentional torts can include causing willful harm through the acts of battery, defamation, invasion of privacy, infliction of mental distress, and malicious prosecution and false imprisonment (Huber & Baruth, 1987).

Counselors can minimize their chance of being sued by practicing in a responsible and ethical manner, including the following:

- Providing clients with a professional disclosure statement that covers the counselor's qualifications, guarantees and limits of confidentiality, fee structures, and therapy cancellation and termination policies
- Securing ongoing supervision or forming peer supervision groups
- Belonging to professional organizations and following their codes of ethics
- Using legal consultants in making difficult ethical decisions
- Practicing ongoing continuing education
- Keeping excellent and accurate records of all treatment sessions, other client contact, supervision suggestions, consultations with consultants and colleagues, and updated treatment plans and progress

Special Issues for Counselors Who Are A.A. Members

Although some of these issues were discussed previously in the context of dual relationship and A.A. members who work in the chemical dependency counseling field, further differentiation may be necessary to avoid confusion. Counselors sometimes confuse the ethical and legal concept of confidentiality with the A.A. tradition of anonymity. Although there is overlap, they are not the same. Both of these principles protect the alcoholic or addict and the profession, and confidentiality allows people to seek treatment without fear of being stigmatized. The public, however, might see the tradition of anonymity as further perpetuating the stigma of substance abuse and see members of A.A. as hiding behind this tradition. The tradition of anonymity in A.A. is utilized as a strategy to address the stigma associated with alcoholism, as reassurance to newcomers that their identities will be protected, and as a method to protect members and ensure equality (Alcoholics Anonymous World Services, 2011). The main purpose of the tradition is the protection of the fellowship. There is a fine balance between protecting A.A. and educating the public about the organization so others can benefit from the program. The tradition allows a person to identify as an alcoholic but not as a member of A.A. through the public media. In regard to outside-group communications (including all types of media), traditions 11 and 12 prohibit any unauthorized disclosure of another member's identity as an A.A. member. It is not required that members use only first names in meetings, as A.A. advises members that "we may use last names within our group (Alcoholics Anonymous World Services, 2005).

Another area of concern is court-mandated attendance at A.A. meetings. While some people may get exposed to the program and go on to a life of sobriety, many will not. People who are only at a meeting to avoid jail usually do not participate in the meeting and may hinder others from getting maximum benefit. They also have no stake in keeping information that is shared at the meeting confidential or keeping other members' anonymity. Even worse, they may perceive A.A. as an extension of a coercive system that spies on them and reports back to the authorities (Bissell & Royce, 1987). This negative experience may rule out A.A. as an option for people when they are truly ready for its help. This is especially true for adolescents, who feel overcontrolled by the world. If they are forced to attend, it may rule out this option for the rest of their lives.

Counselors who are also members of A.A. need to help their clients understand the difference between therapy and A.A. and being a counselor and a sponsor. They should also protect the A.A. program from social pressure to use it as mandatory treatment.

References

Alcoholics Anonymous World Services. (1986). *If you are a professional, A.A. wants to work with you.* New York: Author.

Alcoholics Anonymous World Services. (2005). *The A.A. group…Where it all begins.* New York: Author.

Alcoholics Anonymous World Services. (2011). *Understanding anonymity.* New York: Author.

Alcoholics Anonymous World Services. (2013). *For A.A. members employed in the alcoholism field (A.A. Guidelines).* Retrieved May 29, 2014, from http://www.aa.org/lang/en/en_pdfs/mg-10_foraamembers.pdf

American Counseling Association. (2014). *ACA Code of ethics.* Retrieved May 27, 2014, from http://www.counseling.org/resources/aca-code-of-ethics.pdf

Berton, J. (2014). *Ethics for addictions professionals.* Hoboken, NJ: Wiley.

Bissell, L., & Royce, J. (1987). *Ethics for addiction professionals.* Minneapolis, MN: Hazelden Foundation.

Bonitz, V. (2008). Use of physical touch in the 'talking cure': A journey to the outskirts of psychotherapy. *Psychotherapy: Theory, Research, Practice, Training, 45*(3), 391–404.

Child Abuse Prevention and Treatment Act of 1974 (42 U.S.C.A. § 5106g) (1974) (amended 2010)

Comprehensive Alcohol Abuse and Alcoholism Prevention, Treatment and Rehabilitation Act of 1970 (42 U.S.C. § 290 *et seq.*) (1970)

Corey, G. (1991). *Theory and practice of counseling and psychotherapy.* Pacific Grove, CA: Brooks/Cole.

Corey, G. (2012). *Theory and practice of counseling and psychotherapy* (9th ed.). Pacific Grove, CA: Brooks/Cole.

Corey, G., Corey, M. S., Corey, C., & Callanan, P. (2014). *Issues and ethics in the helping professions* (9th ed.). Stamford, CT: Cengage Learning.

Corey, G., Corey, M. S., & Haynes, R. (2015). *Workbook for ethics in action* (3rd ed.). Stamford, CT: Cengage Learning.

Culbreth, J., & Cooper, J. B. (2008). Factors impacting the development of substance abuse counseling supervisors. *Journal of Addictions & Offender Counseling, 29*, 22–35.

DiMarco, M., & Zoline, S. S. (2004). Duty to warn in the context of HIV/AIDS-related psychotherapy: Decision making among psychologists. *Counseling and Clinical Psychology Journal, 1*(2), 68–85.

Drug Abuse Office and Treatment Act of 1972 (21 U.S.C. § 290 *et seq.* (1972)

Gallagher, J. (2009). Ethical violations: A quantitative study comparing human services professions. *Recovery Online Today*. Retrieved June 7, 2014, from http://www.recoverytoday.net/Mar09/gallagher.html

Gallagher, J. (2010). Licensed chemical dependency counselors views of professional and ethical standards: A focus group analysis. *Alcoholism Treatment Quarterly, 28*(2), 184–197.

Geppert, C., & Roberts, L. W. (2008). Ethical foundations of substance abuse treatment. In C. Geppert & L. W. Roberts (Eds.), *The book of ethics: Expert guidance for professionals who treat addiction* (pp. 1–28). City Center, MN: Hazelden Foundation.

Health Providers Service Organization. (2014). *Understanding counselor liability and risk*. Retrieved on June 3, 2014, from http://www.hpso.com/resources/claim-studies.jsp

Herlihy, B., & Dufrene, R. L. (2011). Current and emerging ethical issues in counseling: A Delphi study of expert opinions. *Counseling and Values, 56*, 10–24.

Huber, C. H., & Baruth, L. G. (1987). *Ethical, legal and professional issues in the practice of marriage and family therapy*. Columbus, OH: Merrill.

Lambert, B., Scheiner, M., & Campbell, D. (2010). Ethical issues and addiction. *Journal of Addictive Diseases, 29*, 164–174.

Lawson, A., & Lawson, G. (2004). *Alcoholism and the family: A guide to treatment and prevention* (2nd ed.). Austin, TX: PRO-ED.

Lawson, G., & Lawson, A. (1989). *Alcoholism and substance abuse in special populations*. Gaithersburg, MD: Aspen Publishers.

Meyers, L. (2014). A living document of ethical guidance. *Counseling Today, 56*(12), 32–40.

National Association of Alcoholism and Drug Abuse Counselors. (2011). *NAADAC code of ethics*. Retrieved May 25, 2014, from http://www.naadac.org/code-of-ethics

Neukrug, E., Milliken, T., & Walden, S. (2001). Ethical complaints made against counselors: An updated survey of state licensing boards. *Counselor Education and Supervision, 41*, 57–70.

Schultz, B. (1982). *Legal liability in psychotherapy*. San Francisco: Jossey-Bass.

Shallcross, L. (2011). Do the right thing. *Counseling Today*. Retrieved May 29, 2014, from http://ct.counseling.org/2011/04/

Tarasoff v. Regents of the University of California, 17 Cal. 3d 425, 551 P.2d 334, 131 Cal. Rptr. 14 (1976)

CHAPTER 3

Counselor Certification and Licensure

CHAPTER OBJECTIVES

- Explore a brief history of the substance abuse counseling profession
- Understand the advantages of being considered a profession
- Discern similarities and differences between licensure and certification
- Ascertain training and educational requirements for CD counselors
- Appreciate state-to-state differences in CD counselor requirements
- Understand future directions for licensure and certification and their implications

It would be great if you could begin your career as a substance abuse counselor the minute you finished your coursework or degree. After all, aren't you ready? You've studied all the different treatment modalities, familiarized yourself with the DSM, learned what differentiates an upper from a downer, and more. Why, after all, would you need to go through the byzantine process of becoming credentialed and securing a license? Isn't it enough to hang a shingle outside your office door, let potential clients know about your newly acquired expertise, and offer your counseling services? Now that you know what you know, shouldn't you be able to provide your services anywhere you like—whether in California or Mississippi, Dubuque or New York City?

Although these questions are commonly asked by soon-to-be clinicians entering the substance abuse profession, the answers are not as straightforward as they might seem. Take the word *profession,* for example. What does it mean when we say we are members of the substance abuse treatment profession? Why is it important to even be considered a member of the profession? For that matter, how did the substance abuse profession form—and why?

Answers to these and other important questions will be provided in this chapter, including discussions about the differences between certification and licensure and the different training and educational requirements expected of counselors treating substance use disorders (SUDs). Finally, we will examine the differing state requirements expected of chemical dependency counselors.

This chapter aims to provide a clear roadmap for getting from here to there—how one transitions from being a student to becoming an independent counseling professional who is able to stand on his or her own two feet. Specifically, this chapter deals with the various hoops you, as a chemical dependency counselor, will be required to jump through in your travels. It is hoped that by spending time on this topic, we will be able to make your journey a little less bumpy.

A Brief History of the Substance Abuse Counseling Profession

Prior to 1974, when various counseling-related professions—including the substance abuse counseling profession—began the process of credentialing counselors, the development of these professions was anything but straight-forward. Counseling professions arose in response to historical forces and from a variety of related but distinct fields, including medicine, psychology, nursing, and social work. Indeed, many of these and the related counseling fields that correspondingly developed in the United States can trace their roots to the Industrial Revolution of the mid-1800s, which forced seismic shifts upon what had historically been a largely agrarian populace (Capuzzi & Gross, 2009).

These shifts included the development of new technologies for the production of textiles, agriculture, transportation, and the mining of coal, as well as an expansion in public education and a large infusion of immigrants, all of which encouraged increasing numbers of people to live in cities and develop new ways of, and systems for, living and working together (Montagna, 2012). As a result of these various large-scale disruptive forces and the stressors they imposed upon the populace, new methods of working with individuals and groups, such as counseling, were developed as a way to support these people as they adapted to the changes and their social repercussions (Gintner, 2002). Many of these new methods developed groups of like-minded individuals who eventually formed different but not necessarily unrelated professions.

All these professions seem to have developed in a similar manner. That is, a group of individuals with a common set of concerns and/or interests eventually came together to organize on behalf of their emerging profession, and once a critical mass was established, it became an earnest field of inquiry, as well as an established pathway for interested others to follow. At the same time, the process of establishing a profession allowed for the cultivation of standardized practices and helped to protect the interests of both the practitioners and the beneficiaries (e.g., clients, patients, students).

Accordingly and appropriately, the substance abuse counseling profession owes a debt of gratitude to the many similarly interested individuals from a variety of backgrounds—paraprofessionals, doctors, activists—who early on recognized there existed a need to provide help to those with alcohol and drug problems. As the following timeline demonstrates, the substance abuse counseling profession developed in fits and starts, and through specific legislation, developments in pharmacology, and more. (Unless otherwise noted, these timelines are taken from Capuzzi & Gross [2009] and White [1998], who also provide a more expansive listing and detail specific efforts that were undertaken prior to 1914.)

A Timeline of Historical Forces Leading to the Establishment of the Profession

1914—*The Harrison Tax Act* federally regulated opiates and cocaine. It further stipulated that only physicians could legally dispense such drugs.

1917—*The Smith-Hughes Act* supported the development of a nation-wide program for vocational education.

1935—Bill W. and Dr. Bob met for the first time and began their way of working with other alcoholics that would form the basis for Alcoholics Anonymous (A.A.).

1943—The Veterans Administration established a vocational rehabilitation program to assist veterans of World War II. Further services authorized included education and training (Department of Veterans Affairs, 2006).

1944—Marty Mann was the first woman to regain her sobriety through A.A. To help others, she founded what is today known as the National Council on Alcoholism and Drug Dependence around three very specific declarations: (1) *Alcoholism is a disease and the alcoholic a sick person; (2) the alcoholic can and should be helped; and (3) alcoholism is a public health problem and a public responsibility* (National Council on Alcoholism and Drug Dependence, n.d.).

1946—The National Institute of Mental Health was established with the passage of the *National Mental Health Act*, which also provided assistance to states for the use of effective methods of prevention, diagnosis, and treatment of people with mental health disorders.

1951—Disulfiram (Antabuse) was approved by the U.S. Food and Drug Administration for the treatment of alcoholism. Antabuse is utilized as an aversive therapy, as it creates severely distressing symptoms if a patient drinks alcohol.

1951—Anne B. and Lois W., wife of A.A. co-founder Bill W., began consolidating the various family groups that grew alongside A.A. through the 1940s under the umbrella of Al-Anon Family Groups.

1954—*The Vocational Rehabilitation Act* (VRA) expanded upon earlier versions of the VRA to cover those with disabilities. It further required and allocated funding for the development of personnel (including counselors) who specialized in assisting persons with disabilities.

1954—Ruth Fox, MD, established what is today known as the American Society of Addiction Medicine (ASAM). A "Counselor on Alcoholism" was the title for the first formal state job classification position of its kind, approved in the United States by the Minnesota State Civil Service Commission.

1958—The halfway house movement which was started in Lincoln, Nebraska, by Ralph Fox, coalesced to become the Association of Halfway House Alcoholism Programs of North America.

1960—*The Disease Concept of Alcoholism* was published by E. M. Jellinek. In this book, Jellinek introduced his models of the different types of alcoholism (i.e., alpha, gamma, and delta, two of which he reported as being a disease).

1963—*The Community Mental Health Centers Act* mandated the creation of mental health centers across the nation. In addition, it provided for direct counseling services to people in the community (as opposed to those in an institution), as well as outreach and coordination of other services. Alcoholism and addiction counseling were included in this legislation.

1964—Dr. Vincent Dole, an endocrinologist, and Dr. Marie Nyswander, a psychiatrist specializing in addiction, conducted studies that demonstrated the efficacy of utilizing methadone to blunt the cravings experienced by people addicted to heroin.

1964—The insurance industry began reimbursement of the treatment of alcoholism so that it was on par with the treatment of other illnesses. This had the effect of substantially increasing the number of both private and hospital-based inpatient treatment programs.

1966—In two separate cases before the Federal Appeals Court, the disease concept of alcoholism was affirmed. Additionally, President Johnson not only appointed the first National Advisory Committee on Alcoholism but also was the first U.S. president to address the country about alcoholism: "The alcoholic suffers from a disease which will yield eventually to scientific research and adequate treatment."

1968—The Federal Advisory Committee on Traffic Safety acknowledged the substantial role alcohol plays in car crashes. New laws for dealing with impaired driving would be pushed by federal agencies in the early 1970s. This time period also saw an increase in remedial education and other services for those arrested for being under the influence of alcohol.

1970—*Congress passed The Comprehensive Alcohol Abuse and Alcoholism Prevention Treatment and Rehabilitation Act.* As a result, the National Institute on Alcohol Abuse and Alcoholism (NIAAA) was established as part of the National Institute of Mental Health (NIMH). States are required to create a State Alcohol Authority (SAA) and a Single State Authority (SSA) for drug abuse to manage formula grants and plan for the delivery of treatment services (U.S. Department of Health and Human Services, 2005).

1972—The Food and Drug Administration approved methadone to treat opiate (heroin) addiction.

1974—Roy Littlejohn conducted the first of a series of studies on credentialing counselors working in alcohol and drug treatment programs. This began a years-long process of certification and licensure of addiction counselors that coincided with similar efforts on behalf of other counseling disciplines, such as professional counseling and marriage and family therapy.

Today, all 50 U.S. states and the territories of Guam and Puerto Rico have developed standards for certification and/or licensure that substance abuse treatment professionals must meet in order to provide services (U.S. Department of Health and Human Services, 2005). Before looking more specifically at these standards, it will be helpful to spend some time looking at why so many have worked together over the past century to develop a cohesive, single profession dedicated to treating substance use disorders.

The Advantages of Being Considered a Profession

According to BusinessDictionary.com, the definition of *profession* is thus: "Occupation, practice, or vocation requiring mastery of a complex set of knowledge and skills through formal education and/or practical experience. Every organized profession (accounting, law, medicine, etc.) is governed by its respective *professional body*" ("Profession," n.d.).

Professional body is further defined by BusinessDictionary.com as follows:

> Trade association of an organized profession (accounting, law, medicine, etc.) that certifies successful completion of its requirements, and thereupon awards a license and bestows a recognized appellation (Chartered Accountant, Attorney at Law, Doctor of Medicine, etc.). Professional bodies usually prescribe a discretionary or mandatory code of conduct for their members.

> These bodies exercise political control over their membership,
> and have monopoly over the profession's formal education,
> certification, licensing, symbols, etc. ("Professional body," n.d.)

And finally, there is this:

> Governmentally sanctioned credentialing is usually called
> licensure and is based on the legal concept of the regulatory
> power of the state. This power holds that the state has the right
> and obligation to pass laws and take other such actions as it may
> deem necessary to protect the health, safety and welfare of its
> citizens. Passage of a state licensure or credentialing law for a given
> profession restricts or prohibits the practice of that profession by
> individuals not meeting state-determined qualification standards,
> and violators may be subject to legal sanctions such as fines, loss
> of license to practice, or imprisonment. (American Counseling
> Association, n.d.)

Now that the reference points are set, let us take a look at some of the most
important reasons for organizing a profession.

- **To protect the public**—The establishment of professional guidelines means
  that people seeking treatment for substance use disorders can be assured that
  their providers are adequately trained. Furthermore, it allows credentialing
  bodies, such as state licensing/credentialing boards, to sanction those who
  do not meet such standards and/or engage in unethical practices.

- **To advocate on a systemic level**—There is political strength in numbers, and
  the more members a particular profession has, the more that policymakers,
  politicians, and others with influence are likely to listen. This is important
  for at least two reasons. One, it allows members of the substance abuse
  treatment profession to advocate for systemic changes (e.g., more funding,
  better policies and laws) that will benefit those with substance use disorders.
  Two, it additionally provides members the parallel process of advocating for
  the legitimacy of their profession.

- **To provide a roadmap for professional development**—Because standards
  have been identified, those who are interested in becoming substance abuse
  counselors have a template to follow for acquiring the necessary education,
  training, and supervision. These standards often serve as figurative rungs
  on a ladder for career enhancement that can help provide incentive for
  professionals remaining in the field.

- **To provide simplification**—There is a "shorthand" that is created through
  professionalization that benefits and protects the public and bestows certain

advantages to providers themselves. As an example, agencies who employ providers know that their employees meet minimum standards for providing treatment to those with substance use disorders. Substance abuse treatment professionals, too, know that their credentials will serve as a sort of "stamp of approval" that will affirm to others their abilities to provide such services; it helps to create an easily recognized professional identity.

This is not to say, however, that there are no other important ancillary advantages of being a profession, such as established and standardized training programs that are easily accessible for those interested in such training, access to reduced-cost liability insurance, reimbursement for services from third-party payers (e.g., insurance plans), and so forth. These benefits clearly spell out the advantages of being a member of the substance abuse treatment profession.

Similarities and Differences Between Licensure and Certification

If licensure is government-sanctioned credentialing and is thus a compulsory credential for any person wishing to practice in a particular field, all other forms of certification can be considered voluntary:

> Separate from state laws and regulations, voluntary certification from independent professional certification organizations for counseling and a host of specializations within the counseling profession have been created to establish recognition of those practitioners as having met the minimum standards of education and supervised clinical experience as set by the profession. *Certification is not required; rather it is strictly voluntary.* This certification attests to the fact that the holder of this certification has met the standards of the credentialing organization and is therefore entitled to make the public aware of this as further documentation of his or her professional competence. In and of itself, however, this certification is not a practice credential but rather a professional credential in that it does not give the holder permission to practice. That permission is given only by the governmentally sanctioned entity. (American Counseling Association, n.d.)

The similarities between licensure and certification are numerous. There is typically an organization that has created a set of minimum standards for training and education that a practitioner must meet in order to secure a particular credential. Once in hand, this certification serves to let others know that the holder of the credential has demonstrated a level of professional competence high enough to secure the credential—it serves, in other words, as a sort of shorthand for advertising a particular specialty. Just a few of these certifications and their credentialing organizations' websites are listed in Table 3.1 to provide some insight into the breadth of possibilities.

Professionals who are interested in these or other voluntary certifications and who meet the minimum education and training standards the credentialing organizations have outlined simply need to apply for, and pay a fee to receive, the applicable certification.

That licensure is *mandatory* while other forms of certification (such as those listed in Table 3.1) are *voluntary* is the most significant distinction between the two concepts. Any treatment professional desiring to address substance use disorders must have a license from the corresponding body responsible in a particular jurisdiction (i.e., a state) for regulating the practice of substance abuse practitioners. Without this practice license, a would-be substance abuse counselor will be unable to treat clients, no matter how many other certifications the counselor may hold.

Table 3.1
Examples of Certifications and Credentialing Organizations

Type of certification	Credentialing organization	Website
Bioenergetic Therapist	International Institute for Bioenergetic Analysis	www.bioenergetic-therapy.com
Group Psychotherapist	American Group Psychotherapy Association	www.agpa.org
Employee Assistance Professional	Employee Assistance Professionals Association	www.eapassn.org
Eating Disorders Specialist	International Association of Eating Disorders Foundation	www.iaedp.com
Forensic Traumatologist	American Academy of Experts in Traumatic Stress	www.aaets.org
Dance Therapist	American Dance Therapy Association	www.adta.org
Sex Therapist	American Association of Sexuality Counselors and Therapists	www.aasect.org

Training and Other Requirements for Chemical Dependency Counselors

First, the good news... If variety is the spice of life, then chemical dependency counselors are the luckiest practitioners on the planet. Every state has developed its own standards for what is expected of practitioners. The bad news? Every state has its own standards for what is expected of practitioners. This means that to make sense of these training and educational standards, they have to be considered from a birds-eye view. Once we have a good feel for the general landscape, we can then look at how such requirements vary from state to state, using the most recent national review, conducted in 2005 for all states and the territories of Puerto Rico and Guam, as our point of reference (U.S. Department of Health and Human Services).

States commonly have at least three levels of licensure made up of four primary components: education, experience, training, and supervision (as can be seen in Table 3.2). Prior to proceeding, a word of caution is warranted. The hours in Table 3.2 represent only an example across states. Because standards for each state were developed independently, they will most likely vary in their specifics.

Before looking at the numbers more directly, it will be helpful to understand how the scopes of practice for each of these levels of certification and licensure differ.

An *associate/intern* will be required to work under the supervision of a professional who holds a higher level of certification or is an approved supervisor. The associate may be required to provide ongoing documentation that he or she is enrolled in an institution of higher education to earn a bachelor's degree. Commonly allowable activities as adapted from the U.S. Department of Health and Human Services (2011) report entitled *Scopes of Practice and Career Ladder for Substance Use Disorder Counseling* include the following:

- Diagnostic impression, and Screening, Brief Intervention, Referral to Treatment (SBIRT)
- Monitor treatment plan/compliance
- Referral
- Service coordination and case management for substance use disorders (SUDs)
- Psychoeducational counseling of individuals and groups
- Client, family, and community education
- Documentation
- Professional and ethical responsibilities

Table 3.2
Comparison of Requirements for Different Levels
of Chemical Dependency Credentialing

	Associate/ Intern	Certified	Licensed
Education	High school diploma /GED	Bachelor's degree in related field	Master's degree in related field
Hours of Experience	2,000	4,000	6,000
Hours of Training	250	325	300
Hours of Supervision	200	200	300

A *certified counselor* will frequently be able to practice independent of any supervision requirements. A counselor at this level, however, is typically unable to qualify as an approved supervisor and is thus unable to provide needed supervision services. Commonly allowable activities include the following:

- Clinical evaluation, including diagnostic impression or Screening, Brief Intervention, and Referral to Treatment (SBIRT)
- Treatment planning for substance use disorders, including initial care, ongoing care, continuity of care, discharge, and planning for relapse prevention
- Referral
- Service coordination and case management for substance use disorders and for co-occurring disorders
- Counseling, therapy, trauma-informed care, and psychoeducation with individuals, families, and groups
- Client, family, and community education
- Documentation
- Professional and ethical responsibilities

A *licensed counselor* will be able to practice independent of any supervision requirements (though it is still a good idea to utilize both ongoing supervision and peer support), will frequently be able to collect third-party payments, and will be able to provide approved supervision services to both interns and certified counselors. Commonly allowable activities include the following:

- Clinical evaluation, including screening, assessment, and diagnosis of substance use disorders (SUDs)

- Treatment planning for SUDs
- Referral
- Service coordination and case management in the area of SUDs
- Counseling, therapy, trauma-informed care, and psychoeducation with individuals, families, and groups in the area of SUDs
- Client, family, and community education
- Documentation
- Professional and ethical responsibilities
- Clinical supervisory responsibilities for all categories of SUD counselors

In addition to these three core levels of licensure, many states have even more levels of certification and licensure. These commonly include licenses to provide supervision services (i.e., an "approved supervisor"), treat co-occurring disorders, provide prevention services, teach DUI courses, or work in a criminal justice context. Each of these other licenses has its own requirements that would need to be met in order for such a license to be issued. Practitioners will frequently pursue these other licenses and certifications to expand their scope of work so that they can provide more services to more clients, thus making themselves both more marketable and more versatile.

Besides allowing a practitioner to be licensed at the highest and most independent level, another advantage of having an advanced degree is that it will frequently warrant a reduction in the number of hours of experience that need to be documented for a particular level of certification. In some cases, this may work out to 2,000 hours (essentially 1 year's worth of experience) credited for a bachelor's degree and 4,000 (2 years' worth) for a master's degree.

All of these hours of experience will require either a mandated frequency and/or a total number of hours of supervision in order to qualify as recordable hours. As an example, a total of 200 hours of supervision may be required by a particular state at a rate of 1 hour of supervision per 40 hours worked. Both the required frequency and total number of hours for any other state may be more or less.

The standard for required training hours is for all of these hours to be addiction-specific. Examples of acceptable coursework include counseling theories and techniques, group counseling, family counseling, individual counseling, ethics, HIV/AIDS, confidentiality, multicultural understanding, assessment, case management, screening and intake, and pharmacology of psychoactive drugs. These hours are frequently fulfilled through the coursework taken to fulfill a minor in Addictions, with 18 semester hours through an accredited university.

How to Apply to Be a Certified/ Licensed Chemical Dependency Counselor

Because each state has its own standards for counselor certification and licensure, the steps will differ depending on where you live. Having said that, here are typical steps common to almost every state.

1. **Request an Application**—To request an application, you must first identify which agency in your state is responsible for issuing practice certifications and licenses. The application will ask you to provide basic contact information, and will include forms with which to document your education, training, supervision, and exam scores. All of these will need to be completed and returned to the state's licensing agency, along with a fee and transcripts or other verification forms that are needed (e.g., letters of reference, documentation of supervision, exam scores).

2. **Take and Pass an Exam**—At some point in the certification process, you will most likely have to take an exam. Many states utilize those managed and proctored by national certification organizations such as the National Certified Addiction Counselor and Master Addiction Counselor exams offered by the National Association for Alcoholism and Drug Abuse Counselors (www .naadac.org), and the Alcohol and Drug Counselor and Advanced Alcohol and Drug Counselor exams offered by the International Certification and Reciprocity Consortium (www.internationalcredentialing.org). The written portion of an exam will typically test your knowledge in a number of domains relevant to substance abuse counseling. If an oral exam is required, it will typically be given if the written portion is passed and may involve the analysis of a case study by the examinee before a review board.

3. **Secure a Supervisor**—The most common scenario is for clinical supervision to be provided through your employer. If it is not, it will be necessary to secure such supervision privately, and this will usually carry an additional financial obligation to the intern. The supervisor will commonly be responsible for ensuring that all necessary follow-up documentation is sent to the credentialing body and will be a point of contact between this body and the intern in case issues arise. You will want to track the numbers of hours of supervision you accrue to prove that you have met and/or are meeting the state's requirement.

4. **Complete the Necessary Trainings**—Complete all required trainings, such as those detailed earlier, within the state's time frame. Ongoing continuing education hours will also be required, usually about 20 hours annually. Depending on the state and the credential being applying for, it is sometimes possible to complete the necessary trainings as you accrue experience hours, as detailed below.

5. Earn the Needed Experience Hours—Once the previous steps have been accomplished, it will be necessary to earn the needed experience hours through employment at an agency that treats substance use disorders. If working full-time, a counselor can typically accumulate 2,000 hours annually. It will be necessary to document these hours and may even be required to track both direct client contact and incidental/ancillary hours separately.

Because things don't always go as planned—the mail doesn't go through, someone forgets to file the appropriate piece of paper in the proper folder, supervisors become ill and/or move on to other jobs—our suggestion is that interns keep copies of files in which all necessary hours (supervision, training, experience) are tracked, and back up documentation (copies of school transcripts, trainings attended) and copies of reports sent to the licensing board. In this way, interns will learn more about both their and their supervisors' responsibilities, be less likely to be taken advantage of, have a better ability to hold their supervisors and employers accountable, and experience more ownership and control over what happens in their careers.

Once all the necessary thresholds have been crossed (i.e., the needed experience, supervision, training, education, and exam requirements have been met), and once written documentation has been submitted to the licensing body, the state will provide you with the appropriate practice license or certification. This will allow you to practice within the legislatively defined scope of practice allowable in that state.

To practice in another state, it will be necessary to repeat the application process. If a state's practice law has been written with "portability" in mind (sometimes referred to as "reciprocity," or, in other words, how well a license "travels" from one state to the next), this will be reflected in a truncated application process, which will commonly ask for proof of licensure from another state. Until there is a universal, national standard that applies to all states, it will be necessary to apply for and receive the needed state practice credential before you can begin offering services.

Apply as early as possible before moving to another state. This will minimize the likelihood of being unable to work due to not having the necessary credential. Follow up with the licensing agency throughout the process to ensure that things do not get held up because of missing documentation or other issues. If your application languishes for no known reason, consider having someone with more experience intercede on your behalf, such as your employer, supervisor, or a board member serving on the licensing agency's board.

Future Directions for Licensure and Certification

Given the twists and turns that have marked the substance abuse treatment profession's history, it will be helpful to consider where things may be in regard to licensure and certification.

Here are three things we know.

1. The substance abuse treatment profession is not alone—Other professions, like professional counseling, have similar concerns regarding licensure portability and reciprocity (Erford, 2012):

> Now we are squarely focused on the building blocks to licensure portability, which will allow counselors from one state to transfer their licenses to practice in another state without having to jump through a new set of qualification hoops. The major stumbling block is the widely disparate licensure qualifications that currently exist. To practice in any state, a professional counselor must qualify under the laws existing in that particular state. Obviously, to achieve reciprocity and portability, some states are going to need to change qualification laws and regulations. It is unlikely that those states on the higher end of the continuum are going to lower their standards.

In these and other human service professions (e.g., occupational and physical therapies, nursing, social work), there is movement toward requiring a master's degree as the minimum degree needed to practice independently. It is possible that addictions professionals will see a similar requirement. One benefit of this would be to help ensure that parity exists between addictions and other professionals (marriage and family therapists, professional counselors, etc.) who provide addictions treatment.

2. The Affordable Care Act may provide further incentive toward increased professionalization—With implementation of the Patient Protection and Affordable Care Act (ACA, 2010), there will be pressure to expand the pool of providers so that clients have access to qualified personnel:

> The advent of healthcare reform has created increased interest and pressure for licensure of addiction professionals. Healthcare reform is driving the need for licensure of addiction professionals to compete in the primary healthcare marketplace for Medicare and third-party reimbursement. (NAADAC, 2011)

It is unclear, though, exactly how the opportunities created by the ACA will affect addictions professionals. One possibility is that, as was previously pointed out, a master's degree will become the minimum degree accepted in order for a provider to be considered for a practice license.

3. The substance abuse treatment profession is unique—On the other hand, the provision of addictions treatment services could diverge from a "master's-only model" into many different but related directions, as evidenced by what has happened in the recent past:

> Licensing of addiction counselors has been a "hot" issue over the past five years. Licensure bills have been introduced and passed in many states. They range from legislation to codify addiction professional licensing requirements, exempt addiction counselors from licensure, certify employee assistance and other counseling professionals and to expand addiction counselors' scope of practice. (NAADAC, 2011)

It is conceivable, then, that there will be pressures (i.e., the need to have as many qualified providers as possible to meet the expected increase in demand) in place to ensure that non-master's addictions counselors are able to provide needed addictions services. This could end up looking a lot like the career ladder for social workers, where those with bachelor's degrees are able to do one level of work, those with a master's do another level, and those with a clinical endorsement have the most expansive scopes of practice. Other possibilities include ensuring that a variety of professionals have the ability to provide addictions services, and providing addictions counselors with enhanced scopes of practice (e.g., the ability to treat co-occurring disorders).

How, then, is a budding substance abuse treatment professional supposed to plan for the future? We believe that there will always exist a need and avenue for individuals without a master's degree to provide addictions-related services. For a more expansive scope of work that allows for increased job security and flexibility, however, a master's degree will probably be the minimum degree needed.

Regardless of how exactly the future unfolds, the bottom line is that we are likely to see increased standardization as it applies to the preparation of addictions professionals, "help to raise the bar of professional practice, better protect the public, and realize our…goals of portability" (Erford, 2012).

References

American Counseling Association. (n.d.). *Licensure and certification.* Retrieved from http://www.counseling.org/counselors/LicensureAndCert.aspx

Capuzzi, D., & Gross, D. (2009). *Introduction to the counseling profession* (5th ed.). Columbus, OH: Pearson.

Cogan, M. (1955). The problem of defining a profession. *Annals of the American Academy of Political and Social Science, 297,* 105–111.

Department of Veterans Affairs. (2006). *The VA history in brief* [VA Pamphlet 80-97-2]. Washington, DC: Author.

Erford, B. (2012, December). Raising the bar: The power of standardization. *Counseling Today, 5*(6), 5.

Ginter, E. J. (2002). Journal of Counseling & Development (JCD) and counseling's interwoven nature: Achieving a more complete understanding of the present through 'historization' (musings of an existing editor—An editorial postscript). *Journal of Counseling & Development, 80*(2), 219.

Jellinek, E. M. (1960). *The disease concept of alcoholism.* New Haven, CT: Hillhouse Press.

Montagna, J. (2012). *The Industrial Revolution.* New Haven, CT: Yale-New Haven Teachers Institute.

NAADAC, the Association for Addiction Professionals. (2011). *Licensing of addiction professionals in states.* Alexandra, VA: Author.

National Council on Alcoholism and Drug Dependence. (n.d.) *Our founder, Marty Mann.* Retrieved from http://www.ncadd.org/index.php/about-ncadd/testimonials-from-the-media

Patient Protection and Affordable Care Act, 42 U.S.C. § 18001 *et seq.* (2010).

Profession. (n.d.). In *BusinessDictionary.com.* Retrieved from http://www.businessdictionary.com/definition/profession.html

Professional body. (n.d.). In *BusinessDictionary.com.* Retrieved from http://www.businessdictionary.com/definition/professional-body.html

U.S. Department of Health and Human Services. (2005). *A national review of state alcohol and drug treatment and certification standards for substance abuse counselors and prevention professionals.* Rockville, MD: National Clearinghouse for Alcohol and Drug Information.

U.S. Department of Health and Human Services. (2011). *Scopes of practice and career ladder for substance use disorder counseling.* Rockville, MD: National Clearinghouse for Alcohol and Drug Information.

White, W. (1998). *Slaying the dragon: The history of addiction treatment and recovery in America.* Bloomington, IL: Chestnut Health Systems.

CHAPTER 4

The Counseling Process

CHAPTER OBJECTIVES

- Understand the transdisciplinary foundations of understanding addiction, treatment knowledge, application to practice, and professional readiness
- Understand the clinical evaluation skills of screening and assessment, treatment planning, and referral
- Understand the case management skills of treatment plan implementation, consulting, and continuing assessment and treatment planning
- Understand the core elements of individual counseling: empathy, genuineness or congruence, attentiveness, respect, immediacy, concreteness, and warmth
- Understand the counseling skills of reflecting, questioning, confrontation, self-disclosing, interpreting, and clarifying
- Seek and select a personal approach to counseling
- Understand clinical practices of documentation, supervision, and client and community education

In the field of chemical dependency counseling, the counseling process is more than making friends with clients, giving information, and referring them to self-help groups. Knowledge, skills, and attitudes all play important parts in the practice of substance abuse counseling and the treatment of addictions. Chapter 1 discussed the use of self in the counseling process, which is a very powerful skill. However, it is one thing for a counselor to know what attitudes, beliefs, and behaviors are therapeutic and another thing to be able to implement them to create change in others. This requires learning the skills that allow you to use yourself in the counseling process to create change. Chemical dependency counselor skills and competencies have been described by various certification groups.

This chapter will describe the clinical evaluation skills of screening and assessment, treatment planning, and referral, and the case management skills of implementation of a treatment plan, consulting, and continuing assessment and treatment planning. Other competencies that are covered in this chapter are using individual counseling, including rapport building, empathy, genuineness, attentiveness, respect, immediacy, concreteness, and warmth; and developing core relationship abilities, such as listening, reflecting, questioning, confronting, self-disclosing, interpreting, and clarifying; selecting a treatment approach; documenting and charting; using supervision; and accessing client and community education.

Chemical Dependency Counselor Skills

Basic chemical dependency counseling skills have been defined by several certification and accreditation organizations to help educators develop a curriculum for training chemical dependency counselors and a criterion for evaluating these trainees for certification. A set of skills has been developed and updated by the Center for Substance Abuse Treatment, a part of the Substance Abuse and Mental Health Services Administration, U.S. Department of Health and Human Services, through the work of the Addiction Technology Transfer Centers' National Curriculum Committee (Center for Substance Abuse Treatment, 2011). Committee members included representatives from the Addiction Training Centers, the Center for Substance Abuse Treatment, and the Project for Addiction Counselor Training. They have attempted to describe the knowledge, skills, and attitudes essential to chemical dependency counseling in today's health care environment in a technical assistance publication, *Addiction Counseling Competencies: The Knowledge, Skills, and Attitudes of Professional Practice*, which has been referred to as the TAP 21 (Technical Assistance Publication #21). This publication, DHHS Publication No. (SMA) 08-4171, can be downloaded without cost from the U.S. Department of Health and Human Services, Public Health Service, Substance Abuse and Mental Health Services Administration at their online store at www.store.samhsa.gov.

The first section of this publication describes Transdisciplinary Foundations, which are described as knowledge and attitudes that are prerequisite to the development of competency in the professional treatment of substance use disorders. They form the basis of understanding upon which discipline-specific proficiencies are built (Center for Substance Abuse Treatment, 2011). These include the following:

Understanding Addiction

• Understanding a variety of models and theories of addiction and other problems related to substance use, including terms and concepts of theory research and practice; theoretical models from other disciplines, such as sociology, medicine, psychology, and religion; how to access this literature; and how to evaluate and apply these models and theories.

The attitudes needed for this are openness to and valuing of information from different fields of study, especially if they differ from one's personally held views; an appreciation of the complexity involved in fully understanding addiction; and, a willingness to apply critical thinking to form personal concepts.

- Recognizing the social, political, economic, and cultural context within which addiction and substance abuse exist, including risk and resiliency factors that characterize individuals and groups and their living environments; how this impacts drug-taking activity; the history of licit and illicit drug use; research identifying risk and resiliency factors; and statistics of incidence and prevalence or substance use disorders in the general population and the major demographic groups.

    The attitudes needed include recognition of the importance of contextual variables and an appreciation for differences between and within cultures.

- Knowing the behavioral, psychological, physical health, and social effects of psychoactive substances for the user and significant others, including the fundamental concepts of pharmacological properties and the effects of all psychoactive substances; and knowledge of the continuum of drug use, the various effects of psychoactive substances, the varying courses of addiction, the effects of chronic use on consumers and others, and the relationship between infectious diseases and substance use.

    The attitudes needed include a sensitivity to multiple influences in the developmental course of addiction and an interest in scientific research findings.

- Recognizing the potential for substance use disorders to mimic a variety of medical and mental health conditions and the potential for medical and mental health conditions to coexist with addiction and substance abuse, including knowledge of normal human growth and development, symptoms of substance use disorders that are similar to medical symptoms and/or mental health conditions and their interaction; knowledge of common disorders that exist with addictions; and methods for differentiating between medical disorders and addictions.

    The attitudes that are needed include the willingness to reserve judgment until completion of a thorough clinical evaluation, the willingness to work with people who might display and/or have mental health conditions, the willingness to refer cases outside one's expertise to other professionals, and a willingness to appreciate the contribution of multiple disciplines in the evaluation process.

Treatment Knowledge

- Knowing the philosophies, practices, policies, and outcomes of the most generally accepted and scientifically supported models of treatment, recovery, relapse prevention, and continuing care for addiction and other substance-related problems, including knowledge of generally accepted models; the philosophy, practices, policies, and outcomes of these models; and alternate models that demonstrate potential.

The attitudes needed are that a variety of approaches and models are valid, and being open to new, evidence-based treatment approaches, including pharmacological interventions.

• Recognizing the importance of family, social networks, and community systems in the treatment and recovery process, including understanding the role of these groups as assets or obstacles in the treatment and recovery process, and methods for incorporating family and social dynamics in treatment and recovery processes.

The attitude needed is an appreciation for the significance and complementary nature of various systems in facilitating treatment and recovery.

• Understanding the importance of research and outcome data and their application in clinical practice, including knowledge of research methods in the social and behavioral sciences, sources of research literature relevant to the prevention and treatment of addiction, benefits and limitations of research, and scientific research on epidemiology, etiology, and treatment efficacy.

The attitudes necessary include a recognition of the importance of scientific research to the delivery of addiction treatment and an openness to new information.

• Understanding the value of an interdisciplinary approach to addiction treatment, including the roles and contributions of multiple disciplines to treatment efficacy, the terms and concepts necessary to communicate effectively across disciplines, and the importance of communication with other disciplines.

The attitudes necessary include a desire to collaborate, respect for the contributions of multiple disciplines to the recovery process, and commitment to professionalism.

Application to Practice

• Understanding the established diagnostic criteria for substance use disorders and knowing treatment modalities and placement criteria within the continuum of care, including established diagnostic criteria, such as the *Diagnostic and Statistical Manual of Mental Disorders* (DSM) and the *International Classifications of Diseases* (ICD) criteria; knowing established placement criteria developed by various states and professional organizations; understanding strengths and limitations of various diagnostic and placement criteria; and knowing the continuum of treatment services and activities.

The attitudes needed include an openness to a variety of treatment services based on client need and a recognition of the value of research findings.

- Knowing a variety of helping strategies for reducing the negative effects of substance use, abuse, and dependence, including, but not limited to, evaluation methods and tools, stage-appropriate interventions, motivational interviewing, involvement of family and significant others, mutual-help and self-help programs, coerced and voluntary care models, and brief and longer-term interventions.

  The attitudes needed include an openness to various approaches to recovery and an appreciation that different approaches work for different people.

- Tailoring helping strategies and treatment modalities to the client's stage of dependence, change, or recovery.

  The attitudes needed include flexibility in choice of treatment modalities and respect for the client's racial, cultural, economic, and sociopolitical backgrounds.

- Providing treatment services appropriate to the personal and cultural identity and language of the client, including knowledge of various cultural norms, values, beliefs, and behaviors; cultural differences in verbal and nonverbal communication; and resources to help develop individualized treatment plans.

  The attitudes needed include respect for individual differences within and among cultures.

- Adapting practice to the range of treatment settings and modalities, including knowledge of the strengths and limitations of available treatment settings and modalities, and how to access and make referrals to them.

  The attitudes needed are flexibility and creativity in practice application.

- Being familiar with medical and pharmacological resources in the treatment of substance use disorders, including knowledge of current medical and pharmacological interventions; the assets and liabilities of these interventions; health practitioners in the community who are knowledgeable about addiction and addictions treatment; and the role that medical problems and complications can play in the intervention and treatment of addiction.

  The attitudes needed include an openness and flexibility with respect to the potential risks and benefits of pharmacotherapies for the treatment and recovery process.

- Understanding the variety of insurance and health maintenance options available and the importance of helping clients access those benefits, including knowledge of existing public and private payment plans; methods for gaining access to available payment plans; policies and procedures used by available payment plans; and key personnel, roles, and positions within plans used by the client populations.

Attitudes needed include a willingness to cooperate with payment providers, a willingness to explore treatment alternatives, and an interest in promoting cost-effective, high-quality care.

- Recognizing that crisis may indicate an underlying substance use disorder and may be a window of opportunity for change, including knowledge of the features of crisis, which may include but are not limited to the following: family disruption, social and legal consequences, physical and psychological panic states, and physical dysfunction; substance use screening and assessment methods; intervention principles and methods; principles of crisis case management; post-traumatic stress characteristics; critical incident debriefing methods; and available resources for assistance in the management of crisis situations.

   Attitudes needed include a willingness to respond and follow through in crisis situations and a willingness to consult others when necessary.

- Understanding the need for and use of methods for measuring treatment outcome, including knowledge of the treatment outcome research literature, scientific process in applied research, appropriate measures of outcome, and methods for measuring the multiple variables of treatment outcome.

   The attitudes needed include recognition of the importance of collecting and reporting on outcome data and an interest in integrating research findings into ongoing treatment design.

Professional Readiness

- Understanding diverse cultures and incorporating the relevant needs of culturally diverse groups, as well as people with disabilities, into clinical practice; the unique influence the client's culture, lifestyle, gender, and other relevant factors may have on behavior; the relationship between substance use and diverse cultures, values and lifestyles; assessment and intervention methods that are appropriate to culture and gender; counseling methods relevant to the needs of culturally diverse groups and people with disabilities; and the (1990) American With Disabilities Act and other legislation related to human, civil, and client rights.

   The attitudes needed include willingness to explore and identify one's own cultural values, and the acceptance of other cultural values as valid for other individuals.

- Understanding the importance of self-awareness in one's personal, professional, and cultural life, including knowledge of personal and professional strengths and limitations and cultural, ethnic, or gender biases.

Attitudes needed include openness to constructive supervision and a willingness to grow and change personally and professionally.

- Understanding the addiction professional's obligations to adhere to ethical and behavioral standards of conduct in the helping relationship, including knowledge of state and federal regulations related to the practice of addiction treatment, scope-of-practice standards, and a discipline-specific ethics code.

  The attitudes needed include a willingness to operate in accordance with the highest ethical standards and a willingness to comply with regulatory and professional expectations.

- Understanding the importance of ongoing supervision and continuing education in the delivery of client services, including knowledge of the benefits of self-assessment and clinical supervision for professional growth and development, the value of consultation to enhance personal and professional growth, resources available for continuing education, and supervision principles and methods.

  Attitudes necessary include a commitment to continuing professional education and a willingness to engage in a supervision relationship.

- Understanding the addictions professional's obligation to participate in prevention as well as treatment, including knowledge of research-based prevention models and strategies, the relationship between prevention and treatment, environmental strategies and prevention campaigns, and the benefits of working with community coalitions.

  Attitudes necessary include an appreciation of the inherent value of prevention and an openness to research-based prevention strategies.

- Understanding and applying setting-specific policies and procedures for handling crises or dangerous situations, including safety measures for clients and staff and knowledge of setting-specific policies and procedures, what constitutes a crisis or danger to the client and/or others, the range of appropriate responses to a crisis or dangerous situation, universal precautions, legal implications of crisis response, and exceptions to confidentiality rules in crises or dangerous situations.

  Attitudes include an understanding of the potential seriousness of crisis situations, awareness of the need for caution and self-control in the face of a crisis or danger, and a willingness to request help in potentially dangerous situations.

The second section of *Addiction Counseling Competencies: The Knowledge, Skills, and Attitudes of Professional Practice* (Center for Substance Abuse Treatment, 2011) outlines eight practice dimensions of professional practice of addiction counseling. The dimensions are supported by counselor competencies.

The counselor's success in carrying out a practice dimension depends on his or her ability to attain the competencies underlying that component.

Clinical Evaluation

Evaluation is a crucial part of the counseling process. It involves screening and assessment. Without a good assessment, the counselor does not have a roadmap of how to proceed. This process is so important that an entire chapter (Chapter 5) has been devoted to it. Clinical evaluation involves a multitude of skills, from testing to diagnosing, that precede treatment planning or goal setting.

Screening

Screening is defined as the process through which counselor, client, and available significant others determine the most appropriate initial course of action, given the client's needs, characteristics, and available resources within the community. The counselor should first establish rapport with the client and assess if there is a crisis situation and if there is a need for additional professional assistance. This might include law enforcement, medical assistance, or care for dependent children.

Counselors should then systematically gather information from the client and other available sources, using screening instruments and other methods that are sensitive to culture and gender. Age should also be a factor in choosing assessment instruments. Screening instruments such as the *Michigan Alcohol Screening Test* (MAST) were designed for adults with a history of alcohol abuse. A number of questions on the MAST are irrelevant for adolescents. Questions concerning being arrested for driving while intoxicated or being hospitalized for alcohol-related physical problems do not apply to adolescents without driver's licenses and who have not been drinking long enough to develop major physical problems.

A screening interview should include current and historic substance use and abuse, a health history, previous or current mental health problems, a history of mental health or substance abuse treatment, mental status—an orientation to time and place—a social and family history including who might be available for conjoint treatment (marital or family counseling), and any current social, environmental, and/or economic constraints on the client's ability to successfully follow through with an action plan. These constraints might be a lack of insurance or financial resources to pay for treatment, inability or unwillingness to enter inpatient treatment for fear of loss of job or income, or lack of childcare. The scope of this history taking should involve only the information that will be necessary for crisis intervention and to make an appropriate diagnosis and referral for treatment. More in-depth history taking will be done during the treatment process.

The first consideration with a plan of action is the safety of the client and others. Alcohol and other drug toxicity and withdrawal symptoms should be evaluated for the need of detoxification under medical supervision. The danger of harm to others (homicide) and harm to self (suicide) must be evaluated to determine the need to warn potential victims or to intervene in a possible suicide attempt.

Once these issues of danger are eliminated or resolved, counselors need to help clients identify the role of substance use in their current life problems. During the history taking, counselors can make note of the problem areas that the client is self-identifying, such as arrests, loss of employment, divorce, abuse, and physical problems. They can then return to these problem areas and inquire about their connection to substance abuse.

One technique that can be used to help clients see this connection is a life-history graph. Clients are asked to make a graph of the ups and downs of their lives, labeling each peak and valley. They then take a different color marker or pen and draw a drinking history line on the same graph, indicating amount of alcohol and other drugs used during their lifetime. Often this graphic display of an increase in substance use during the same time period that problems increased helps clients make the connection.

When the client has decided that substance abuse has created problems in his or her life, the counselor can assess the client's readiness for treatment or change and can suggest the treatment options that are relevant to the client's needs, characteristics, and goals. Recommendations for treatment should be made on the basis of ethnic, gender, and age considerations; financial resources; employment issues; severity of the problem; social supports; needs of family members for treatment; and available resources.

The next step is to construct with the client and appropriate others an initial plan of action. Once the plan has been agreed upon, specific steps should be taken to initiate an admission to a treatment program or a referral to other types of treatment. The final part of the screening process is to follow up on the admission or referral to ensure that the client successfully began an appropriate course of treatment.

Assessment

Assessment is defined as an ongoing process through which the counselor collaborates with the client and others to gather and interpret information that is necessary for planning treatment and evaluating client progress. In this process, counselors select and use comprehensive assessment instruments that are sensitive to age, gender, and culture. The following is a list of areas of assessment and suggestions of possible evaluation instruments:

- **Alcohol and other drug use history**—After taking a treatment history, counselors should obtain releases of information to request treatment records from previous physicians, therapists, and drug treatment programs. These reports can be invaluable in learning what worked and what failed with this client and can save valuable treatment time.

- **Family issues and dynamics**—A family genogram (see Chapter 7) for charting intergenerational addiction, alliances, coalitions, co-existing problems, and adaptive consequences is an example of one helpful tool.

- **Work history and career issues**—For clients who need career counseling, there are several instruments that can assess interest and potential success in various careers. A referral to a career-counseling center or a vocational rehabilitation program may also be appropriate.

- **Psychological concerns**—A variety of assessment instruments and other personality tests may be useful in assessing mental disorders. A referral to a psychologist or a psychiatrist may be useful if there is a history of previous mental illness or a current report of symptoms of depression or other mood disorders, such as a change in sleeping and eating habits and depressed or manic moods that do not subside 30 days after detoxification; symptoms of thought disorders, such as hallucinations or delusions not associated with withdrawal; symptoms of anxiety disorder and phobias; or other mental illness symptoms. It is often challenging to make a mental illness diagnosis while a person is under the influence of substances or is in the process of detoxification.

- **Physical and mental health status**—A physical examination by a health care professional and a mental heath status exam determine if the client is reality based and is oriented with respect to current time and place.

- **Educational and basic life skills**—This may involve an intelligence test or various aptitude tests to evaluate reading and mathematical skills. A general evaluation of self-care ability and mobility may also be needed.

- **Socioeconomic characteristics, lifestyle, and current legal status**—This data can be compiled from an interview that questions financial resources; employment status; resources for shelter, food, and clothing; family supports; relationships with significant others; any pending criminal or civil court actions; and probation or parole status.

- **Use of community resources**—The evaluation interview may include questions about current use of resources, such as shelters, food programs, health care programs, support groups, churches, mental health centers, aid for dependent children, welfare, or other community agencies or programs.

- **Behavioral indicators of problems in the domains listed above**—One of the best tools a counselor has is his or her observation skills. Assessment has two parts: what the client reports through written or oral modalities and what the counselor observes. These two parts may contradict each other and indicate the need for further evaluation.

Once the data has been gathered, the counselor analyzes and interprets the data to determine treatment recommendations. This is often done in consultation with other professionals, other treatment team members, and supervision. Assessment findings should be completely documented in the client's file along with treatment recommendations that can lead to an individualized treatment plan.

Treatment Planning

The treatment plan is as important as a good evaluation, and it should follow directly from the information that was gathered and interpreted in the clinical evaluation process. *Treatment planning* is defined as a collaborative process through which the counselor and client develop desired treatment outcomes and identify the strategies for achieving them. At a minimum, the treatment plan addresses the identified substance-related disorder(s) plus issues related to treatment progress, including relationships with family or friends, employment, education, spirituality, health concerns, and legal needs. It is important to note the word *collaborative*. In the past, counselors have been guilty of using the same treatment plan for everyone and presenting it to the client, instead of co-evolving the treatment plan. Chemical dependency is complicated and does not affect everyone in the same way. Counselors should not expect a universal treatment plan that is created prior to the evaluation process to work for very many of their clients or to address individual problems.

In co-creating a treatment plan, the counselor needs to assemble and interpret all of the evaluation data and explain this information to the client. The counselor should clarify any areas of misunderstanding or confusion, gather any further information needed, and explain the implications of treatment with the client. The counselor should then confirm the client's readiness to participate in treatment and make certain that the client is aware of what the commitment entails.

Once the counselor gets a commitment from the client, he or she can then begin to prioritize the client's problems and needs that were outlined in the evaluation. Using the prioritized list, the client and counselor need to agree upon the treatment outcomes for each need; decide what strategy will be applied to attain the outcomes; match treatment activities and community resources to the needs; and develop a mutually acceptable plan of action and method for monitoring and evaluating progress. Strategies for change should be measurable, so the counselor and the client can see progress. Vague treatment goals like "becoming happy" or "learning about myself" are very difficult to measure. Treatment goals like "getting my driver's license back" or daily journal writing for self-evaluation are more easily measured. Sometimes goals need to be divided into small achievable steps.

While it is preferable to inform clients as soon as they begin the treatment process of their confidentiality rights, the program procedures that safeguard them, and the exceptions to these rights that are imposed by law—such as child-abuse reporting and danger to self and others—(see Chapter 2 for a complete discussion on disclosures), now is a good time to review program-specific rules for conduct concerning outside contact, visitation, and what is expected of them while in the treatment program. The client should be given a written statement about patients' rights, limitations to the rights, and program rules.

The treatment plan should be a flexible document that can be evaluated and changed at regular intervals or when circumstances change. For instance, it may be necessary to change a health need to a higher priority, or it may become evident that marital or family work may need to be done earlier than was planned because of the family system's involvement with the addiction. Counselors may be overwhelmed by the list of needs generated by the evaluation and the length of time the client's insurance allows for treatment. Given these limitations, the treatment plan may need to differentiate between short-term goals and long-term goals. The counselor may only be able to meet the first few priorities that will probably involve intervening with the substance abuse and stabilizing the client. However, if the treatment plan is for long-term recovery in many areas of the client's life, the counselor can provide referrals to community resources that will help the client continue with the treatment plan after he or she is discharged from the program.

Referral

Familiarity with community resources and a willingness to refer clients to these resources are essential for the chemical dependency counselor who wants long-term success for his or her clients. *Referral* is defined as the process of facilitating the client's utilization of available support systems and community resources to meet the needs identified in clinical evaluation and/or treatment planning.

The first step in becoming skilled at the referral process is to identify and establish relationships with civic groups, agencies, other professionals, government entities, and the community at large to ensure appropriate referrals, to identify service gaps, to expand community resources, and to help address unmet needs. This process takes time, but it is worth the effort. Many communities may have already compiled referral books that are regularly updated either online or in print. If there are not any current directories, counselors can create their own referral books by collecting business cards, brochures, and information about community resources and professionals. The internet can be a starting place to find out what is available in a community. Professional associations can also provide information about their members in cities across the country if referrals are to professionals outside the community where the treatment was provided.

Because many resources are funded by shifting tax bases or grants and because there is a high degree of turnover in the substance abuse treatment field, these referral sources should be continually evaluated to determine their appropriateness. When these resources are identified, counselors can then make referrals for their clients in order to meet the needs that were identified in the treatment plan. Counselors should explain in clear and specific language the necessity for and process of referral to increase the likelihood of client understanding and follow-through. It may even be necessary for the counselor initially to accompany the client to the referral source.

Part of the referral process is obtaining appropriate releases of information from the client prior to making the referral so that relevant information can be exchanged between the counselor and the agency or professionals to whom the referral is being made. The amount and type of information that is shared with the referral source by the counselor should be consistent with confidentiality regulations and generally accepted professional standards of care (see Chapter 2). The release to disclose information is also important, because it allows the counselor to follow up on the referral and to evaluate the outcome. If a referral did not meet the client's need, then a different referral can be made.

Case Management/Service Coordination

Once the treatment plan has been established and referrals have been made to outside resources, the process of treatment can begin. Case management is similar to quarterbacking a football team: The case manager does not do all the work, but takes direction from a coach or program director, utilizes a team treatment approach, gets consultation from various sources, and implements the game plan. *Case management* is defined as the administrative, clinical, and evaluative activities that bring the client, treatment services, community agencies, and other resources together to focus on the issues and needs that were identified in the treatment plan. Case management establishes a framework of action for the achievement of specified goals. It involves collaboration with the client, coordination of treatment and referral services, liaison activities with community resources and managed care systems, and ongoing evaluation of treatment progress and client needs.

Implementing the Treatment Plan

Implementing the treatment plan is the core of the case management process. Counselor activities associated with this process include (a) initiating collaboration with referral sources; (b) obtaining and interpreting all relevant screening, assessment, and initial treatment planning information; (c) confirming the client's eligibility for admission and continued readiness for treatment and change; (d) completing necessary administrative procedures for admission to treatment; and (e) establishing accurate client expectations for treatment, including the nature of services, program goals, program procedures, rules regarding client conduct, schedule of treatment activities, costs of treatment, factors affecting duration of care, and the client's rights and responsibilities.

Once all of the administrative duties have been completed, there is an ongoing expectation that the case manager will coordinate all treatment activities with services that are provided to the client by other resources. This may include doing individual therapy with the client; referring the client to appropriate group therapy, marital therapy, or family therapy; referring the client to educational presentations; monitoring progress in all of the program modalities with external resources; and evaluating the client's readiness to move to higher levels in the program or to terminate treatment.

Consulting

Another facet of case management is *consulting* with other treatment providers. Counselors' skills in this area include being able to summarize a client's background, treatment plan, recovery progress, and problems inhibiting progress for the purpose of assuring quality of care; gaining feedback from the client and other treatment providers; and planning changes in the course of treatment. In this process, counselors are working with professionals in many specialized fields, and they need to be aware of the terminology they use and the roles they play in the treatment of chemical dependency.

Case managers are also a part of a multidisciplinary treatment team and make significant contributions to this process. They are the contact person between the treatment program and the outside community. As such, they must be responsible for guarding the client's right to confidentiality and to demonstrate respect and nonjudgmental attitudes toward their clients in all contacts with professionals and other agencies.

Continuing Assessment and Treatment Planning

Case management is an ongoing process that includes *continuing assessment and treatment planning*. Counselors maintain ongoing contact with clients to ensure that they are adhering to the action plan. They need to watch for stages of change and signs of treatment progress. If progress is stalled or it appears that the treatment plan that was initially created at intake is no longer appropriate, both the counselor and the client need to negotiate a new plan. Although relapse prevention should begin at the initial treatment planning stage, this is a good time to evaluate this part of the program. It is a mistake to wait until the last therapy session to develop a relapse prevention plan (see Chapter 10). Any treatment plan change or addition to the treatment plan needs to be well documented in the client's chart so that the rest of the treatment team is aware of the changes.

Individual Counseling

There are many different theories of counseling, including cognitive-behavioral theories (e.g., rational-emotive therapy), psychoanalytic theories, existential therapy, person-centered therapy, Gestalt therapy, transactional analysis, behavioral therapy, reality therapy, and many integrated theories. It is beyond the scope of this book to describe each of these theories, and the reader should consult a counseling-theories book (e.g., Corey, 2012) for the details of each of them. All of these counseling theories, however, agree that the establishment of a quality relationship between counselor and client is of utmost importance. Other common elements of counseling theories are the skills that create change. This section will discuss the core elements that facilitate counseling—*rapport, empathy, genuineness, attentiveness, respect, immediacy, concreteness,* and *warmth*—and the skills of *listening, reflecting, questioning, confronting, self-disclosing, interpreting,* and *clarifying.*

Core Elements

The core elements of counseling are the qualities of the counseling process that make the counselor–client relationship unique. They involve behaviors and attitudes and set the stage for the counseling process to begin.

Rapport

Shertzer and Stone (1980) offer the following explanation of *rapport*:

> Rapport is described most simply as a condition essential to a comfortable and unconditional relationship between counselor and counselee. It is established and maintained through the counselor's genuine interest in and acceptance of the client. It cannot be forced or contrived. It is a bond characterized by interest, responsiveness, and a sensitive emotional involvement. (p. 261)

Rapport needs to be established from the beginning of client contact and carried through to the last minute of contact. It is the counselor's behavior, tone, choice of words, and topics that say to the client, "I care about you, and you are safe here." The therapeutic relationship is not like any other. The 50-minute hour has different rules and expectations than time spent in general life activities. It is a safe place for people to be vulnerable, to be in pain, to try new behaviors, and to find solutions to their problems. Initially, many clients experience ambivalence about coming to therapy, and they need reassurance. Counselors should not overwhelm clients in the beginning by jumping into problem solving too soon, yet they need to establish what will happen during their time together. Counselors can be too casual, talking about the weather or sports, which gives clients the impression that counseling is merely a social visit.

Opening introductions should be brief, with the counselor being attentive and demonstrating interest in the client, while moving to the purpose of the therapy. Counselors can ask, "How can I help you?" or "What brings you here?" The counselor develops rapport by being interested, attentive, and understanding. The time it takes to establish rapport varies with clients and is dependent on the counselor's skills and experience, as well as the client's motivation. Clients who are mandated to counseling may be more resistant to developing a trusting relationship with counselors.

Empathy

Empathy is a counselor's putting himself or herself in the client's shoes (Greason & Cashwell, 2009). It is different from sympathy. Empathy is comprehending the emotions of another, not feeling the same emotions, as in sympathy. Empathy is also the counselor's communicating back to the client what the counselor perceives the client is describing. It is an interrelationship between two who understand the experience being shared.

Empathy requires good listening skills that involve listening to not only what is being said but also how it is being said. Counselors listen to the process, as well as to the content, of communication. Nonverbal behavior can be as important as verbal behavior. When reflecting his or her observations back to the client, the counselor can summarize what is being said and what he or she is observing the client doing, for example:

> CLIENT: (wringing her hands) "Every time I try to tell my husband what's bothering me, he just shuts down and leaves the room."

> COUNSELOR: "I hear that you are very upset with your husband, and I can see you wringing your hands in concern."

> CLIENT: "Yes. I don't know what else to do."

Even if the counselor is wrong or misses the point, he or she is still creating a healing environment by becoming intensely involved with the client. "The communication that is important is taking place on a subterranean, therapeutic level" (Small, 1990, p. 29).

In addition, empathy is the counselor's ability to not lose him- or herself in the process. Rogers (1961) believed that empathy was one of the six necessary conditions of counseling. He described it as a sensing of the client's world "as if it were your own, but without ever losing the 'as if' quality" (p. 284). It is not possible to completely understand or experience another person's position. Counselors who become over-identified with their clients lose the perspective they need to help them. If they become overwhelmed with emotion or hopelessness, they cannot communicate hope and the possibility of change.

Elliott, Bohart, Watson, and Greenberg (2011) describe some roadblocks to empathy that counselors need to guard against. First, clients will not feel heard if counselors do not utilize good listening skills and interrupt them or fail to maintain appropriate eye contact. Second, empathy does not include counselors' analyzing clients and assuming they are experts on how clients are feeling. Third, when counselors are preoccupied with their own issues or life problems, they are unavailable to be truly with their clients. Although it may be useful for a counselor to share his or her addiction and recovery story with clients, real empathy is hearing the uniqueness of each client's path of addiction. The areas of similarity will give the counselor a good picture of what the client has experienced. Counselors, however, need to be flexible enough to discard their ideas, tactics, or goals if they do not fit the client's situation.

Genuineness or Congruence

Genuineness is also referred to as *congruence*. Rogers (1967) described it as the counselor's being himself or herself and not denying himself or herself. "By this we mean that the feelings the counselor is experiencing are available to him, available to his awareness, that he is able to live these feelings, be them in the relationship, and to communicate them if appropriate" (p. 90). When counselors are congruent and genuine, they are free to be themselves without phoniness. They are not playing a role or wearing a mask. Genuineness "cannot be faked" and is present to the degree "the relationship is empathic and not phony" (Egan, 2014, pp. 47, 79). This suggests that counselors who know themselves and are able to be fully truthful will do better than those not comfortable with who or how they are in the world.

There are times when the genuineness concept can be distorted. It does not mean that counselors communicate everything they are thinking or feeling. For example, boredom or hostile feelings toward the client may not facilitate a therapeutic environment for clients and may come from the counselor's projections or countertransference. If these feelings are real and persistent, however, the counselor should refer the client to another therapist. Genuineness is also not total self-disclosure, but if counselors use self-disclosure, it should be honest. Genuineness and congruence allow counselors to help their clients put down their masks and face their difficult or defended feelings. It is easier for clients to acknowledge their genuineness if counselors are modeling this quality.

Genuineness is especially important in chemical dependency counseling because of, in part, the shame surrounding having an addiction. Alcoholics and addicts are familiar with the cultural stigma surrounding addiction and have had plenty of experience with those who disapprove of their behavior. Alcoholics and addicts are masters at masking feelings and playing games. Many expect to be seen as "less than" and despised (Gray, 2010). Counselors who can risk being real in every way with these clients can have a major impact and create real contact.

Attentiveness

Attentiveness requires an ability to strategically control attention and focus and not be distracted by irrelevant internal or external variables (Greason & Cashwell, 2009). Attentiveness requires counselors to listen and observe in order to try to understand the client's feelings and perspectives that are being presented. Egan (2014) indicated that counselors communicate attending behaviors through both verbal and nonverbal channels to their clients. The counselor is not dividing his or her attention between the client and other extraneous variables. Non-attending behaviors include frequent breaks in eye contact, and topic-jumping verbal behavior.

When counselors are truly listening to their clients, they can pick up subtle nuances of the conversation and will be more accurate in their observations and reflections, which will foster the counseling relationship. Attentiveness is communicated through facial expressions, body positions and movement, and verbal response (Egan, 2014). This "attentive presence," when experienced by clients "invite[s] or encourage[s] them to trust you, open up, and explore the significant dimensions of their problem situations" (Egan, 2014, p. 76). Facial expressions communicate messages that are meaningful to the client. These include eye contact, welcoming body posture, and manipulation of facial muscles to produce positive connotations of smiles or negative responses of frowns (Egan, 2014). Eye contact has different meanings for different cultures. Some cultures (e.g., Native American) find eye contact rude, but other cultures see it as a sign of attentiveness. This does not mean staring at the client. A counselor's eyes can move slightly away from the client's and then return. Head nodding can be an affirmation of the client, but it should not be overdone, and facial expressions provide a mirror for the client and communicate that the counselor is alert and interested. Body position also gives messages to the client. Tension and an upright position may imply a working state, while a relaxed posture may communicate comfort with the counseling process.

Verbal behaviors can also reflect an attentive state. Counselors who stay with the topic and help the client develop the theme he or she is exploring will be more facilitative to the counseling process than those who interrupt their clients or who jump from topic to topic. The tone and pitch of the counselor's voice also communicate a sense of comfort and acceptance. The use of minimal responses, such as "mm-hmm" or "ah," can be used to let clients know that they are being heard, but much like the head nod, they can be overused.

Respect

Unconditional positive regard is one of the elements that Rogers (1957) believed was necessary to bring about personality change. Depending on the counselor's theoretical orientation, change can include surface or deep changes in an individual's personality structure, behavior or thoughts, level of acceptance, and/or ability to live more completely in the present (Corey, 2012). This positive regard is seen as unconditional because it does not depend on the client's behavior. In the face of the client's imperfections, the counselor is nonjudgmental and accepts the client for who he or she is, assuming the client has done the best possible with the circumstances given. Counselors may not *agree* with a client's perspective, but they must *respect* it and affirm the client's right to arrive at his or her own decisions, solutions, and understanding (Corey, 2012).

Respect includes acting in the best interests of clients, expressing care and concern, and knowing when to help and when to refrain from helping (Gibson, 2006). Truax and Carkhuff (2007) developed a scale to measure positive regard, called "nonpossessive warmth," which was later labeled "respect." The level of respect toward which to aspire is that which esteems the client "regardless of the client's particular characteristics" (Gibson, 2006, p. 85). Furthermore, "respect is precisely the quality that the professional calls upon when the client is anything but estimable" (Gibson, 2006, p. 85).

To communicate respect to clients, counselors need to believe that clients have the capacity to solve their own problems. It is the counselors' responsibility to help clients find their own inner strengths and solutions. For instance, if a client is struggling with a decision about whether or not to leave his wife, a counselor who respects his client will allow him to struggle with the decision and support his struggle, not give him the answer. For example:

> CLIENT: "I just don't think I can live with Judy any longer. All we do is fight, and there never seem to be any good times between us. But I keep remembering how good our marriage used to be before we got caught up with drugs. What should I do? Stay or go?"

> COUNSELOR: "Why do you think it is so difficult for you to make this decision?"

> CLIENT: "I keep thinking that maybe the drugs have caused the problems. If we can both get clean and sober, we might be able to go back to the way it used to be."

> COUNSELOR: "It sounds like you still have hope for your marriage."

> CLIENT: "I guess I do."

COUNSELOR: "What can you do to make it better?"

CLIENT: "Well, first I need to work on my own recovery."

An important part of chemical dependency counseling is helping clients with addictions to take responsibility for themselves. Often they have cognitive distortions about their real strengths and weaknesses and jump from a position of powerlessness to omnipotence. Counselors who can demonstrate respect can help their clients find their real strengths and weaknesses and support them in taking responsibility for both. This respect will help to give those with addictions problems hope that they may actually be worthwhile people with the ability to make choices and govern their lives (Gibson, 2006).

Immediacy

Immediacy is a term that describes the counselor's ability to communicate feelings and experiences that are happening between the counselor and the client in the here and now. It is sharing with the client what the counselor believes is happening on many levels at the moment. This helps the client clarify what he or she may be feeling about the counselor or the counseling process. Immediacy takes the focus off of the content of the communication and brings it to the process of what is happening between the counselor and the client, that is, talking about their relationship. By doing this, the counselor helps the client better understand what is happening.

By being aware of the multiple levels of communication in counseling, counselors can listen to both the content of their client's speech and the way it is spoken. For example, if a client brings up how angry he is about what is happening at work and rambles on for some time, the counselor might suspect that he is filling up time with this complaint to avoid something else. The dialogue might go like this:

CLIENT: "I just don't think my boss understands how hard I work. He's always on my back."

COUNSELOR: "You seem quite upset about work, but I have a feeling you might be avoiding me with these complaints and afraid that I might bring up something you don't want to deal with."

CLIENT: "You may be right. I was afraid you would be disappointed in me because I didn't show up for the group meeting last night."

COUNSELOR: "I think we need to clear the air about that."

It might have been easier for this counselor to empathize with the client about his work situation and ignore the uncomfortable feeling he was experiencing. By taking the risk of confronting the lack of here-and-now communication, the counselor was able to really connect with the client and allow him to be honest about his fear. In the field of chemical dependency counseling, this is an important skill. Many with a history of drug and alcohol problems are experts at verbal manipulation. They use denial and projection as defense mechanisms to avoid pain, which deprives them of genuine human connection. These clients can learn to deal with the immediate reality of their lives when their counselors take the risk to model this honest, direct communication.

The here and now is the focus of several theories of counseling, such as person-centered counseling and Gestalt therapy. There are techniques for staying in the present and bringing clients back to the here and now, but the best resource is the counselor's knowledge of self. Chapter 1 describes the use of self and the knowledge of self as it applies to counselors. When counselors know themselves and understand what issues are difficult for them or where their blind spots are, they are better able to identify what they bring to the counseling relationship and what belongs to their clients—a very useful skill for developing immediacy in the counseling process.

Concreteness

The purpose of concreteness "is to help clients be as accurate and precise as possible when discussing their problems" (Kuntze, Molen, & Born, 2009, p. 2). Counselors' responses to their clients need to be specific about the feelings, experiences, and behaviors that the clients are describing. This allows the counselor to help clients see to what degree their choices are helping them to achieve their goals, to turn abstract and vague thoughts into something clear and concise, to stay focused on meaningful issues, and to move through the change process (Egan, 2014).

Counselors should avoid going off on tangents or allowing clients to get into abstract discussions, to gossip, or to speculate about others. They need to direct clients who do this back to relevant issues and the process of the moment. For example:

COUNSELOR: "Last time we met, you were very angry at your wife."

CLIENT: "Well, John was saying in group last night that all men have trouble understanding women. Women don't even know what they want most of the time."

COUNSELOR: "Well, that's all well and good, but I am interested in what is happening between you and your wife."

This client is avoiding the painful subject of his marital problems by reporting someone else's opinions and making global statements about men and women. The counselor pulls the client back to the original question about the client's relationship with his wife. This may be sufficient for the client to then get to the avoided subject, or he may again avoid it by bringing up something else or by dismissing it as not important. The client may not be ready to deal with the painful issue, and the counselor should then respect his wishes for the time being. The counselor can also be concrete by bringing the topic of conversation to the here and now of what is happening between the counselor and the client. For example:

> COUNSELOR: "I think you need to talk to your wife about your feelings."
>
> CLIENT: "Yes, but she doesn't listen."
>
> COUNSELOR: "Maybe if you picked a good time and told her it was important to you . . ."
>
> CLIENT: "Oh, she doesn't care about anything important to me."
>
> COUNSELOR: "I'm feeling frustrated right now, and I don't know how to help you. It seems like you're very upset with your wife, yet you seem to reject all of my suggestions of how to work this out."

By returning the content of the conversation to what is happening for the counselor at that moment, it puts the responsibility of change back on the client. It is an acknowledgement by the counselor that he cannot change the client.

Chemical dependency counselors may find that their clients are very astute at intellectualization and generalization. This keeps the focus off them and helps them avoid taking responsibility for themselves. Many people with addictions have used mind-altering substances to avoid the real world and all of the responsibilities that come with being an adult. They will resist taking responsibility for themselves in the here and now in favor of talking about the *idea* of taking responsibility. People with alcohol and drug problems may also take longer than other clients to trust counselors, and they may test the waters with irrelevant or safe topics in counseling sessions. As counselors stay concrete and connected to these clients, the clients will begin to take responsibility for their thoughts, beliefs, and actions.

Warmth

Warmth is similar to respect. Showing warmth is one way of showing respect for a client. The opposite of a counselor with warmth is one who is cold, aloof, and too businesslike. Particularly in the beginning of counseling, clients like to have a counselor whom they perceive as friendly and warm.

Warmth is generally communicated through non-verbal behavior, such as smiles, gestures, tone of voice, touches, and posture. Warmth, however, can be overused, which can make clients feel uncomfortable. The counseling relationship is not a real friendship. It is a unique relationship with special rules, and there must be clear boundaries between the counselor and the client. An overuse of touching, for instance, may make the client uncomfortable and feel that his or her personal space is being invaded. On the other hand, a counselor who has a strict rule of never touching a client may miss an opportunity to make a human connection with his or her client.

Being genuine is also a part of appropriate warmth. If a counselor is genuinely a warm person, this will be communicated through the use of genuineness and immediacy. If the counselor is not naturally a warm person, he or she should not try to be falsely warm toward the client. It is more important to be genuine. Clients differ in the amount of warmth they need from their counselors. Counselors should gear the amount of warmth expressed to the need of the client, not to their own need to be seen as warm.

Counselor Skills

Counselor skills are learned behaviors that promote client self-exploration, understanding, and change. They go hand in hand with the core elements of counseling and guide the counselor in the therapy process.

Listening

Therapeutic listening has been described as being a "part of the whole engagement with the other person" (Lee & Prior, 2013). It is a different kind of listening than listening to a speech or lecture or social listening in a conversation. In these instances, people are listening with only part of their minds. They may be processing what they are hearing or formulating a response to the speaker. In counseling, the client requires the counselor's complete attention. This is called "active listening" on the part of the counselor. This requires the counselor to be fully present and to set aside habitual attitudes, perceptions, and beliefs (Lee & Prior, 2013). Effective counselors do several things, including listening not only for clients' problems but also for their strengths and resources; listening to and understanding both the clients' verbal and nonverbal messages; listening to all aspects (emotions, thoughts, behaviors) of the lives of their clients in the context of their social settings; and attending to their clients' nonverbal behaviors (Egan, 2014).

Nonverbal behavior is important because it can give the counselor another avenue for gaining information about the client. By observing posture, body movements, facial expressions, physical characteristics, and physiological responses such as facial flushing or pupil dilation, or listening for changes in the tone, pitch, or level of voice; pauses; silences; and inflections or spacing of words, the counselor can gain information about the congruence of verbal and non-verbal behavior. Chemical dependency clients, who are experts at manipulating words, may be more truthful with their non-verbal behaviors or, at least, may not be able to conceal their non-verbal communication.

Listening to the client's verbal messages requires full attention to the client and hearing the verbal descriptions of his or her experiences, behaviors, and affect (Egan, 2014). The counselor's job is to help the client be specific about experiences. Most verbal expression has a cognitive aspect and an affective aspect. The cognitive part is the fact of the experience or the thought process connected with the experience (i.e., what the client thought about the experience). The affective part is the feeling or emotion that was evoked by the event or the thought about the event. Counselors should listen to both aspects of the verbal message and begin to sort out the core messages or themes that keep recurring in the verbal part of the communication.

Communication may be made up of verbal and non-verbal processes, but clients are more than their words and behaviors. They do not live in a vacuum. They live in contexts, surrounded by other people who have influences on their lives, and, thus, the context of their experiences is part of who they are and what they say. Counselors can develop empathy for their clients when they begin to understand what life is like for them and how it may be different from what the counselors have experienced. When counselors can listen in such a way that they see the world as their clients do, they have a better understanding of the clients' struggles, support systems, and values.

"Full listening" as defined by Egan (2014) means listening actively, accurately, and for meaning. This includes times when things don't always seem to "add up" for clients. Sometimes clients have a false perception of themselves. They think that they are ugly, when they are not, or helpless, when they are not; or they may even over-estimate their abilities, when they should not. Part of listening is evaluating the content of verbal communications and comparing the content with the observable reality. It may not be appropriate to challenge clients the moment they say something that is distorted. The counselor can make a mental note of the distortion and bring it up at a time when it will be most useful to the client.

Another type of listening is listening to self, or what might be called "intuitive listening." This process can happen in several ways. When counselors are intently listening, they will have a sensation that the rest of the world has disappeared. This is like having tunnel vision that is focused on the client, with the rest of the world out of focus. This intense process often creates a physiological reaction in the counselor, such as muscle tension, or an emotional reaction. When counselors can tune in to a client's verbal and non-verbal behavior, they can get other clues about the client and about how others may experience the client. Intuitive flashes may also occur that seem unrelated to the content of the conversation. It is difficult for counselors to trust these intuitions because they seem to come from nowhere, but they may contain the most real information. When counselors can step back and check their own reactions to clients, they may also find that they are mimicking their clients' postures and voice intonations. This is a process that may be automatic, but it is also a way to give feedback to clients, telling them that you are trying to get into their world.

Reflecting

The skill that is coupled with active listening is reflecting or restating. Counselors can restate the content of what they think they heard the client say, or they can reflect the feelings that the client is emoting. A simple reflection involves the verbal repeating of the content contained in a client's statement and can be focused on the main thought or feeling just expressed by the client. There is little interpretation involved on the part of the counselor in utilizing a simple reflection. For example:

> CLIENT: "I don't know whether I can go back to the stress of my job after completing this treatment program. It's a pretty demanding job, but I don't know what other kind of job I could get."

> COUNSELOR: "You don't know whether to go back to your job, but you don't know what else you might do."

In this example, the client had two thoughts: concern about returning to his or her stressful job and not knowing about other options. It is tempting for counselors to reflect the last thing said by clients, but this may not represent the theme of the conversation. The counselor in the example tried to reflect both parts of the client's dilemma. Although this may let the client know that the counselor is listening, if it is overused, it can sound like the counselor is simply parroting back the client's words.

Counselors can also reflect the affective content of the communication. "Reflection of feeling literally means the reproducing or mirroring of feeling. The helper pays attention to and shows understanding for the more emotional aspects of the client's story" (Kuntze et al., 2009, p. 2). For example:

> CLIENT: "I don't know whether I can go back to the stress of my job after completing this treatment program. It's a pretty demanding job, but I don't know what other kind of job I could get."

> COUNSELOR: "You're afraid to return to a stressful job, but you're worried about what else you might do."

In this case the counselor did not restate the content of the client's communication, but reflected the feelings that he thought the client had about the content. This is useful when working with someone with an addiction who has difficulty talking about feelings or who may be unaware of these feelings.

Rogers (1951) defined reflection of feeling as an attempt "to understand from the client's point of view and to communicate that understanding" (p. 452). Reflection is an attempt to communicate the core of what the client is feeling or experiencing. When this is done in a non-threatening way, clients can then see their feelings as a part of themselves. Often an accurate reflection of feelings comes from the intuitive level of listening, when a counselor can sense a feeling or have an emotional reaction to the client's feelings. Even if the counselor does not accurately reflect the client's feelings, the client has to focus on real feelings. The counselor can then ask for a clarification from the client to get a clearer picture of what the client is feeling.

Questioning

Questioning is a technique used by counselors to obtain information from clients. Ideally this is done with open-ended questions that allow clients to fully describe their experiences. Questioning can be overused and can become problematic. Inexperienced counselors ask many more questions than do those with experience.

If questions are phrased in such a way that the client can answer them with a "yes" or a "no," the counselor will learn little about the client, and the client will feel as though the counseling process is an interrogation. This also limits the client's responsibility to work in the session and exaggerates the work done by the counselor. It is the counselor's job to structure the rhythm of the counseling process. A good way for counselors to check this is to listen to an audiotape of a counseling session and note the amount of time the counselor is speaking and the amount of time the client is speaking. Counselors who are questioning excessively will also feel drained at the end of the session. Questions that redirect should be open-ended but target relevant areas that the client may be avoiding or that may be difficult to explore.

Questions that say to the client that the counselor is interested are empathetic types of questions. They are often tentative statements of reflection that happen to be in the form of a question. When the counselor is ahead of the client and is groping for understanding, a request for clarification will tell the client that the counselor is trying to understand. For example:

CLIENT: "I'm looking forward to graduating from the drug treatment program, but I feel nervous about it."

COUNSELOR: "Are you frightened about having to return to your old environment where your friends that you used to hang out with and use drugs with live?"

The counselor is anticipating that this is why the client might be nervous about completing the program, and leads the client to talk about the fear of returning home. This could help clients understand their feelings and direct them to discuss relapse prevention skills.

Confronting

Confrontation, though it has come under scrutiny as of late, is often associated with drug and alcohol counseling. The use of heavy confrontation techniques was thought to be necessary to confront the denial of those with alcohol and drug problems. This led to a type of group therapy for addiction dubbed "hot-seat" therapy. Group members would take turns being in the hot seat while other group members confronted them with their behavior. Although this may have been effective for some, particularly those who were reluctant to recover, it was damaging to the self-esteem of others in part because of its judgmental tone. This practice led to the misunderstanding in the field of chemical dependency treatment that confrontation must be of the hot-seat type. Confrontation, however, can be done differently, in such a way that it not only helps clients come more directly in contact with their own experience but also creates a situation whereby they can grow (Gibson, 2006).

Confrontation is used to help clients face reality when the counselor perceives minimization, dismissal, or false ideas in his or her client. Confrontation occurs when the counselor observes a discrepancy between any number of things regarding a client (i.e., differences between what they say and how they act, their beliefs and their actions, their values and their actions, and their goals and how to achieve them; Gibson, 2006). Another way to think about the focus of confrontation is "on the failure of someone to live up to his or her own expectations or the legitimate expectations of the culture or community, however defined, in which the person lives" (Egan, 2014).

Confrontation is often thought of as tearing down a person by attacking his or her defenses, but it can be used to "enable the client to recognize and move away from ways of being that are self-defeating or self-limiting" (Gibson, 2006, p. 91). For example:

CLIENT: "I've never been successful at anything in my life."

COUNSELOR: "Wait a minute. You told me that you got a college degree in business, and you started your own consulting firm."

CLIENT: "Yeah, but I lost that business last year."

COUNSELOR: "Do you think that might have had something to do with your drinking?"

CLIENT: "I suppose you're right."

COUNSELOR: "It seems to me that you can be quite successful when you're not preoccupied with drinking."

Egan (2014) has indicated some areas where clients might need to be challenged or invited to challenge themselves:

- Failure to own problems
- Failure to define problems in solvable terms
- Faulty interpretations of critical experiences, behaviors, and feelings
- Evasions, distortions, and game playing
- Failure to identify or understand the consequences of behavior
- Hesitancy or unwillingness to act on new perspectives (p. 187)

It is not surprising that confrontation is frequently used in chemical dependency treatment. Those with alcohol and drug problems often have distorted senses of themselves due to years of living in a fog and using the defense mechanisms of denial, rationalization, minimization, intellectualization, and manipulation of others in order to maintain their addiction. One of the main goals of chemical dependency treatment is to help clients take responsibility for their own behavior and stop blaming others. These defensive behaviors have also pulled distorted responses from family members and friends who are angry, upset, and confused about the behaviors and blaming statements of their loved one with an alcohol or drug problem. These significant others often resort to distorted accusations to try to get the loved one to wake up and stop abusing alcohol and other drugs. These accusations are often internalized, creating even more of a sense of failure in the person who has an addiction, even though it is not accurate, and perpetuating the addiction.

Ellis (1985), in his rational-emotive therapy, described the need to challenge inner thoughts that sustain self-defeating behavior. He believed that people have some common self-defeating thoughts about how life should be. When reality does not match up with these *shoulds*, the individuals get depressed and give up. A common theme of these irrational thoughts is absolutism (i.e., *always*, *never*, *should*, and *must* statements). Counselors who hear these self-defeating, irrational ideas need to confront this type of thinking and help their clients modify their thoughts to more closely resemble reality.

Self-Disclosing

Chemical dependency counselors frequently have concerns about how much of their own recovery process or their personal connections with addiction to share with their clients. In some ways it may be helpful to the client to know that the counselor has successfully struggled with the same problem that he or she is facing, but this should be done cautiously, because doing so may "interfere with treatment, such as clients censoring themselves out of fear they might negatively impact their therapist or a sense of competition between client and therapist" (Henretty & Levitt, 2010, p. 72).

Self-disclosure involves sharing feelings, attitudes, and experiences with the client in order to help that person. Because both too much and too little self-disclosure can be detrimental, such sharing should be done thoughtfully and intentionally and be meaningful and pertinent in context and content in order to be therapeutic (Henretty & Levitt, 2010). Self-disclosure can be very effective if it is used sparingly and with a good sense of timing and appropriateness. It works well when the counselor is aware of how to use a sense of self as a therapeutic tool, and it can come in several forms. As per Henretty and Levitt (2010), research supports disclosures about the following:

- Demographic information, such as education, theoretical orientation, and professional and marital status
- Feelings and thoughts about the client and/or therapeutic relationship
- Mistakes made in therapy
- Past struggles that have been successfully overcome and are related to what the client is going through
- Client and therapist similarities

When the counselor gives clients feedback or discusses their reactions to the relationship, self-disclosure is usually very helpful so that the clients can know how they are perceived by others. Self-disclosures about the counselor's own problems are more difficult to evaluate as to their helpfulness.

A general rule about self-disclosure is to ask, "Who is really benefiting from this self-disclosure—the counselor or the client?" The answer to this question must be "the client." Counselors should not disclose personal problems that they need help with. These issues should be discussed in the counselor's personal therapy. Disclosures by the counselor of personal success, however, may be helpful in both connecting with the client on a human level and providing role modeling for a client who is struggling with a similar problem. Caution should be used, however, in an overreliance on self-disclosure. The client needs to see the counselor as a relatively healthy and successful human being. Counselors who overuse self-disclosure may be seen by their clients as unhealthy and unable to help.

Clients are often interested in their counselors and may ask about their personal lives or their training. These questions can be answered briefly to satisfy casual curiosity, but if the client shifts the focus of the counseling process to an interrogation of the counselor, he or she may be avoiding being the focus of the therapy. When this happens, the counselor can shift the focus back to the client with statements such as, "You're asking a lot of questions today."

Interpreting

Interpretations point out the underlying feelings or attitudes of the client and attempt to integrate feelings, thoughts, and actions. It is the counselor's attempt to imply meaning or cause-and-effect reasoning to the client's description of self—to create insight.

Interpretation is a technique used after the counselor has gotten to know the client and has spent time listening to his or her view of self and the world. If the counselor is correct in his or her interpretation and the client is ready to accept the interpretation, it may speed the client to insight. Insight, however, does not always lead to a change in behavior. Clients also reject interpretations if they believe that they are incorrect or if they are not ready to accept the interpretation of their behavior.

Client-centered therapies do not put much emphasis on interpretations because it puts the responsibility for change more with the counselor than with the client. Interpretation is also seen as a cognitive process that ignores the affective component. Rogers (1942) listed some issues for counselors concerning interpretation: (1) Counselors should avoid interpretation if they are unsure of themselves; (2) counselors should use the client's symbols and terms in the interpretation; (3) interpretations should deal with attitudes that have already been expressed; (4) it is not useful to argue about the correctness of the interpretation with the client; (5) if the client has gained genuine insight, he or she will be able to spontaneously apply it in new areas; and (6) after the client has achieved a new insight, he or she may temporarily relapse to old behaviors.

Clarifying

Clarifying techniques are related to reflection and interpretation. Clarifying helps clients to better understand their feelings, as well as the options they have to choose from (Evans, 2013). Clarifications are more than mere reflections of the content of the client's speech. They are statements that elicit more information so that the client's meaning can be understood. Clarifications can also be utilized to help clients be more concrete and to help identify important issues to enable deeper understanding on the part of the client (Evans, 2013).

Clients from cultures other than the counselor's may use unique words or speech patterns to explain themselves. Clarifications can be helpful in allowing clients to teach counselors about how they see the world and how they think.

Seeking and Selecting a Personal Approach to Counseling

Counselors must choose a style or approach to counseling that fits their own personality. This should involve their own models or theories of why people change addictive behaviors and how they can best use their skills to enhance this change in their clients. If counselors do not have a solid belief in what they are doing during the counseling process and what their role is in that process, a positive outcome for the client will be a matter of luck or of the client's motivation, rather than of what the counselor does.

New or beginning counselors are limited by their lack of education and experience. They do not always know what the options are, and they are often limited to what their supervisors or instructors do or tell them to do. Counseling is a skill that involves the counselor's beliefs, values, motivation, education, and personality. The more experience counselors have, the more they should be able to use their personal attributes to enhance their ability to assist clients with a positive change. As new counselors combine experience with additional education, counseling will become more natural and will begin to involve all of their personal attributes to make the most out of their relationship with the client.

The most important beginning step is for counselors to take an inventory of their values, beliefs, skills, and personalities and to ask themselves what theory or model best fits these attributes. For example, some counselors are very confrontational with clients, because they believe that this confrontation motivates clients to change. Other counselors are more supportive and believe that clients are more likely to change in a supportive environment. Counselors should choose a style that they believe in and that they believe will be useful to their clients. Clients can usually sense that their counselors are not operating out of belief systems that support what they are doing. Some counselors may be comfortable being both confrontive and supportive in different situations. That is effective as long as the counselor is able to wisely choose which client will respond best to which approach. That is also a skill that takes experience.

The more options for treatment and counseling approaches that counselors have to choose from, the more likely it is that they will chose one that maximizes their abilities and that enhances treatment for their clients. It may take several years before a new counselor is completely comfortable with his or her approach. This process is shortened if the new counselor continues to learn new skills and receives regular supervision.

There are many approaches to counseling and to the treatment of chemical dependency. Some of them have been briefly presented in this text. It is up to the individual counselor to learn about the many approaches to treating chemical dependency. Training through workshops and other continuing-education events will give the new counselor additional information regarding what is available. As counselors gain experience and receive supervision, they can make adjustments to their approaches in order to find the one that is comfortable.

Documentation

Documentation is the recording of the screening and intake process and the assessment and treatment plan, as well as preparation of written reports, clinical progress notes, discharge summaries, and other client-related data. This is often the least-liked part of the counseling process, but it can be the most important. The purpose of keeping accurate and complete records is to clearly document the entire treatment process, which begins with written screening and assessment data, the treatment plan, releases of information, and any previous records from prior admissions or prior treatment. The documentation continues with treatment plan updates, progress notes concerning the client's progress on the treatment plan, reports from adjunctive therapies or referral sources, and any other written documents that are relevant to the therapy. The file is completed with an accurate, concise, and informative discharge summary, aftercare plan, and any referrals made to other professionals or programs.

Each facility has its own set of forms for documentation, but there are some generally agreed-upon materials that should be placed in a client's file. Documentation serves an important function as a written record of the client's treatment. It is a record of what was done in treatment, what failed, and what succeeded. If the client is re-admitted at a later date, the new counselor has a wealth of information about the previous treatment and does not have to start from the beginning.

A client's records can also be used in non-therapeutic ways that can be damaging to the client and to the treatment process. Records are protected by confidentiality regulations and should not be available to anyone other than members of the treatment staff who need access to the file in order to maintain a consistent treatment plan and to document progress. Requests by third parties for copies of records must follow the confidentiality guidelines of having appropriate, signed releases of information that conform to the regulations. Even with the appropriate procedures, client records often fall into the hands of people who are not governed by confidentiality regulations or who are unaware of them. That is why it is especially important to carefully write evaluations, treatment plans, and progress notes in a professional style that clearly indicates what is observed behavior, client communication, and counselor interpretation or hunch. Progress notes should directly reflect a client's progress in relation to treatment goals and objectives. Client files are not a place for keeping secrets or elaborating on the opinions of the counselor.

Clients should be involved in all parts of their treatment. This includes understanding their evaluation results, co-creating and signing their treatment plan, clearly understanding the progress they are making in treatment, and being aware of any referrals or third-party involvements. Thus, there should not be anything in a client's record that he or she is not aware of. Clients do have a right to know what is in their records. It may not be in their best interest for counselors to give the clients the actual records to read, but counselors should be able to explain everything in the chart to the client.

Counselors should be timely and accurate in charting a client's progress. A study of successful chemical dependency counselors indicated that counselors who performed their duties in a concerted and organized manner had better success rates in enabling clients to stabilize their lives and to use the other social and medical services available to them (McLellan, Woody, Luborsky, & Goehl, 1988). McLellan et al. described the charts from the most successful counselors as "notable for the thorough and accurate charting of all pertinent aspects of patient contact" (p. 429). The charts indicated clearly formulated plans of rehabilitation created through consultation with the treatment team and client. The plans were followed and documented at all points.

Supervision

Supervision is a very important part of counselor education and training. However, it is not always easy to find a good supervisor in a chemical dependency treatment setting. Some counselors are supervisors because they have worked in an agency longer than anyone else. Longevity does not necessarily make them good supervisors. In fact, in some cases, these individuals may not even meet current requirements to be a counselor, because they were grandfathered in when chemical dependency counselor certification was just beginning. Some of these individuals may be outstanding supervisors, but many are not.

In other situations, agencies that are underfunded and understaffed take on trainees to help with the workload. In these cases, there are usually not enough staff to provide the necessary therapy, much less adequate supervision. Trainees may be put into counseling situations with little or no supervision. Clients may suffer as a result.

Supervision is often approached in the chemical dependency field from an apprenticeship model. That is, the supervisor gives the message, "Do just like I do, and don't question my approach." This is contrasted with the scientific model, which encourages individuals to seek what is best for them and their clients. The scientific model also encourages all questions, even if the supervisor is being questioned about his or her approach. Supervision should be a tutorial process by which principles are transformed into practical skills. The supervisor should monitor and assist the supervisee in a minimum of these areas:

- Record keeping, including all agency requirements
- Counseling activity via audio, video, or direct observation
- Referral
- Assessment and diagnosis
- Ethics and professional issues
- Presentations in case conferences

- Client evaluation of performance
- Issues of diversity among clients

The supervisor should talk to the counselor-in-training about such issues as client motivation, covert sexual issues, transference and countertransference issues, termination procedures, unconscious material that may be interfering with counseling, and other issues related to the process of counseling.

There are several models of supervision, some of which include:

- Lecturer
- Teacher
- Case Reviewer
- Collegial-Peer
- Monitor
- Therapist

Each approach has its advantages and disadvantages. It is important that the supervisor choose an approach that the counselor being supervised is comfortable with and a process that he or she will gain from. The supervisor will need to choose the modality of supervision, emphasis and focus of supervision, style of supervision, and form of evaluation of the supervisee. These things should be decided in consultation with the supervisee.

In some cases, a trainee might be in supervision with someone who is not providing quality supervision. The supervisor may have an entirely different idea about a treatment approach than the trainee. The trainee may even have more formal education than the supervisor, in which case the trainee should keep an open mind. It is best for the trainee to deal with issues like these directly with the supervisor. If the problems cannot be worked out directly with the supervisor, the situation will dictate the appropriate course of action. Trainees may have no choice other than to accept the poor supervision until they have reached their goal in training (i.e., number of hours for certification, or a certificate). One option for trainees in this situation is to arrange for some supplemental supervision with someone who can provide appropriate training. One hour of good supervision may be better than 100 hours of bad supervision. The trainee needs to acknowledge that the supervisor has an authoritative position, and it would not be in the trainee's best interest to undermine that position. To avoid a negative training situation, trainees should choose training sites and supervisors carefully. It is a good idea for trainees to visit the prospective training site, talk to the staff, find out who the supervisor will be, and speak directly to him or her. Trainees need to interview the staff and supervisors to determine if the site will be able to provide the training and experiences that they want. If the site or the supervisor is not what the trainees need, they should try other agencies.

Taking courses, reading, and role-playing are all necessary and valuable learning experiences for the counselor-to-be. However, working as a counselor with real clients and with good supervision is the only way that one becomes an accomplished counselor. It is the student's responsibility to seek out good supervision in a treatment setting that meets his or her training needs.

Client and Community Education

This is the process of providing clients, individuals, and community groups with information on the risks related to alcohol and other drug use, as well as available prevention, treatment, and recovery resources. Education is often an important component of drug and alcohol treatment programs. It is also essential in combating the stigma of addiction by informing the public about prevention strategies, warning signals, symptoms, the course of recovery, and treatment opportunities and successes. Chemical dependency counselors will be expected to design and provide culturally relevant formal and informal education programs that raise awareness and support substance abuse prevention and/or the recovery process. These presentations may include factors that increase the likelihood that an individual, community, or group will be at risk for alcohol and other drug problems. Further, there is a need to sensitize others to issues of cultural identity; ethnic background; age; and gender role or identity in prevention, treatment, and recovery.

Counselors will need information about the many subjects that are related to chemical dependency and that affect the individual, the family, and the community. These include how addiction affects the family and concerned others; the principles and philosophies of prevention, treatment, and recovery; and related health and behavioral problems, such as HIV/AIDS, tuberculosis, sexually transmitted diseases, and other communicable diseases. Counselors should also be able to teach basic life skills to their clients, such as stress management, relaxation, communication, assertiveness, and refusal skills.

It is frequently difficult to separate counseling and education. Counseling is focused on helping the client find his or her own solution; education is the process of giving others didactic information. In chemical dependency treatment, counselors may have to learn to blend these two processes to maximize their treatment success. Clients who want to remain sober will be more successful if they are taught stress management and refusal skills. Family education programs are usually part of a treatment process as well. These can be very helpful to families in breaking the blame-and-revenge cycle; but when family education is augmented with systemic family therapy, the outcome is even better.

References

American With Disabilities Act of 1990, 42 U.S.C. § 12101 *et seq.* (1990).

Center for Substance Abuse Treatment. (2011). *Addiction counseling competencies: The knowledge, skills, and attitudes of professional practice.* Technical Assistance Publication (TAP) Series 21. HHS Publication No. (SMA) 08-4171. Rockville, MD: Substance Abuse and Mental Health Services Administration.

Corey, G. (2012). *Theory and practice of counseling and psychotherapy* (9th ed.). Pacific Grove, CA: Brooks/Cole.

Egan, G. (2014). *The skilled helper: A systemic approach to effective helping* (10th ed.). Belmont, CA: Brooks/Cole.

Elliott, R., Bohart, A. C., Watson, J. C., & Greenberg, L. S. (2011). Empathy. *Psychotherapy, 48*(1), 43–49.

Ellis, A. (1985). Expanding the ABCs of rational-emotive therapy. In M. Mahoney & A. Freeman (Eds.), *Cognition and psychotherapy* (pp. 313–323). New York: Plenum.

Evans, G. (2013). *Counseling skills for dummies* (2nd ed.). West Sussex, UK: Wiley.

Gibson, S. (2006). Respect as esteem: The case of counseling. *Res Publica, 12*(1), 77–95.

Gray, R. (2010). Shame, labeling and stigma: Challenges to counseling clients in alcohol and other drug settings. *Contemporary Drug Problems, 37,* 685–703.

Greason, P. B., & Cashwell, C. S. (2009). Mindfulness and counseling self-efficacy: The mediating role of attention and empathy. *Counselor Education and Supervision, 49*(1), 2–19.

Henretty, J. R., & Levitt, H. M. (2010). The role of therapist self-disclosure in psychotherapy: A qualitative review. *Clinical Psychology Review, 30,* 63–77.

Kuntze, J., Molen, H. T., & Born, P. M. (2009). Increase in counseling communication skills after basic and advanced microskills training. *British Journal of Educational Psychology, 79,* 175–188.

Lee, B., & Prior, S. (2013). Developing therapeutic listening. *British Journal of Guidance & Counselling, 42*(2), 91–104.

McLellan, A. T., Woody, G. E., Luborsky, L., & Goehl, L. (1988). Is the counselor an "active ingredient" in substance abuse rehabilitation? An examination of treatment success among four counselors. *Journal of Nervous and Mental Disease, 176*(7) 423–430.

Rogers, C. (1942). *Counseling and psychotherapy.* Boston: Houghton Mifflin.

Rogers, C. (1951). *Client-centered therapy.* Boston: Houghton Mifflin.

Rogers, C. (1957). The necessary and sufficient conditions of therapeutic personality change. *Journal of Consulting Psychology, 21,* 95–103.

Rogers, C. (1961). *On becoming a person.* Boston: Houghton Mifflin.

Rogers, C. (1967). The interpersonal relationship: The core of guidance. In C. Rogers & B. Stevens (Eds.), *Person to person* (pp. 89–98). Lafayette, CA: Real People Press.

Shertzer, B., & Stone, S. C. (1980). *Fundamentals of counseling* (3rd ed.). Boston: Houghton Mifflin.

Small, J. (1990). *Becoming naturally therapeutic* (Rev. ed.). New York: Bantam Books.

Truax, C. B., & Carkhuff, R. R. (2007). *Toward effective counseling and psychotherapy.* Chicago: Aldine Transaction.

CHAPTER 5

Characterizing Clients and Assessing Their Needs

The eyes believe themselves. The ears believe other people.

~ Chinese Proverb

CHAPTER OBJECTIVES

- Examine the rationale for a diagnosis
- Examine the options for diagnosing chemical dependency
- Examine areas that should be included in a diagnosis
- Encourage the reader to match patient diagnoses to appropriate treatment plans
- Examine different classification approaches
- Review the DSM-IV and DSM-5 approaches to diagnosis

There is no such thing as a "typical person with chemical dependency issues"; members of this group are as different as fingerprints (see Chapter 8 on diversity). There is no specific personality type, family history, socioeconomic situation, or stressful experience that has been found to categorically predict the development of chemical dependency, although all of these play a part. People with chemical dependency issues include doctors, ministers, chemical dependency counselors, lawyers, truck drivers, teachers, homemakers, and members of virtually every profession known. In some cases, treatment programs are designed for certain professions. For example, there are inpatient treatment programs designed just for medical doctors and Catholic priests. Chemical dependency transcends race, religion, social class, intelligence, and ethnic affiliation. Chemical dependency is a complex disorder not seemingly reducible to a common cause, and attitudes and concepts about chemical dependency are changing for those who work in the field (Straussner, 2014). As more objective information concerning chemical dependency accumulates, the total picture will become clearer. The issues of use, misuse, and abuse are now being examined from many perspectives: legal, clinical, professional, personal, social, and cultural, among others. Chemical dependency is now seen as a series of complex interactions among people, their environment, neurobiology and genetic factors, and the chemical(s) they choose to use. Chemical dependency problems should be seen on a continuum. For example, alcohol problems are not limited just to "alcoholics": Problem drinkers, pre-alcoholics, and families of alcoholics are included. Not only are there different types of people who have chemical dependency problems, but also there are many types of chemical dependency problems. There are also a variety of treatment choices available to a person with chemical dependency issues. The type of person, his or her environment, the chemical involved, and the use pattern should all be considered in the diagnosis and treatment plan for the chemically dependent person, which often fall to the chemical dependency counselor. This information should be used to match the patient to an appropriate treatment setting. Simple definitions and simple methods of diagnosis sacrifice important scientific and clinical distinctions. Quality treatment is preceded by quality diagnosis. Counselors must know their clients and be able to assess their needs with accuracy.

Diagnosis

The therapeutic relationship that a counselor establishes with a client is usually called "counseling" or "therapy." This process is discussed in detail in Chapter 4. The importance of this relationship should be self-evident. The relationship may be therapeutic to a greater or lesser degree depending on its quality; however, in most instances, therapy does not end with the counseling relationship. Therapy can include many things, for example, relaxation training, assertiveness training, group counseling, recreation therapy, or bibliotherapy (utilizing an online or in-print program). The counseling session, besides providing some direct therapeutic value, is the appropriate place for the counselor to assess the client's diverse therapeutic needs. During the initial counseling sessions, the counselor should evaluate the client and his or her therapeutic needs. The direction of this initial interview is likely to be determined by the setting in which it is done.

Treatment Settings

Addictions counselors work in a variety of settings. These include but are not limited to the following:

- Inpatient drug or alcohol treatment programs (usually 30 days or less)
- Long-term residential programs
- Outpatient drug and alcohol treatment programs
- A private practice setting
- Family clinics
- Mental health programs
- Corrections settings
- Therapeutic communities

- Methadone maintenance programs
- High school and college settings
- Military addictions programs (inpatient and outpatient)

Counselors have different backgrounds and training experiences depending on what is required by the program and the regulatory agency in the state where the treatment program is located (Gallagher, 2009). Decisions regarding which programs patients are sent to are sometimes predetermined by the setting. For example, an inmate in a corrections setting will stay in the available program because there is no choice. However, treatment plans and specific goals can be individualized, and this is usually done by the counselor. In other situations, the counselor may choose among several program options for each individual. An example of this is a drug counselor who works in an outpatient mental health center. The choice might be to send a patient to a therapeutic community or a methadone maintenance outpatient program, or just to see them in outpatient counseling. In any situation, assessment and diagnosis are very important in relation to the eventual outcome.

The Process of Diagnosis

The quality of an assessment will be based on the quality and depth of the counseling relationship. Likewise, the outcome of treatment (or therapy) will be directly related to the accuracy of the diagnosis and how it has been reflected in the treatment plan. Therefore, diagnosis becomes an integral part of the outcome, or prognosis. Counselors who know how to diagnose and how to translate this diagnosis into an individualized treatment plan are maximizing the benefits of their efforts.

Mee-Lee (2013) recommends that the diagnosis process focus on six primary areas:

- **Dimension 1: Acute Intoxication and/or Withdrawal Potential**—This involves assessing an individual's risk from intoxication or withdrawal by collecting information related to past and current use of substances.

- **Dimension 2: Biomedical Conditions and Complications**—This area is assessing risk as it relates to possible health problems and involves collecting information related to health history and current physical functioning.

- **Dimension 3: Emotional, Behavioral, or Cognitive Conditions and Complications**—As it implies, this area assesses risk (e.g., thoughts of suicide or homicide, lack of capacity to guarantee one's safety) by collecting information related to one's mental health and capacity, thoughts, and emotions.

- **Dimension 4: Readiness to Change**—This area is assessing risk as it relates to an individual's desire to make a change.

- **Dimension 5: Relapse, Continued Use, or Continued Problem Potential**—Risk as it relates to an individual's likelihood of relapse or continued use is examined here by collecting information related to the presence or absence of skills and resources for preventing and responding to such an event.

- **Dimension 6: Recovery/Living Environment**—Risk as it relates to an individual's recovery or living situation is assessed in this area by collecting information related to social support and available resources.

Many of these areas are discussed in detail in Chapter 8, particularly those that relate to emotional, social, and spiritual functioning.

Physical symptoms usually involve the changes in physical health one experiences after using a toxic substance for a period of time. A medical examination is recommended in most cases. The primary issues a counselor should ask about include physical health related to vital organs; physical damage acquired while drinking or using; and poor overall health due to an inadequate diet, lack of exercise, and the possibility of diseases like TB, hepatitis, and AIDS. Additional important physical symptoms include blackouts, an increased or decreased tolerance for the drugs he or she uses, a change in sex drive, and ataxia or tremors. Advanced physical problems can be used to help motivate the patient to stop using if there are no other complicating factors. However, the counselor should be leery of using statements such as, "If you continue to use like this, you're going to die!" In some cases, that may be just what the patient wants to do. The counselor's reminder might give cause for the patient to use even more.

Assessing Readiness to Change

In the Transtheoretical Model of Change put forth by Prochaska, Norcross, and DiClemente (2006), there are six well-defined stages of change that everyone—including someone with chemical dependency issues—goes through when considering and making changes. The five stages that relate directly to chemical dependency are as follows:

1. Precontemplation—In this stage, someone is not aware of a problem she or he may have, or an opportunity of which she or he may take advantage.

- *Non-chemical dependency (Non-CD) example:* On a trip through Northern California for the first time, not until Raymond sees Mt. Shasta does he even realize it exists.

- *Chemical dependency (CD) example:* Until her doctor mentions the damage that her use of alcohol is causing to her liver, Lora has never really thought that it might be a problem.

2. **Contemplation**—The preoccupation in this stage is weighing the pros and cons of making a change.
- *Non-CD example:* Once he sees Mt. Shasta, Raymond begins to think about whether to climb it.
- *CD example:* Now that she is aware of the damage to her liver, Lora begins to consider whether to cut back or quit.

3. **Preparation**—In this stage, a person has decided to make a change and examines the different options and strategies for doing so. It is here that commitment to change is solidified.
- *Non-CD example:* Raymond has decided that he wants to climb Mt. Shasta, so he researches the best routes to climb, the gear he'll need, and so forth.
- *CD example:* Lora has decided that she doesn't want to make her health worse, so she makes an appointment with a chemical dependency counselor to review her options.

4. **Action**—This is where a person puts the different options and strategies into play.
- *Non-CD example:* Raymond has his gear in hand, his route in mind, and has begun hiking up Mt. Shasta.
- *CD example:* Lora has decided to start with outpatient counseling to learn additional skills and information to help her remain sober.

5. **Maintenance**—Once someone gets past the initial excitement of starting a new behavior, maintaining it and the motivation to continue becomes the next challenge.
- *Non-CD example:* Halfway up the mountain, Raymond has blisters, is sunburned, and is questioning why he should continue when it would be so much easier to turn around and go home. He remembers how important this is to him and trudges onward.
- *CD example:* Lora has been sober for over six months and runs into some old friends who invite her to join them at what used to be her favorite bar. She is tempted, but remembers how important this is to her and decides not to go.

Assessing clients' readiness for change can help counselors to better match treatment options to optimize the likelihood of their success. Rather than viewing motivation to change as a fixed variable, counselors are invited to see it as something malleable and influenced by their interventions.

Chemical Dependency Behavior Classification and Symptoms

There are two major ways to classify deviant behavior such as chemical dependency: as immoral or sinful, or as amoral and beyond the individual's control. This deviant behavior is addressed either through the social institutions of the judicial system or through the social institutions of the health care system. If the judicial system is involved, this often means jail versus a hospital treatment program. Alcoholism and the abuse of medically prescribed drugs are now viewed less as immoral, sinful behavior (legal diagnosis) and more as personal sickness (medical diagnosis). The use or abuse of illegal drugs, however, has been slower to make this transition. "Alcoholism is a disease" is a slogan that has a great deal of public acceptance. "Heroin addiction is a disease" or "Drug addiction is a disease" have less chance for such acceptance because of the legal status of the substance involved. Addiction may be addiction; however, the social context of use has special meaning when the legal and political aspects of diagnosis are considered.

Diagnosis as a Social Process

At issue is how a specific society or segment of society creates and uses social rules to define chemical *use* versus *abuse*. These rules may be narrow or broad, depending on the drug and the particular society. The abuse of alcohol, for example, is defined rather consistently in American culture as a pattern of repetitive, heavy drinking with obvious personal deterioration; consequently, almost anyone can make an accurate "social" diagnosis of alcoholism. However, this process of collective identification of "alcoholics" or of seeing those with serious problems related to alcohol as only those who have shown obvious deterioration, such as "skid-row" alcoholics, has probably done more to deter progressive treatment and rehabilitation of individuals with alcohol problems than any other single variable, for two reasons. First, anyone can compare him- or herself to someone else who appears in worse shape and, in doing so, conclude that they don't really have a problem, or that their problem isn't really that bad. Second, persons may resist being labeled as "alcoholic" because they view alcoholics as down-and-outers, something "less than." They may refuse treatment with that label, though they might accept treatment without the label.

Diagnosis as a Clinical Process

The counselor is primarily involved with diagnosis from a clinical or treatment perspective. The first aspect of this diagnosis is to establish that chemical dependency problems are present. This screening diagnosis is conducted to establish whether or not the client is appropriate for the counselor and his treatment agency. Some agencies have intake specialists to make these evaluations, but many other agencies place this responsibility on the person who will be the client's individual counselor. A key question here is, "Are mood-altering chemicals involved?" or "Does this person ingest drugs?" (Lewis, 2014). After this has been established, the counselor can proceed to the second phase of diagnosis.

Diagnostic Classifications

Where treatment is general and imprecise, there is little need for a detailed diagnosis. This has, in the past, been the case in the field of alcoholism and drug abuse. Until recently most treatment approaches for alcoholism and drug abuse have been global and imprecise. Each person would go through the same treatment program, regardless of diagnosis. As further explained later in this chapter, however, assessment and diagnostic processes will need to become more sophisticated as different treatment methods and treatment approaches are identified, established, and updated (Insel, 2011).

There are two major types of diagnosis: binary diagnosis and multivariate diagnosis. The binary type of diagnosis is an either/or method: One is either chemically dependent or one is not. The multivariate approach considers many factors and degrees of addiction. The binary approach may be based on either a unitary or a multivariate framework. When the assumption is that there is a discrete entity termed "chemical dependency" or "drug addiction" or "alcoholism," the diagnostic goal is simply to find an effective way to distinguish those who are dependent on chemicals from those who are not. However, even though many still believe such entities exist, the research data of the past 20 years clearly demonstrate that the unitary concept is incorrect. The adverse effects of chemical use depend on many factors, and the binary diagnosis of chemically dependent persons leaves much to be desired.

Conjunctive and Disjunctive Classifications

Concepts or categories can either be conjunctive or disjunctive. A conjunctive classification is one in which all the defining attributes must be present for any individual to be classified in that category. For example, one must be over 18 and registered to be classified as a voter. This does not occur in the classification of alcoholism: Alcoholism is disjunctively categorized. That is, a person classified as "alcoholic" can have a number of different defining attributes: blackouts, legal problems, family problems, physical problems, or any of the many other problems related to alcohol use. The alcoholic may have experienced any one or any combination of these problems (American Psychiatric Association, 2013; Manubay & Horton, 2010).

As might be expected, a person with alcohol and/or drug problems in treatment frequently denies having trouble with alcoholism or drug abuse and focuses on the areas where no problems exist. The focus for the counselor is on the addictive problems. The following exchange is typical:

> COUNSELOR: "You appear to have an alcohol problem, because you were picked up twice for drinking and driving."

> CLIENT: "Yes, but I still have a good job and my family life is fine; besides, many of my friends have been picked up for drinking and driving."

These encounters often end with the counselor's concluding that the client is in denial and that nothing can be done until the client drinks some more and "hits bottom." The client is left feeling that "the counselor does not understand the situation and has only one goal, and that is, to diagnose me as an alcoholic." These sessions often end without resolution, with both counselor and client feeling frustrated. Too often, the binary method of either/or diagnosis identifies only those in the late stages of alcoholism. Problem drinkers and those in the early stages of developing a drinking problem frequently are not treated and are even sent on their way until they "hit bottom." Those who do enter treatment are likely to drop out or exhibit resistance. This approach is not acceptable, given the different types of treatment interventions available for all types of alcohol and drug problems (Lewis, 2014; Nathan & Gorman, 2007; Straussner, 2014).

Multivariate Syndromes

Most scientific authorities in the field of chemical dependency agree that the factors involved in chemical dependency, drug addiction, and alcoholism are most accurately viewed as multivariate syndromes (i.e., multiple patterns of dysfunctional chemical use that occur in many different types of personalities, with multiple combinations of adverse consequences and multiple outcomes, that may require different treatment interventions). Pattison and Kaufman (1982) listed six implications of multivariate syndromes that apply to alcoholism. These are presented here in adapted form to show their relevance to chemical dependency. Note how accurately these continue to resonate more than 30 years later.

1. There are multiple patterns of use, misuse, and abuse that may be denoted as a pattern of chemical dependency.
2. There are multiple interactional etiological variables that combine to produce a pattern of chemical dependency.
3. All persons are vulnerable to the development of some type of chemical dependency problem.

4. Treatment interventions must be multimodal to correspond to the particular pattern of alcoholism or chemical dependency in a specific person.

5. Treatment outcomes will vary in accord with specific chemical-use patterns, persons, and social contexts.

6. Preventive interventions must be multiple and diverse in order to address diverse etiological factors.

The future of the chemical dependency field will, no doubt, include the description of consistently interrelated sets of symptoms with implications for etiology, prognosis, treatment, and prevention. The chemical dependency counselor will contribute to this by providing a multivariate diagnosis that is free of imprecise and ambiguous definitions that binarily impose a diagnosis of chemical dependency. The chemical dependency counselor is and will be expected to identify and treat all manner of people on all points of the chemical dependency continuum.

Defining the Problem

How is "the problem" defined? Many terms are used in the field of chemical dependency. Some have clear meanings, others are confusing and less well-defined. It is difficult for counselors to talk to one another (or to clients or other professionals) if they are using similar words but those words have different meanings to each person.

To begin with, what is chemical dependency? Does it refer only to physical dependency, or does it also include psychological dependency? What is considered a chemical? Alcohol? Nicotine? Caffeine? For the purpose of this book, and as a general guide for the counselor, the following definition is offered: *Chemical dependency is a condition in which there are perceivable signs or indications that the ingestion of a psychoactive or mood-altering chemical is causing the individual continuous life problems, yet this individual continues to use the chemical.* Although this is a rather broad definition, it does not fully encompass the range of clients that a chemical dependency counselor is likely to see.

The important aspects of this definition of chemical dependency are the phrases *life problems* and *continues to use.* What are these life problems, and which treatment approach is best suited to assist the client in dealing with them? What role does chemical use play in these problems, and what is the payoff because of continued use? Note that the rationale behind this definition is not to seek an either/or diagnosis, but to determine at what level these problems exist. For the individual who is beginning to experience problems related to chemical use, the counselor may only want to point out the relationship between the problems and the chemical use. The counselor may imply that the use must change or the problems will remain or get worse. It can no longer be assumed, however, that the only choice available to the client is to give up chemical use or progressively develop more and more problems. Chemical dependency problems are similar to other chronic medical disorders in that the condition may improve, remain stable, or become worse. As is also the case with most behavioral disorders, the client's economic, intellectual, and personal resources are often a major determinant of outcomes, with or without therapeutic intervention (Straussner, 2014). The prognosis for problem drinkers, for example, is far more encouraging than once believed. Rapid, spontaneous remission or gradual disappearance of alcohol-related problems may occur in a relatively high number of people. Walters (2000) reported spontaneous remission rates to be as high as 26.2% from alcohol, tobacco, and other drugs of abuse even without formalized help or treatment.

Others have reported on those who've "cured" themselves of addictions, those who've reduced their alcohol intake to non-problem levels, and those with addictions to heroin who returned from Vietnam to a drug-free life without treatment (Peele, 1982). It is true that many factors are now clear regarding chemical dependency; however, other pertinent issues remain unclear. One reason for this is the use of circular definitions. The counselor should avoid these semantic traps. For example, if, by definition, an alcoholic is a person who cannot drink alcohol without experiencing problems, it is impossible for an alcoholic to return to non-problem drinking, and the only acceptable treatment goal for an alcoholic is total abstinence. If an alcoholic should, by chance, return to non-problem drinking, then by definition he or she was not really an alcoholic. This definition eliminates the possibility of scientific inquiry and is called "circular thinking."

Denial

Denial is a concept that can be used to distort issues. If alcoholism is a "disease of denial," as many contend, then the only logical diagnosis that can be made of the problem drinker is alcoholism. If a problem drinker or a pre-alcoholic, diagnosed as alcoholic, rightfully denies his alcoholism, the denial is seen as the first stage of alcoholism (denial). If the problem drinker does not deny alcoholism, the only alternative is to accept it. These "yes-you-are–no-I'm-not" games only cloud the issues with regard to a specific diagnosis. They also detract from the counselor–client relationship.

The degree to which denial seems to be present in the context of a therapeutic relationship has been found to be largely correlated with choices made by the therapist (Miller & Rollnick, 2013). When a therapist tries to convince clients of something (e.g., they must accept a label, change friends, eat better, exercise), it is frequently, if not always, counterproductive for the resistance it brings forth. Nor is this unique to clients. Imagine you, dear reader, are hungry and you have two choices before you: a banana and a donut. Though you want the donut, you reach for the banana because you know it is the healthier choice. As you do so, a well-meaning friend walks in and says with a slightly scolding tone, "You know, you really shouldn't eat the donut." Almost automatically and instinctively, you change course and eat the donut.

Are you being difficult? Resistant? Are you unable to make healthy choices for yourself? Well, your friend could certainly accuse you of all those things, just as counselors have blamed clients for being "in denial" for decades. When we perceive someone attempting to limit our choices and freedoms—such as in the example above, when your friend said, "You shouldn't"—we tend to resist, even if it means going against our own best interests. The resistance that is engendered through this interaction has been labeled "psychological reactance," and, as suggested earlier, the degree to which it is present is largely within the therapist's control (Miller & Rollnick, 2013).

Definitions, then, should be for the benefit of both the client and the counselor, and they should not detract from the therapeutic process. They should be flexible, yet understandable to both the client and the counselor. As relates to diagnosis, we have found it helpful in our own work with clients that when we make the process open and collaborative with the client in a manner that is informed and participatory, then clients are much more likely to understand and be accepting of labels and/or diagnoses.

Defining Terms

Some of the words that counselors should examine for themselves are *use, misuse, abuse, addiction, habituation,* and *dependence.* The following brief definitions are offered to assist counselors in developing meanings for these words relative to their own personal, social, and physical criteria:

- **Use**—The intake of a chemical substance into the body with the goal of somehow altering one's state of consciousness. (Use may or may not cause problems.)

- **Misuse**—Using a chemical with some physically, psychologically, socially, or legally adverse consequence. (The word *misuse* often carries unnecessary moral implications.)

- **Abuse**—Chronic, recurrent misuse of chemicals.

- **Addiction**—A cellular change that occurs with the increased use of most depressant drugs. The primary clinical features are the development of tolerance and the development of withdrawal symptoms upon removal of the drug.

- **Habituation**—The repetition of a behavior. (This behavior is often anxiety-reducing for the individual.)

- **Dependence**—Physical dependency is much the same as addiction. Psychological dependence is a state that occurs when there is a strong urge to alter one's state of consciousness through the use of a chemical. These two types of dependence may occur independently or in combination with each other.

These are not the only terms that the chemical dependency counselor needs to clarify; there are many others. The point is that the counselor cannot be too clear or too specific about a client's problems and how these problems relate to a treatment plan.

Definitions and Diagnoses

Even though alcoholism and drug abuse have so many commonalities such that little practical distinction is now thought to exist between the two, historically alcoholism and drug abuse were regarded as distinct and separate disorders. We begin, therefore, by first examining some alternate ways of considering alcoholism and drug addiction before looking at how they are currently considered. It is important to understand the different ways in which alcoholism and drug addiction have changed over the years so that clinicians will anticipate and not be surprised to see future changes and approaches, one of which is discussed further into this chapter.

Historical Perspectives for Diagnosing Alcoholism and Chemical Dependence

Many approaches have been presented in the literature for evaluating and diagnosing alcoholism over the years. There have been biological methods, but these are indirect because they reflect consequences of alcohol use, and many persons may have alcoholism syndromes without biological damage.

There have been psychological methods of diagnosis that included indirect psychometric measures, such as the McAndrews Alcoholism scale of the *Minnesota Multiphasic Personality Inventory* (2nd ed., MMPI-2; 1989). There have also been direct psychometric methods, such as the *Michigan Alcoholism Screening Test* (MAST; 1971). Though it no longer makes such a distinction, the National Council on Alcoholism once had a list of major and minor criteria for the diagnosis of alcoholism, presented here as an example:

- **Diagnostic Level 1**—Classical, definite, obligatory. A person who fits this criterion must be diagnosed as alcoholic.

- **Diagnostic Level 2**—Probable, frequent, indicative. A person who satisfies this criterion is under strong suspicion of alcoholism; other corroborative evidence should be obtained.

- **Diagnostic Level 3**—Potential, possible, incidental. These manifestations are common in people with alcoholism but do not by themselves give a strong indication of its existence. Other significant evidence is needed before the diagnosis is made.

Criteria such as these were helpful but not foolproof in diagnosing alcoholism. One of the problems was false positives; while some of these measures have a 99% accuracy rate for identifying those in an alcoholic population, they diagnosed almost 50% of those who were not alcoholics as alcoholics. Often, the results from measures such as these did not translate well into treatment plans. Each of these measures has shown some degree of success in diagnosing a certain type of alcoholic, but often this is to the exclusion of many other types. Several authors have made an attempt to differentiate between these types of alcoholics. One such differentiation was reported by Greenblatt and Shader (1978). They suggested that alcoholism be divided into three distinct conceptual entities:

1. A pathologic psychosocial behavior pattern, characterized by deteriorating function in occupation, family, and citizenship, resulting from excessive alcohol ingestion.
2. A drug addiction of the classic type. Cessation of alcohol ingestion is followed by withdrawal.
3. A medical disease with certain characteristic sequelae, such as cirrhosis, nutritional disorders, and neurological damage.

They suggested that for those alcoholics who have all three characteristics, a diagnosis of alcoholism is easy. However, the alcoholic may have only one of these disorders or perhaps a combination of two. (For example, the heavy-drinking executive may have characteristic two but not one or three; the skid-row alcoholic may have one and two but not three, and so on.) These classifications were, perhaps, most useful for physicians.

Kuanert (1979) divided alcoholism into three somewhat different categories. He classified alcoholism as *reactive, secondary,* or *primary.* Reactive alcoholics were those who become preoccupied with alcohol only after being overwhelmed by some external stress. Secondary alcoholics were those suffering from a major psychiatric illness (e.g., schizophrenia), who medicated for this illness with alcohol. Primary alcoholics were those who found, from their first drinking experience, that their relationship with alcohol was extremely positive and highly desirable. They chose to involve themselves with alcohol and to capture the feelings evoked from this special relationship time and time again, and they disregarded any negative consequences of their drinking. What was fundamentally useful about Kuanert's approach was that he supplied a different and varied treatment plan for the underlying psychiatric illness than the alcoholism.

Wright (1982) presented a useful profile of the chemically dependent person. Each of the areas in the profile (below) could be addressed in a diagnostic interview and could also be included in a treatment plan:

- **Risk factors**
  1. Alcoholic relatives
  2. Disorder in family of origin
  3. Unusual early life history
- **Physical symptoms**
  1. Diseases related to substance usage
  2. Physical signs of usage
  3. Tolerance
  4. Withdrawal
  5. Stress-related or obscure illnesses
- **Mental symptoms**
  1. Decreased cognitive ability
  2. Memory failure
  3. Psychological dependency
  4. Obsession
  5. Defensiveness
  6. Delusioned denial
- **Emotional symptoms**
  1. Compulsive use
  2. Unstable moods
  3. Powerlessness
- **Social symptoms**
  1. Job
  2. Relationships
  3. Legal
  4. Financial
  5. Psychiatric
- **Spiritual symptoms**
  1. Rigid negative attitudes
  2. Low self-image
  3. Negative God concept
  4. Unusual religious observances

5. Failure of humility

6. Failure of love

Wright's (1982) list did not delineate all the potential problem areas of the chemically dependent person, but it did provide an excellent starting place. To provide more detail, each area would need to be expanded; for example, under Relationships might be Spouse and under that might be Sexual, Recreational, and so on.

A more extensive set of criteria for chemical dependency diagnosis that has been published was the diagnostic manual of McAuliffe and McAuliffe (1975). It is much too detailed to present here; however, the major areas covered are:

- Symptoms of mental obsession
- Symptoms of emotional compulsion
- Symptoms of low self-image
- Symptoms of rigid, negative attitudes
- Symptoms of a rigid defense system
- Symptoms of delusion
- Symptoms of powerlessness
- Physical symptoms

Although this manual was considered to be quite thorough, it might not have translated as well into a specific treatment plan as other, less complicated approaches to diagnosis. However, both the beginning counselor and the more advanced counselor could find this manual very useful with some adaptation to his or her own situation, if nothing else for better understanding the thinking of pioneers in the field and how it has evolved compared to our current understanding of addiction.

Current Understanding of Substance Use Disorders

Because of research advances, both alcoholism and chemical dependency—collectively referred to these days as "substance use disorders"—are understood in the context of how each similarly affect the brain's reward system. We now know that alcohol and other substances profoundly affect the level of chemicals (e.g., dopamine) that have the effect of making alcoholics and addicts want to use more of a substance (Begun & Brown, 2014). This suggests then that substance use disorders are, at least in part, diseases of the brain, as other mental health disorders are also thought to be. Genetics are thought to play an important contributory role; multiple studies have confirmed the contribution of genetics to substance use disorders, accounting for nearly 50% of an individual's vulnerability to addiction (Begun & Brown, 2014).

With these advances in understanding, and as further discussed in Chapter 9, the Research Domain Criteria project, launched by the National Institute of Mental Health, has as its goal the transformation of diagnosis by "incorporating genetics, imaging, cognitive science, and other levels of information..." (Insel, 2013, para. 3). This project hopes to identify relevant biomarkers and to collect the "genetic, imaging, physiologic, and cognitive data to see how [it] cluster[s] and how these clusters relate to treatment response" (para. 4).

The National Academy of Sciences has developed an effort with a goal of "precision medicine" that would utilize "genomic, epigenomic, exposure, and other data to define individual patterns of disease, potentially leading to better individual treatment" (Insel, 2011, para. 3). As a reference point for how transformative such a shift in thinking is, the National Academy of Sciences report references how the treatment of cancer has been "revolutionized by the application of molecular biology." Instead of utilizing less precise and traditional diagnostic labels, such as "kidney cancer" or "lung cancer," doctors are now looking for particular genetic mutations specific to tumors. When specific "driver mutations" are identified, medications can be developed to specifically target and block the growth of related cancerous tumors (Insel, 2011). It is hoped that the same will be possible for diagnosing substance use disorders in the future.

Even with the new knowledge such advances may bring, there is still an understanding that addiction takes place within a sociocultural context with all the variables previously identified in the historic models for assessing addiction as mentioned previously. This is why it is important, in order to have the most accurate diagnosis possible, to do a thorough biopsychosocial assessment to collect the necessary information and identify the requisite areas of concern.

Other Diagnostic Manuals

A diagnostic manual must be mentioned here because of its wide acceptance by the mental health field and by insurance companies who need a specific diagnosis to evaluate claim payments. This is the *Diagnostic and Statistical Manual of Mental Disorders* of the American Psychiatric Association, commonly referred to as "the DSM." This manual bases diagnosis on a description of the clinical features of the dysfunction. The chapter titled "Substance Abuse Disorders" lists the specific criteria for addiction and related problems.

Because this manual was recently updated, it will be useful for students and clinicians to be familiar with how both the previous and current editions approached diagnosis. The earlier edition, the DSM-IV, divided substance-related disorders into two categories, substance dependence and substance abuse (American Psychiatric Association, 1994). It will be helpful for students and clinicians to locate the DSM-IV criteria either online or in print.

The newest edition of the manual, the DSM-5, did away with these distinctions, collapsed the criteria, and added craving to the list, for a new, unified category—substance use disorder—which is rated as either mild, moderate, or severe, depending on how many criteria are met (American Psychiatric Association, 2013), which is parallel with the different diagnostic approaches discussed earlier in this chapter that also differentiated amongst three types of alcoholics.

Both the DSM-IV and the DSM-5 also list the criteria for substance intoxication and substance withdrawal; the criteria for each are substance specific in the DSM-5. As well, both the DSM-IV and DSM-5 separate drugs by class. As stated earlier, it will be useful for students and clinicians to compare and consult both of these manuals; it is highly recommended that those considering becoming counselors acquire one or both manuals for easy reference in their professional libraries.

The diagnostic criteria presented in the different versions of the DSM are accurate from the perspective of those who established them. Chemically dependent persons' symptoms can be evaluated, split up, divided, and diagnosed in hundreds of ways: All of these ways could conceivably be correct. Most likely, chemical dependency counselors will be expected to follow the DSM-5 or DSM-IV or the rules that their agency has established with regard to diagnosis. However, the beginning counselor will soon be the experienced counselor and, in that regard, can have an effect on the agency's policies, including how diagnosis is used and what criteria are followed. There is one simple rule to follow when making these decisions: Make sure the diagnosis is helpful to the client and leads to an appropriate treatment plan.

Case Examples

To best illustrate the type of in-depth diagnosis that we encourage, we will present two case examples. The first example has been taken directly from the case file of a very traditional alcoholism treatment program. Note that almost anyone would fit into this treatment plan and that the treatment recommended does not necessarily relate to the patient as presented in the history. It is not at all unusual to see this traditional kind of diagnosis and treatment plan. Specific data have been changed to protect the individual and the agency.

CASE #1

Date of Admission: 3/14/14

Date of Discharge: 4/10/14

Data Base: Patient is a 25-year-old male from San Diego, California; height, 75 inches; weight, 200 pounds. Patient came in voluntarily on 3/14/14.

Chief Complaint: Patient was pushed by authorities, after second DWI, to seek treatment at the present time. Went through detoxification.

History of Illness: Patient drinks only scotch, a pint per day. Drinks three or four days a week at a bar and at home. Some hangovers. Blackouts denied. No delirium tremens. Had one period of sobriety for three months.

Physical Examination: Liver was not enlarged.

Laboratory Report: SGOT, 19; GGT, 18; Hemoglobin, 18; MCV, 84; Ua, negative; VDRL, negative.

Chest X-Ray: 3/14/14, normal.

Psychological: Assessment on 3/16/14. IQ was 110. Test readministered on 4/1/14, and IQ was 121. A total of two hours with psychology department.

Observations: On entry, patient was cooperative, detoxification was not needed, no withdrawal symptoms.

Medications: 500 mg. Antabuse, three times a week; Unicap T, two daily; Tennes lotion to back (patient's own medication), as needed.

Medication on Discharge: 250 mg. Antabuse daily; B-complex daily; Tennes lotion to back (patient's own medication).

Ward: Patient was alert and compliant and cooperated reasonably well. Well aware of problems. Self-esteem improved. Patient was definitely serious about program. Family contacts—active girlfriend who picked him up after discharge.

Social Worker: Mr. Smith entered treatment as the result of a DWI. He was verbally skilled throughout his stay. Felt he has gained maximum benefit. His recovery plans include Alcoholics Anonymous (A.A.), Antabuse, and continued individual counseling. Did have three consents that were signed.

Counselor: Mr. Smith completed program, including A.A. steps one through five. During the third week, he continued to play with the idea that a cured alcoholic could return to social drinking. His intellectualization and avoidance of responsibility for his recovery are a strong defense against accepting alcoholism. He made statements that his girlfriend and mother would keep him sober. No visible change in behavior or attitude was observed; unless he follows a supervised recovery plan, his prognosis is poor.

Medical: Patient was present when the medical goal was set to confront legal problems ensuing from alcohol ingestion. Patient needs very closely supervised follow-up or he will not do well. Was very compliant, a junior at the university, and used intellectualization as a defense. Would plan to return to school. Only mildly involved in program.

Final Diagnosis: Alcohol dependence

Problems and/or Solutions:

Alcohol dependence—Patient was educated on alcoholism and completed the routine program. Patient was compliant throughout.

Legal problems ensuing from abnormal alcohol use and/or illegal drug use—Patient received second DWI. Patient faces court date to determine punishment and must pay all fees connected to case.

Anxiety—Patient reduced anxiety level slightly through participation in individual and group therapy.

Lacks understanding in the dynamics of addiction—He was urged to follow recovery plan but was never able to work on a feeling level.

Intellectualization—Patient was always wondering whether he would be able to drink socially further. This attitude remained unchanged. Patient needs a supervised environment to stay sober.

Treatment Modalities: Lectures, 21 hours; Group, 12% hours; Movies, 8% hours; Religious therapy, 8% hours; A.A. orientation, 6 hours; Reading and tapes, 25 hours; Social skills, 5 hours; Counselor, 2% hours; Social Worker, 1% hours; Team, completed fifth step; Testing, 2 hours; and Medical exam, ½ hour.

Aftercare Plan:

Date of Discharge—4/10/14

Placement—San Diego; Family; Own finances; Student at university

Legal—Second DWI in county; Follow-up A.A. in city of residence

Staff Recommendations: A.A. meetings twice weekly; Antabuse daily for two years with supervision; outpatient counseling; seek sponsorship in A.A. and become active in A.A. or patient will not make it.

Summary of the Case: Participation good. Problems identified and treatment plan completed. Patient received moderate detoxification benefit from treatment. Awareness of problems related to drinking were poor on entry—good on discharge. Plans for dealing with problems related to drinking were poor on entry—good on discharge. Changes in self (attitude, behavior, feelings) related to drinking were moderate.

Prognosis: Poor, unless follow-up is closely supervised.

CASE #1 DISCUSSION

Note that the presentation omits a great deal of information relating to this individual (for example, his feeling of self-worth, his sexuality, his family, his work history, his development, etc.). The treatment plan was not specific and did nothing or very little to meet the patient's specific needs.

The diagnosis was alcohol dependence, yet there was nothing to indicate that the patient was physically addicted. (Detoxification was noted as unnecessary, though he did go through a detoxification procedure. It is not uncommon for inpatient programs to require all new patients to go through detoxification as a medical precaution.) Psychological addiction, if it existed, was not mentioned.

Drinking occurred only three to four times weekly. Very little was mentioned regarding his family. Anxiety daily was mentioned, but with no specifics. (It is not unusual for a person to be anxious because of being in a treatment program.)

Treatment consisted mainly of lectures, group therapy (which some people respond to and others do not), movies, and A.A. orientation. Aftercare was simply "A.A. in city of residence."

Although the patient seemed poorly motivated, nothing was done to improve his motivation. Little wonder, then, that his prognosis is listed as poor; however, the poor prognosis is made to look as if it is the patient's fault. Statements such as, "Patient was always wondering whether he would be able to drink socially," "Lacks understanding in the dynamics of addiction," and "Never able to work on a feeling level" were used to focus on the patient's deficiencies, but these issues were apparently never dealt with in treatment.

It is also interesting to note the counselor's conclusion that "no visible change in behavior or attitude was observed." What did happen in treatment to change anything in the life of this patient? One would suspect very little by reading his records. A more appropriate statement to sum up what happened in treatment would be the following: A thorough diagnosis was never completed, and the patient was run through the standard treatment program.

To illustrate a more thorough approach that relates diagnosis to treatment, we will present this case again, with a narrative of what diagnosis and treatment could have been like.

CASE #2

Upon admission, a complete personal history was taken to determine basic demographic data; educational, vocational, health, treatment, social, and judicial histories; relationships with family and friends; recreational and community involvement; personality and emotional development; sexual functioning; and motivation for treatment.

A behavioral assessment of alcohol abuse was completed that included, in detail, what goes on before, during, and after the client consumes alcohol. This also includes the people he is with, when and where he drinks, the amount and type of available alcohol, concurrent activities, and any emotional state that could have influenced his drinking. The specific reinforcers for drinking were also identified.

Personal Data

Joe is an unmarried 25-year-old white male, third-year university student majoring in business. Joe presented March 14, 2014, for treatment of alcohol abuse, motivated by authorities due to a second DWI. At time of presenting, Joe had been drinking over a pint of scotch, three to four times per week. This pattern had existed for over a year.

Personal History

Joe is the oldest of three children. He has two brothers, five and seven years younger than he. He was born in Yuba City, California. His attitude toward his parents and siblings, on the surface, appears positive. However, he reports that as a child he found it difficult to approach his father and that he never seemed able to please him. Most of his communications in the family were through his mother. He did report some resentment toward his brothers because he had to help his father, a farmer, with the chores, and his brothers did not because they were too young. This often involved getting up at 4:30 in the morning while his brothers slept in.

The youngest brother is a senior in high school, and the middle brother is a junior in college preparing to go to medical school.

His father, now 69, continues to farm but at a reduced level. His mother is a retired schoolteacher. Neither parent drinks, because of religious beliefs.

Joe does have a girlfriend whom he plans to marry sometime after college. Their relationship seems tenuous due to his drinking behavior. He is often verbally abusive to her when he drinks heavily.

Joe is in the third year of college as a business major. However, his grades have been falling because of his drinking and sleeping through class. He is unsure about his business major and reports that he majored in business because he thought his father wanted him to. He has never seen a guidance counselor about his career plans, nor has he spoken to his parents or teachers. He has worked as a sales clerk in a clothing store for the past two years to help pay his way through school. He hates the job but needs the money.

Joe spent two years in the Army, stationed in Europe as a tank gunner during most of that time. He receives some military benefits to assist him through school. He loved Europe and hated the Army.

Joe's only encounters with the police are the two DWIs, which were approximately two years apart.

Joe has some interest in music, sports, reading, and movies. He seems to have led a fairly normal, middle-class, small-town existence.

Joe seems reluctant to adopt a treatment goal of total abstinence. However, he does seem anxious to attend to the other aspects of his life (i.e., vocation, sexual relationships, personal satisfaction in social relationships, and family relationships).

Joe attended A.A. after his first DWI, but he "didn't like it or the people in it." "A bunch of burned-out drunks" was the way he described it. The religious aspects reminded him of his Baptist upbringing, which he has rejected.

Behavioral Assessment

Joe's problems are:

- Alcohol abuse
- Vocational dissatisfaction
- Relationship problems with girlfriend and family
- Skill defect in expression of positive and confrontational statements to peers and family
- Anxiety in presence of strangers and crowds

Etiological Description

Alcohol Use—Joe's immediate concern is his inappropriate use of alcohol, the DWIs, and the problems that drinking causes between him and his girlfriend. He first drank alcohol while in basic training in the Army seven years ago. He found that alcohol made him feel at ease around other people. He drank nearly every day during his two years in the Army. Although he reported some hangovers, he had no blackouts or other alcohol-related problems. He has smoked marijuana but did not find it enjoyable. He reports no other drug use.

His beverage of choice is scotch, which accounts for 90% of his alcohol intake. Seventy-five percent of his drinking is done at bars, with friends. He reports that he drinks the equivalent of a pint of scotch, three to four times per week. He has had no suicide attempts, no psychiatric treatment, and no formal treatment for his alcohol abuse.

Vocational Potential

Joe is also very concerned about his vocational future. He is afraid that a degree in business will limit him in his career choices. He is not sure what he wants to do. He does not particularly like school, and he did not like the Army. He does not feel that he is capable of much more in school than he is already doing. He does not see himself as bright; "close to average intelligence" is how he described himself. His teachers in high school always told him that he was not working up to his potential, but he thought he was.

Interpersonal Relationships

Joe does not seem to have much insight into the nature of relationships. Often he does not see the cause-and-effect relationship between his behavior and the way other people treat him. He also has given little thought to the relationship between how he feels about himself now, his personal needs, and his early family life. He feels that others just "don't understand him." In this way, he seems to externalize his problems, placing the responsibility for his happiness on those around him. He appears to have many unverbalized expectations of others, and he is hurt when these others do not live up to these expectations. This hurt is also hard to verbalize and is often expressed inappropriately as anger during a drunken episode. He later regrets this behavior and feels guilty about it. This, in turn, makes him feel unworthy of any positive regard from others.

Joe indicated that while his home life as a child was mostly satisfactory, little, if any, real communication existed. He believes that strong emotions of any type were discouraged. His mother and father never fought; there was never a raised voice in the household. The only time his father showed any emotion was when his mother (Joe's grandmother) died. Even then, there was very little; just one short crying episode, then things were back to "normal."

Joe has indicated that he has felt ill at ease with other people most of his life. As a child, he was physically smaller than most of his classmates and, as such, was not invited to participate in competitive sports; in adolescence, he felt that his size led to his frustrated attempts at dating.

More recently, Joe has expressed skill deficit and anxiety when speaking with strangers and expressing himself in crowds. Joe is also unassertive in various social situations.

Treatment Techniques

Joe is a candidate for Motivational Enhancement Therapy (MET; Miller, Zewben, DiClimente, & Rychtarik, 1999), during which he will be asked to undergo an extensive assessment battery requiring approximately seven to eight hours. This battery is designed to assess his drinking compared to others', his normal level of intoxication, his risk factors, his negative consequences, hidden liver functioning via a blood test, and any neuropsychological damage he may have sustained as a result of his drinking. Motivational Enhancement Therapy is based on principles of motivational psychology and is designed to produce rapid, internally motivated change. This treatment does not attempt to guide and train the client step by step through recovery; instead it employs motivational strategies to mobilize the client's own resources. MET consists of four carefully planned and individualized treatment sessions. The first two sessions focus on structured feedback from the initial assessment, future plans, and motivation for change. The final two sessions allow the therapist to reinforce progress, encourage reassessment, and provide an objective perspective on the process of change.

As it happens, Joe meets all the criteria for success on a controlled drinking program:

- He has, at times, practiced social drinking.
- He is under 40 years of age.
- He was never physically addicted to alcohol.
- He has few life problems related to alcohol (in comparison to most alcoholics).
- He has a relatively short problem-drinking history (less than 10 years).
- He does not see himself as an alcoholic.
- He does not subscribe to the disease concept of alcoholism.
- He prefers the controlled drinking option to abstinence.
- He has no family history of alcoholism.
- He has environmental support (girlfriend, peers) for controlled drinking.

He will be offered a controlled-drinking program on an outpatient basis, but he must remain abstinent for 30 days before beginning the program. If he is unsuccessful at controlled drinking, he has agreed to accept total abstinence as an alternative goal.

The following program will be adopted to deal with Joe's abuse of alcohol wherein Joe will:

- Investigate situations, feelings, or thoughts that occur before, during, and after excessive drinking.
- Arrange effective alternative responses to excessive drinking.
- Learn how controlled drinking differs from alcoholic drinking.
- Practice drink refusal.
- Establish contract with the outpatient counselor, girlfriend, and family to reward a period of controlled drinking and to levy penalties (e.g., loss of attention, monetary fines) for excessive drinking.
- Set up a reading program on controlled drinking, including the book *Controlling Your Drinking* by Miller and Munoz (2013).
- Complete a drinking questionnaire that links frequency and amount of drinking to consequences experienced by client at outset of program with counselor, and once every three months thereafter.
- See a vocational counselor for testing and evaluation to set career and educational goals that Joe feels good about based upon the test results and vocational counseling.

- See a family therapist in family therapy with his parents and brothers, as well as his girlfriend.
- Modify through assertiveness training his skill deficit in interpersonal relationships.

In this example, the treatment plan is directly related to the diagnostic information. All of a person's problems cannot be dealt with in a short time period, so the client in consultation with his counselor must decide which problems should be selected for treatment to achieve the best overall results. This decision will depend, in part, on the resources of the treatment agency. Some treatments might include educational and vocational counseling; marital counseling; family counseling; sexual dysfunction, obesity, exercise, nutrition, or recreational counseling; and education as to non-alcoholic ways of getting "high."

Goal Setting

To be maximally effective, alcohol and drug and non-use–related treatment goals, objectives, and interventions must be established as part of the treatment plan. The following five key elements were identified as part of a National Institute on Drug Abuse (NIDA) blending initiative involving a team made up of researchers, clinical treatment providers, and trainers (Stilen, Carise, Roget, & Wendler, 2007):

1. *Measurable*—Can change or progress toward meeting the objectives be documented/evaluated? Will the counselor/treatment program be held accountable for the service(s)?

2. *Attainable*—Can the client take steps toward meeting the objectives? Do interventions reflect the level of care available, or are outside referrals used when needed?

3. *Time-Limited*—Is the time frame specified for the objectives and interventions?

4. *Realistic*—Can the client meet the objectives of the current situation? Do the interventions reflect the client's level of functioning or functional impairment?

5. *Specific*—Are specific activities included? Could the client understand what is expected?

Once goals, objectives, and interventions have been outlined and set, treatment may begin as outlined. Consider both the assessment and treatment planning processes to be ongoing throughout the client's course of treatment, and continue to gather data on the client's progress and revise accordingly. Some sample problems and goals are provided in Table 5.1.

Table 5.1
Sample Problems, Goals, Objectives, and Interventions

Problems	Goals	Objectives	Interventions
"I am overweight."	"I will lose weight."	"I will lose 15 pounds in 3 months."	"I will increase the amount I exercise from 2 to 4 days per week by (insert due date)."
Client has earned first DUI and expressed concern over amount she drinks (at least one pint of whiskey daily for the past 2 years).	Client will achieve and maintain an alcohol-free lifestyle.	Client will remain alcohol-free for 30 days from admission (as evidenced by daily urinalyses and self-report).	Client will attend the Legal Consequences group one time per week for 4 weeks and write one page per week on her reactions to the information in group and share with her counselor.
Client stated she lacks the ability to remain drug-free.	Client will develop skills for relapse prevention.	Client will complete a relapse-prevention plan by (give date) with at least 10 different skills and strategies in the following areas: refusal skills, cognitive restructuring, alternative recreation skills, and time management.	Client will attend weekly individual sessions for the next 3 months at which client will identify, share, and discuss a prevention skill from her relapse prevention plan with her counselor.
"I lost my job when I went to jail."	"I will find work."	"I will make a plan for securing employment within 30 days."	Counselor will have client sign release of information form. Counselor and client will call Vocational Rehabilitation for an appointment by (give date).
The client states, "My wife and I are still arguing a lot about my past drinking."	As per client, "I want to get along better with my wife and argue less."	The client will develop three healthy ways to handle conflict in his marriage by (give date).	The client and the counselor will meet within 4 days of the completion of his 8-week conflict resolution group to review his use of three ways to handle conflict in his marriage.

Client Motivation

It is useful to divide clients into one of these two categories: motivated to change or not motivated. It is true that there are degrees of motivation; but, basically, either clients come to the counselor's office willingly or they do not. There are two types of motivation: intrinsic (motivation from within the individual) and extrinsic (motivation from outside sources, such as the courts and family members). Clients who seek treatment because they will be fired if they do not are usually extrinsically motivated; clients who are just sick and tired of their lifestyles are intrinsically motivated.

The counselor can have a great deal of influence on both kinds of motivation. First, it is important to establish what motivation is already there. Then, build on that and expand to the other area of motivation. Counselors who tell clients, "You're the only one who can motivate yourself to stay straight" do not know much about motivation or their clients. Counselors can motivate their clients, and clients cannot do it all by themselves. (If they could, they would not need to see a counselor.) The counselor can motivate a client in many ways: by example, by providing hope where there is none, and by providing information and education where myths and misconceptions exist. The counselor can also aid in motivation by doing family therapy, by working with the client's employer, or by helping to find the client an employer.

Motivational Techniques

Miller and Rollnick (2013) discuss four particular processes to which counselors should attend, to directly affect their clients' desire for change:

- **Engaging**—As discussed in previous chapters, the quality of the therapeutic alliance is directly related to its ability to influence motivation.

- **Focusing**—This process helps to center the course of therapy around clients' goals and what they want to change in their lives.

- **Evoking**—The focus here is on helping clients to identify their own reasons for change, to let them explore their own thoughts and feelings, and to consider ways and strategies for how they might change.

- **Planning**—This involves solidifying clients' desires for change and developing a specific roadmap for moving forward.

As previously identified by Miller et al. (1999), specific principles that can help counselors support their clients through these processes include the following:

- **Expressing Empathy**—As it suggests, this involves relating to the client in an empathic manner.

- **Developing Discrepancy**—This is also referred to as "amplifying ambivalence" and is thought to enhance motivation for change by increasing a client's cognitive dissonance between their perceptions of where they are currently and where they want to be in the future.

- **Rolling With Resistance**—Along with another principle called "avoiding argumentation," a therapist should seek to "roll with" the perspectives of their clients such that resistance is minimized. Ambivalence is welcomed, explored, and normalized.

- **Supporting Self-Efficacy**—The degree to which clients feel they can change is thought to be directly related to the likelihood of making that change. Therapists address and help to support the strengthening of their clients' self-efficacy.

Examples of other motivational techniques include what is known as contingency management (further described in Chapter 13), wherein clients are provided rewards and negative consequences in response to the choices they've made. Another example is aversive therapy, which can help to enhance motivation by associating the use of a substance with discomfort of some kind. An example of this is the use of Antabuse (disulfiram), a prescription medication that creates unpleasant sensations—including flushing, throbbing headaches, nausea, vomiting—when alcohol is ingested.

The important thing to remember here is that the counselor must not rely totally on the chemically dependent person to be self-motivated. Without outside assistance, some people will never succeed.

Summary

Persons with chemical dependency issues come in all ages, shapes, and sizes, and they have various physical, psychological, and sociological problems. They use various chemicals, and their chemical use interferes with their life in various ways. It is the counselor's job to assess these many conditions and symptoms and to put them into a useable diagnosis that will translate into an effective treatment plan. The counselor uses his or her knowledge of the treatment approaches available and his or her assessment of the client to match the client to the treatment approach that will result in the best outcome for the client.

In the past, this was rarely done. Simplistic definitions led to general, non-specific treatment programs. The person with a drinking problem was diagnosed as either alcoholic or not alcoholic. Alcoholics were sent to A.A. or entered treatment where they learned about A.A.; non-alcoholics went back to drinking, as did many alcoholics who would not admit to being powerless or alcoholic. Drug addicts were sent to Narcotics Anonymous (N.A.), Cocaine Anonymous (C.A.), or inpatient drug programs. There was only one goal for all of these programs—total abstinence through living the 12 steps. It was assumed that if abstinence was maintained, the other problems would go away. This did not happen. Many patients could not maintain abstinence, and for many who did, the real problems were just beginning.

Can a person diagnosed as chemically dependent ever return to non-problem drug or alcohol use? The answer to this question and others is being researched every day, and answers are being found. In some cases, they may not be the answers everyone would like to have. But counselors who want to accurately assess their clients must have all the information that is available—and they must be able to adjust to the complex problems of each client with an individualized treatment plan. A thorough diagnosis is the key to that treatment plan.

References

American Psychiatric Association. (1994). *Diagnostic and statistical manual of mental disorders* (4th ed.). Washington, D.C.

American Psychiatric Association. (2013). *Diagnostic and statistical manual of mental disorders* (5th ed.). Washington, D.C.

Begun, A., & Brown, S. (2014). Neurobiology of substance use disorders and implications for treatment. In S. L. Straussner (Ed.), *Clinical work with substance-abusing clients* (pp. 39–66). New York: Guilford Press.

Butcher, J. N., Dahlstron, W. G., Graham, J. R., Tellegen, A. M., & Kreammer, B. (1989). *The Minnesota multiphasic personality inventory: Manual for administration and scoring* (2nd ed.). Minneapolis, MN: University of Minneapolis Press.

Center for Substance Abuse Treatment. (2013). *Enhancing motivation for change in substance abuse treatment.* Treatment Improvement Protocol (TIP) Series, No. 35. HHS Publication No. (SMA) 13-4212. Rockville, MD: Substance Abuse and Mental Health Services Administration.

Gallagher, J. (2009). Ethical violations: A quantitative study comparing human services professions. *Recovery Online Today.* Retrieved from http://www.recoverytoday.net/Mar09/gallagher.html

Greenblatt, D. I., & Shader, R. I. (1978). Treatment of alcohol withdrawal syndrome. In Shader, R. (Ed.), *Manual of psychiatric therapeutics* (pp. 50–59). Boston: Little, Brown.

Insel, T. (2011, November 15). Director's blog: Improving diagnosis through precision medicine [Blog post]. Retrieved from http://www.nimh.nih.gov/about/director/2011/improving-diagnosis-through-precision-medicine.shtml

Insel, T. (2013, April 29). Director's blog: Transforming diagnosis [Blog post]. Retrieved from http://www.nimh.nih.gov/about/director/2013/transforming-diagnosis.shtml

Kuanert, A. P. (1979). Perspectives from a private practice: The differential diagnosis of alcoholism. *Family and Community Health—Alcoholism and Health, Part II, 2*(2), 1–11.

Lewis, T. (2014). *Substance abuse and addiction treatment: Practical application of counseling theory.* New York: Pearson.

Manubay, J., & Horton, T. (2010). Common medical illnesses in patients with substance use and psychiatric disorders. In E. V. Nunes, J. Selzer, P. Levounis, & C. A. Davies (Eds.), *Substance dependence and co-occurring psychiatric disorders* (pp. 14/4–14/37). Kingston, NJ: Civic Research Institute.

McAuliffe, R. M., & McAuliffe, M. B. (1975). *Essentials for the diagnosis of chemical dependency.* Minneapolis, MN: American Chemical Dependency Society.

Mee-Lee, D. (Ed.). (2013). *The ASAM criteria: Treatment criteria for addictive, substance-related, and co-occurring conditions.* Chevy Chase, MD: American Society of Addiction Medicine.

Miller, W. R., & Munoz, R. F. (2013). *Controlling your drinking* (2nd ed.) New York: Guilford Press.

Miller, W. R., & Rollnick, S. (2013). *Motivational interviewing: Helping people change* (3rd ed.). New York: Guildford Press.

Miller, W. R., Zewben, A., DiClemente, C., & Rychtarik, R. G. (1999). *Motivational enhancement therapy manual.* (National Institute on Alcohol Abuse and Alcoholism Project MATCH Monograph Series Vol. 2). Rockville, MD: U.S. Department of Health and Human Services.

Nathan, P. E., & Gorman, J. M. (2007). *A guide to treatments that work.* New York: Oxford University Press.

Pattison, M. E., & Kaufman, E. (Eds.). (1982). *Encyclopedic handbook of alcoholism.* New York: Gardner Press.

Peele, S. (1982, August). The human side of addiction: People who cure themselves of addictions. *The U.S. Journal,* p. 7.

Prochaska, J. O., Norcross, J. C., & DiClemente, C. C. (2006). *Changing for good: A revolutionary six-stage program for overcoming bad habits and moving your life positively forward.* New York: HarperCollins Publishers.

Selzer, M. L. (1971). The Michigan alcoholism screening test: The quest for a new diagnostic instrument. *American Journal of Psychiatry, 127,* 1653–1658.

Stilen, P., Carise, D., Roget, N., & Wendler, A. (2007). *Treatment planning M.A.T.R.S.: Utilizing the Addiction Severity Index (ASI) to make required data collection useful.* Kansas City, MO: Mid-America Addiction Technology Transfer Center in residence at the University of Missouri-Kansas City.

Straussner, S. L. (2014). Assessment and treatment of clients with substance use disorders. In S. L. Straussner (Ed.), *Clinical work with substance-abusing clients* (pp. 3–38). New York: Guilford Press.

Straussner, S. L. (Ed.). (2014). *Clinical work with substance-abusing clients.* New York: Guilford Press.

Walters, G. D. (2000). Spontaneous remission from alcohol, tobacco, and other drug abuse: Seeking quantitative answers to qualitative questions. *American Journal of Drug Abuse, 26*(3), 443–460.

Wright, C. (1982, August 29–September 1). *New patterns in alcohol and drug addiction: The physician as a pusher.* Paper presented at the 33rd Alcohol and Drug Problems Association of North America (ADPA) annual meeting, Washington, DC.

CHAPTER 6

Group Counseling in the Treatment of Chemical Dependency[1]

CHAPTER OBJECTIVES

- Examine reasons to use group therapy
- Examine advantages and limitations of groups
- Review different types of groups
- Examine the therapeutic nature of groups
- Review goals and objectives of groups
- Examine attributes of good group leaders
- Examine issues in choosing group members
- Examine stages of group process

Perhaps the best way to begin this chapter is with a statement of what it is not: It is not all you have ever wanted to know, or will ever need to know, about groups. It would be impossible, in one short chapter, to provide the reader with the skills to be an effective group leader (i.e., a leader who consistently produces therapeutic results when leading a group). It takes study and practice to develop into a first-rate group facilitator.

There have been hundreds of books and articles written about groups; so why should a chemical dependency counselor read this particular chapter about groups? First, this chapter is being written specifically with the beginning chemical dependency counselor in mind. Second, it provides a structure for your future study and practice of group counseling in the treatment of chemical dependency. This chapter should be viewed as a map for chemical dependency counselors to use to help themselves toward a greater understanding of the group process and, in turn, toward improved skills as group leaders. The point is to encourage you, as a chemical dependency counselor, to continue your study of group counseling far beyond the scope of this chapter—and to have you recognize that group counseling is not just individual counseling done with more than one person. The dynamics and usefulness of group counseling go far beyond those of individual therapy in the treatment of the chemically dependent client. The clinical pros and cons of this will be discussed later in this chapter. Like all forms of therapy, however, groups that are used inappropriately

---

1 Portions of this chapter have been adapted from *Group Process and Practice*, by G. Corey and M. S. Corey, with permission from Brooks/Cole Publishing © 2006.

can be harmful to the group member and can detract from (rather than add to) movement toward the individual group member's treatment goals. This negative effect will be discussed in more detail later.

Why Use Groups?

The first question that should be addressed is of major concern for all chemical dependency counselors, and that is, Why use groups at all? This leads to many other questions, for example:

- How is group therapy different from individual therapy?
- What are some advantages of groups?
- What are some limitations of groups?
- What kinds of groups are there?
- What makes a group therapeutic?
- What is the group process?
- Are there stages that groups go through?
- What are the stages?
- Are there general rules and goals for a group?
- How much should a group leader structure the group session?
- What are the qualities of a good group leader?
- Who are appropriate group members?
- What are some specific models for alcohol or drug groups?
- What are some group dynamics that can make a member feel worse, rather than better?
- What are the ethical issues involved in groups?

These and other questions will be discussed in the following pages. Read these pages not from the perspective of, "At last, I have found the answers!" but rather, "At last, I have begun to understand the questions!"

So why should the chemical dependency counselor use groups as a treatment approach? This can be answered from many different perspectives. First and foremost in the heart of the program administrator is the fact that groups make sense economically. A counselor who can see six individual clients per day can run three groups instead and see over 20 clients. In a field such as chemical dependency, where there are many more clients than counselors, group counseling may be the only way for counselors to effectively handle their caseloads. This would not be an acceptable solution to the time bind if there was evidence that those attending groups received significantly less therapy than those who attended only individual sessions. This, however, is not the case, and group psychotherapy is the treatment of choice for those with addictions (Eaves & Sheperis, 2011). Although most treatment programs include both group and individual therapy, often it is in the group that the client or patient makes the most progress toward significant therapeutic movement. Why is this? The reason is that essentially humanity is an indivisible, social, decision-making being whose actions have a social purpose (Dreikurs & Sonstegard, 1968). As social beings, we are influenced more by a group of people than by just one person. (That is unless that person is very special to us, such as a child, a parent, or a spouse. See Chapter 7 on family counseling.) This group effect is also true for chemically dependent clients; however, they have often had very poor experiences in social relationships and desperately need positive social interaction to enable them to give up the self-destructive patterns of chemical use that have developed over a lifetime. Substance abusers often feel socially isolated, and they lack certain prosocial interpersonal skills. Because of this, within the context of the group, they will often recreate the coping skills (i.e., manipulating, denying, blaming, rationalizing, or distracting) they utilized that served them so well while using (Corey & Corey, 2006). Groups, particularly ones including savvy peers, are the ideal place to provide the therapeutic impact to confront and change these traits while providing support and structure (Eaves & Sheperis, 2011).

Fulfilling Individual Needs Through the Group

To be more specific, individual needs that can potentially be fulfilled in the group include the following (Yalom, 1995):

- Discovering and accepting formerly unacceptable and unknown parts of themselves
- Being able to say what needs to be said
- Hearing others provide honest feedback
- Learning how to express their feelings
- Learning the kind of impression they make on others
- Expressing both negative and positive emotions to others
- Learning that they are ultimately responsible for ways in which they live their lives
- Learning how they come across to others
- Seeing that others could benefit from sharing embarrassing things and taking risks, and learning how to do the same
- Feeling more trusting of other groups and people

Each theoretical approach to group counseling (e.g., transactional analysis, rational emotive therapy, behavioral therapy) provides its own rationale for using groups as a therapeutic technique. Each type of group (e.g., Adult Children of Alcoholics [ACOA] groups, encounter groups, t-groups, educational groups) has separate reasons why it should be used. It is not appropriate in this chapter to detail when, and why, each different type of group or theoretical model should be used; however, it is important to note that the reason a counselor chooses to use groups as part of a treatment plan should be congruent with the type of group chosen. For example, if one of the major individual treatment goals is to build self-esteem, a group that involves a great deal of personal confrontation might not be the most appropriate type of group to reach this goal—a more supportive group would be more appropriate.

The answer to the original question becomes this: The chemical dependency counselor should consider the use of group therapy as part of an overall treatment plan because it is economically the best use of time, and groups are often the best method for reaching many of the social goals of a complete treatment plan for the chemically dependent client.

The Advantages of Groups

Therapeutic groups have certain distinct advantages over other intervention strategies. Corey and Corey (2006) mention these advantages:

- Participants are able to explore their style of relating to others and to learn more effective social skills.
- The group setting offers support for new behavior and encourages experimentation.
- There is a re-creation of the everyday world in some groups, particularly if the membership is diverse with respect to age, interests, background, socioeconomic status, and type of problem. When this occurs, a member has the unique advantage of being in contact with a wide range of personalities, and the feedback received can be richer and more diverse than that available in a one-to-one setting.
- Certain factors that facilitate personal growth are more likely to exist in groups. Members of groups, for instance, have the opportunity to learn about themselves through the experience of others, to experience emotional closeness and caring that encourage meaningful disclosure of self, and to identify with the struggles of other members.

The Limitations of Groups

While there are some distinct advantages to group methods, as reported by Gladding (2009), there are some limitations to the effectiveness of therapeutic groups. These are expanded on next:

- Groups are not cure-alls and cannot help all people nor address all possible problems. Unfortunately, systemic pressures (e.g., staffing constraints, agency policies) frequently dictate the use of groups for all clients. Counseling and therapy are difficult forms of work, and we believe that shortcuts are not necessarily fruitful.

- There is often a subtle pressure to conform to group norms, values, and expectations. Group participants sometimes unquestioningly substitute group values and norms for norms and values that they had unquestioningly acquired in the first place. This is mindlessness. Rigid adherence to values without careful consideration of why is not healthy, no matter what values a person has selected.

- Some people become hooked and make the group experience an end in itself. Instead of using the group as a laboratory for human learning and as a place where they can learn behavior that will facilitate their day-to-day living, they stop short, savoring the delights of the group for its own sake.

- Not all people are suited to groups. The idea that groups are for everybody has done serious harm to the reputation of the group movement. Some people are too suspicious, too hostile, or too fragile to benefit from a group experience. Some individuals are psychologically damaged by attending certain groups. Before a person is accepted into a group, all the factors need to be carefully weighed by both the counselor and the client to increase the likelihood that the person will benefit from such an experience.

- Improperly facilitated groups may result in reinforcing non-productive and dysfunctional, even destructive, behaviors of the group members. This is why we believe it so very important that the only therapists who should be doing group counseling are those properly trained in group counseling techniques.

The chemical dependency counselor who knows the most about the different types of groups and the different theoretical approaches will be the most effective at helping chemically dependent persons to reach their treatment goals.

Types of Groups

There are many types of groups, as well as many theoretical approaches to groups. Among the varieties of group psychotherapy, there is enormous diversity of format, goals, and the roles of the leader (Erford, 2011). There are also many ways to select the members of a group. They could be homogeneous and have the same problem, such as cocaine addiction. They could be selected by age, as in children's or adolescents' groups. They might be a combination of both, as in elderly, prescription-drug-abuser groups. They could be the same sex or unisex groups. Members could be heterogeneous with regard to problems and have several different problems, such as depression, drug abuse, and phobias. The group's makeup should be decided by the leader based on the goals of the group. There are advantages and disadvantages to every combination. (For more on this, see Chapter 8.)

It would go beyond our purpose here to list and describe every type of group, but we will mention a few that are often used in chemical dependency treatment. One of the major types of groups that the chemical dependency counselor is likely to become involved with is the treatment group, sometimes called the "focal group," that is often used during an inpatient treatment program in conjunction with individual therapy. Sometimes these groups are used mostly to "break the denial" of the patient, using heavy confrontation by the group leader and other group members. Sometimes this is called the "hot-seat" method. Often this simply leads to compliance rather than to the individual's actually getting in touch with the reality of his or her chemical dependency; it becomes easier for the patient to falsely admit to a belief that he or she is alcohol or drug dependent than to be confronted by the group. This might be one reason for a high dropout or recidivism rate among chemically dependent clients in treatment. An alternative to the hot-seat model might be a less threatening, more supportive group that would allow patients to explore their life situations with honest and open feedback. Certainly not all therapy groups that use confrontation conclude with high dropout rates and recidivism; the majority are supportive, as well as confrontational, and end with a positive result. It is important, however, to remember that groups can be harmful, as well as helpful, and that extremes, whether in confrontation or support, are subject to negative results.

Educational Groups

The second type of group often used in the treatment of chemical dependency is the educational group. This is a modified lecture format, where patients learn about new ways to look at old problems. For example, a group topic might be sex and recovery. The facilitator or group leader might make several remarks about the importance of sex and its relationship to the recovery process and then lead a discussion among group members about the topic. These groups are often very meaningful to the members, both from the perspective of the information they provide and from the feeling of having shared problems with other group members. Members often find that they are not, as they thought, the only ones with a particular problem. In addition, these groups are often used in the addictions field with those with co-dependency issues, rather than persons with addiction. The motto of many treatment programs seems to be, "Treat the addict and educate the family." This approach is better than not involving the family at all. However, we suggested some time ago that the family is in as much need of treatment as the person with the addiction, and both should receive education and therapy (A. Lawson & Lawson, 1984; G. Lawson & Lawson, 1998).

Multifamily Groups

Another type of group offered at treatment centers across the country involves getting several families together for a group session. These groups have been used for the treatment of adolescent substance abuse, and in the treatment of families of members with alcohol or drug problems. Although there is little research on their effectiveness, the clinical reports of the outcomes of these groups have been very positive. In one study comparing multifamily therapy groups with multifamily education groups, both groups showed improvement in family functioning and in the overall mental health of the family members (Valentine, Lawson, & Lawson, 1995). Other studies have found multifamily psychoeducational groups to (a) support success in decreasing hospitalizations for those with schizophrenia, (b) assist adolescents in their treatment of eating disorders, and (c) improve family functioning (Erford, 2011).

Self-Help Groups

Although not technically "therapy" or "counseling," another type of group that helps members not to feel alone with their problem is the self-help group. The self-help group has a long and successful history in the field of chemical dependency. Many people around the world are sober and leading productive lives as a result of a wide diversity of groups, including the following (Fewell & Spiegel, 2014):

- Alcoholics Anonymous (A.A.)
- Narcotics Anonymous (N.A.)
- Cocaine Anonymous (C.A.)
- Marijuana Anonymous (M.A.)
- Crystal Meth Anonymous (C.M.A.)
- Heroin Anonymous (H.A.)
- Groups for those with co-occurring substance use and mental disorders
- Al-Anon groups, for families and friends of those with addictions
- Self-Management and Recovery Training (SMART), based on the principles of rational-emotive behavior therapy
- Moderation Management for problem drinkers, rather than those addicted to alcohol
- Women for Sobriety

A broad body of research—most of it investigating A.A. and its effect on drinking—has supported the finding that lower levels of addictive behaviors are associated with attendance at more A.A. meetings, whether concurrent or subsequent to attendance (Miller, Forcehimes, & Zweben, 2011). Level of involvement showed a stronger benefit than merely attending meetings just to attend them; in other words, those who participated more deeply in both the 12-step program and fellowship appeared to benefit the most from A.A. (Miller et al.). Those without social networks that promote abstinence seem to get the most benefit from attendance at such groups because it gives them a ready-made and easily accessible social support system for maintaining their sobriety (Miller et al.). In light of these studies, Miller et al. conclude the following:

> There is good reason to encourage substance-dependent clients, whether religious or not, to sample 12-step meetings. As stated earlier, we do not think that anyone should be required or coerced to attend, but there is good reason to expect that such mutual help groups may improve clients' chances for stable recovery. (p. 229)

It is incumbent upon chemical dependency counselors, then, to become knowledgeable about all of the self-help options available to their clients.

Aftercare Groups

Perhaps a blend of the qualities of the self-help group and the therapy group has been reached in the aftercare group. These groups are used to support the chemically dependent person after inpatient treatment and are sometimes offered in conjunction with individual outpatient counseling. Unlike self-help groups, they usually have a trained group leader and an identified goal, possibly stated in the client treatment plan. The aftercare group can be run using any number of theoretical models.

The Behavioral Approach to Groups

Some good reasons have also been presented to use a behavioral approach in groups. According to Varenhorst (1969, p. 131), the behaviorist's use of learning principles in group process makes groups more effective than individual therapy for the following reasons:

- There is greater variety of models within a group.
- There are greater numbers of sources of reinforcement within the group.
- There are more opportunities for creating realistic social enactments whereby role rehearsal can be practiced, changed, and strengthened.

- There is an immediate situation in which generalization, as well as discrimination, can be learned with greater efficiency.
- Membership in the group itself can be utilized as a powerful reinforcing agent.

The behaviorists suggest that persons in groups need to perform certain specific behaviors. They are as follows:

- Share feelings openly.
- Suggest ideas and actions.
- Reinforce others as the need occurs.
- Give feedback.
- Participate in demonstrations or role playing of alternative actions.
- Be willing to accompany group members on assignments outside the group.
- Make a commitment to one's goals and the purposes of the group.

These are only a few of the many possible theoretical approaches to groups. Whether the chemical dependency counselor leads a treatment group, an educational group, an aftercare group, or another type of group, several theoretical approaches should be explored in an attempt to find the one most compatible with the group goals and the skills and style of the facilitator. Besides the ones mentioned above, a chemical dependency counselor might consider these additional theoretical models:

- Transactional Analysis (TA) groups
- Group-centered or humanistic groups
- Gestalt groups
- Rationale emotive therapy groups
- t-groups
- Reality therapy groups
- Focal groups

For a detailed description on how to run a beginning group with addicted populations, see Chapter 20 in *Treating Addiction: A Guide for Professionals* (2011), by Miller, Forcehimes, and Zeben.

What Is Therapeutic About Groups?

In one of the most widely read and quoted books ever written about groups, Yalom (2005) has identified 11 curative factors of groups: They are presented here with regard to the chemically dependent client. The first of these is the instillation of hope. This is a crucial factor in the treatment of chemically dependent clients because, so often, they have given up all hope. They have tried many things to deal with their condition, without success. The family doctor, their minister or priest, self-control, and all manner of internal and external assistance for the problem have been sought and tried. Hope is important because it keeps the patient in therapy and fosters high expectations, which have been shown to correlate highly with success. In other words, the more a person believes in a treatment approach, the more likely it is to work. By observing the improvement of other group members, each member draws hope from the other members; thus, hope can be enhanced in chemical dependency groups by including patients more advanced in treatment.

The second curative factor is universality, that is to say, a sense of shared problems. Often chemically dependent persons enter therapy with the disturbing thought that they are the only ones alive with their particular problem; they are plagued with the thought that what they have experienced is unacceptable. Usually, just realizing that they are not unique in their problems is a powerful source of relief. After hearing others disclose problems similar to their own, group members report feeling more in touch with the world; simply put, the feeling that "we're all in the same boat" is very comforting. Statements reinforcing this by the group leader are effective in chemical dependency groups.

The third curative factor is the imparting of information. This includes information about chemical dependency (the dynamics involved in the chemical dependency condition, as well as advice to clients about how to cope with their problems) offered by the group facilitator or other group members. It is important for the group leader to be aware of the group member who seeks advice from other group members, only to reject their advice: This should be pointed out to that member. Other dynamics include making a bid for attention and nurturance by constantly asking for group suggestions for a problem that is insoluble or that has already been solved. Other types of groups give advice and guidance directly through slogans (e.g., "One day at a time," asking that the person remain sober for only the next 24 hours). There is much misinformation and myth regarding chemical dependency; the counselor should have accurate facts in this area.

The fourth curative factor is altruism. Simply put, you receive through giving. When a group member is able to help another group member, it is hard to distinguish who receives the most benefit from the exchange. There is nothing that does more to build self-esteem than the act of unselfishly giving help to another. This wisdom has long been shared and proven by A.A., with the twelfth step—"We try to carry this message to alcoholics." Many an alcoholic has maintained a high level of sobriety by helping others. In short, people need to feel needed; the group can fulfill this need.

The fifth curative factor is described as the corrective recapitulation of the primary family group. Chemically dependent persons often enter group therapy with a history of a highly unsatisfactory experience in their first and most important group—their family of origin. Over half of those who enter treatment have parents who themselves are chemically dependent. For many patients, working out problems with therapists and other group members means also working through unfinished business from long ago. The role of the family is explained in more detail in Chapter 7.

The sixth curative factor is the development of a socializing technique that includes the development of basic social skills. Many chemically dependent persons either never learned basic social skills or lost them sometime during their period of chemical abuse. For these people, the group often represents the first opportunity for accurate interpersonal feedback. The changes gained in level of social skills are not an end in themselves, but they are often exceedingly instrumental in the initial phases of therapeutic change.

It is often apparent that senior members of a group have acquired some highly sophisticated social skills. They are aware of group process and have learned how to be helpfully responsive to others. They have acquired methods of conflict resolution and are less prone to be judgmental. They are also more capable of experiencing and expressing accurate empathy. These skills cannot but help to improve their future social interactions; these senior members should be pointed out as models of behavior for newer group members.

The seventh curative factor, imitating behavior, is an important therapeutic force. The healthy behavior of the group leader often becomes the model for the rest of the group. Imitating another group member, even if it turns out that the role does not fit, is a therapeutic process. Learning what one is *not* is often progress toward learning what one *is*.

The eighth and ninth curative factors as listed by Yalom (2005) are interpersonal learning and group cohesiveness. He includes an entire chapter on each of these concepts. Interpersonal learning involves the corrective emotional experience involved in a group, as well as the therapeutic value of experiencing the group as a social microcosm. Group cohesiveness pertains to the source of stability that one feels from being a part of a cohesive group. This has been described as a "oneness" with the group.

The tenth curative factor, catharsis, has assumed the role of a therapeutic process from the early time of Freud. This is the purging of oneself to cleanse away excessive emotions. But this expulsion alone is not enough; it is the process of "learning how to express feelings" that is the most therapeutic aspect of catharsis, not the expulsion itself.

Finally, the eleventh curative factor, the existential factors of group therapy, are considered. This is basically a compilation of factors not included in the categories above. There are five of them, and they seem particularly important for the chemically dependent client:

1. Recognizing that life is at times unfair and unjust
2. Recognizing that ultimately there is no escape from some of life's pain or from death
3. Recognizing that no matter how close I get to other people, I still face life alone
4. Facing the basic issues of my life and death, and thus living my life more honestly and being less caught up in trivialities
5. Learning that I must take ultimate responsibility for the way I live my life, no matter how much guidance and support I get from others

It is highly recommended that the chemical dependency counselor read Yalom's book in its entirety.

The ideas of Corey and Corey (2006), who have also addressed the therapeutic factors that operate in groups, bear mentioning here. Although there is some overlap among their factors and the ones listed above, they are worth listing again:

- **Hope**—This is the belief that change is possible, that one is not a victim of the past, and that new decisions can be made. Hope is therapeutic in itself, for it gives members confidence that they have the power to choose to be different.

- **Commitment to change**—A resolve to change is therapeutic in itself. If one is motivated to the point of becoming an active group participant, the chances are good that change will occur. This commitment to change involves a willingness to specify what changes are desired and to make use of the tools offered by the group process to explore ways of modifying one's behavior.

- **Willingness to risk and to trust**—Risk involves opening oneself to others, being vulnerable, and actively doing in a group that which is necessary for change. The willingness to reveal oneself is largely a function of how much one trusts the other group members and the group leader. Trust is therapeutic, for it allows persons to show the many facets of themselves, encourages experimental behavior, and allows persons to look at themselves in new ways.

- **Caring**—Caring is demonstrated through the listening and involvement of others. It can be expressed via tenderness, compassion, support, and even confrontation. If members sense a lack of caring from either group members or the group leader, their willingness to lower their masks will be reduced.

Clients are able to risk being vulnerable if they sense that their concerns are important to others and that they are valued as persons.

- **Acceptance**—This involves a genuine support from others that says, in effect, "We will accept all of your feelings. You do count here. It's OK to be yourself. You don't have to strive to please everyone." Acceptance involves affirming a person's right to have his own feelings and values and to express them.

- **Universality**—The realization that certain problems (such as loneliness, need for acceptance, fear of rejection, fear of intimacy, and hurt over past experiences) are universal lessens the feeling that one is alone. And, through identification with others, one is able to see oneself more clearly.

- **Confrontation**—Through careful and considerate confrontation, group members are able to better learn about themselves, to become aware of both their potential and their hang-ups, and to explore ways of utilizing this awareness to grow.

- **Power**—This feeling emerges from the recognition that one has untapped reserves of spontaneity, creativity, courage, and strength. In groups, personal power may be experienced in ways that were formerly denied, and persons can discover ways in which they block their strengths. This power is not a power over others; rather, it is the sense that one has the internal resources necessary to direct the course of one's life.

- **Freedom to experiment**—The group situation provides a safe place for experimentation with new behavior. After trying new behavior, persons can gauge how much they want to change their existing behavior.

- **Feedback**—Members gauge the effects of their behavior on others from the feedback they receive. If feedback is given honestly and with care, members are able to understand more clearly the impact they have on others. Then it is up to them to decide what to do with this feedback.

- **Catharsis**—The expression of pent-up feelings can be therapeutic in that energy can be released that has been tied up in withholding certain threatening feelings. Catharsis may allow a person to realize that negative and positive feelings toward others may co-exist. A woman may be suppressing a great deal of resentment toward her mother and by releasing it, may discover a need for her mother's affection and a feeling of love for her mother.

- **The cognitive component**—Catharsis is even more useful if a person attempts to find words to explain the feelings that are expressed. Some conceptualization of the meaning of intense feelings associated with certain experiences can give one the tools to make significant changes.

- **Self-disclosure and the group member**—Participants in groups can discover and deepen their understanding of themselves by sharing personal details about themselves with group members. Thus, a woman who feels isolated from others may come to understand the concrete things she does that lead to these feelings and may learn to lessen this isolation by asking others for what she needs.

- **Self-disclosure and the group leader**—Too much self-disclosure on the part of the group leader can be counterproductive. Group leaders must remember that their job is to facilitate and otherwise direct and evaluate the group members' interactions.

- **Humor**—Laughing at oneself can be extremely therapeutic. This requires seeing one's problems in a different perspective. Thus, a man who sees himself as stupid may eventually be able to laugh at the stupidity of continually convincing himself that he is stupid. People who are able to laugh at themselves are better able to cope with seeing themselves clearly.

- **Cohesion**—A group is characterized by a high degree of "togetherness" at times, providing a climate in which participants feel free to share problems, try new behaviors, and in other ways reveal the many dimensions of themselves. Group cohesion is influenced by many variables, a few of which are the attraction of the group for its members, the enthusiasm of the leaders, the trust level of the group, and the extent to which the members identify with one another.

It can be concluded that the goal of a group is to provide its members with the therapeutic factors discussed above. But, to maximize the use of these therapeutic forces, it is wise to be even more specific about group goals.

Failures in Groups

With all that groups have to offer, they can fail to provide the necessary conditions for a member to improve. In some instances, they can even be harmful. Failures in group therapy are well known by those who are practitioners in the field. In a review of the available literature, Roback (2000) identified three specific areas of therapist characteristics that are thought to be significant contributors to failures in group psychotherapy: (1) therapist leadership styles that were either too aggressive and interrogative, or passive and non-directional; (2) poor matching on the part of the therapist of clients with the group treatment modality, as when a client is unable to tolerate group dynamics due to the underlying issues he or she is facing; and (3) therapist negative transference and personality maladjustment, whereby therapists meet their own needs, whether known or unknown, at the expense of their clients. As Roback (2000) pointed out, because of a lack of research, definitive conclusions cannot be too heavily drawn regarding negative group outcomes. Even so, there are things counselors can do to minimize their contribution to negative group experiences. First, therapists should receive training to reduce non-therapeutic confrontation techniques. Second, therapists should examine and modify their own styles of leadership if found to be problematic. Third, therapists should not be so quick to blame treatment failures on the patients. And finally, group leaders profit by having ongoing supervision regardless of how much experience they have had.

Group Goals and Objectives

For the chemically dependent client, the group provides a chance for self-exploration that can lead to a reassessment of one's values and behaviors. This process should be an invitation to examine seriously a segment of one's selfhood or behavior. It is up to the group member to decide what, how much, and when he or she wishes to explore and change; if this invitation becomes a command, the likelihood of real self-exploration is diminished. Far too many chemical dependency counselors believe that clients need to be coerced or forced to look at themselves before they will avail themselves of this opportunity. Chemically dependent clients are in a great deal of pain emotionally, physically, and spiritually. Given the opportunity of self-exploration and change by a group leader who is accepting and permissive, and at the same time confronting and encountering, the chemically dependent person will most often welcome the opportunity to change.

Goals for Group Members

Some general types of goals that are appropriate for any type of group and are universal to all group members have been listed by Corey and Corey (2006). They include:

- Become aware of how one interacts with others
- Increase awareness of behaviors and feelings that prevent intimacy
- Learn how to trust oneself and others
- Become aware of cultural externalities (i.e., "should's" and "must's" — and their effect on personal decisions)
- Increase self-awareness and thereby increase the possibilities for choice and action
- Free oneself from the inappropriate early decisions that keep one less than the person one would like to be
- Recognize that others struggle too
- Clarify the values one has and decide whether and how to modify them

- Become both independent and interdependent
- Find ways to solve personal problems
- Become more open and honest with selected others
- Support and challenge others appropriately
- Learn how to ask others for what one wants
- Become sensitive to the needs and feelings of others
- Provide others with useful feedback

All of these are appropriate goals for the chemically dependent person. Additional goals listed by Corey and Corey (2006) for a substance-abuse group are to help the abuser confront difficult issues and learn to cope with life stresses more effectively, to provide a supportive network, and to learn more appropriate social skills.

Goals for Group Leaders

Corey and Corey (2006) identified 15 broad goals for group leaders. Group leaders can help members to do the following:

1. Understand how they interact with others
2. Understand how to have more intimacy
3. Learn how to trust both themselves and others
4. Develop awareness around how their culture influences their choices
5. Become more self-aware and increase choices
6. Examine earlier decisions and beliefs that may no longer be helpful
7. Recognize they are not alone in the problems they face or with the feelings they have
8. Clarify and modify values as needed
9. Become independent and interdependent
10. Learn strategies for resolving problems
11. Be more open and honest
12. Balance between support and challenge
13. Ask others for the help and the things they want
14. Be sensitive to what others are going through
15. Provide helpful feedback to others

Guidelines for Group Leaders

At this point it will be helpful to list some guidelines for chemical dependency counselors to follow when leading a group. Corey and Corey (2006) have also listed these.

- It is important to teach group process to the members. This need not involve giving a lecture; rather, issues can be discussed as they arise in the course of a group discussion.

- The issue of confidentiality should be emphasized in the group. The dangers of inappropriate sharing of what occurs during a session need to be highlighted, and members need to have an opportunity to express their fears or reservations concerning the respect of the rest of the group for the disclosures that are made.

- Instead of talking about a group member, the leader and other members should speak directly to the person in question.

- Each member is free to decide for himself what issues to work on in the group, and each person may decide how to explore a problem. A person's right to say, "I pass" should be respected. It is the member who is responsible for the decision to disclose or not to disclose.

- Confrontation is an essential ingredient in most groups, but members must learn how to confront others in a responsible manner. Essentially, confrontation is a challenge to look at the discrepancy between what one says and what one does, or to examine the degree to which one is being honest.

- Questioning is more often a distraction than a help in group process, and members should be warned of this. Generally, questions of a probing nature have the effect of pulling the questioned participant away from the experience of feeling. Asking questions can generate a never-ending series of "why's" and "because's." Questioning is an impersonal way of relating that keeps the questioner at a safe distance.

- If members are to engage in any personal work, it is imperative that a climate of trust and support be established. If people feel that they can be themselves and be respected for what they feel, they are far more inclined to take the risk of sharing intimate aspects of themselves than if they expect to be harshly judged.

- Members need to learn how to listen without thinking of a quick rebuttal and without becoming overly defensive. We do not encourage people to accept everything they hear, but we do ask them to really hear what others say to them and to seriously consider those messages—particularly those messages that are repeated consistently.

- The issue of how what is learned in a group can be translated into out-of-group behavior should be given priority. Contracts and homework assignments can help members carry the new behaviors that they develop in a group into their daily lives.

By following these guidelines, the counselor should achieve the group's goals. It is worth mentioning here that just reading this material will not make a person an excellent group counselor; practice and experience, along with the oversight of a well-trained supervisor, are essential. However, there are certain individuals who learn group counseling more readily than others (those who are almost naturally therapeutic and who have very little problem learning the group model). There are also those who find it difficult to lead a successful group.

The Group Leader

It is overly simplistic to say that a good group leader is one who has strong leadership skills. Yet the fact remains that this is true. That which separates those professionals who are therapeutic from those who are not is the quality of their leadership skills. This discussion, then, becomes one of *what are good leadership skills*, not *what is a good leader*. In terms of such factors as client satisfaction, smooth group operation, and positive client change, the following skills are offered by Gladding (2009). They are discussed here in terms of the chemical dependency counselor:

- Effective group counselors are caring. They demonstrate a true interest in the lives of their clients and work earnestly on their behalf.

- Effective group counselors are like interpreters in that they help to provide a clearly articulated roadmap of change through clarification and explanation. This not only provides helpful reassurance to group members that their leader knows what she or he is doing but also helps give them a framework for being successful in their own lives.

- Effective group counselors are like referees in that they strive to maintain a balance between stimulation and safety. This is to say that effective group members look for opportune times to challenge group members to take risks and to self-disclose. At the same time, counselors understand the need for structure and safety. As such, the leader must minister to the needs of all members, challenging some, encouraging others, and blocking or reducing the potential impact of harmful interaction.

- Effective group counselors understand the dynamics at play within a group, how to increase its therapeutic value, and are able to act intentionally because they have a good framework for anticipating what may come next. If a group member has as a goal, as but one example, the exploration of the possibility of controlled drinking in the future, and a major goal of the group leader is total abstinence for all members, neither the group leader nor the group member is likely to meet his goals. In group counseling, as in individual counseling, the goal is not necessarily first and foremost to change behavior;

this is difficult for chemical dependency counselors to accept. When it is obvious to all but a particular group member that chemical use is causing that group member continued problems, it is easy for the group leader and members to insist on abstinence as the primary goal for this individual. Unless the individual has accepted this goal, however, it is likely that he will leave the group feeling out of place and identified by other group members as not ready to work on his problem, even when this person may have been ready to work on his problem as he saw it. In this instance the group might have been able to influence an attitude change and thus a change of goals and behavior. But if the original goals are not accepted by the group and the member does not return to the group, there will be no continued group influence, and the member may discontinue treatment. Effective group counselors will be comfortable in tending to these sometimes dissimilar mutual group and idiosyncratic goals for the benefit of all.

- Effective group counselors are invested in constantly improving themselves. They do this by tending to their needs, both personal and professional, so that they can live more authentically and empathically.

- Effective group counselors are well versed in the theory, practice, and techniques of group therapy.

Evaluating Group Counseling Skills

The skills mentioned above (and, in fact, all the group counseling skills) should be thought of as existing in various degrees, rather than on an all-or-none basis (i.e., they may be highly, or only minimally, developed). Corey and Corey (1992, 2006) have developed rating scales for counselors to use to rate themselves and for group members to use to rate group leaders. These scales are most beneficial for counselors who wish to improve their skills and are included here with that purpose in mind.

Self-Rating Scale

Rate yourself from 1 to 3 on the following items:

3 = *I do this most of the time with a high degree of competence.*

2 = *I do this some of the time with an adequate degree of competence.*

1 = *I do this occasionally with a relatively low level of competence.*

1. Active listening—I am able to hear and understand both direct and subtle messages.

2. Reflecting—I can mirror what another says, without being mechanical.

3. Clarifying—I can focus on underlying issues and assist others to get a clear picture of some of their conflicting feelings.

4. Summarizing—When I function as a group leader, I am able to identify key elements of a session and to present them as a summary of the proceedings.

5. Interpreting—I can present a hunch to someone concerning the reason for his behavior without dogmatically stating what the behavior was.

6. Questioning—I avoid bombarding people with questions about their behavior.

7. Linking—I find ways of relating what one person is doing or saying to the concerns of other members.

8. Confronting—When I confront another, the confrontation usually has the effect of getting the person to look at his behavior in a non-defensive manner.

9. Supporting—I am usually able to tell when supporting another will be productive and when it will be counterproductive.

10. Blocking—I am able to intervene successfully, without seeming to be attacking, to stop counterproductive behaviors (such as gossiping, story-telling, and intellectualizing) in the group.

11. Assessing—I can generally get a sense of what specific problems people have, without feeling the need to label people.

12. Modeling—I am able to model desirable behaviors in group that support self-disclosure and considerate confrontation.

13. Suggesting—I offer suggestions, not prescriptions, for group members that provides options and their right to choose.

14. Initiating—I approach group pro-actively to ensure that the work of the group and its members is continuously progressing in a productive manner.

15. Evaluating—I appraise outcomes when I am in a group, and I make some comments concerning the ongoing process of any group I am in.

16. Facilitating—In a group, I am able to help others openly express themselves and work through barriers to communication.

17. Empathizing—I can intuitively sense the subjective world of others in a group, and I have the capacity to understand much of what others are experiencing.

18. Terminating—At the end of group sessions, I am able to create a climate that will foster a willingness in others to continue working after the session.

Rating Scale for Group Counselors

The following evaluation form can be used in several ways. Group leaders can use it as a self-evaluation device, supervisors can use it to evaluate group leaders in training, group leaders can use it to evaluate their co-leaders, and group members can use it to evaluate their leader.

Rate the leader from 1 to 7 on the following items:

1 = *to an extremely low degree*

7 = *to an extremely high degree*

1. Support—To what degree does the group leader allow clients to express their feelings?
2. Interpretation—To what degree is the group leader able to explain the meaning of behavior patterns within the framework of the theoretical system?
3. Confrontation—To what degree is the group leader able to actively and directly confront clients when the clients engage in behavior that is inconsistent with what they say?
4. Modeling—To what degree is the group leader able to demonstrate to members behaviors to emulate and practice both during and after the session?
5. Assignment—To what degree is the group leader able to direct clients to improve on existing behavior patterns or to develop new behaviors before the next group session?
6. Referral—To what degree is the group leader able to make available to clients persons capable of further assisting clients with personal concerns?
7. Role direction—To what degree is the group leader able to direct clients to enact specific roles in role-playing situations?
8. Empathy—To what degree does the group leader demonstrate the ability to adopt a client's internal frame of reference and communicate to the client that he or she is understood?
9. Self-disclosure—To what degree does the group leader demonstrate a willingness and ability to reveal his own present feelings and thoughts to clients when it is appropriate to the group counseling situation?
10. Initiation—To what degree is the group leader able to initiate interaction among members or between leader and members?
11. Facilitation—To what degree is the group leader able to help clients clarify their own goals and take steps to reach these goals?

12. Diagnosis—To what degree is the group leader able to identify specific areas of struggle and conflict within each client?

13. Follow-through—To what degree is the group leader able to implement (and follow through to a reasonable completion) work with a client in an area that the client has expressed a desire to explore?

14. Active listening—To what degree does the group leader actively and fully listen to and hear the subtle messages communicated by clients?

15. Knowledge of theory—To what degree does the group leader demonstrate a theoretical understanding of group dynamics, interpersonal dynamics, and behavior in general?

16. Application of theory to practice—To what degree is the group leader able to appropriately apply a given theory to an actual group situation?

17. Perceptivity and insight—To what degree is the group leader able to sensitively and accurately extract the core meanings from verbal and non-verbal communications?

18. Risk taking—To what degree is the group leader able to risk making mistakes and to profit from mistakes?

19. Expression—To what degree is the group leader able to express thoughts and feelings directly and clearly to clients?

20. Originality—To what degree does the group leader seem to have synthesized a personal approach from a variety of approaches to group leadership?

21. Group dynamics—To what degree is the group leader able to assist a group of people to work effectively together?

22. Cooperation as a co-leader—To what degree is the group leader able to work cooperatively with a co-leader?

23. Content orientation—To what degree is the group leader able to help group members focus on specific themes in a structured type of group experience?

24. Values awareness—To what degree are group leaders aware of their own value systems and of the client's value system, and to what degree are they able to avoid imposing their values on the client?

25. Flexibility—To what degree is the group leader able to change approaches—to modify style and technique—to adapt to each unique working situation?

26. Awareness of self—To what degree is the group leader aware of his own needs, motivations, and problems, and to what degree does

the leader avoid exploiting or manipulating clients to satisfy these needs?

27. Respect—To what degree does the group leader communicate an attitude of respect for the dignity and autonomy of the client?

28. Care—To what degree does the group leader communicate an attitude of genuine caring for the client?

29. Techniques—To what degree is the group leader knowledgeable of techniques and able to use them well and appropriately to help clients work through conflicts and concerns?

30. Ethical awareness—To what degree does the group leader demonstrate awareness of, and sensitivity to, the demands of professional responsibility?

Choosing Group Members

In reality, the chemical dependency counselor often has very little choice about which clients or patients become group members. Inpatient drug and alcohol treatment programs routinely include patients in group therapy as a part of the total treatment program. All of those in treatment attend groups. Whenever possible, however, the chemical dependency counselor can maximize the group's effectiveness by carefully selecting group members. Referrals to self-help groups after, or in conjunction with, treatment should also be done in a selective manner.

For example, despite the widespread recognition that A.A. has enjoyed an exceedingly fine success rate (and A.A. itself has spread widely throughout the world), it must also be recognized that the traditional precepts of A.A. as spelled out in the 12 steps have no appeal for, and may even antagonize, the patient in some populations. More specifically, the traditional A.A. group may be problematic for some people. Heath, Waddell, and Topper (1981) reported that some years ago a Navajo Indian made the simple but eloquent point that "it's not right to tell all them personal things, about what I did to my wife and how I argued with her father, and all that." And by contrast, in a Costa Rican community, many problem drinkers were willing, even eager, to publicly confess the injuries they had caused others, but they could not accept the principle of surrender. As one Costa Rican put it, "Damn, I'm not about to admit that alcohol is stronger than I am. What kind of a man would say that? . . . One's purpose should be again to be strong like a man, to overcome this alcohol with one's own forces."

In instances such as these, routine referrals to a specific self-help group might be unwise. Offering a choice of groups like A.A., N.A., Moderation Management, Women for Sobriety, and so on, would be a much better idea.

Who belongs in what group? How does one determine which combinations of individuals produce optimal conditions for maximum effectiveness?

The first approach one might take is to decide whom to exclude from the group. All manner of individuals have been recommended for exclusion from the group: these include psychotics or prepsychotics; those who are brain damaged, paranoid, extremely narcissistic, hypochondriacal, or suicidal; and even those addicted to drugs or alcohol. For obvious reasons, it would be impossible for the chemical dependency counselor to exclude all of these as group members.

The best approach might be to include individuals who meet the following four criteria:

1. They have a sense of reality.
2. They can be related to interpersonally.
3. They have sufficient flexibility to help reduce, or to heighten, intragroup tensions.
4. They can serve, at times, as a catalyst for the group.

Motivation is another factor to consider; however, many seemingly unmotivated persons have become motivated as a result of their group experience. It would be a mistake to assume that because people do not admit to being alcoholic or drug dependent that they do not desire or value personal change. (It may be that they are unwilling to pay the price of admitting to chemical dependency.) They may also view themselves as deficient in understanding their own feelings or the feelings of others. Admitting one's problems is a step toward solving those problems, but it is not the *only* step, or necessarily the *first* step. The first step might be examining those problems, and this can be effectively done in a group. It is important for group members to express satisfaction with their group if they are to continue membership. Members continue membership for the following reasons:

• They view the group as meeting their personal needs.
• They derive satisfaction from their relationship with group members.
• They derive satisfaction from their participation in the group task.
• They derive satisfaction from group membership vis-à-vis the outside world.

There is yet another factor that should be considered here: Should the group be homogeneous or heterogeneous in makeup? That is, should groups be made up of members with similar problems and backgrounds or different problems and backgrounds? With regard to the chemically dependent client, there are some definite advantages to homogeneous groups:

• Group identification takes place rapidly.
• Re-education takes place rapidly, and insight develops quickly.

- Psychodynamics are laid bare more rapidly.
- Duration of treatment is lessened.
- Attendance is more regular.
- Interferences, resistances, and interactions of a destructive nature are lessened.
- Intragroup cliques are uncommon.
- Recovery from symptoms is more rapid.

There are advantages to heterogeneity within groups as well, but for the chemically dependent client, the advantages of a homogeneous group are far greater. Yalom (1995) has cited alcoholics as an example of a population that does poorly in mixed outpatient group settings. This is not because of their drinking, but because of their interpersonal behavior (which he describes as "destructive"), which will ultimately have a deleterious effect on the group and its members.

Yalom (1995) also sees the selection of group therapy members with specialized goals such as obesity, alcoholism, or addiction as relatively uncomplicated. The admission criterion, he states, may simply be the existence of the target symptom—chemical dependency.

We would again remind chemical dependency counselors that there are many different reasons why people become chemically dependent and that chemical dependency manifests itself in numerous behaviors. The counselor who remains constantly aware of this and who meets each client's needs on an individual basis (including what group to refer a client to) will have the most success. The point is, some kind of screening and selection process is necessary; counselors who do not pay attention to this phase of group work unnecessarily increase the psychological risk for the group members.

Group Process

What is group process? Group process refers to the stages of development of a group and the interactions that go on during each stage of the group (Corey & Corey, 2006).

All groups are different. The leadership styles and personalities of the leader or co-leaders and the makeup of the group members affect the direction in which the group will go. However, a typical group goes through four stages:

1. The initial stage
2. The transition stage
3. The working stage
4. The ending or final stage

Each of the stages has certain characteristics that a leader can observe to determine if the group is progressing at an appropriate rate. In order to help members get the most from a group experience, the leader should know and understand these stages and assist the group in its journey through them.

The Initial Stage

The initial stage is perhaps the most important because it will establish the future direction that will ultimately lead to the success or failure of the group. The initial stage could last for several sessions or for just one session, depending on the members' makeup and the leaders' skill. During this period, the leader should help establish the goals of the group; but the first item on the agenda should be to establish the rules of the group. Most leaders offer only a few rules at the beginning and add others if it is necessary. The fewer the rules at the beginning, the better. Some examples are:

- No physical violence during group.
- What goes on in group is not discussed outside of group.
- Do not talk over someone else; wait until he or she is finished.
- Do not be late for group.

During this stage, the leader wants to establish the structure of the group, set guidelines for opening and closing the session, help establish goals, foster group cohesion and trust, and deal with resistance and hidden agendas. It is also important to encourage members to be active participants and not just observers. One way to begin this process is by having members tell a little about themselves and then have the group talk about their reservations about being in the group.

The characteristics of the initial stage as listed by Corey and Corey (2006) are:

- Members test the atmosphere and get acquainted.
- Members learn what is expected, how the group functions, and how to participate in the group.
- Risk taking is relatively low, and exploration is tentative.
- Group cohesion and trust are gradually established if members are willing to express what they are thinking and feeling.
- Members are concerned with whether they are included or excluded, and they are beginning to define their place in the group.
- Negative feelings may surface as members test to determine if all feelings are acceptable.
- A central issue is trust versus mistrust.

- There are periods of silence and awkwardness; members may look for direction and wonder what the group is about. Members are deciding whom they can trust and how much they will disclose, how safe the group is, whom they like and dislike, and how much to get involved.
- Members are learning the basic attitudes of respect, empathy, acceptance, caring, and responding—all attitudes that facilitate the building of trust.

For details on all of the stages, see Corey and Corey (2006), *Group Process and Practice.*

The Transition Stage

The transition stage of a group is perhaps the most difficult for the leader or leaders of the group. They must deal with increasing anxiety in the group as more and more personal issues are discussed. They must deal with defensiveness and resistance as group members become threatened by the material or the process of the group. As members begin to trust each other and begin to share, there are always members who are fearful of rejection, of making a fool of themselves, of losing control, of disclosing too much, as well as other such fears. There are always struggles for the control of the group. There is conflict, there are challenges to the group leader, and there is confrontation. Some other problem behaviors and difficult behaviors among group members that often occur during the transition stage, according to Corey and Corey (2006), are the following:

- Silence and lack of participation
- Members who monopolize the group
- Members who tell long stories
- Members who are always asking questions as if they were interrogating someone
- Members who always have advice to give
- Members who soothe over everything because they cannot stand conflict or stress
- Members who are hostile
- Members who are dependent
- Members who act superior
- Members who socialize outside of group as a form of resistance
- Members who intellectualize everything

These issues can be dealt with in group or outside of group by speaking directly with the member involved. If they are not dealt with appropriately, the group will have a difficult time moving to the working stage.

During the transition stage, the members of the group are sizing up the leader. There are several inappropriate ways that group members may see the leader, and these must be dealt with as well. Members may view leaders as experts who have all the answers. They may see them as authority figures, which may get in the way of establishing trust. They may see them as superpersons, infallible or perfect, which makes it hard on their own self-esteem. They may view them as friends, which is unrealistic. Finally, group leaders may be seen as lovers. Even if the leader has given no evidence of wanting a relationship with the member other than as group leader, some members may want to convert the therapeutic relationship into a romantic one. Adherence to relevant ethical codes that prohibit this from happening is required (Thomas & Pender, 2007).

These issues need to be dealt with by the group leader, achieving an appropriate balance between support and confrontation. Too much of either may be destructive to the group member. Too much support leaves the member unchallenged, and aggressive confrontation has been shown to be directly related to negative outcomes in groups (Corey & Corey, 2006; Roback, 2000).

The transitional stage of a group's development is marked by feelings of anxiety and defenses in the form of various resistances. Corey and Corey (2006) list member resistances and stage characteristics as follows:

- Being concerned about what they will think of themselves if they increase their self-awareness, and concerned about others' acceptance or rejection of them
- Testing the leader and other members to determine how safe the environment is
- Struggling between wanting to play it safe and wanting to risk getting involved
- Experiencing some struggle for control and power and some conflict with other members
- Observing the leader to determine if he or she is trustworthy
- Learning how to express themselves so that others will listen to them

The Working Stage

Earlier in this chapter, the therapeutic factors that operate in a group were presented. There are similar factors in play during the working stage of a group. Corey and Corey (2006) point out that working groups:

- Have members who trust the leaders and other group members
- Have members who take risks
- Have clear goals and move toward those goals

- Have members who feel included
- Have an accurate expression of what is being experienced
- Focus on the here and now
- Share leadership functions
- Have members who initiate activities
- Have members willing to share threatening material
- Have high cohesion
- Have members who can resolve conflict in the group
- Have members who accept responsibility for solving their problems
- Have members who give feedback freely
- Have members who feel hopeful
- Have members who deal with needed confrontation without an attack
- Have members whose communication is clear and direct
- Have members who use each other as resources
- Have members who encourage diversity
- Have members who have cooperatively developed norms
- Have members who use out-of-group time to work on problems raised in group
- Have members who emphasize thinking as well as feeling

The Final Stage: Ending a Group

The end of a group can be as meaningful an experience as the working phase. A wise leader will take advantage of this phase to consolidate the learning by clearing up unfinished business, giving an opportunity for members to say good-bye, reviewing, and making referrals where necessary. Termination of the group experience more specifically includes the following: dealing with feelings of separation, dealing with unfinished business, reviewing the group experience, helping other members to practice for behavioral change, and giving and receiving final feedback. To assist in transferring the group experience to real life, the leader may want to make a contract with each member about how they will use the information they have gained in group in their lives. Finally, leaving the members with the following information may be helpful.

- Realize that the group is a means to an end.
- Realize that change may be slow and subtle.
- Do not expect one group alone to renovate your life.

- Decide what to do with what you learned.
- Think for yourself!

Corey and Corey (2006) also acknowledge a few other important final-stage characteristics of a group:

- There may be some sadness and anxiety over the reality of separation.
- Members are likely to pull back and participate in less intense ways, in anticipation of the ending of the group.
- Members are deciding what courses of action they are likely to take.
- There may be some fears of separation as well as fears about being able to carry over into daily life some of what was experienced in the group.
- Members may express their fears, hopes, and concerns for one another.
- Group sessions may be devoted partly to preparing members to meet significant others in everyday life. Role playing and behavioral rehearsal for relating more effectively to others are common.
- Members may be involved in evaluations of the group experience.
- There may be some talk about follow-up meetings or some plan for accountability so that members will be encouraged to carry out their plans for change.

Ethical and Professional Issues

The group leader is the one who is primarily responsible for the direction that the group takes with regard to ethics. The group leader sets the tone and models behaviors for group members. Some issues and responsibilities that a group leader should consider are these:

- What does a group leader need to tell potential members about the group?
- Were members screened? How?
- Is group membership voluntary or involuntary?
- What does a group member need to do if he wishes to leave the group?
- Are there any consequences attached to leaving the group?

Confidentiality

Confidentiality is a major issue for the group leader. It is not only that the group leader must keep confidences, but also that he or she must get the group members to do so as well. Group leaders should emphasize the importance of confidentiality at various stages of the group's development. If, at any time, any member gives an indication that confidences have been broken, the group leader should explore this matter with the group.

Group leaders owe it to their clients to specify at the beginning of a group the limits on confidentiality. For example, group leaders should let the members know that they may be required to testify against them in court unless the leader is entitled to privileged communication. In general, licensed psychologists, psychiatrists, and licensed clinical social workers are legally entitled to privileged communications. This means that these people cannot break the confidence of a client unless in their judgment the client (1) is a danger to himself or others, (2) may do serious harm to someone else, or (3) reports child or elder abuse (Corey & Corey, 2006). Many an A.A. meeting place has a sign that sums up confidentiality. It says: "Let what is said here stay here." That is generally good advice for group members in any group.

Psychological Risk

Another ethical and professional issue is psychological risk to the group members. The therapeutic forces at work in a group are powerful ones, and their unleashing involves a certain amount of risk. These forces have the potential to be just as harmful as they are helpful. The leader must not assume that the members of a group are aware of them. Members of a group may be subject to scapegoating, group pressure, breaches of confidence, inappropriate reassurance, and hostile confrontation; the group process may even precipitate a crisis in the group member's life. These hazards should be discussed and examined during the initial session, focusing on ways that these hazards can be avoided. For more information on ethics, see Chapter 2.

Evaluating Oneself as Group Leader

Another issue that the group leader must confront is that of her or his own competence as a group leader. Counselors should ask themselves questions such as, What kind of clients am I capable of dealing with? What are my areas of expertise? What techniques do I handle well? How far can I safely go with clients? When should I refer? Truly competent group leaders have answers for why they do what they do in a group. They can explain the theory behind their group work. They can express the goals of their group. They can provide a relationship between the way they lead a group and the goals that they hope to achieve. And, finally, they know how to evaluate how well these goals are being met.

As you might imagine, one does not become an effective group leader without extensive training and experience; that is the idea that we began this chapter with and the one we will end it with. The group experience can be one of the most therapeutic tools that the chemical dependency counselor has to work with. But it takes time and effort for the counselor to learn to maximize the group experience for the therapeutic benefit of its members. However, it will be time and effort well spent, especially considering that group therapy is evolving into the treatment of choice due, as was previously discussed, to its cost-effectiveness (Eaves & Sheperis, 2011; Miller et al., 2011).

Seven Common Questions From New Group Leaders

Since there are no real right or wrong answers to most of these questions, you may want to discuss them in class or with your colleagues.

1. *When should you use a co-therapist?*
One of the best ways to learn to do group therapy is to co-lead a group with a trained, experienced group leader. New counselors should have several hundred hours of time co-leading a group before attempting a group on their own. Then those leaders should have a year or more of experience before attempting to train another person as a co-leader.

From a therapeutic standpoint, it is usually a good idea to have a co-leader. In most cases, two heads are better than one; one person may see something the other does not or each person may offer a different, but equally valuable, perspective. The exception to this is if the co-leaders have unresolved personal issues. In this case, group process is usually more productive if there is only one leader. For mixed-sex groups, male and female co-leaders are ideal.

The other consideration is always economics. Can the agency afford to put two counselors in one group? Are you willing to split your fees if you are in private practice? It would be nice to believe that everyone makes the co-leader decision based on what is best for the patients or clients; however, cost will always be a factor. For a detailed description of the advantages and disadvantages of co-leadership, see Corey and Corey (2006).

2. *Should my group be open or closed?*
Open groups have a constantly changing membership, whereas closed groups have the same members and are usually time limited in some way. Do not confuse this with A.A.'s open and closed meetings. The group setting usually is the determining factor in the open- or closed-group decision. Some settings lend themselves to open groups and others to closed groups. The group leader often has no say in the decision.

Adding new members and having some members leave a group is disruptive to the group process. There are, however, some advantages to this. For example, the older members can help newer members progress quickly to the working stage of group. Also the departing members can model appropriate separation for those who will follow them. As members come and go, the dynamics of the group will change—sometimes for the better, sometimes for the worse.

If a treatment program has patients at different phases of treatment, that is, people coming into and leaving the program all the time, it is difficult to have anything other than an open-ended group. If, as a leader, you have a choice, try to decide which would be more therapeutic based on the group's goals.

3. *Should I mix those with drug problems with those with alcohol problems in a group?*

Some in the field feel that those with alcohol and drug problems are essentially alike and the issues are the same. As you will learn in Chapter 8, diversity of any kind should be considered. Again there are positive and negative aspects to both sides. Those with alcohol problems sometimes do not like to be compared to those with drug problems because they may not have broken the law in a similar manner. Some of those with drug problems do not like those with alcohol problems because they seem self-righteous. Other times, members have both drug and alcohol problems. If there is a problem mixing the two, it is a prime issue that can be dealt with during group. An experienced group leader will use group friction as a tool in therapy and as a learning experience for group members.

4. *What about mixing sexes, races, ethnic groups, or those with co-dependency issues with those with addictions?*

The chapter on diversity addresses this question; and the answer to the question above also applies. Determine the setting and goals for the group, and then decide on the type of membership that will be best to meet those goals.

5. *Should I see a group member in individual therapy as well?*

If you do see group members in individual therapy, it may be best to see all of them, to avoid the feeling of special status about the ones you do see. There are also issues regarding bringing up things you talked about individually in the group setting. Is that all right with the client? If not, you could damage your relationship by revealing something of a personal nature in group. On the other hand, different clients have different needs and the time in individual therapy may be helpful, for example, in times of crisis. If you choose to see group members in individual therapy, be sure to consider the clinical ramifications for both the individual and the other group members, as well what it might do to group process.

6. *What about simultaneous membership in groups, like A.A. and a therapy group?*

It is common for substance abusers, family members, and adult children of alcoholics to be members of 12-step or other self-help groups when they enter group therapy. It is good to encourage such contact as helpful support, but it is also important to underscore the ways in which the ground rules of group therapy differ. During the initial stage of the group, this should be explained to everyone in the group since the likelihood is that there are several members who have self-help group experience.

When discussing A.A. or other self-help experience with group members as a possible adjunct to group therapy, the differences between the two should again be highlighted, as well as what members can expect if they've never attended previously (Miller et al., 2011). Not only can therapists remind clients that simultaneous membership may increase their likelihood of success, but they can also pair first-timers with volunteers who will take them to their first meeting as a way to increase the likelihood that they will attend at least one meeting (Miller et al., 2011).

7. What training do I need before I can ethically lead a group on my own?

When the field of chemical dependency treatment was emerging and groups were becoming a popular method of treatment, many people ran groups with little if any training or experience. This author is aware of a newly sober individual in treatment who was a group member one week and working in the same treatment center as a group leader the next week. His total training and experience consisted of group membership for a total of 16 sessions during a 28-day inpatient treatment program. The reality is that this individual turned out to be a very good group leader, and he helped many with addictions issues recover over the years. But that was some time ago, when hardly anyone had training in any aspect of chemical dependency treatment. Someone had to fly the first plane without the benefit of instruction. Someone performed the first liver transplant without instruction. Because of those who went before, it is not necessary to fly, do a liver transplant, or do group therapy without instruction.

Because the potential for harm is equal to or greater than the potential for positive therapeutic movement in a group, only those who know what they are doing should lead therapy groups. Some people, such as the one mentioned above, can be naturally therapeutic, just as some people are naturally harmful to be around. Training will weed out harmful individuals and sharpen the skills of those who are naturally therapeutic.

There are those who believe only someone with a graduate degree should be allowed to do group therapy. But many people—with the right motivation (see Chapter 1), with a course in group counseling, and with several hundred hours of supervision with a co-leader—have become outstanding group leaders. As they begin to lead groups on their own, they should continue to be supervised during a probationary period. Anything less than this would be unadvisable. The section on credentials and certifications has additional information on this topic.

With regard to group therapy, the Curriculum Review Committee of the Addiction Training Centers Program, funded by the Center for Substance Abuse Treatment (CSAT; 2011), recommends that a CD counselor be able to:

1. Describe, select, and appropriately use strategies from accepted models for group counseling with substance use disorders

2. Perform the actions necessary to start a group, including determining group type, purpose, size, and leadership; recruiting and selecting members; establishing group goals and clarifying behavioral ground rules for participating; identifying outcomes; and determining methods for termination or graduation from the group

3. Facilitate the entry of new members and the transition of exiting members

4. Facilitate group growth within the established ground rules and precipitate movement toward group and individual goals by using methods consistent with group type

5. Understand the concepts of "process" and "content" and shift the focus of the group when such an intervention will help the group move toward its goals

6. Describe and summarize client behavior within the group for the purpose of documenting the client's progress and identifying needs and issues that may require a modification in the treatment plan (p. 184)

References

Center for Substance Abuse Treatment. (2011). *Addiction counseling competencies: The knowledge, skills, and attitudes of professional practice.* Technical Assistance Publication (TAP) Series 21. HHS Publication No. (SMA) 08-4171. Rockville, MD: Substance Abuse and Mental Health Services Administration.

Corey, G., & Corey, M. S. (1992). *Group process and practice* (4th ed.). Pacific Grove, CA: Brooks/Cole Publishing.

Corey, G., & Corey, M. S. (2006). *Group process and practice* (7th ed.). Pacific Grove, CA: Brooks/Cole, Cengage Learning.

Dreikurs, R., & Sonstegard, M. (1968). Rationale for group counseling. In D. C. Dinkmeyer (Ed.), *Guidance and counseling in the elementary school: Readings in theory and practice* (pp. 278–287). New York: Holt, Rinehart & Winston.

Eaves, S. H., & Sheperis, C. J. (2011). Group work with adult populations. In B. T. Erford (Ed.), *Group work processes and applications.* Upper Saddle River, NJ: Pearson.

Erford, B. T. (Ed.). (2011). *Group work processes and applications.* Upper Saddle River, NJ: Pearson.

Fewell, C. H., & Spiegel, B. R. (2014). 12-step programs as a treatment modality. In S. L. Straussner (Ed.), *Clinical work with substance abusing clients.* New York: Guilford Press.

Gladding, S. T. (2009). *Counseling: A comprehensive profession.* Upper Saddle River, NJ: Pearson.

Heath, D. B., Waddell, J. D., & Topper, M. D. (Special Eds.). (1981). Cultural factors in alcohol research and treatment of drinking problems. *Journal of Studies on Alcohol* (Suppl. 9).

Lawson, A., & Lawson, G. (1998). *Alcoholism and the family* (2nd ed.). Austin, TX: PRO-ED.

Lawson, G., & Lawson, A. (1984). Treating the whole family: When intervention and education aren't enough. *Focus on the Family and Chemical Dependency, 7*(1), 14–16.

Miller, W. R., Forcehimes, A. A., & Zweben, A. (2011). *Treating addiction: A guide for professionals.* New York: Guilford Press.

Roback, H. B. (2000). Adverse outcomes in group psychotherapy. *Journal of Psychotherapy Practice and Research, 9*(3), 113–122.

Thomas, R. V., & Pender, D. A. (2007). Association for specialists in group work: Best practice guidelines 2007 revisions. *Journal for Specialists in Group Work, 33*(2), 111–117.

Valentine, D., Lawson, A., & Lawson, G. (1995, May). *A comparison of family education and family therapy in treatment of spouses of alcoholics.* Seventh International Congress on Treatment of Addictive Behaviors, Leevenhorst, Netherlands.

Varenhorst, B. (1969). Behavioral group counseling. In G. M. Gazda (Ed.), *Theories and methods of group counseling in the schools* (pp. 119–156). Springfield, IL: Charles C. Thomas.

Yalom, I. D. (1995). *The theory and practice of group psychotherapy* (4th ed.). New York: Basic Books.

Yalom, I. D. (2005). *The theory and practice of group psychotherapy* (5th ed.). New York: Basic Books.

CHAPTER 7

Family Counseling:
Seeing the Family as the Client

CHAPTER OBJECTIVES

- Provide counselors with an introduction to systems thinking
- Provide a history of systems thinking
- Help counselors apply this thinking to family dynamics that foster or maintain addictive behaviors
- Define family therapy terminology as it applies to substance abusing families
- Provide a brief overview of several family therapy theories
- Describe typical patterns of alcoholic and addicted family systems

It is beyond the scope of this book to give counselors all the information they need to become family therapists. It takes years of training and supervision to become a competent family therapist. Counselors, however, may find themselves in a treatment setting that does not employ a family therapist or in a geographical area where referral to a family therapist is not possible, and they will need to provide help to the families of their clients. Counselors should therefore know as much as possible about family systems and how they are affected by chemical dependency. People do not develop an addiction in a vacuum. They are influenced by their families, peers, and society as a whole, which have an impact on addicted individuals as well.

Counselors who understand the systemic, intergenerational process of chemical dependency are more likely to intervene in factors that hold families in repeated patterns and reduce the risk of relapse, especially if the substance abuser is being treated in a program separate from the family. Family therapy does not always mean that the entire family must be treated. Counselors can work with individual clients on family issues and change the way he or she interacts with the family, which will produce changes in others.

The goal of this chapter is to provide counselors with an introduction to systemic thinking and to help them apply this thinking to family dynamics that foster or maintain addictive behaviors. In contrast to *linear thinking*, which states that A causes B, *systems thinking* involves A causing B that causes C that affects D and interacts with E that affects A and B, and so on. There is no real beginning and no real ending, just a constant state of interaction among the parts of the system. Systems thinkers also see symptoms or problems as not existing within an individual but among individuals. They are interested in understanding people's behavior in a context. These ideas grew out of several sources from various fields of study.

The Roots of Family Therapy

Family therapists took from the anthropological approach of functionalism the notion that deviant behavior may serve as a protective function for a social group, and applied this to the symptoms of family members (Nichols & Schwartz, 2013). Functionalists believed that families needed to adapt to their environment. Symptoms in family members meant that the family was not adapting to the environment and was unable to meet its needs.

Ludwig von Bertalanffy, a biologist, developed a model of General Systems Theory that related to any system, whether physical (a machine), biological (a dog), psychological (a personality), or sociological (a labor union or set of laws). A system could be made up of smaller systems or be a part of a larger system (Davidson, 1983). These systems also had properties, or rules, such as, "A system is more than the sum of its parts." In other words, when the parts of a system come together, they create something like a watch, which tells time when all of its parts are assembled. Thus, therapists should not concentrate on just the people in a family but should observe the interaction and process of these family parts. Bertalanffy espoused that living systems, people, were not machines and had special properties. *Equifinality* was the idea that organisms had the ability to reach final goals from different initial conditions and in different ways, and had the ability to protect and restore their wholeness (Davidson, 1983). Bertalanffy also promoted a belief in the importance of values and the ecological protection of the environment.

Cybernetics, another major influence on family therapy, was developed by Norbert Weiner, a mathematician studying machines. The core of this theory is the *feedback loop,* which is a process of a system's getting information for self-correction to maintain a balance or progress toward a goal (Nichols & Schwartz, 2013). These can be *positive feedback loops,* which amplify deviation from a course or state, or *negative feedback loops,* which reduce deviation. An example of how this works is the effect of rising temperature outside a house, which creates a negative feedback loop that activates the thermostat and starts the air conditioner to bring the temperature back to the original state. Gregory Bateson, an anthropologist, brought cybernetics to family therapy with the notion of *circular causality:* Psychopathology is not caused by events in the past but it is part of ongoing circular feedback loops (Nichols & Schwartz, 2013). These ideas are applied to families by studying (a) their rules that govern behavior, (b) negative feedback loops or the process families use to enforce the rules, (c) the sequence of events around the problem or how the family reacts and in what order to a problem, and (d) what happens if the negative feedback does not solve the problem or positive feedback loops do not push for new solutions. This is evident in alcoholic families when the family has a set pattern in reaction to the intoxication of the alcoholic member. Rules are established to attempt to solve the problem: "Don't make noise. It will disturb your father." The non-alcoholic spouse takes on most of the responsibility for running the family. All family members learn not to talk about the alcoholic behavior. Secrets are kept and role behaviors develop in an attempt to fix the problem. All of this leads to a balance or status quo in the family in an attempt to keep the family together, but the sequences of family behavior become part of the problem. Instead of the drinking behavior being the deviation from that stable state, it becomes part of the status quo of the family. Family members learn how to adapt to it, thus keeping it stuck. This usually results when negative feedback about the drinking behavior (nagging or complaining) has failed to correct the deviation. An example of a negative feedback loop that does not work is the classic communication pattern "I drink because you nag" and "I nag because you drink." This usually leads to an increased, or at least a continued, pattern of drinking.

Murray Bowen, a psychiatrist, was strongly influenced by biological sciences because he wanted to draw his concepts from a science that concerned living organisms. His concept of *differentiation of self* (or how one is differentiated from his or her family of origin), which is the core of this theory, was taken from the process by which cells differentiate from each other or are fused together. He saw this process in families whose members included children with schizophrenia and who appeared highly emotionally reactive to each other and formed what Bowen called an *undifferentiated family ego mass,* like one undifferentiated cell (Nichols & Schwartz, 2013). Bowen was also influenced by the theory of evolution in adopting his premise of the *multigenerational transmission process,* whereby low levels of differentiation were passed down through the generations, creating symptoms in family members. This concept is relevant to chemical dependency that has become part of a multigenerational process in families. Bowen describes the transmission of alcoholism across generations in the only paper he wrote about a specific symptom or problem (Bowen, 1974).

These early explorations of various fields of study led to the development of key concepts that are common to many of the theoretical models of family therapy. Each theory has special concepts of its own to explain problems in families and to explain how these key concepts fit into their theories.

Key Concepts in Viewing the Family as the Client

The following are some definitions of commonly used family therapy terms. It is important for counselors to understand this terminology, which may be new to them, before moving on to the various theoretical models and techniques of family therapy.

Homeostasis

A common bond or thread runs through family members. Jackson (1957) coined the term *family homeostasis* to define a balancing behavior in families. "This balance or equilibrium shifts in response to changes which occur within the family (illness, aging, death, unemployment) and influential forces from without (economic, political, social)" (Meeks & Kelly, 1970, p. 400). Ewing and Fox (1968) adopted theoretical concepts from Jackson's theory of homeostasis in families. They viewed the alcoholic marriage as a "homeostatic mechanism" that is

> established . . . to resist change over long periods of time. The
> behavior of each spouse is rigidly controlled by the other. As
> a result, an effort by one person to alter typical role behavior
> threatens the family equilibrium and provokes renewed efforts by
> the spouse to maintain status quo. (p. 87)

Alcohol is often a key part in the balance of the alcoholic family. Wegscheider (1981a) drew a parallel between the alcoholic family and an art form—the mobile—that is made up of rods and strings upon which are hung the parts. There is balance and flexibility, and when influenced by an outside force, such as the wind, it shifts position but remains in a balance. In families where there is stress, the whole family shifts to bring a balance for stability and survival. This balance can be healthy or unhealthy. According to Wegscheider, in the chemically dependent family, each person is affected by the chemical abuse of one member, and "in an attempt to maintain balance, members compulsively repress their feelings and develop survival behaviors and walls of defense to protect them from pain" (p. 37).

Family balance is often achieved in the alcoholic or addicted family with drinking or other drug use as a central point. When this drinking or other drug use is removed through treatment, the family is thrown into turmoil, as if it were a mobile in a windstorm. Mom is not needed as the overly responsible martyr when Dad returns to take over running the household. Brother has no reason to stay away from home and must reevaluate his relationship with Dad. The family suddenly notices Little Sister's hyperactive mannerisms. The emotional distance of the marriage may still exist, and the precipitating environment that encouraged the drinking may remain. Without family intervention, relapses may occur, the family may separate, or a new family member may become symptomatic.

Family Roles

The basic principles of homeostasis include predictable roles for family members to act out and a set of rules—both overt and covert—for interaction of these roles. Family roles include husband, wife, father, mother, daughter, son, grandmother, grandfather, aunt, uncle, cousin, stepfather, stepmother, stepbrother, stepsister, and many more. Each of these roles comes with a set of expectations, depending on the cultural and ethnic backgrounds of the families and the current societal parameters of appropriate behavior.

Other roles played by family members are more subtle and derive from a person's birth order and the requirements of the family. Many firstborns, for instance, are high achievers. They are born into a family of adults who have high expectations of the first child. A son may be groomed to take over the family business or follow in his father's footsteps. Oldest daughters are often encouraged to be responsible and help parent younger siblings. They become little adults who make the family proud and give stability to the system. The second-born children come along and dethrone the firstborn, and competition is set up. This can be a healthy or unhealthy competition. If the oldest is academically good in school, the second may excel in sports or music. If the family needs a focus for its problems, the second born can fill a need for a scapegoat and be the family's worst child. Youngest children are born into a system that has established rules and patterns of operation. They are often left out of family matters because they are too young, and they usually have many bosses. They may tend to act out to get attention from this established family. If the youngest is the third child, the second born becomes a middle child. Middle children can be concerned with finding their place and making certain they are treated fairly. These birth position roles shift with the demands of the family. Middle children become like the oldest when the oldest leaves home. Families with large gaps between children's ages have two oldest children.

In all families, members take on role behaviors; however, in families of individuals with alcoholism or addiction, normal role behavior becomes rigid in response to the family's alcoholism, which helps the family members cope (Black, 1979; Booz-Allen & Hamilton, Inc., 1974; Nardi, 1981; Wegscheider, 1981a, 1981b). This does not mean they are pathological role behaviors; they are simply attempts to rigidly play out expected role behaviors to protect the family in a time of stress. Virginia Satir, a pioneer in family therapy, identified role behaviors that family members play when they are under stress (as cited in Bandler, Grender, & Satir, 1976). Satir labeled people in these roles the blamer, the placater, the irrelevant, and the superreasonable. Family members work hard at these roles to save the family system at the expense of their own emotional and physical health. The roles hide the true feelings of these people and interfere with clear, congruent communication. When these role behaviors fail and the stress continues, family members change roles in a desperate attempt to cope.

Wegscheider (1981a, 1981b), a student of Satir, identified role behaviors specific to an alcoholic family. These are seen as defenses that cover a person's true feelings and make communication difficult. The roles include the dependent, or alcoholic; the enabler, or spouse; the family hero, who is usually the oldest or most responsible and a high achiever; the scapegoat, or problem child; the lost child, who is a loner and lives in a fantasy world; and the mascot, or clown, who pretends to be carefree.

These theories emphasize the negative aspects of these roles in children of alcoholics—self-denial, repression of feelings, and denial of needs. But a number of investigators (Nardi, 1981; Thornton & Nardi, 1975; Wilson & Orford, 1978) have asserted that there is a positive component to this role acquisition. These roles may help children of alcoholics develop important life skills like responsibility, initiative and independence, and insight into people's problems.

Black (1979, 1981a, 1981b) places the roles that children of alcoholics assume in two categories: (1) misbehaving, obviously troubled children and (2) mature, stable, overachieving, behaving children, who Black believed were in the majority. They have also been called the responsible ones, the adjusters, and the placaters. Black (1979) stated that the roles adopted by children of alcoholics may appear to be functional, but they really serve to cover up problems that may emerge in adulthood when these roles are no longer sufficient for coping. She stated, "These adults often find themselves depressed, and they do not understand why life seems to lack meaning. They feel loneliness, though many are not alone. Many find great difficulty in maintaining intimate relationships. And many become alcoholic and/or marry alcoholics" (Black, 1979, p. 25).

Of all of the theories of the family movement in substance abuse, the idea of "role behaviors" has been the most popular. The idea that a child of an alcoholic was a family hero or a scapegoat or any of the other roles gave meaning to the Adult Children of Alcoholics' (ACOA's) struggle. If the clinical notion that ACOAs have an identity problem is correct, then these ACOAs without identity can claim one from the list of role behaviors. However, identifying each child with a role behavior does not help the counselor or the family to understand the family dynamics that helped set the stage for alcoholism or drug abuse in a family member or the dynamics that maintain the symptom or the problems of recovery.

The field of chemical dependency has stopped short in the understanding of alcoholism and addiction as a family system problem by identifying each member as diseased and in need of individual treatment. This is counterproductive to healing the system and halting the intergenerational transmission of addiction, and it is harmful to the individuals in the system who are searching for an identity. They do not need a diagnosis of pathology.

This emphasis on role behaviors often leads to a lifelong search for recovery from what is a natural birth-order role. The current emphasis on individual recovery and inpatient treatment of ACOAs is often based on these individual pathology theories. These theories usually lump all ACOAs together and imply that they all have the same types and severity of problems. Recent research studies have dispelled this uniformity myth and have found many variables that distinguish them: the gender of the alcoholic parent; number of alcoholic parents; the age of the child at the onset of parental addiction; birth order; co-existing problems of poverty, sexual abuse, and violence; number of siblings; availability of mentors or family members with resources; maintenance of family rituals during active alcoholism; and levels of individual resiliencies (Barry & Blane, 1977; Bennett, Wolin, & Reiss, 1988; Bennett, Wolin, Reiss, & Teitelbaum, 1987; Booz-Allen & Hamilton, Inc., 1974; O'Sullivan, 1991; Simmons, 1991; Wolin & Bennett, 1984; Wolin, Bennett, & Noonan, 1979, 1980). ACOAs are also not predisposed to marry heavy drinkers, and their marriages are no less intimate than those of children of non-alcoholics (Boye-Beaman, Leonard, & Senchak, 1991).

Role behaviors are a natural part of living in a family. They become harmful only when they are acted out in a rigid manner with little or no other option for problem solving. Roles are only one of several parts of systems theory. It is equally important to understand family rules, family values, cultural issues, alliances, coalitions, homeostatic mechanisms, and intergenerational transmissions and projections.

Family Rules

Decisions are made or not made according to the rules, boundaries, and alliances of family members. Families have rules about the expression of feelings such as love, hurt, or anger. Some rules are spoken about and others are not, but everyone knows them. These rules include who can express feelings, how they are expressed, and how they are received. In an alcoholic family, the unspoken rule may be that anger can only be expressed during intoxication or that affection and intimacy can occur only when one or both spouses are drinking. Barnard (1981) believed other areas where rules are formulated for family functioning are (1) what, when, and how family members may comment on what they see, feel, and think; (2) who can speak to whom and about what; (3) how a member can be different; (4) how sexuality can be expressed; (5) what it means to be male or female; and (6) how a person can acquire self-worth and how much is appropriate to possess. Typical rules that govern families of individuals with alcoholism or addiction concern the best way to deal with the intoxicated or high person, secret keeping, and family preservation. Black (1981b) listed three rules that children of alcoholics often live by: "Don't talk. Don't trust. Don't feel." Talking, especially about the substance abuse, might cause even more problems. Trusting usually leads to disappointment when parents do not come through with their promises. Feeling is too painful, and expression of feelings is not allowed because it might cause more trouble. These rules are the basis for dyadic and triadic relationships and interactions in the family subsystems that are formed by generation, sex, mutual interest, or duties.

Family Subsystems

The first subsystem in the family is the marital subsystem that has a closed membership in which duties are performed by the husband and wife. The second subsystem, the parental subsystem, emerges with the birth of the first child. These duties are usually carried out by the husband and wife, but in a family of a person with alcoholism or addiction, the parents may abdicate their roles to a grandparent or sibling who fills the parental gap. This may blur the generational boundaries or turn the child into a parent. This child who takes on early parenting responsibilities is at risk of losing his or her childhood when strapped with the adult responsibilities of raising their siblings.

The third main category is the sibling subsystem. There may be one or many subsystems, depending on the number of children, gender of the children, age differences, and common interests. In healthy families, the subsystems are fluid, and members can flow between them as the overall system changes and balances. Children can act like adults when they learn to do chores or babysit for their younger siblings for short times. Parents can act like children and play and be silly for short times. Flexibility is important in defining subsystems; however, these shifts to other subsystems need to be temporary. In an alcoholic family, these systems may become rigid and create uncertainty with regard to tasks. Children get stuck in the parent subsystem; people with addiction and alcoholism become rigidly childlike and irresponsible. Parenting may be ignored, children may take on adult roles, and children may be allowed into the marital subsystem if incestuous relationships occur between a parent and one or several children.

Boundaries

This concept has been misused in the popular literature and in the chemical dependency field. Boundaries are not rules for the behavior of children, nor are they processes of limit setting. Boundaries exist between each member of the family and between subsystems. They describe levels of comfort with closeness and connectedness within the family and with the family and the larger society. Minuchin (1974) defined three types of boundaries: enmeshed, clear, and disengaged. In reality most boundaries fall somewhere on a continuum from the very rigid (disengaged) to the very diffuse (enmeshed), with the clearly defined boundaries falling in the center.

Clear boundaries are found in most healthy relationships that are based on mutual respect. Clear boundaries allow separateness for each member, yet maintain closeness and connectedness. Freedom and flexibility in these relationships promote clear and direct communication patterns.

Enmeshed or diffuse boundaries leave no room for flexibility and no room for differences. Sameness and unity are stressed in these relationships, and a sense of belonging does occur. However, adolescents, whose job it is to individuate and pull away from their parents in order to find individual identities, become smothered and may turn to alcohol or drugs to set up a distancing mechanism. The fused marital relationship is an example of the loss of self-identity that occurs when the individual personality of one or both partners is sacrificed for the sake of the marriage. Ethnic and cultural factors have an effect on the amount of connectedness a family should have and can tolerate. Many families with a cultural heritage of close relationship with extended families can tolerate a great degree of diffuse boundaries without causing problems for the family members.

Disengaged or rigid boundaries are often seen in alcoholic families and are identified as the isolation of the members or isolation of the family from society. The rules in these families are (1) do not talk about the alcoholism or drug addiction, (2) do not confront drinking or drug behavior, and (3) protect and shelter the person with alcoholism or addiction so that things do not become worse. These rules perpetuate the drinking or using, which maintains the need for isolation. Often, marital relationships in these families have arrived at a fixed distance where neither partner is getting his or her needs met from the other. Similarly, siblings in this situation lack a sense of belonging, and very little love is transmitted to build self-worth. These children may use alcohol and other drugs to numb the pain of rejection, or they may act out inappropriately to try to get the recognition they want. This pattern of rigid boundaries can be found in families who have children in their twenties who have not left home. They often have chronic drug problems that keep them from gaining steady employment and, thus, moving out. Research has indicated that these young adults and adolescents with drug problems have never felt connected to their families and hang on to try and get those needs met (Friedman, Tomko, & Utada, 1991; Olson & Killorin, 1987). Olson and Killorin (1987) compared chemically dependent families and non-dependent families using the circumplex model of measuring family cohesion. One-third of the chemically dependent families perceived their families as disengaged compared to seven percent of the non-dependent families. On the outside looking in, these families might look enmeshed and stuck together. It would be tempting for a counselor to tell the parents to kick these drug-abusing kids out, and although this may be an end goal, it can be disastrous if the children do not first feel connected to the family. Too often drug-abusing young adults only feel connected to their families when the families give them money or bail them out of trouble.

Family Values

As family roles, rules, and boundaries begin to develop, so do family values. These values are a blend of those values transmitted from the spouses' families of origin. These values may be shared by the couple or be more strongly supported by one spouse or the other. Things that are valued in families are athletics, music, money, work, education, power, control, winning, social status, military service, conservatism, or radicalism, to name just a few. Conflict can occur when the mother embraces music and education as her strong values and wants her son to become a musical virtuoso, while the father longs for an athlete who is competitive and values winning. In some cases, children make adaptations and combine values to please both parents, but when the values are in direct opposition, the child must choose one or none of the conflicting values. This is a no-win situation for the child because one of the parents will withhold approval. The children in the family have the option of accepting or rejecting any or all of the family values and are not bound by pure imitation of their parents. However, it is often true that the parent who sees his or her values mirrored in the child will come forth with more approval. Depending on the boundaries and rules of the family, children who choose different values may be allowed this differentiation, or they may defy a family rule that says family members must not be different.

Other conflicts arise when a female child is born into a family that values boys and needs an heir for the family business or when a male child is born to a family that needs a girl for balance or to satisfy a parent's psychological need.

As the family develops, it takes on an overall atmosphere, depending on the amount of conflict involved in the balancing of roles, family values, and interaction rules. The interactions produce atmospheres that are friendly, competitive, or cooperative or environments that are hostile, autocratic, or permissive.

Although it is important for counselors to understand the values of families and family members, it is also important for counselors to understand their own values. In the early years of family therapy, the effort to understand each family member's perspective, treat each fairly, and not blame any one person for the family's problems ignored societal realities of power and gender differences in families. Recent criticisms of this pure systems thinking have caused family therapists to be more aware of the values and belief systems that they bring with them to the therapy session. Therapists do not check them at the door. For instance, in working with a married couple, the gender of the therapist is a fact that is easy for the couple to see and may make the person of the couple with the same gender feel more understood. Counselors who try to hide their belief that women are not treated equally in society are not being fair to the woman by assuming everyone is equal in the therapy. Counselors should be aware of their values and biases and address the inequality of men and women in the society with their clients in order to be most effective.

Alliances and Coalitions

Alliances are connections between two people in a family about an issue or a position. Mom and Dad, for instance, can be in alliance about their children's bedtimes. Two sisters can form an alliance as a power base to defend themselves against their brothers. Families, however, most often work in triangles that can operate in many ways: two against one, two for one, one pulled between two others, one bridging a gap between two others, and so forth. It is very difficult for two family members to talk for very long without "triangulating" a third member into the discussion. For instance, if two sisters are debating an issue, it is common to hear, "But Mom said . . ."

Coalitions form in a family when two people are allied against a third. When a wife is afraid to confront her husband directly because he hits her, she may entice her son to fight her battles with her husband for her. A daughter who feels that her father treats her mother badly may pick fights with him to even the score. Many coalitions are problematic because they cross generational boundaries and shift people into inappropriate subsystems.

In healthy families, alliances form in a horizontal pattern within generations. That is, grandparents have an alliance between themselves, parents have a marital and parental alliance, and the children have special alliances among themselves. These alliances can become vertical in nature if, for instance, there is a cross-generational alliance between one spouse and his or her parent or an alliance between a parent and a child that takes the place of marital closeness. "Whenever generational boundaries are consistently violated and members of one generation supply what should be received in another generation, pathology can be expected" (Haley, 1976, p. 39).

These cross-generational alliances disturb the balance of the family by changing role definitions and pulling members of the family of origin into the dynamics and workings of the nuclear family. Marital issues cannot be resolved if they are only discussed between the wife and her mother. If the maternal grandmother was overprotective of her daughter and is reluctant to allow her to break away and become an independent person, this attachment may continue through their adult lives. If the daughter married and had children because the expectations of society were stronger than the overprotective tie with her mother, she may be very angry with her husband for taking her away from her mother and angry with her children for keeping her in a difficult position. This anger often is not shown directly but is manifested in the same overprotective parenting style with which the mother was raised. The mother's underlying wish to be rid of her husband and children must be repressed and covered with over-concern. Her anxiety and overprotection often produce symptoms in one of the children and may cause an over-involvement between the parent and child, thus passing on a cross-generational alliance and maladaptive behavior. Overprotective parenting has been identified as one of the parenting styles that increase the risk of children becoming addicted to drugs and alcohol (Lawson & Lawson, 1998).

As the family of procreation develops as a social system, the spouses define themselves in terms of their relationships with their families of origin. Framo (1976) identified four categories of relationships with families of origin. The first category is the overinvolved relationship, which may resemble the enmeshed subsystems in the nuclear family. These families may live close together—maybe even down the street. The people in these families will often talk daily on the telephone. In some families that are forced to move apart, this daily phone contact may continue long distance. These families usually have very little social life outside their own confines and are closed off from the rest of society. The (other) spouse in these relationships may resent the spouse's over-involvement or may welcome the relationship with a parent substitute. Difficulty occurs in these situations if grandparents give advice on home management, parenting, marital relationships, and areas that are typically roles of the marital and parental subsystems. Self-identity and self-worth as a spouse and parent are sabotaged with messages from the family of origin to the effect that "you are inadequate, and you need our help." What the family of origin may really mean is "we need you to need help so we can busy ourselves with your problems and not look at our own marital difficulties."

The second category is the superficial relationship. It involves infrequent, non-personal contact, usually revolving around ceremonies or family rituals. Framo (1976) believed that people in these relationships see themselves as having resolved their difficulties with their families in a mature way. They have used space, distance, and time to reduce conflict.

The third category occurs when people completely cut themselves off from their families. They proclaim that the absence of contact is the only way to maintain their own sanity and virtually deny the existence of other family members, treating them as if they were already dead. Framo (1976) believes that these people have the greatest chance of repeating the irrational patterns of their parents.

The last category is a positive one in which a person establishes an identity within the family of origin before leaving. This differentiation or individuation occurs when families have clear boundaries and parents can solve their own problems without projecting them onto their children or involving their children in the resolution process. These children consequently have no need to stay in the family or to escape its clutches. There is neither an over-attachment nor an angry rebellion. These families do have a sense of belonging, but it is balanced with respect for independence. The parents in this type of family of origin love their children enough to let them leave. In transactional-analysis terms, these adult children relate more in adult-to-adult transactions with their parents than in adult-to-child transactions.

"In general, the more a nuclear family is emotionally cut off from parental families, the higher the incidence of problems and symptoms in the nuclear family" (Bowen, 1978, p. 264). Children from families with alcoholism and drug addiction may leave their families in many ways, but usually they feel like they never really belonged to the family, though they can never really leave. This task of leaving the family is crucial and has an effect on all subsequent relationships. Carter and McGoldrick (1980) stated:

> We see a new family life cycle beginning at the stage of the "unattached young adult," whose adequate or inadequate completion of the primary task of coming to terms with his or her family of origin will most profoundly influence whom, when and how he or she marries and all succeeding stages of the new family life cycle. Adequate completion of this task would require that the young adult separate from the family of origin without cutting off or fleeing reactively to a substitute emotional refuge. (p. 13)

Symptoms

The family roles, rules, boundaries, values, atmosphere, alliances, and coalitions all combine to constitute the family homeostasis. Meeks and Kelly (1970) stated:

> Any attempt to shift the family equilibrium either from within (i.e., change in a member) or from without (i.e., input from a therapist) may evoke resistance from the family system which seeks to maintain the status quo (equilibrium). No matter how sick it may appear to the outside observer, the established equilibrium represents that family's attempt to minimize the threats of disruption and pain. (p. 400)

In the alcoholic family, a balance is maintained with the presence of alcohol, and the family may resist any attempts to remove this part of the balance, though they may ask for the drinking to cease. They believe that change may be worse than the pain they are already suffering. At least they know how to cope with the problem, and the pattern of coping is familiar. According to Steinglass (1976), "the presence or absence of alcohol becomes the single most important variable determining the interactional behavior not only between the identified drinker and other members of the family but among non-drinking members of the family as well" (p. 106).

When families present themselves to a therapist, it is usually due to a symptom in one member resulting from a disturbance in family homeostasis, or it is the result of the suggestion of someone outside the family. Bowen (1978) defined three areas within the nuclear family in which symptoms are expressed: (1) marital conflict, (2) dysfunction in a spouse, and (3) projection to one or more children. Bowen labels this third area the family-projection process, which he believes exists to some extent in all families. In this process, families project their problems onto their children, who become symptom bearers for the family. The symptom bearer often unconsciously volunteers for this position and may be instrumental in bringing a family into therapy where alcohol abuse or dysfunctional family patterns can be corrected, thus relieving the symptoms in the child. These children have a stake in saving their families and themselves in the symptom-bearer role. "Children, and adults as well, will forgo their own nature in order to save a parent from going crazy or in order to become the kind of person a parent (or parent representative) can love" (Framo, 1976, p. 207). Children may mirror the behavior of the parent to gain acceptance, but instead they receive rejection. The child's symptoms may be labeled inappropriate, thus causing conflict and anxiety in the child.

Family therapy has evolved around the notion of the identified patient or the symptom bearer as the person who expresses a particular dysfunction for the whole family. Therefore, the context of the person addicted to alcohol or drugs is reframed as the alcoholic or addicted family, with the person with alcoholism or addiction as the identified patient. Steinglass (1976) pointed out that, uniquely, symptoms occur in the parental subsystem in the alcoholic or addicted family. This is in contrast to the majority of dysfunctional families in which children are the symptom bearers. The adult with alcoholism or drug addiction, however, may have developed the seeds of his or her addiction as an adolescent in response to disruption in the family of origin and has just brought it into his or her current family as part of an intergenerational family process. This does not mean that the children are not symptomatic. Children of people addicted to drugs or alcohol suffer from a variety of problems.

The alcoholic or addicted family may also be unique in the process of triangulation, in which the tension between two people is displaced onto an issue or a substance (e.g., alcohol or other drugs) instead of being projected onto the child. Unfortunately, the removal of the substance may result in a worsening of tension or another displacement. Posttreatment divorces are common.

Because of the intergenerational nature of addictions, however, there is usually more than one person in a family with substance abuse problems. It is not unusual for a family to have issues with drug abuse, alcoholism, compulsive overeating, addiction, and anorexia. Chemical dependency is a unique symptom in that it can take on a life of its own. Changing the family system may not stop the addictive behavior. Often, the addiction needs to be treated in conjunction with changing the family patterns that maintain the addiction. It can be just as counterproductive to treat the family and ignore the addictive behavior as it is to treat the addiction and ignore the family dynamics and problems of other family members.

Theories of Family Therapy

This section will provide a brief description of four schools of family therapy. As the field of family therapy developed, family therapists created their own family therapy models. These models were influenced by the therapists' personalities; cultural backgrounds; previous training in psychology, psychiatry, or social work; social trends; and the zeitgeist. Historical events that led the way for these theorists included the child guidance movement, where children were usually seen with their mothers; the failure of psychoanalysis to treat juvenile delinquency and schizophrenia; and the ending of World War II, with an emphasis on families reuniting. The pioneering schools of family therapy discussed in this section are Structural Family Therapy, Strategic Family Therapy, Intergenerational Family Therapy, and Experiential Family Therapy.

Structural Family Therapy

The founder of structural family therapy was Salvador Minuchin, a psychiatrist from Argentina. His theory grew out of his work with boys with juvenile delinquency at the Wyltwyck School, where he worked with poor, multiproblem families. These families required techniques that were concrete and action oriented. Minuchin would have these families enact their problems in the therapy sessions so he could see, firsthand, what was happening in the family in order to determine its organization and structure. Structural family therapists are interested in the structure (rules, roles, and sequences of behaviors), subsystems, and boundaries of families. Minuchin was also concerned with environmental factors and found the family to be the interpreter of societal values, rules, and behaviors. Children, he felt, learn either functional or dysfunctional behaviors in the family through observing and interpreting the family structure.

The family structure is defined as transactions that are unique to a family—levels of authority, power structure, and mutual expectations. The structure is created with the marriage and the agreement of the spouses to satisfy each other's needs. The evolution of spousal functions creates the core of the nuclear family. The structure changes when the first child is born and parental functions are negotiated. With this child rides the potential for family growth or possible destruction. If the family cannot clearly differentiate the spousal and parental functions, dysfunction in the family may occur. This theory is similar to Bowen's concepts of the family projection process and cross-generational alliances.

Within the family structure, Minuchin defined *subsystems* as one or more family members who share something in common: generation, sex, interests, or family duties. He defined *boundaries* as the rules of the subsystems that are either rigid, diffuse, or clear. Dysfunction occurs with rigid boundaries that create isolation and discourage family communication, or with diffuse boundaries that do not clearly define areas of authority or responsibility, as when children are running the family. These diffuse boundaries discourage individual responsibility and promote random and confused problem solving.

Minuchin's Structural Therapy categorized the family's method of experiencing stress in four ways:

1. Stress can be caused in one family member by someone outside the family, such as a boss, which is then transmitted to other family members.

2. Stress may be caused in the entire family by an outside force, such as economic conditions or a move to a new location.

3. Stress can be caused by life crisis transitions, such as the birth of a child, a child attending school for the first time, adolescence, a child leaving home (particularly the last one), or midlife crises of the parents, which may coincide with adolescence of the children.

4. Stress may result from the presence of a chronically ill person in the family, including a member with alcoholism or addiction.

Minuchin feels that dysfunction in the family occurs when there are unclear levels of authority and power, when expectations are misunderstood, when there is confusion as to the functions of subgroups, or when rigid or diffuse boundaries exist in the family.

The goal of Structural Family Therapy is to alter the family structure so that the family can solve its problems. The therapist alters boundaries and realigns subsystems to change the behavior and experiences of each of the family members (Nichols & Schwartz, 2013). A common goal is to help parents function as a single parental unit without division or conflict. Parents, also, need to be in charge of the children and not act as their buddies or peers.

There are three main overlapping processes in Structural Family Therapy (Minuchin, 1974). First, the therapist joins the family as a director of the therapy process. Minuchin has referred to this as joining the family like a wise uncle. Second, the therapist maps the underlying structure of the family. Minuchin has devised a system of symbols to graphically map out the family structure, boundaries, and interactions. Third is the intervention to change the family structure, in which the structural therapist follows seven steps:

1. Joining and accommodating—This is the process of the therapist's connecting with the family and establishing rapport. The therapist greets each member and uses his or her position to respect the parents' authority by first asking them to describe the problem. Children are also respected and given a chance to tell their perspectives. Therapists try to match the family's tone and way of speaking, using their language—even their coping mannerisms and postures. This is an important part of the therapy. The therapist must be accepted by the family members before they will allow him or her to change them.

2. Working with interaction—This is the process of getting family members to talk with one another so the therapist can observe the interactions. This process is called "enactment." The therapist may give a directive, for instance, for the parents to have a conversation about their concerns for their son, or have a parent try to get a child to behave. This gives the therapist a chance to see how they behave at home and to observe boundaries and rules for behavior.

3. Diagnosing—This is a process that begins with the first contact with the family. Hypotheses about family structure and interaction are formulated with the first phone call. The therapist carefully watches what the family does, where members sit, whom they talk to, how they talk, and what they say. The goal of the diagnosis is to move the family from seeing only one person as having a problem to spreading the problem to all family members and then to finding a solution that will benefit all family members. The diagnosis is established in the first session but is refined and revised as more data are gathered and interventions are tried.

4. Highlighting and modifying interactions—Once unhealthy patterns have been diagnosed, the therapist must point them out and begin to change them. This can be done by using the therapist's directive position to intensify the problematic interaction and react strongly to it. The other method of modifying interactions is to highlight the times when the family is working in a positive way and get them to do more.

5. Boundary making—Structural family therapists are concerned with altering boundaries so they are clear. If boundaries are diffuse and relationships enmeshed, therapists find ways of marking boundaries. This can be done in the sessions by changing where people are sitting or between sessions by assigning tasks. If the daughter, for instance, always sits between the parents and seems overinvolved in their relationship, the therapist might ask her to change seats with one of her parents, putting the parents together, with the daughter outside the subsystem. Therapists also block family members who interrupt others, thus marking a clear boundary. Homework assignments might include assigning the couple to go on a date by themselves. Rigid boundaries can be opened up by connecting family members. During a session, the therapist might ask family members who are distant from the family to become more involved in the process of the session, as well as challenge conflict avoidance by family members. A homework assignment might include having a non-involved father spend time with his daughter. The goal of this process is not only to create clear boundaries but also to move family members from thinking about their problems in a linear way to helping them understand circular causality and how all of the family members influence each other.

6. Unbalancing—Families become stuck in patterned behaviors that keep them from solving their problems. Unbalancing is an attempt to arbitrarily add importance or weight to one person's perspective in order to make a shift in the process and shake the homeostatic balance. Although this may seem like the therapist is making a value judgment about who is right, it is done simply to shake things up. The therapist takes turns showing preference with other family members at other times to even things up.

7. Challenging the family's assumptions—As part of changing the family structure, structural therapists may use a cognitive or educational approach to normalize behaviors that the family may see as terrible or to reframe behavior or problems with a positive twist. A child whom the parents describe as "into everything" may be described by the therapist as "bright and inquisitive." It is the same behavior with different labels. Sometimes the therapist will teach the family about their structure and what needs to be changed to help them see themselves in a different light.

Structural Family Therapy is the most common family approach used in the treatment of chemical dependency. Research in treatment outcome has indicated that this method of treatment is very successful with individuals with drug addiction, adolescents who abuse drugs, and children with anorexia. Stanton and Todd (1992) compared a structural-strategic model of family therapy with a placebo condition and individual therapy in treating drug addiction. The level of positive change and symptom reduction in the family therapy condition was double that achieved in the other conditions, and the changes were maintained at 6- and 12-month follow-up evaluations.

Treatment outcome studies have also been conducted using family therapy based on a structural approach in treating adolescent drug abuse. The Purdue Brief Therapy Model (Lewis, Piercy, Sprenkle, & Trepper, 1991; Piercy & Frankel, 1989) was one of the projects that integrated family therapies that had previously demonstrated their effectiveness and applied this model to adolescent substance abuse. The models included theory from Stanton and

Todd (1982), who demonstrated the effectiveness of structural-strategic family therapy with adult heroin addiction; Szapocznik and his colleagues (Szapocznik, Kurtines, Foot, Perez-Vidal, & Hervis, 1983, 1986), at the University of Miami School of Medicine, who found strategic therapy effective in decreasing adolescent drug abuse; Minuchin, Rosman, and Baker (1978), who found that structural family therapy decreased symptoms of psychosomatic illnesses such as asthma and anorexia nervosa; Alexander (1974), who used functional family therapy to work with juvenile delinquents; and Patterson (1982), who repeatedly demonstrated the effectiveness of behavioral contracting with delinquent adolescents. This brief twelve-session model was geared to help change the entire family into a healthier supportive environment. Its goal was to stem the current drug abuse of an adolescent and prevent the development of drug abuse by a younger sibling.

This model was compared to a family drug-education program, Training in Parenting Skills (TIPS), and individual-based drug counseling of adolescents. The results indicated that the two brief, family-based drug interventions together appeared to reduce the drug use of nearly one-half (46%) of the adolescents who received them. In commenting on this success, Lewis (1991) stated the following:

> We suspect that this success was due partly to the fact that both of these outpatient interventions focused on the systemic treatment of *entire* family groups. In contrast, however, the family therapy intervention seems to have been more effective in significantly reducing adolescent drug use for a greater percentage of the adolescents (54.6%) than the family education intervention (37.5%). An even more dramatic result of the study was this: Although more than twice as many adolescents in the family therapy condition (40%) were hard drug users at their pretest, *twice as many of these hard users (44.4%) moved to no use at all* by the posttest time, compared to only the 25% of the hard users in the family education condition who moved to no drug use. (pp. 2–3)

A similar adolescent treatment outcome study was conducted by Joanning and associates (Joanning, Quinn, Thomas, & Mullen, 1992). They compared Family Systems Therapy to Adolescent Group Therapy and Family Drug Education. The Family Systems Therapy was based on the structural-strategic model that Stanton and Todd (1982) used with adults addicted to drugs. The Family Systems Therapy produced twice as many apparently drug-free clients (54%) as did the Family Drug Education model (28%) and three times as many as did the Adolescent Group Therapy approach (16%).

Strategic Family Therapy

Strategic Family Therapy grew out of the Communications Model that was developed by the Mental Research Institute (MRI) in Palo Alto, California. Gregory Bateson began working with interpersonal communications in schizophrenic families and applying cybernetics to family therapy. Bateson was joined in this project by Jay Haley, John Weakland, and Don Jackson, who developed a belief that communication between members was the most important factor of family life (Bateson, Jackson, Haley, & Weakland, 1956). These theorists believed that blocked forms of communication in the individual were symptoms of overall dysfunctional communication in the family. They proposed that dysfunctional communication patterns produced family tension that was projected onto one or more family members.

The MRI group developed the theory of the "double bind" and later related it to clinical work. The double bind is a communication pattern involving a victim or scapegoat and a message sender. The sender gives two messages at the same time; often one is verbal and the other is non-verbal. In order for these messages to be defined as a double bind, they must be conflicting and be repeatedly sent over a long period of time. One message must carry a negative connotation or punishment message (which may seem life threatening), whereas the other is more abstract and contradictory. The victims are trapped in this pattern by their need for love and approval.

Haley (1976) developed a philosophy involving personal alliances in the family. In the healthy family, he noticed mutually satisfying and need-fulfilling relationships. In the dysfunctional family, he found confused communication patterns and shifting alliances. Haley hypothesized that confused, out-of-order communication patterns can lead to misinterpretation, assumption, guessing, and misunderstanding among family members. If children cannot interpret what their parents' needs and wishes are, they certainly cannot fulfill them. Haley also found that cross-generational alliances produced confused communication and misunderstanding in the power hierarchy of the family. He believed that change in communication patterns and alliances in the family would change the overall functioning of the family and reduce symptoms in the symptom bearer.

Haley was highly influenced by the work of Milton Erickson and Salvador Minuchin, as well as that of Gregory Bateson. It is the combination of these influences of communication theory, cybernetics, Ericksonian hypnosis, and structural theory that became Haley's strategic approach. Strategic therapists are more concerned with changing a family's behavior than in changing their understanding; consequently, they are very interested in technique (Nichols & Schwartz, 2013). The goal of therapy is to resolve the presenting problem. The therapists are not interested in insight or understanding. The strategic therapist takes on most of the responsibility for change in the family and devises novel strategies for bringing about change. Strategic therapists have been criticized for being manipulative and for deceiving the family, but they have responded to these criticisms with treatment outcome data indicating the power of their techniques in producing change.

Strategic therapists borrow concepts from cybernetics and are interested in positive feedback loops, family rules, creating second-order change, and reframing behavior to expose the "function of the symptom." This means the adaptive function that the problem serves in the family and why it is so hard to give up. This is another way of trying to understand why people do things that are apparently opposite the goal they are trying to achieve. Strategic therapists use paradoxical techniques to bypass a family or a family member's resistance to change. A simple paradox is prescribing the symptom. If, for instance, a daughter is doing poorly in school, the therapist might suggest that she continue to fail at her school work. If she continues to fail, she has followed the therapist's directive. If she begins to succeed, that intervention has also worked. If there is strong resistance to change, sometimes going with the resistance will produce more change than confronting it directly. If the therapist believes that the daughter is failing because it gets her mother involved with her around homework and studies and takes her mother's focus away from a failing marriage or her alcoholic husband, the therapist may say, "You really need to continue to fail at school, because your mother feels needed when you do," or the therapist might compliment the daughter for being so sensitive to her mother's need and being willing to sacrifice her schoolwork for her mother. Haley also believes that the symptoms that are presented by the symptom bearer are metaphors for what is really wrong with the family or the marriage, and without changing the family structure, the symptom will either return or change to another one. Another type of paradoxical message is the restraint of change. Since families are used to their homeostatic balance, even if it is unhealthy, change may be very frightening for them. The therapist can acknowledge this ambivalence to change by instructing the family to go slow with change, because it can be dangerous. There is an art to devising paradoxical interventions, and they should not be used if a straightforward directive will be followed or if the therapist has not had sufficient training and supervision in these techniques.

Haley has developed a four-stage process for a first session of Strategic Family Therapy, which he calls Problem Solving Therapy. The stages are (1) social, (2) problem, (3) interaction, and (4) goal setting. This method would be useful with families of persons recovering from alcoholism and addiction, with families in which alcoholism or other drug addiction is not the presenting problem and is not the central issue of therapy, or with families in which the adolescent child is abusing alcohol or other drugs. If the family's presenting problem is not addiction and the therapist redefines the problem as alcohol or other drug abuse, the family may become anxious or may feel unheard and pull out of therapy. It is important to initially begin with what the family has identified as their problem, but without forgetting about the addiction. If the therapist can remain flexible and spontaneous, an initial solvable problem can be a good starting point, and then the therapy can shift to the addictive behavior or recovery issues. Usually, the presenting problem can be easily linked to active abuse or unresolved problems from previous addictive behavior.

The beginning period allows the family to experience the "familiness" of their problems. The entire family should attend the early sessions, and the network of support people who are involved with the family are useful for the initial interview. Sometimes, it is useful to include the sponsor of the person with alcoholism or addiction. Strategic therapists, however, will work with whoever comes to the sessions.

The first stage is the social stage, and it establishes a comfort level and provides a naturalizing of the social environment. Family members are allowed to sit where they wish. The therapist has a greeting exchange with family members to get their names, ages, and additional innocuous information. The idea is to demonstrate that each person is important and can contribute to the session. At this point, it can be determined who is missing from the family and whether any members of the extended family would be important contributors.

The issue of blame may arise at this time with the alcoholic family. Either the family is uncomfortable with the unstated alcohol problem and blames a child for their presence in therapy, or the family continues to scapegoat the addicted person and remains uninterested in his or her contributions to the family problems. The therapist should focus on the here and now and initially avoid discussions of specific problems. The family will present a dominant mood that the therapist should attempt to match.

With parents and children all in one room, parent–child interactions, discipline modalities, and sibling relationships may also be noted. This, however, only represents how family members act in front of others and may be different from behavior at home. Also, at this time, parents may be openly in disagreement, in agreement, or overly agreeable about the child's problems. One of the spouses may be reluctant to participate in the session.

Additionally, the therapist can observe the seating arrangement to see if the identified patient is isolated or sitting between the parents or if the parents have an allied child near them.

It is best at this time to keep all conclusions about the family interaction tentative, and therapists should not share their observations with the family. At some level, the family is aware of these dynamics and would see this as an invasion. Haley (1976) said, "To point out something like a seating arrangement is asking the family to concede something they might prefer not to concede, and thus that action could arouse defensiveness and cause unnecessary difficulties in the therapy" (p. 19).

The second stage is the problem stage, and it begins with an inquiry about the family's view of the problem that has brought them in for therapy. It signals the end of the social atmosphere stage and indicates that it is time to get down to business. It may be very confusing to the alcoholic or addicted family to be in family therapy when it is obvious to them who has the problem. The therapist must clarify why the entire family has been asked to participate. The problem orientation can remain, but the therapist may state that it is important to get everyone's opinion of the problem. Usually the therapist has some prior knowledge of the family from a referral source or from the family member who called for the appointment. If the family seems secretive, it is beneficial for the therapist to share this prior information with the family.

During questioning about the problem area, the therapist needs to decide whom to ask and in what way. If the family is simply asked what the problem is, the therapist may receive a long history of all of the negative behavior of the identified patient. The therapist can offer hope for change and ask questions like, "What do you want to change in your family?" To assess what caused the family to ask for help, the therapist may ask, "How did the decision get made to call for this appointment?" or "What has happened recently that motivated you to call for this appointment?" Haley (1976) suggested, "As a rule, the more general and ambiguous the inquiry of the therapist is, the more room there is for the family members to display their point of view" (p. 21).

It is difficult to present these questions to the family as a whole, and usually there is a therapist bias in selecting who is addressed. If the therapists are chemical dependency counselors, their sympathies may be with the alcoholic or addicted person, who seems victimized by a nagging spouse. If the therapists are child oriented, they may be angry at the parents, who have neglected and hurt the children. A decision about whom to address can best be made by first examining the family hierarchy of power and influence. Usually, one parent is more motivated to work than the other, and one parent has more power to get the family to return for further sessions. Haley (1976) believed that the person who can get the family back to therapy should be treated with respect, but the under-involved parent should be engaged first.

Sometimes, the most detached family member is a child. In this instance, it is best to start talking with the person who is least involved and sits furthest away, and then work through the family to the most involved member. It is inadvisable to begin with the identified patient, as it may look like the therapist is blaming him or her. Identified patients are used to getting attention when the family is anxious, and this pattern must be broken by the therapist. Haley (1976) said, "Every therapist must watch out for a tendency to turn to, or on, the problem person in a benevolent way when he or she [the therapist] is anxious and under stress" (p. 25).

In addition, the problem that brought the family to therapy must be clearly stated and not minimized. If there is a tendency to extend the social stage and not deal with issues, the family will be confused. If alcohol and/or other drug abuse is the presenting problem and a direct discussion of this issue is skirted, the problem will grow in magnitude and take on the aura of being unmentionable. Even if the therapist does not agree that the presenting problem is the main issue, it can be used as a lever to create change. For instance, if the presenting problem is child oriented but the therapist is certain of marital conflict, the marital relationship can be approached by addressing disagreement on parenting issues. Haley (1976) stated, "Usually family members say that one person is the problem. The therapist's job is to think of the problem in terms of more than one person. By thinking that way he [or she] is most able to bring about change" (p. 33).

As the problem is being presented, the therapist should simply listen to the family and observe behaviors. The therapist should avoid making interpretations, giving advice, or encouraging emotional reactions with inquiries about feelings rather than facts. One member of the family must not be allowed to monopolize the discussion. The therapist must have enough control of the session to allow everyone to speak. If the therapist is not in control, things will go as they have in the past, and change will not occur.

If the family requested therapy because of a problem with a child, the chances are good that the parents may be talking metaphorically about marital problems. If the mother says her daughter is unaffectionate, it is possible that the mother is also saying her husband is unaffectionate. These hypotheses should not be shared with the family. There is a reason that things are not talked about directly, and the child's behavior should not be outwardly connected with the marital situation. If the problem statement is left open and ambiguous, it will allow for these dynamics to be expressed to the therapist indirectly through safe subjects.

There are many areas that have become forbidden for families of individuals with alcoholism or addiction to discuss, and the children may be protecting the parents by withholding information or by taking the blame for family troubles. The couple with alcoholism or addiction may be unable to talk about certain subjects in a sober state, but can let the therapist know they exist in indirect ways. The therapist can observe all the levels of communication and interaction and can begin to think about the family's problems in a systems context. The therapist does not have to convince the family of this approach; the family will experience it in the process of treatment.

The third stage that Haley (1976) described is the interaction stage. Here, the therapist begins to direct people to speak to one another, rather than having all comments directed to the therapist. At this stage, family members may be able to act out some of their problems. A role-play situation of family interactions around a problem can be set up, allowing the therapist to observe the structure of the family and the interaction patterns.

The fourth stage is the goal-setting stage, which requires a more detailed definition of the problem. The desired changes are defined, and a clear therapeutic contract is negotiated. In order for the family to begin change, it is necessary to put the problem into terms that are solvable, observable, and measurable. This is important for observing therapy outcomes and for giving the family a clear direction for working. At this stage, the therapist can ask specific questions about the symptoms, such as when they occur, if they are constant or periodic, if they come on quickly or gradually, or how intense they are. It is useful to find out what everyone does in reaction to a problem. If the problem is drinking, questions can be asked about shifts in everyone's behavior and how it is different from their behavior when the family member is sober. In families who present a problem in an area other than substance abuse, the goal of the family may not be to stop the drinking or the using of one member. If the therapist insists on abstinence instead of the family's goal, the family may leave treatment. The therapist should instead see this as an opportunity to carefully tie the presenting problems to times of active use or to times that are complicated by the substance abuse. This is similar to an intervention of several sessions. However, if abstinence is the goal, it is easily observable and can be defined in terms of family behavior. The alcoholic or addicted individual may also be in the victim or scapegoat role in the family, and it would be dangerous to try to convince the family otherwise at this stage. If the therapist has been involved with the individual treatment of the alcoholic or addicted person, the temptation may arise to defend him or her and fight the rest of the family. If the therapist works too hard to free the alcoholic or addicted person from this negative position, the family may have to make the person out to be worse, to show the therapist that they were correct. The therapist needs to listen to the pain of all of the family members concerning the effects of living with an alcoholic or addicted family member and not be too quick to explain all of his or her behavior away with the disease model, which leaves family members with anger about behaviors of the alcoholic or addicted member, such as affairs or abuse, with no outlet except their feeling guilty about justified anger. A situation like this may lead to attempts to sabotage early recovery or retaliate in a more covert way. The same thing is true of a family who has a scapegoat child or adolescent that the therapist wants to save.

In this first session, the therapist is working to join the family by making everyone feel at ease, allowing everyone to contribute, involving everyone with one another, and including everyone in the decision-making process. If done in a genuine manner, this joining allows the therapist to enter the family and to begin to bring about change from within.

If the family seems hesitant about committing to a course of therapy, it may relieve their anxiety to set a certain number of sessions after which an assessment of progress will occur and a decision to continue can be made.

Intergenerational Family Therapy

Although structural and strategic approaches to family therapy are useful in working with chemically dependent families, the process of addiction in families is most clearly understood from an intergenerational perspective. The only definite statement that the chemical dependency field can make is that chemical dependency and other addictions run in families, generation after generation—more in some than in others. Whether this is caused by nature (genetics) or nurture (environment) is really not as important as how to intervene in a family problem that has a tremendous history.

Intergenerational family therapists share an interest in family dynamics across generations and come from a background in psychodynamic theory. Their interest in history is fueled by the belief that people's pasts influence their current behavior and relationships. Three pioneers in the school developed their theories at approximately the same time and were influenced by each other. They are Murray Bowen, Ivan Boszormenyi-Nagy, and James Framo. Bowen was also influenced by biological science, as mentioned earlier. He developed a theoretical model called Bowen Therapy with six interlocking concepts: (1) differentiation of self, (2) triangles, (3) nuclear family emotional process, (4) family projection process, (5) multigenerational transmission process, and (6) sibling position. He added two concepts in the 1970s: emotional cutoff and societal emotional process.

Nagy and Framo worked together at Eastern Pennsylvania Psychiatric Institute developing a process of working with families with schizophrenia. Nagy developed a contextual family therapy, which was based on loyalty, trust, and ethics in family relationships (Boszormenyi-Nagy & Spark, 1973). He emphasized the loyalty commitments people have to their families of origin, which is particularly useful in understanding what appears as undeserved loyalty in families with substance abuse. Framo was influenced by Bowen, but he drew the foundations for his theory from object-relations theory. Framo brings adult children together with their parents and siblings for intensive family-of-origin therapy sessions (Framo, 1991). The goal of these sessions is to heal old wounds, to correct family mythology, and to help the adult children relate on an adult-to-adult level with their parents, instead of regressing to a child in their presence. This is similar to Bowen's concept of differentiation from the family of origin; however, Bowen coaches clients to return to their families and practice a non-reactive response to the presence of their family of origin. Framo brings them all together in the therapy sessions.

Because Bowen directly addressed the intergenerational transmission of alcoholism, this section will cover his theory in more depth. This model can be used with individuals in treatment and is particularly effective with adults who were raised in alcoholic or addicted families. Bowen (1974) saw the transmission process that occurs in families with alcoholism as involved with levels of differentiation of self in the family. This is a function of the relationship that the child has with his or her parents, and the way the child's unresolved emotional attachment to his or her parents is handled in young adulthood. This model of family theory and therapy, which emerged during the birth of the family movement, defines symptoms in one member as a function of the family system of more than one generation (Bowen, 1974).

This theory can be used to understand the etiology of alcoholism in the family (Bowen, 1974). Bowen's theory was developed during his work with schizophrenic families. He began seeing distinctions in affective states and cognitive processes that led to his *scale of differentiation,* or the degree that individuals can differentiate themselves from their family of origin. This early work defined the *family* as a system that is operated by the same principles as other systems, such as societies, corporations, or institutions. Thus, the family is a system in that a change in one family member would be followed automatically by a change in another. Bowen was willing to work with the most motivated individual in the family to bring about change. He further believed that a person's current behavior is caused by a transference process that inappropriately applied past history and behaviors to present situations. Bowen's initial focus was on the mother–daughter relationship, which fostered his theory of the *family projection process*—the projecting of the problems of the parents onto the child. When he began to add grandparents to his sessions, he developed his theories on *multigenerational transmission*—how symptoms or family patterns were handed down through the generations.

Bowen (1974) observed families that exhibited feelings of oneness or lack of individual identities among the members. He further found varying degrees of this oneness in families who seemed overly dependent on one another and labeled it "stuck-togetherness." This stuck-togetherness was the families' defense against crises or tensions; under threat, the family members pulled together to restore balance. A delicate balance was created, with changes in one member affecting all others. If self-destructive behaviors, such as substance abuse, helped maintain balance, the families would tolerate them.

In this system, the smallest unit is a *triangle.* When two people feel stress, they bring in a third person to stabilize the unit. In families with alcoholism, the third member of the triangle can be the alcohol itself. In states of calm, there are two comfortable sides of the triangle and one conflictual side. Over a period of time, these roles become fixed. When conflict occurs between the two comfortable members, they project conflict onto the third, who develops symptoms in a family projection process. A familiar example is the mother, father, and child triangle. When conflict occurs in the marriage, tension rises in the mother and is projected onto the child, who will accept it to maintain the family oneness. In this case, the father may be the adaptive spouse who gives up his identity for the sake of the marriage and supports the other spouse's need, as well as her projection to the child. This father may also withdraw from the conflict by working long hours or drinking with his friends in the local tavern. There are several other patterns of response to stress or conflict that might occur among the three members as well.

The child selected for this projection is often the one closest to the mother. He or she may be the oldest, the only child, a child born during crisis, or one born with a defect. When this child leaves the family, another will take his or her place. When all the children have left, the marital problems may come to the fore, or the projection is passed on to others outside the family.

The adolescent who leaves this family will create a pseudoindependence based on anxiety that will be transmitted to that person's marital relationship in a multigenerational transmission process. Therefore, the patterns of the family of origin will be repeated in the nuclear family.

Families with high degrees of stuck-togetherness produce children who distance themselves from the family in an attempt to gain self-identity. They may (a) become rebellious adolescents or withdraw destructively; (b) gain physical distance by moving away from home; or (c) emotionally distance themselves, which may also create physical distance. These children never differentiate themselves from their parents and are consequently unable to become problem solvers in crisis situations. Some of these children may become substance abusers who say, "I can't take pressure and I can't cope; I'm an alcoholic."

Bowen (1974) devised a scale for determining self-differentiation in family members. This scale ranges from 0 to 100. The range from 0 to 25 encompasses those who are dominated by their emotions. Essentially, they lack a self; their only feeling of self-worth comes from others. The two rules of behavior for these people are (1) Does it make me feel good? and (2) Will others approve of me? Moving up the scale, differentiation is added to this profile to create people who begin to use intellectual processes in decision making and who gain personal opinions. The upper half of the scale reflects goal-orientation and encompasses those who can respond with rational principles and have less need to be defensive. They have achieved a self with a high degree of differentiation from their families. These people are able to achieve intimate relationships and are problem solvers.

In Bowen's (1974) words, self-differentiation is as follows:

> the degree to which the person has a "solid self" or solidly
> held principles by which he lives his life. This is in contrast

> to a "pseudoself" made up of inconsistent life principles that can be corrupted by coercion for the gain of the moment. The "differentiation of self" is roughly equivalent to the concept of emotional maturity. (p. 263)

This rating is based on the amount of a person's differentiation from his or her parents, the type of relationship that exists with the parents, and the quality of emotional separation from the parents in young adulthood.

Bowen (1978) states that people with similar scores tend to be attracted to one another, and they pass on similar degrees of differentiation to their children. The child with the lowest degree of differentiation is at highest risk for the family projection process and later problems. It is common for people to flee their families, blaming their parents for their problems and seeking happiness in their marriages. These two pseudoselves fuse and create impairments in one of the spouses. The most common way that couples handle this marital fusion is by one spouse's becoming dominant and the other adaptive. The adaptive one becomes a "no-self." "If this pattern is continued long enough, the adaptive one is vulnerable to some kind of chronic dysfunction, which can be physical illness, emotional illness, or a social dysfunction such as drinking, the use of drugs, or irresponsible behavior" (Bowen, 1978, p. 263). Families can use marital conflict or the projection of their immaturity onto the children as ways to adapt. This selection of adaptive patterns is not a conscious process. These patterns were programmed into the spouses by their families of origin.

Bowen believed that there is a continuum of behaviors that lead to alcoholism. On one end are the persons who deny the emotional attachment to their families of origin and maintain a superindependent posture. The actual level of emotional attachment, however, is intense. As these persons become increasingly emotionally isolated, they find relief in alcohol. On the other end of the continuum are the persons who are so attached to their parents that they are never able to manage a productive life. These people become "de-selfed" in the emotional fusion with the family of origin. They deny their intense need for their parents and begin drinking heavily early in life. Bowen states that most people with drinking problems fall somewhere in between these two extremes. "A high percentage of adult alcoholism is in people who are married, and who have the same kind of emotional attachment in marriage that they had in their parental families" (Bowen, 1978, p. 265).

Treatment would involve helping the patient differentiate from his or her family of origin and reduce the emotional reactivity to this system. The goal would be to help these patients create their own nuclear families with a minimum of the multigenerational transition process. This is a lengthy process, usually transpiring between the therapist and the family member wishing to differentiate from the family of origin. The therapist coaches the patient in this work with his or her family of origin.

Framo (1972) described a similar process of symptom development. He stated, "Symptoms are concomitants of the universal conflict between individuation, autonomous strivings, and loyalty to the family relationship system" (Framo, 1972, p. 127). In alcoholic families, it is difficult to truly belong and nearly impossible to individuate in a healthy way. The effects of living in a disruptive, alcoholic family system may transmit alcoholism into a second or third generation.

Bowen therapists, in contrast to strategic approaches, are less interested in technique than in theory. Bowen therapy does, however, have some overall therapeutic interventions that are used to achieve the goal of differentiation. Therapists construct a multigenerational family map of symbols called a "genogram" that includes ages, marriages, divorces, deaths, and other important events in family life. These symbols have been expanded to indicate close, conflicted, or cutoff relationships; addictions; and other intergenerational problems and patterns (McGoldrick & Gerson, 1985). The purpose of this genogram is to help clients see what patterns they are acting out from previous generations. When clients have an awareness of their heritage, they are then free to choose to repeat those patterns or to change them (see Figure 7.1). Bowen (1978) also advocated the therapist's taking a non-reactive position in therapy to lower the reactivity of the client or family. He also taught his clients to be non-reactive to their families by helping them distinguish between thinking and feeling and by using "I" statements. This helps clients take responsibility for their reactions and thoughts and reduces blaming. An example of an I statement could be, "When you call me a drunk, I get angry and defensive. I wish you would stop it."

David Treadway (1989) adapted Bowen's model for working with couples with active alcoholism. He chose this model because of the extreme emotional reactivity in these couples and their inability to take personal responsibility for their behavior. He outlined a six-stage model for working with these couples:

Stage 1: Disengagement—The goal of this stage is to shift the responsibility back to the drinker and to help the spouse change standard responses to the substance abuse, which has helped maintain it. Treadway (1989) believed that the chemical abuse is inextricably intertwined with the couple's behavior pattern. This reflects the strategic notion that families develop a circular pattern of behavior around a problem that often becomes part of the problem. He also believed that the spouse may be the most motivated person to change and that a change in his or her behavior would force a shift in the behavior of the person addicted to alcohol. Another goal of this stage is to get the drinker to stop by changing the spouse's behavior, referring him or her to A.A., or creating an intervention. In a way, the therapist is firing the spouse from trying to get the drinker to quit, and he takes on this role, freeing the spouse to take responsibility for his or her own recovery.

Stage 2: Differentiation—The goal of this stage is to help the family members tolerate the discomfort and confusion surrounding sobriety and to reduce their unrealistic expectations about early recovery (Treadway, 1989). Treadway acknowledged that couples who have been organized around the substance will be destabilized by the removal of the substance from the balance. Spouses also become more aware of the pain and hurt associated with the struggle with the substance abuse. Treadway used a Bowen model at this stage to lower the reactivity in sessions by becoming the third point of the triangle and running all of the conversation through him. He did not allow the spouses to attack one another and works to break the fusion of the couple. This is similar to doing individual therapy while the spouse watches. He hoped to develop empathy in each spouse for the other.

Stage 3: Negotiation—Usually, couples in early recovery have difficulty negotiating and problem solving because one spouse has been over-functioning in most areas and the other has been subordinated and treated like a child. Since the over-functioning spouse has developed some sense of worth, if not martyrdom, from the over-functioning, he or she may be reluctant to give up this hierarchical position. However, the other spouse has to find something to do in the family besides drink. Treadway (1989) teaches the couple how to put their feelings aside and work together effectively. He acts as an arbitrator in this process.

Stage 4: Conflict management—One of the most common dynamics of alcoholic or addicted families is the ever-present conflict. Conflict can occur during dry stages or wet stages. Substance abuse either dampens conflict or fuels it. Couples in early recovery try to avoid open conflict at all costs because they fear it will lead to drinking or using (Treadway, 1989). Couples need to learn how to tolerate conflict without letting it escalate out of control. Treadway's approach helps couples learn to tolerate unresolved conflict and to fight fairly.

Stage 5: Resolution of the past—Couples who have been struggling with substance abuse for years have a large storage vault full of hurt, anger, and resentment. As they begin to acknowledge the wasted years of dealing with addiction, unresolved pain from childhood may also emerge in this grief process. Treadway's goals for this stage are to unite the spouses around the shared pain and loss, instead of allowing the typical adversarial blaming of each other, as well as to help the couple come to a position of acceptance. Acceptance is not necessarily forgiveness because some things may not be forgivable, especially physical abuse, sexual abuse, affairs, or refusal to participate in sex (Treadway, 1989).

Stage 6: Intimacy—Intimacy and sexual behaviors are just as intertwined with substance abuse as conflict is. Sexual dysfunction and sexual abuse are common co-existing problems with chemical dependency. Intoxication may

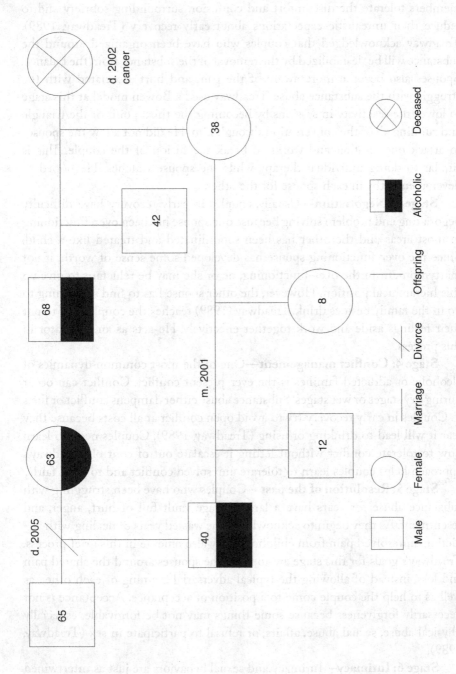

Figure 7.1. Sample of a genogram.

be connected with intimate behavior or avoidance of intimacy, and fear of intimacy can be a problem for adults who were raised in chemically dependent families. It is possible that neither spouse has ever seen a positive model of intimacy in a couple relationship. Treadway (1989) helped couples "separate reasonable expectations for intimacy from attempts to make up for unresolved family-of-origin needs. Coming to terms with their old grief in relationship to their original families is often a prerequisite to setting realistic expectations for their couple relationships" (p. 96). During this last stage of the treatment model, Treadway removed himself from the third point of the triangle and empowered the couple to take more leadership in the therapy and to become more self-reliant.

Couples may not go through all of the stages of the model or may come and go in therapy over a several-year period. This is, however, a good example of how Bowen theory and a focus on intergenerational issues can be used in treating chemical dependency.

Experiential Family Therapy

"Experiential family therapists focus on the subjective needs of the individual in the family and work to facilitate a family process that will address the individuality of each member" (Hanna & Brown, 1995, p. 13). They have elements of the intergenerational theorist, but they put more emphasis on emotional expression and growth. They also resemble the structural and strategic therapist in their focus on the present interactions in the therapy session. Experiential family therapy drew from individual humanistic theories that emphasized here-and-now experiences in therapy, Gestalt therapy, and encounter groups, as well. The arts and psychodrama impacted on techniques of family sculpting and family drawing.

The two most influential therapists in this school were Virginia Satir and Carl Whitaker. Satir began seeing families in her private practice in Chicago, and later joined Bateson, Haley, Jackson, and Weakland in Palo Alto, California, at the Mental Research Institute, where she added her perspectives to the Communications Model. She saw communications as a key factor in functional and dysfunctional relationships and believed that homeostasis was more valuable to a family than was an individual member's well-being. Satir (as cited in Hannah & Brown, 1995) also stated that parents bring their faulty patterns of communication to the marriage from their families of origin and that children learn these patterns in a multigenerational process. Satir's version of the Communications Model, however, grew to be a more holistic health model dedicated to self-esteem building, personal growth, and spirituality. Satir was a dynamic, nurturing therapist who genuinely cared for her fellow human beings. She was a master at creating peak experiences in therapy, with her gift of a healing touch that created family dramas in the therapy sessions. Her technique of *family sculpting* has been adapted by the chemical dependency field to help families experience their connections, boundaries, and hierarchies.

Satir (as cited in Hannah & Brown, 1995) developed four basic role types that family members typically adopt when dealing with crises, such as substance abuse, in the family:

1. The *placater* is a person who reduces tension by smoothing things over. The person may be a martyr, a role often played by the spouse of the person with alcoholism or addiction. The placater would avoid confrontation of abusive drinking behavior and deny personal emotions.

2. The *blamer* role is often played by people with low self-esteem who attack to keep the focus off themselves. The alcoholic plays this role by blaming others and by insisting that his or her drinking behavior was caused by the spouse's nagging or the children's misbehavior. The spouse can also shift to this role when conflict is high.

3. The *irrelevant* role is played by people in the family who avoid conflict by changing the subject, responding inappropriately, distracting others, or having temper tantrums.

4. The *superresponsible* role is characterized by ultareasonable communications. These people act calm, cool, and collected, but internally they feel vulnerable.

Satir would use these roles to create family sculptures so that families could experience from a symbolic and dramatic perspective the roles that they played in the family and how this was all part of a family dance in response to family stress or problems. She believed that these roles covered real feelings that people were afraid to share because of their low self-esteem. In her work, Satir clarified communications, helped families find solutions, supported each family member's self-esteem, and taught families how to touch and be affectionate.

Carl Whitaker was raised on an isolated dairy farm in New York. He attributed this experience of isolation to his shyness and his ability to connect with schizophrenic patients. He was originally trained as a doctor of obstetrics and gynecology but during World War II was pressed into working as a psychiatrist and became fascinated by patients with psychoses. Because he had no formal training in psychiatry, he was unencumbered by traditional ideas. Whitaker went on to establish a training program at Emory University but left with several of his colleagues to establish the Atlantic Psychiatric Clinic, where his version of experiential family therapy—Symbolic-Experiential Family Therapy—was further developed. Whitaker's theory evolved from his work with families with schizophrenia and from collaboration with other family therapists. The goal of his therapy was individual growth, as well as strengthening the family as a whole. He believed that personal growth requires family integration, and family integration depends on the personal growth of its members (Nichols & Schwartz, 2013). Toward this goal of growth, Whitaker created an experience in the therapy process that allowed for the growth. He valued experience for its own sake. He further believed that a therapist should approach a therapy session with the expectation that he or she would also experience growth from these existential encounters.

Whitaker often referred to his therapy as "therapy of the absurd," and he relied on his intuitions and the flashes of thoughts that were created by the encounter with the families. He talked of falling asleep in the sessions and dreaming about the family. Upon waking, he would tell the family what he had dreamed in a symbolic way. He was known to blurt out statements about the undercurrent of process in the family, such as, "Someone is having murderous thoughts!" "Whitaker advocates craziness—non-rational, creative experiencing and functioning—as a proper goal of therapy. If they let themselves become a little crazy, he believes, families will reap the rewards of zest, emotionality, and spontaneity" (Nichols & Schwartz, 1995, p. 299).

As opposed to Bowen, Whitaker liked to raise the anxiety of the family and create emotional exchanges. He believed that sometimes family members had to get angry with each other in order to clear the air and allow for closeness and loving feelings (Nichols & Schwartz, 1995).

Although these experiential therapists are difficult to emulate because their personalities were part of their therapies, their beliefs, goals, and processes can be adapted by others. Focusing on feelings, self-esteem, and the experiences of the therapy process can be useful in working with substance abusing families, who usually have low levels of self-esteem and a strong taboo about expressing feelings. They often need to learn to be spontaneous, loving, and growing individuals and families. Couples who have been struggling with addiction for long periods are full of anger, resentment, disappointment, and fear. Experiential therapy can be useful to help couples get beyond these stockpiles of negative emotions that keep them from growing in their recovery process.

Descriptions of the Alcoholic and Addict Family System

It was important to identify common characteristics of alcoholic families so that assessments and treatment strategies could focus on the recovery of the entire system. Many investigators have looked at the alcoholic family environment (Bowen, 1974; Davis, Stern, & Vandusen, 1978; Killorin & Olson, 1984; McLachlan, Walderman, & Thomas, 1973; Pringle, 1976). McLachlan et al. (1973) studied teenagers with alcoholic parents and found that a sense of secure family cohesiveness clearly differentiated the controls from the alcoholic families. The teenagers from alcoholic families had a much lower sense of family cohesiveness. Pringle (1976) reported that the alcoholic families of origin in his study were controlling, closed systems with little room for self-expression and strongly encouraged competition and achievement, whereas the nonalcoholic families of origin were more cohesive and supportive, and had more open expression and autonomy.

In his extensive writing about the alcoholic family system, Kaufman (1980, 1984, 1986) described four types of family reactivity patterns: (1) the functional family system, where family members have the ability to wall off and isolate alcoholic behavior; (2) the neurotic, enmeshed family system, where drinking behavior interrupts normal family tasks, causes conflict, shifts roles, and demands new adaptation; (3) the disintegrated family system, where the alcoholic is separated from the family, but they are still available for family therapy; and (4) the absent family system, which is marked by total loss of family of origin (Kaufman, 1984). He further stated, "There is now substantial evidence to conclude that family systems play a significant role in the genesis of alcoholism, as for example in the transmission of marital and family roles of alcoholism from one generation to the next" (Kaufman, 1984, p. 7). In his article "Myths and Realities in the Family Patterns and Treatment of Substance Abusers," Kaufman (1980) rejected myths about substance abusers' family patterns. He pointed out that families of drug abusers are very similar to families of alcohol abusers; however, the drug abuser may be a child, while the alcohol abuser may be the adult. In over half of the families with an identified patient with a drug problem, there is also a parent who is an alcoholic. He felt that the family plays an important part in the onset and perpetuation of substance abuse, yet it may not be the cause of all substance abuse. He also cautioned about overgeneralizing about alcoholic families and added that they vary according to ethnic background, sex of the alcoholic, and stage of life cycle of the family. He concluded that there is a need for more research in the area of substance abusing family environments and implications for directions in family therapy.

Kaufman (1991) reviewed his 1980 article on myth and reality in the field and concluded that counselors are learning more and more about the importance of the family in the root and maintenance of substance abuse. The field is acknowledging that there is more to the family system than the mother–son relationship, that the fathers are not all distant, that the mothers are not all enmeshed, and that there are unique dynamics in the family systems of various ethnic groups. Siblings are also incredibly important in family therapy. Kaufman further stated that though there is still controversy about whether one can treat a family with ongoing substance abuse, the majority of therapists working in the field agree that the substance abuse needs to be stopped before doing family therapy. This follows his previous statement that no study has demonstrated the need for abstinence for effective therapy, though many family therapists state that this is necessary (Pattison & Kaufman, 1981). Although in some cases family therapy may be needed as an interventive process to accomplish the sobriety, Kaufman believed this is part of the debate within the field on whether alcoholism or drug abuse is a symptom or a disease.

Kaufman also updated his subgroups of families of individuals with alcoholism or addiction. He thought that there are far fewer of the "functional families systems" than he first believed. These families were able to wall off and isolate alcoholic behavior. Berenson (1976) also proposed a Category 1 and a Category 2 of family systems with alcohol problems. Category 1 was similar to the functional family. These families agreed that alcohol was not a problem or was a minor problem, the problem was acute as opposed to chronic, there was only occasionally a family history of alcoholism, and the behavior change when drinking was slight and infrequent. The Category 2 family had high conflict about drinking, saw it as a chronic problem, usually had a family history of alcoholism, and often had intense behavior change when drinking. It is interesting to note that he describes the amount and pattern of drinking in both of these families as variable. This differentiation of categories was important because different treatment models were proposed for each category.

There was also a differentiation made among various states of operating within a single family in an attempt to understand the dynamics of the alcoholic family. Steinglass, Davis, and Berenson (1977) observed that families tend to maintain alcoholic behaviors. They studied the *adaptive consequences* of alcoholism by observing videotapes of families when the alcoholic was in a dry state and when drinking (the wet state). They found that the family was more relaxed and talkative when the alcoholic was intoxicated and more rigid and closed during dry states. Steinglass et al. further developed a model to demonstrate how drinking behavior is maintained. It is based on three concepts: "interactional behavior cycling between the sober state and the intoxicated state; patterning of behavior that has reached steady state; and the hypothesis that alcohol use in the alcoholic family has become incorporated into family problem solving behavior" (Steinglass, 1979, p. 167). Steinglass (1980) pointed out that chronic alcoholism produces distortions in the normative family lifecycle. Davis, Berenson, Steinglass, and Davis (1974) postulated that "alcohol abuse has adaptive consequences that are reinforcing enough to maintain the drinking behavior, regardless of its causative factors. These adaptive consequences may operate on different levels including intrapsychic, intracouple, or to maintain family homeostasis" (p. 210).

Killorin and Olson (1984) believed that, as a result of these adaptive consequences, the function of the symptom of alcoholism varies and so does the family style. Even though the families may have a common symptom, the way the system interacts can take many forms. Using Olson's Circumplex Model for evaluating family environment, alcoholic families fell into all 16 types of family systems (Olson & Killorin, 1987). They included disengaged as well as enmeshed systems and chaotic as well as rigid systems. Olson and Killorin (1987) compared chemically dependent families and non-dependent families. On the scale of cohesion (how connected families feel), about one-third of the chemically dependent families perceived their families as disengaged compared to 7% of the non-dependent. In terms of family adaptability, over 40% of the chemically dependent families saw themselves as chaotic, while only 8% of the non-dependent families rated themselves as chaotic.

Several studies have evaluated the alcoholic family environment (Moos, Bromet, Tse, & Moos, 1979; Moos, Finney, & Gamble, 1982; Moos & Moos, 1976, 1984). Moos et al. (1979) investigated poor follow-ups for individuals addicted to alcohol 6 to 8 months after inpatient treatment for alcoholism. Their family environments revealed more conflict and control problems and less cohesion, expressiveness, active-recreational orientation, intellectual-cultural orientation, and moral-religious emphasis than those patients who had follow-up treatment. Additionally, Moos and Moos (1984) compared families of re-covered alcoholics and families of relapsed alcoholics two years after residential treatment. The recovered alcoholic families did not differ from the control fam-ilies (families without alcoholism). The relapsed families showed less cohesion (the amount of support family members give and receive), expressiveness (ex-pression of feelings), and recreational orientation (playing together as a family).

Filstead, McElfresh, and Anderson (1981) took a look at the overall family environment of the alcoholic family and compared it to the non-alcoholic fam-ily environment. Data were collected on 42 white families, 59% of which had male members who were alcoholic. Each family member completed the Moos Family Environment Scale covering 10 dimensions of family life conceptu-ally organized around relationships, personal growth, and system maintenance dimensions. These scores were compared to the normal non-clinic group of families previously used by Moos. The alcoholic families perceived their family environments to be much less cohesive and expressive; perceived less emphasis on the independence of individuals, intellectual-cultural activities (like read-ing and valuing the arts), active-recreational concerns, and organizational tasks than did the so-called normal families. The alcoholic families also reported a much higher level of conflict than did the normal families (Filstead et al., 1981). This same pattern was found in the families of origin of adult children of alcoholics who themselves became alcoholic and adult children of alcoholics who did not develop alcoholism, and these ACOAs created similar patterns in their nuclear families (Lawson, 1988).

There appears to be a set of family dynamics that are common to many families struggling with addiction. These include a lack of support for family members and a low sense of belonging; a high degree of conflict and fighting;

an absence of expression of feelings; difficulties in accepting individual differences and opinions; an expectation of achievement from family members but a lack of modeling intellectual and cultural pursuits; and a lack of family recreational experiences and playing. Although not all families battling addictions have these dynamics, these are good areas of assessment for counselors. When these problems are found in families, goals can be set to modify these dynamics.

The Intergenerational Transmission of Alcoholism

The multigenerational aspect of addictions is a consistent finding in the field of families and addiction. The most important question for the field of addiction prevention is: How do alcoholism and other addictions transmit from generation to generation or even jump generations in families? Families that seem to function in the face of addiction and do not transmit these addictions to the offspring hold important clues to prevention and treatment.

To determine how the family environment may be a transmitter of alcoholism, researchers investigated the importance of family rituals (Bennett, Wolin, Reiss, & Teitelbaum, 1987; Steinglass, Bennett, Wolin, & Reiss, 1987; Wolin & Bennett, 1984). Wolin et al. (1979) studied a group of 25 families of middle- and upper-class background and European origin. All families included at least one parent who met investigators' criteria for the identification of an alcoholic or problem drinker. Structured individual interviews that covered personal history of the interviewee and the continuity of family heritage from the grandparents' generation into the current nuclear family provided information into seven areas of family rituals: (1) dinnertime, (2) holidays, (3) evenings, (4) weekends, (5) vacations, (6) visitors in the home, and (7) discipline. These investigators defined family rituals as patterns of behavior that have meaning beyond their practical outcome or function. "Patterned behavior is behavior that is repetitive, stable with respect to roles, and continues over time" (Wolin et al., 1979, p. 590). They believed that these rituals were important because they "stabilize ongoing family life by clarifying expectable roles, delineating boundaries within and without the family, and defining rules so that all family members know that 'this is the way our family is'" (Wolin et al., 1979, p. 590). Steinglass et al. (1987) stated, "Family rituals are, in effect, condensed, prepackaged training modules intended to convey to all family members the important facts about family identity" (p. 309).

Wolin et al. (1979) identified three types of families:

1. **Distinctive families,** in which rituals did not change during drinking episodes

2. **Intermediate subsumptive families**, which rejected intoxicated behavior when it was present

3. **Subsumptive families**, in which drinking changed the "fabric of the family" and disrupted the family life highly

They found that families whose rituals were disrupted or changed during the period of heaviest drinking by the alcoholic parent were more likely to transmit alcoholism to the younger generation than were families whose rituals remained intact. The more alcoholism became a central organizing force in the family and a disruption to the family rituals, the more the children were at risk for developing alcoholism. The non-transmitter families had one outstanding quality in common: "rejection of the intoxication of the alcoholic parent openly or privately, or talking about his or her behavior disapprovingly" (Wolin et al., 1979, p. 591).

To follow up this study, Bennett et al. (1987) interviewed 68 married children of alcoholic parents and their spouses regarding dinnertime and holiday rituals in their families of origin and in the couples' current generations. They identified 14 predictor variables that contributed significantly ($p < .01$) to the couples' alcoholism outcomes. The children of alcoholics who remained nonalcoholic had limited attachments to their families of origin or selective disengagements, and the families of origin had been able to separate the rituals from the alcoholism. Specifically, they found that the couples who were most resistant to transmission lived 200 miles away from their families of origin and visited them two times per year.

In summation of these ritual studies, Steinglass et al. (1987) said the following:

> We believe that the transmission of alcoholism from one generation to the next involves the whole family system over time. The context for transmission is the sum total of interactions, attitudes, and beliefs that define the family. The process is ongoing and dynamic and has no particular beginning, end, or pivotal event. And it often goes on outside the awareness of the participants involved, the "senders" as well as the "receivers." (p. 304)

Another concept that Bennett et al. (1988) proposed as a risk-reducing factor is "deliberateness." They argue that families with serious problems, such as parental alcoholism, that can still impose control over those parts of family life that are central to the family's identity communicate important messages to their children regarding their ability to take control of present and future life events. These messages, in turn, can play an important role in the extent to which the offspring are protected from developing problems in childhood, as well as alcoholism in adolescence and adulthood.

Spouse selection in a deliberate way, establishment by the couple of their own family rituals and heritage, participation in institutions of the community, and selective disengagement from the families of origin are strategies proposed by this group of researchers to reduce the transmission of alcoholism across generations. This is important information for family therapists working with newly constituted families who are concerned about their own risk for addictive disorders and transmission of these disorders to their own children.

A common theme in research on intergenerational transmission of familial alcoholism is that a "supportive other" is less often reported as present by those children of alcoholics who become alcoholic (Booz-Allen & Hamilton, Inc., 1974; Lawson, 1988; O'Sullivan, 1991; Simmons, 1991). Booz-Allen and Hamilton, Inc. (1974) listed "having a supportive person" in the family as a risk reducer for children of alcoholics. Lawson (1988) found that adult children of alcoholics who were not alcoholic themselves perceived their families of origin as more cohesive and supportive than did adult children of alcoholics who became alcoholic themselves. In looking at these supportive others, O'Sullivan (1991) related the presence of a childhood mentoring relationship to resiliency in adult children of alcoholics. Even in families with alcoholic fathers and families with psychiatrically disturbed fathers, the presence of a "healthy" mother produced young adults who appeared as well adjusted as the control group of young adults whose parents had neither alcoholism nor psychiatric problems (Simmons, 1991). Healthy mothers were defined in this study as having no diagnosis of substance abuse or psychiatric disorder. The common message of these studies seems to be that children can emerge from dysfunctional, substance-abusing families with some degree of resilience if they receive some nurturing and guidance from someone in the family or even someone outside of the family system. From a prevention standpoint, this cohesion and support in families seems to provide a buffering effect against the damage done to children in dysfunctional families.

Jacob, Seilhamer, and Rushe (1989) observed intact families under a broad range of conditions, including laboratory observations involving experimental drinking procedures and naturalistic home observations focused on dinnertime interactions. They were interested in the impact of alcoholism on the process and structure of family life, the degree to which varying patterns of family interactions served to potentiate or inhibit the development of alcoholism in children of alcoholics, and the degree that patterns varied in relation to alcoholism versus depression. Steady, in-home drinking seemed to have a more positive impact on family life than did episodic drinking. The steady, in-home drinkers and their wives engaged in more productive problem solving during the drink versus non-drink conditions. This is constant with the "adaptive consequences" theory of alcoholism. They admit that causality cannot be determined, but the study did underscore how the interplay of familial stressors associated with alcohol abuse, parental psychiatric status, and the mother's ability to mediate negative impacts on the child.

In viewing adult children of alcoholics' responses to parental drinking styles, Tarter (1991) found that the same drinking style that Jacob et al. (1989) found to be a productive problem-solving style for the alcoholic couple was the most problem-creating style for the adult child of an alcoholic who grew up in this drinking-style family. As compared to adult children of alcoholics from "binge drinker at home," "binge drinker away," and "daily away drinker" groups, daily at-home drinkers produced adult children of alcoholics who rated their families of origin as the most unhealthy of the four groups (on the Family of Origin Scale). These adult children of alcoholics, who had daily at-home drinking parents, reported that they had more alcohol problems (Michigan Alcoholism Screening Test [MAST]) and depression (Beck Depression Scale) than did members of the other three groups.

The family system studies have added another dimension to the nature-versus-nurture controversy in the etiology of alcoholism. It is quite possible that there is no one etiological prescription for alcoholism. Genetics may play a major role in the father–son transmission of alcoholism, whereas family environment may have more of an impact on women's alcoholism. Finding family environment patterns that predispose children for alcoholism is important because it may be possible to prevent alcoholism in these children by changing patterns through family therapy and parent training.

Resilient Children of Alcoholics

Not all children of alcoholics are the same. Some suffer greatly from living in substance-abusing families, whereas others from similar families appear much less scarred. Wolin and Wolin (1993) and Jacobs and Wolin (1991) identified children who are less affected as resilient children, who as adults are working well, playing well, and loving well. They call their model of resiliency the Challenge Model because these children see the adversity of a troubled childhood as a challenge. This is in contrast to the Damage Model that so much mental health is based on, which says that a troubled family damages the child, who then has childhood pathologies and succumbs to have only pathology in adolescence and adulthood. The Challenge Model says that the troubled family creates damages and challenges that create child pathologies and resiliencies. The child both succumbs and rebounds to having both pathologies and resiliencies in adolescence and adulthood.

The idea that some children of alcoholics are resilient is not a new idea. Werner (1986), in a longitudinal study, focused on child characteristics and the qualities of the caregiving environment that differentiated children of alcoholics who developed serious problems by the age 18 and those who did not. The study consisted of 49 subjects of multiracial backgrounds, born in 1955 on the island of Kauai, Hawaii. They were evaluated at ages 1, 2, 10, and 18. She found that males and offspring of alcoholic mothers had higher rates of psychosocial problems in childhood and adolescence than females and the offspring of alcoholic fathers. Children of alcoholics who did not develop serious coping skills were different from those who did in characteristics of temperament, communication skills, self-concept, and locus of control. These resilient children also experienced fewer stressful life events that disrupted the family unit in the first two years of their lives.

Wolin and Wolin (1993) developed a list of seven resiliencies that they believe develop out of the challenge to maintain self-esteem in the face of the troubled family's neglect, criticism, physical abuse, denial, and pull to engulf its members in the emotional turmoil. These resiliencies may be innate. "Early signs of these resiliencies can be found in the first memories of successful survivors and can be traced in progressive stages through their childhood, adolescence, and adulthood" (Jacobs & Wolin, 1991, p. 9). These seven resiliencies are insight, independence, relationships, initiative, creativity, humor, and morality. Each resiliency has a child, adolescent, and adult manifestation.

Insight—This is a psychological sophistication, an early sensing that something is wrong with the troubled parent(s). By adolescence, this sensing becomes a knowing. Children understand the family dynamics and attribute the family's problems to factors outside of themselves. In adulthood, the knowing becomes understanding about themselves and others.

Independence—This is the ability to live apart yet relate to others without pressures or demands. The early sign of independence is straying away from the family. Adolescents realize that distance feels better than closeness, and they move from staying to disengaging emotionally from their families. As adults, they separate from their families in a freely chosen, rational way. This is reminiscent of Bowen's ideas of a healthy differentiation from the family of origin.

Relationships—This is a connecting, a selective process where children can bond with parents or others. Early in life, children with this resiliency begin interacting with the healthier parts of their families. As they get older, they begin connecting with neighbors, teachers, coaches, and other substitutes for parents. As adults, they bond with friends, spouses, children, and siblings. The two resiliencies of independence and relationships can be seen as a common goal of all of the family therapy theories. Family therapists try to help families develop a sense of belonging or cohesion, while allowing for the independence and individuality of their members.

Initiative—This is the ability to recover from adversity, with an accompanying deep sense of self-trust and personal control—survivor's pride. Survivors love a challenge. This begins with optimistic exploring, grows in adolescents to working, and, in adulthood, becomes generating.

Creativity and Humor—These resiliencies are linked and share common processes. Creativity is the ability to express and resolve inner conflicts in symbolic form through the arts or in ways that have aesthetic value. Humor is the ability to laugh at oneself and use play as an emotional healer. Young children play with their imaginations to protect them from the trauma of their family life. Shaping is the refinement of playing in adolescence. It adds discipline and effort to art production. The adult version of creativity is composing, and the adult version of humor is laughing. Wolin and Wolin (1993) describe creativity as making nothing into something, and humor as making something into nothing. Children with this resilience could benefit greatly from creative arts therapies.

Morality—This is the activity of an informed conscience. Young children want to know why things happen, and begin judging the rights and wrongs of daily life and their parents. In adolescence, this judging changes into valuing decency, compassion, honesty, and fair play. In adulthood, these survivors serve others even though they did not receive what they deserved in their families. They restore themselves by helping others.

Wolin and Wolin (1993) outlined Challenge Model Therapy in a presentation. The goal of the therapy is to change a survivor's view of him- or herself from damaged goods to one who prevails. This is a five-step process:

Step 1: Begin with damage—This stage begins with building trust and empathy and allowing the damage to be discussed and felt. The therapist takes a complete history of the damage story and helps the survivor see how the consequences are experienced in adulthood.

Step 2: Select one resiliency—The therapist identifies the most easily accepted resilience; returns to the history of damage and questions the resilient behavior in detail; and acknowledges both the damage and the strength. The therapist should expect resistance to acceptance of the resilience and should compliment appropriate behavior.

Step 3: Explore remaining resiliencies—The therapist should know all three stages of each resilience and try to reframe all seven to fit with the survivor's story. The therapist should work with the resistances and accept areas of moderate to little resilience.

Step 4: Build a new narrative—At this stage, the therapist offers explanations of the resiliencies and the damage. The therapist teaches that the survivor had a false mirroring of blame from his or her family, yet somehow has been inoculated against contracting all of the problems of the family. Therapists need to foster survivor's pride and should observe the shifting balance between damage and resilience.

Step 5: Apply resiliencies to current problems—The therapist can use the "chunking down" technique of Gravitz and Bowden (1984) to break problems into smaller components. Therapists at this stage apply insight to the weakest areas of resilience; help survivors attempt independence, more or less, and create healthy relationships; and instruct survivors on how to initiate and establish family rituals.

Evaluation of Family Therapy Treatment of Alcoholism

Treatment outcome research is even more limited than the acceptance of family therapy as a treatment for alcoholism. Treatment outcome data are needed to establish family therapy as a proven successful model. Some studies look at progress by measuring family problems pre-, post-, and during follow-up treatment. Other studies compare family therapy to individual or group treatment. This research is difficult, expensive, and time-consuming.

Edwards and Steinglass (1995) conducted a meta-analysis of 21 of these studies of family-involved therapy for alcoholism. They evaluated them for design adequacy, clinical significance, and effect size. They divided the studies into three phases of treatment: (1) initiation of treatment, (2) primary treatment/rehabilitation, and (3) aftercare.

They found in the first phase that family therapy was effective in motivating alcoholics to enter treatment. These studies included three approaches: The intervention model, unilateral family therapy, and community reinforcement training. The intervention model involved training friends of the alcoholic and family members in four to five 2-hour sessions to stage a formal confrontation of the alcoholic. This was the method used by the Long Beach Naval Station to get Betty Ford into treatment. A single study was done to compare families who used this confrontation method with those who did not (Liepman, Silvia, & Nirenberg, 1989). The families who used interventions had more success in getting the alcoholic person to enter alcohol detoxification or rehabilitation programs than those who did not (86% vs. 17%). The confronted alcoholics were continually abstinent for 11 months compared to 2.8 months for those who did not have an intervention.

Unilateral family therapy (UFT) is a more-extensive model of treatment, and includes an intervention option. The model includes an initial assessment, alcohol education, unilateral relationship enhancement, disenabling, neutralizing old alcohol-control behaviors, preparation for alcoholic-directed interventions (such as confrontation), request and contracting, support for maintenance of gains, relapse prevention training, and help for the spouse in disengaging from his or her alcoholic partner and the drinking problem, combined with help for dealing with emotional problems. Two studies tested the effect of UFT in getting the alcoholic to enter treatment and in reducing drinking. Thomas, Santa, Bronson, and Oyserman (1987) reported that if the spouses of alcoholics participated in UFT, the alcoholics were more likely to be rated "improved" than those whose spouse did not participate (61% vs. 0%). UFT participation also decreased drinking by 53% and reduced spouses' life distress. A larger study (Thomas, Yoshioka, Ager, & Adams, 1993) also found improved motivation to enter treatment, reduction in drinking, and, at follow-up, that the UFT was more improved (57% vs. 31%).

A study by Sisson and Azrin (1986), the last study in the first phase, evaluated community reinforcement training (CRT). CRT for non-drinking spouses instructed participants on how to reduce physical abuse, how to encourage sobriety by reinforcing the alcoholic for periods of sobriety and giving negative consequences for drinking, and how to encourage treatment. CRT, similar to UFT, is based on social learning principles. When CRT was compared to traditional treatment for spouses, it was more successful in getting alcoholics into treatment (86% vs. 0%) and increased the amount of abstinence in the alcoholics—even though they were not in treatment—from 20% to 63%.

The second-phase studies examined primary treatment or rehabilitation. Family-therapy treatment models fell into two categories: (1) family systems–orientated approaches, characterized by a focus on interaction patterns and the regulation of internal and external environments, and (2) behaviorally oriented approaches, all of which are based on social learning theory and include concepts such as reinforcement, reciprocity, and coercion (Edwards & Steinglass, 1995).

The family systems group comprised four studies. The first was a study of a psychoeducational couples group (CT), which was compared to treatment without spouse involvement (Corder, Corder, & Laidlaw, 1972). At a 6-month follow-up, the CT subjects were more abstinent than those without CT were (58% vs. 15%).

Cadogan (1973) tested a longer program that involved having alcoholics and their spouses attend weekly multiple-couples therapy for 3 to 6 months. When they compared this group to a waiting-list group, they found no differences in marital satisfaction, but they did find a higher abstinence rate (45% vs. 10%).

McCrady, Paolino, Longabaugh, and Rosi (1979) compared individual therapy for alcoholics (I) with treatment that involved individual group therapy for the spouse and the alcoholic combined with couples group therapy (CI) and with joint admission therapy (JA) where both the alcoholic and spouse participated in the entire program. In a 6-month follow-up, both couples groups were more abstinent (61% for JA and 83% for CI) than the subjects in individual treatment (43%). Although there was improvement from pre- to posttest on marital measures, there was no difference between groups. In a four-year follow-up of these subjects (McCrady, Moreau, & Paolino, 1982), there were no differences between the groups. Abstinence rates had dropped below the 50% baseline for clinical significance (33% for JA, 13% for CI, and 14% for I). The effectiveness of these treatments diminished with time.

The fourth study evaluated a treatment program for couples designed to impact the adaptive consequences of alcoholism and the role it played in the family's typical patterns of living (Zweben, Perlman, & Li, 1988). This eight-session program (CT) was compared to a single session of advice counseling (AC) attended by the spouse and alcoholic. At the 6-month follow-up, subjects in both groups had increased abstinence (36% to 52% for CT and 29% to 58% for AC). They also decreased their percentage of heavy-drinking days. In general, family systems models seem to do better than individual treatment initially, but the results diminish in the long run.

Six groups of researchers have conducted studies of family-involved treatment models. The earliest was Hedberg and Campbell (1974), who tested four types of behavioral treatment. One treatment involved the entire nuclear family, the members of which were allowed to pick either abstinence or controlled drinking as a goal—behavioral family therapy. The other three treatments were electric shock treatment, covert sensitization, and systematic desensitization. All four treatments consisted of 20 sessions conducted over 6 months, with 14 of these sessions occurring in the first 8 weeks of treatment. Behavioral family counseling (80%) and systematic desensitization (60%) were more effective than the other two treatments in achieving abstinence (36% for covert sensitization, 0% for electric shock).

The community reinforcement approach (CRA) involves increasing social reinforcers to interfere with drinking, including marital counseling. A series of studies were done comparing CRA with a traditional program (Azrin, 1976; Azrin, Sisson, Meyers, & Godley 1982; Hunt & Azrin, 1973; Sisson & Azrin, 1986). At 6-month follow-up, the first study showed a higher abstinence rate in the CRA group (86% vs. 21%). The model was improved, and the next study reported 96% abstinence compared to 45% in the traditional treatment group. Antabuse was added as a component to the behavioral treatment (BTDA) and, at 6-month follow-up, there was again an increase in abstinence rates (97% for BTA, 74% for Antabuse only, and 45% for traditional treatment).

The third group of investigators compared various behavioral couples treatments (McCrady, Noel, & Abrams, 1986). These models were minimal spouse involvement (MSI), alcohol-focused spouse involvement (AFSI), and alcohol behavioral marital treatment (ABMT). The pretreatment to 6-month follow-up percentages of abstinent days were 26% to 88% for MSI, 36% to 75% for AFSI, and 25% to 80% for ABMT. At 6-month follow-up, however, none of the groups had significant abstinence levels. This model was also tested with the addition of an occupational component by the fourth group of investigators, who found significant improvements (Stout, McCrady, Longabaugh, Noel, & Beattie, 1987).

The fifth group of researchers compared behavioral marital therapy (BMT) to a more systemic marital, interactional couples therapy (ICT) and to a standard individual treatment (ST) (O'Farrell, Cutter, & Floyd, 1985). At posttreatment, all three groups increased abstinence (43% to 99% for BMT, 46% to 83% for ICT, and 21% to 91% for ST). The couples in the marital therapy groups showed improvements in their marriages, and the couples in the standard treatment did not. Gains in abstinence and marital adjustment diminished at both follow-up surveys.

In Phase III studies, researchers investigated the value of involving families in the aftercare portion of the treatment. One aftercare study looked at a group of inpatients discharged from a 28-day treatment program. The experimental contingent of these patients received a contract/calendar (CC) intervention, which involved a contract between the spouses to reward attendance at aftercare and to display a calendar with the dates or meetings marked in red. This group did better at 6 months posttreatment than those who did not get the intervention. They attended more sessions of aftercare. At 12 months, the CC group was significantly more abstinent (61% vs. 21%) and had more functioning days when they consumed less than two ounces of alcohol (Ahles, Schlundt, Prue, & Rychtarik, 1983).

Two groups of couples were compared by O'Farrell and his colleagues (O'Farrell, Choquette, Cutter, Brown, & McCourt, 1993) to determine if adding a relapse prevention component to behavioral marital therapy (BMT), which included an Antabuse contract, would improve abstinence rates. The group that received the relapse prevention at the end of the program was more abstinent than the group who received only BMT was (94% vs. 82%).

In summary, Edwards and Steinglass (1995) concluded that family therapy was effective for motivating alcoholics to enter treatment. But, once the drinker enters treatment, the effect of family therapy is just slightly better than individual treatment. They believe that three factors mediate the effectiveness of family therapy: gender, investment in the relationship, and perceived support from the spouse for abstinence. Also, modest benefits have been demonstrated from spouse involvement in aftercare. The most-recent studies are addressing these issues by developing treatment models for women alcoholics and identifying factors that could be used to match appropriate treatments to alcoholics and their families.

In this chapter, we have attempted to help counselors view the entire family as a client in need of treatment. Counselors interested in developing their family therapy skills and working with families should continue to research family therapy practices, attend workshops or take classes in family therapy, and find a good supervisor. A list of suggested reading for counselors who want to learn more about becoming a family therapist is included at the end of this chapter.

References

Ahles, T. A., Schlundt, D. G., Prue, D. M., & Rychtarik, R. G. (1983). Impact of aftercare arrangements on the maintenance of treatment success in abusive drinkers. *Addictive Behaviors, 8,* 53–58.

Alexander, J. F. (1974). Behavior modification and delinquent youth. In J. C. Cull & R. E. Hardy (Eds.), *Behavior modification in rehabilitation settings* (pp. 79–92). Springfield, IL: Charles C. Thomas.

Azrin, N. H. (1976). Improvements in the community reinforcement approach to alcoholism. *Behavior Research and Therapy, 14,* 339–348.

Azrin, N. H., Sisson, R. W., Meyers, R., & Godley, M. (1982). Alcoholism treatment by disulfiram and community reinforcement therapy. *Journal of Behavior Therapy and Experimental Psychiatry, 13,* 105–112.

Bandler, R., Grender, J., & Satir, V. (1976). *Changing with families.* Palo Alto, CA: Science & Behavior Books.

Barnard, C. P. (1981). *Families, alcoholism and therapy.* Springfield, IL: Charles C Thomas.

Barry H., & Blane, H. T. (1977). Birth positions of alcoholics. *Journal of Individual Psychology, 33,* 62–69.

Bateson, G., Jackson, D., Haley, J., & Weakland, J. (1956). Toward a theory of schizophrenia. *Behavioral Science, 1,* 251–264.

Bennett, L. A., Wolin, S. J., & Reiss, D. (1988). Deliberate family process: A strategy for protecting children of alcoholics. *British Journal of Addiction, 83,* 821–829.

Bennett, L. A., Wolin, S. J., Reiss, D., & Teitelbaum, M. A. (1987). Couples at risk for transmission of alcoholism: Protective influences. *Family Process, 26,* 111–129.

Berenson, D. (1976). Alcohol and the family system. In P. Guerin (Ed.), *Family therapy: Theory and practice* (pp. 284–297). New York: Gardner Press.

Black, C. (1979, Fall). Children of alcoholics. *Alcohol Health and Research World,* 23–27.

Black, C. (1981a). Innocent bystanders at risk: The children of alcoholics. *Alcoholism,* 22–25.

Black, C. (1981b). *It will never happen to me.* Denver: M. A. C. Publishers.

Booz-Allen & Hamilton, Inc. (1974). *An assessment of the needs of and resources for children of alcoholic parents.* Rockville, MD: National Institute on Alcohol Abuse and Alcoholism.

Boszormenyi-Nagy, I., & Spark, G. (1973). *Invisible loyalties.* New York: Harper & Row.

Bowen, M. (1974). Alcoholism as viewed through family systems theory and family psychotherapy. *Annals of the New York Academy of Science, 233,* 115–122.

Bowen, M. (1978). Alcoholism and the family. In *Family therapy in clinical practice* (pp. 45–50). Northvale, NJ: Jason Aronson.

Boye-Beaman, J., Leonard, K. E., & Senchak, M. (1991). Assortative mating, relationship development, and intimacy among offspring of alcoholics. *Family Dynamics of Addiction Quarterly, 1*(2), 20–33.

Cadogan, D. A. (1973). Marital group therapy in the treatment of alcoholism. *Quarterly Journal of the Study of Alcohol, 34*, 1187–1194.

Carter, E., & McGoldrick, M. (1980). *The family life cycle: A framework for family therapy.* New York: Gardner Press.

Corder, B. F., Corder, R. F., & Laidlaw, N. C. (1972). An intensive treatment program for alcoholics and their wives. *Quarterly Journal of the Study of Alcohol, 33*, 1144–1146.

Davidson, M. (1983). *Uncommon sense: The life and thought of Ludwig von Bertalanffy.* Los Angeles: J. P. Tarcher.

Davis, D.I., Berenson, D., Steinglass, P., & Davis, S. (1974). The adaptive consequences of drinking. *Psychiatry, 37*, 209–215.

Davis, P., Stern, D. R., & Vandusen, J. M. (1978). Enmeshment-disengagement in the alcoholic family. In F. A. Seixas (Ed.), *Currents in alcoholism: Vol. 4. Psychological, social and epidemiological studies* (pp. 197–199). San Diego: Grune & Stratton.

Edwards, M. E., & Steinglass, P. (1995). Family therapy treatment outcomes for alcoholism. *Journal of Marital and Family Therapy, 21*(4), 475–509.

Ewing, I. A., & Fox, R. E. (1968). Family therapy of alcoholism. In A. Messerman (Ed.), *Current psychotherapies* (pp. 279–280). San Diego: Grune & Stratton.

Filstead, W. J., McElfresh, O., & Anderson, C. (1981). Comparing the family environments of alcoholics and "normal" families. *Journal of Alcohol and Drug Education, 26*, 24–31.

Framo, J. L. (1972). Symptoms from a family transactional viewpoint. In C. Sager & H. S. Kaplan (Eds.), *Progress in group and family therapy* (pp. 125–171). New York: Brunner/Mazel Publishers.

Framo, J. L. (1976). Family of origin as a therapeutic resource for adults in marital and family therapy: You can and should go home again. *Family Process, 15*, 193–209.

Framo, J. L. (1991). *Family of origin therapy: An intergenerational approach.* New York: Brunner/Mazel Publishers.

Friedman, A. S., Tomko, L. A., & Utada, A. (1991). Client and family characteristics that predict better family therapy outcome for adolescent drug abusers. *Family Dynamics of Addiction Quarterly, 1*(1), 77–93.

Gravitz, H., & Bowden, J. (1984, Summer). Therapeutic issues of alcoholic children of alcoholics: A longitudinal study. *Journal of Studies on Alcohol, 47*(1), 34–40.

Haley, J. (1976). *Problem solving therapy.* New York: Harper & Row.

Hanna, S. B., & Brown, J. H. (1995). *The practice of family therapy: Key elements across models.* Pacific Grove, CA: Brooks/Cole Publishing.

Hedberg, A. G., & Campbell, L. (1974). A comparison of four behavioral treatments of alcoholism. *Journal of Behavioral Therapy and Experimental Psychiatry, 5*, 251–256.

Hunt, G. M., & Azrin, N. H. (1973). The community reinforcement approach to alcoholism. *Behavior Research and Therapy, 11*, 91–104.

Jackson, D. D. (1957). The question of family homeostasis. *Psychiatric Quarterly Supplement, 31*, 79–90.

Jacob, T., Seilhamer, R. A., & Rushe, R. H. (1989). Alcoholism and family interaction: An experimental paradigm. *American Journal of Drug and Alcohol Abuse, 15*(1), 73–91.

Jacobs, J., & Wolin, S. J. (1991, October). *Resilient children growing up in alcoholic families*. Paper presented at the National Consensus Symposium on Children of Alcoholics and Co-Dependence, Warrenton, VA.

Joanning, H., Quinn, W., Thomas, F., & Mullen, R. (1992). Treating adolescent drug abuse: A comparison of family systems therapy, group therapy, and family drug education. *Journal of Marital and Family Therapy, 18*(4), 345–356.

Kaufman, E. (1980). Myths and realities in the family patterns and treatment of substance abusers. *American Journal of Drug and Alcohol Abuse, 7*(3 & 4), 257–279.

Kaufman, E. (1984). Family system variables in alcoholism. *Alcoholism: Clinical and Experimental Research, 8*(1), 4–8.

Kaufman, E. (1986). The family of the alcoholic patient. *Psychosomatics, 27*(5), 347–358.

Kaufman, E. (1991). An interview with Edward Kaufman, M.D. *Family Dynamics of Addiction Quarterly, 1*(3) 1–11.

Killorin, E., & Olson, D. (1984). The chaotic flippers in treatment. In E. Kaufman (Ed.), *Power to change: Alcoholism* (pp. 184–187). New York: Gardner Press.

Lawson, A. (1988). The relationship of past and present family environments of adult children of alcoholics. (Doctoral dissertation, U.S. International University, San Diego) *Dissertation Abstracts International, 49*(07), 1989.

Lawson, A., & Lawson, G. (1998). *Alcoholism and the family: A guide to treatment and prevention* (2nd ed.). Austin, TX: PRO-ED.

Lewis, R. A. (1991). Testimony before the house select committee on children, families, drugs and alcoholism. Hearing on adolescent substance abuse: Barriers to treatment, 101st Cong.

Lewis, R. A., Piercy, F. P., Sprenkle, D. H., & Trepper, T. S. (1991). The Purdue brief family therapy model for adolescent substance abusers. In T. Todd & M. Selekman (Eds.), *Family therapy approaches with adolescent substance abusers* (pp. 29–48). Boston: Allyn & Bacon.

Liepman, M. R., Silvia, L. Y., & Nirenberg, T. D. (1989). The use of family behavior loop mapping for substance abuse. *Family Relations, 38*, 282–287.

McCrady, B. S., Moreau, J., & Paolino, T. J. (1982). Joint hospitalization and couples therapy for alcoholism: A four-year follow-up. *Journal of Studies on Alcohol, 43*, 1244–1250.

McCrady, B. S., Noel, N. E., & Abrams, D. B. (1986). Comparative effectiveness of three types of spouse involvement in outpatient behavioral alcoholism treatment. *Journal of Studies on Alcohol, 47*, 459–467.

McCrady, B. S., Paolino, T. F., Longabaugh, R., & Rosi, J. (1979). Effects of joint hospital admission and couples treatment for hospitalized alcoholics: A pilot study. *Addictive Behaviors, 4*, 155–165.

McGoldrick, M., & Gerson, R. (1985). *Genograms in family assessment.* New York: W. W. Norton.

McLachlan, J. F. C., Walderman, R. L., & Thomas, S. (1973). *A study of teenagers with alcoholic parents* (Research Monograph, No. 3). Toronto, Canada: Donwood Institute.

Meeks, D., & Kelly, C. (1970). Family therapy with the families of recovering alcoholics. *Quarterly Journal of Studies on Alcoholism, 31*(2), 399–413.

Minuchin, S. (1974). *Families and family therapy*. Cambridge, MA: Harvard University Press.

Minuchin, S., Rosman, B., & Baker, L. (1978). *Psychosomatic families: Anorexia nervosa in context*. Cambridge, MA: Harvard University Press.

Moos, R. H., Bromet, E., Tse, V., & Moos, B. S. (1979). Family characteristics and the outcome of treatment of alcoholism. *Journal of Studies on Alcohol, 40*(1), 78–88.

Moos, R. H., Finney, J. W., & Gamble, W. (1982). The process of recovery from alcoholism. *Journal of Studies on Alcohol, 43*(9), 888–909.

Moos, R. H., & Moos, B. S. (1976). A typology of family social environment. *Family Process, 15*(4), 357-70.

Moos, R. H., & Moos, B. S. (1984). The process of recovery from alcoholism: 3. Comparing functioning in families of alcoholics and matched control families. *Journal of Studies on Alcohol, 45*(2), 111–117.

Nardi, P. (1981). Children of alcoholics: A role-theoretical perspective. *Journal of Social Psychology, 115*, 237–245.

Nichols, M. P., & Schwartz, R. C. (1995). *Family therapy: Concepts and methods*. Boston: Allyn & Bacon.

Nichols, M. P., & Schwartz, R. C. (2013). *Family therapy: Concepts and methods*. (10th ed.). Boston: Allyn & Bacon.

O'Farrell, T. J., Choquette, K. A., Cutter, H. S. G., Brown, E. D., & McCourt, W. (1993). Behavioral marital therapy with and without additional couples relapse prevention sessions for alcoholics and their wives. *Journal of Studies on Alcohol, 54*, 652–666.

O'Farrell, T. J., Cutter, H. S. G., & Floyd, F. J. (1985). Evaluating behavioral marital therapy for male alcoholics: Effects of marital adjustment and communication from before to after treatment. *Behavior Therapy, 16*, 147–167.

Olson, D. H., & Killorin, E. A. (1987). *Chemically dependent families and the circumplex model*. Unpublished research report, University of Minnesota, St. Paul, MN.

O'Sullivan, C. (1991). Making a difference: The relationship between childhood mentors and resiliency in adult children of alcoholics. *Family Dynamics of Addiction Quarterly, 1*(3), 46–59.

Patterson, G. R. (1982). *A social learning approach to family intervention: Coercive family process*. Eugene, OR: Castalia.

Pattison, E. M., & Kaufman, E. (1981). Family therapy and the treatment of alcoholism. In M. R. Lansky (Ed.), *Family therapy and major psychopathology* (pp. 117–129). New York: Grune and Stratton.

Piercy, F. F., & Frankel, B. R. (1989). The evolution of an integrative family therapy for substance-abusing adolescents: Toward the mutual enhancement of research and practice. *Journal of Family Psychology, 3*(1), 5–25.

Pringle, W. J. (1976). The alcoholic family environment: The influence of the alcoholic and nonalcoholic family of origin on present coping styles (Doctoral dissertation, California School of Professional Psychology, Fresno). *Dissertation Abstracts International, 37*(11), 5812 (University Microfilms No. AAC7710809).

Simmons, G. M. (1991). Interpersonal trust and perceived locus of control in the adjustment of adult children of alcoholics. (Doctoral dissertation, U.S. International University). *Dissertation Abstracts International, 52*(3), 1703. (University Microfilms No. AAC9122858).

Sisson, R. W., & Azrin, N. H. (1986). Family-member involvement to initiate and promote treatment of problem drinkers. *Journal of Behavior Therapy and Experimental Psychology, 17,* 15–21.

Stanton, M. D., & Todd, T. C. (1982). *The family therapy of drug abuse and addiction.* New York: Guilford Press.

Stanton, M. D., & Todd, T. C. (1992). Structural family therapy with drug addicts. In E. Kaufman & P. Kaufman (Eds.), *The family therapy of drug and alcohol abuse* (2nd ed.; pp. 46–62). New York: Gardner Press.

Steinglass, P. (1976). Experimenting with family treatment approaches to alcoholism, 1950–1975, a review. *Family Process, 15*(4), 97–123.

Steinglass, P. (1979). Family therapy with alcoholics: A review. In E. Kaufman & P. Kaufman (Eds.), *Family therapy of drug and alcohol abuse* (pp. 147–185). New York: Gardner Press.

Steinglass, P. (1980). Life history model of the alcoholic family. *Family Process, 19*(3), 211–226.

Steinglass, P., Bennett, L. A., Wolin, S. J., & Reiss, D. (1987). *The alcoholic family.* New York: Basic Books.

Steinglass, P., Davis, D., & Berenson, D. (1977). Observations of conjointly hospitalized "alcohol couples" during sobriety and intoxication for theory and therapy. *Family Process, 16,* 1–16.

Stout, R. L., McCrady, B. S., Longabaugh, R., Noel, N. E., & Beattie, M. C. (1987, June). *Marital therapy enhances the long-term effectiveness of alcohol treatment: Replication of an outcome crossover effect.* Paper presented at the Joint Meeting of the Research Society on Alcoholism and the Committee on Problems of Drug Dependence, Philadelphia, PA.

Szapocznik, J., Kurtines, W. M., Foot, F., Perez-Vidal, A., & Hervis, O. (1983). Conjoint versus one-person family therapy: Some evidence for the effectiveness of conducting family therapy through one person. *Journal of Consulting and Clinical Psychology, 51,* 889–899.

Szapocznik, J., Kurtines, W. M., Foot, F., Perez-Vidal, A., & Hervis, O. (1986). Conjoint versus one-person family therapy: Further evidence for the effectiveness of conducting family through one person with drug-abusing adolescents. *Journal of Consulting and Clinical Psychology, 54*(3), 395–397.

Tarter, J. (1991). *The effects of parental alcohol drinking patterns on adult children of alcoholics.* Doctoral dissertation, U.S. International University, San Diego, CA.

Thomas, E. J., Santa, C., Bronson, D., & Oyserman, D. (1987). Unilateral family therapy with spouses of alcoholics. *Journal of Social Service Research, 10,* 145–162.

Thomas, E. J., Yoshioka, M., Ager, R. D., & Adams, K. B. (1993). *Experimental outcomes of spouse intervention to reach the uncooperative alcohol abuser: Preliminary report.* Manuscript submitted for publication.

Thornton, R., & Nardi, P. M. (1975). The dynamics of role acquisition. *American Journal of Sociology, 80*(4), 870–885.

Treadway, D. (1989). *Before it's too late.* New York: Norton.

Wegscheider, S. (1981a). *Another chance: Hope and help for the alcoholic family.* Palo Alto, CA: Science & Behavior Books.

Wegscheider, S. (1981b, January/February). From the family trap to family freedom. *Alcoholism,* 36–39.

Werner, E. E. (1986). Resilient offspring of alcoholics: A longitudinal study. *Journal of Studies on Alcohol, 47*(1), 34–40.

Wilson, C., & Orford, J. (1978). Children of alcoholics. *Journal of Studies on Alcohol, 39,* 121–142.

Wolin, S. J., & Bennett, L. A. (1984). Family rituals. *Family Process, 23,* 401–420.

Wolin, S. J., Bennett, L. A., & Noonan, D. L. (1979). Family rituals and recurrence of alcoholism over generations. *American Journal of Psychiatry, 136,* 589–593.

Wolin, S. J., Bennett, L. A., & Noonan, D. L. (1980). Disrupted family rituals: A factor in the intergenerational transmission of alcoholism. *Journal of Studies on Alcohol, 41,* 199–214.

Wolin, S. J., & Wolin, S. (1993). *The resilient self: How survivors of troubled families rise above adversity.* New York: Villard Books.

Zwebin, A., Perlman, S., & Li, S. (1988). A comparison of brief advice and conjoint therapy in the treatment of alcohol abuse. The results of the marital systems study. *British Journal of Addiction, 83,* 899–916.

CHAPTER 8

Dealing With Diversity

CHAPTER OBJECTIVES

- Examine the major types of diversity
- Examine how each type of diversity might impact chemically dependent patients
- Identify areas of diversity that may lead to high risk in individuals with chemical dependency problems
- Examine how knowledge of individual diversity issues can be useful to the counselor in treatment planning

When the first edition of this text was written, diversity was not given much consideration in the chemical dependency counseling field. Most treatment programs were inpatient and offered a standard treatment that included education on the disease of alcoholism and the 12 steps, as well as individual and group counseling. Women, men, Native Americans, adolescents, the elderly—everyone went through the same program. The belief was that one program fits all. Everyone who had an addiction was seen as basically the same. They were believed to suffer from the same disease, and the treatment was simple: Break the denial in group and individual counseling, introduce patients to the 12 steps, give them a Big Book and a 30-day medallion, and send them off to be sober "one day at a time" and to attend "30 meetings in 30 days." The cost for this "McTreatment" was usually around $10,000. Insurance companies willingly paid for it. As single-minded as these programs were, some people began a successful recovery in them. But many did not, and the heyday of inpatient treatment programs was short lived. Today, insurance companies are no longer willing to pay for what people needing help with their addictions can get for free in a self-help group.

Today, fortunately, things are changing in chemical dependency treatment. Individual differences, or what is termed here *individual diversities*, have become important issues in most treatment programs. Issues such as race, gender, age, sexual orientation, and cultural background are considered when treatment programs are designed, and the dynamics of addiction are considered when individual treatment plans are developed. There are many books, chapters, and articles that address issues in special populations and discuss how to adapt treatment for certain groups with substance abuse problems, such as adolescents (Eaves & Sheperis, 2011), women and men (Gladding, 2009), older adults (Farkas, 2014), members of the LGBTQ community (Senreich

& Vairo, 2014), and individuals with HIV/AIDS (Gant, 2014). The authors of these books and articles discuss diversity among individuals and how these diversities make a difference when treatment for addiction is planned and implemented. Lawson and Lawson address many of these populations and more in the second edition of *Alcoholism and Substance Abuse in Diverse Populations* (Lawson & Lawson, 2011).

This chapter will cover more than just cultural diversity. Many forms of diversity that affect chemical dependency will be discussed specifically in relation to the etiology and treatment of chemical dependency, and case histories will be given to illustrate the important issues. The following areas of diversity will be included in this chapter:

- Age and developmental level
- Family history and genetics
- Gender and sexual functioning
- Mental health and personality
- Employment and related issues
- Racial and cultural affiliations
- Sexual orientation
- Religion
- Medical problems
- Criminal justice system exposure
- Emotional stress or a history of personal trauma
- Drugs of choice
- Other addictions

By understanding diversity among clients and viewing the individual as part of a system (as discussed in the previous chapter), it will be possible for counselors to interpret addictive behavior in a context that will help determine *all* of the issues that need to be addressed in treatment. This will also help the counselor understand how this diversity can be addressed in issues of recovery. This is not done so the counselor can determine where the patient is wrong; it is done from the perspective of using a knowledge of diversity to help the client recover. It is not really feasible for a counselor to know everything about the culture or race or religion of a client or patient; however, if the counselor is aware of the issues and asks the right questions, the client or patient can help the counselor with what he or she needs to know.

It is important to note that an individual with an addiction can attend a self-help group or a treatment program where only the substance use is addressed, and yet the individual will still be able to stop using and turn his or her life around. This has happened thousands of times and will continue to happen. Many people have stopped destructive behaviors such as smoking, drinking, and using drugs without any help at all. If the substance abuse is the individual's only or major problem, he or she may be quite successful doing this. However, the majority of people with addiction problems often have many other related problems and issues to deal with. In addition, there are degrees or stages of recovery, and the ability to stop using drugs without also having opportunity for a meaningful, happy, and fulfilling life does not offer much. This "unfulfilling recovery" often leads to relapse or even suicide. It is the counselor's job not only to help clients achieve sobriety and maintain it, but also to assist them in the search for happiness and meaning in life. This is best done with an understanding of the issues of diversity as described in this chapter.

Each approach to counseling has a theory about how and why people change. There are basically three things that people can change: They can change their *behavior* (i.e., change from using drugs to not using drugs); they can change their *cognitions or thoughts* (i.e., thinking of drug abuse as a disease, rather than as a moral weakness), and, finally, they can change their *feelings or emotional response to something or someone* (i.e., feeling they cannot control their use of alcohol, whereas earlier they felt that they could). Most people who make significant changes in their lives do so in all three areas. Someone with an addiction who just changes drug-using behavior by quitting drugs, without changing their thinking and feelings about drugs, has little chance of maintaining that behavior change. A counselor with an understanding of the issues of diversity will be much better equipped to assist in this change.

The next section of this chapter will examine some specific areas of diversity. There is a great deal of overlap. For example, family background and religious affiliation overlap. Most people do not choose a religion; they are born into a family where they are expected to follow the religion of the family. If they choose not to, this may or may not be a major family issue. Because there is overlap, some of the sections on specific diversities will be much longer than others. This has nothing to do with their importance. They are all important to consider in relation to etiology and treatment.

Age and Developmental Stage

An individual's age and developmental stage are related to substance abuse in many ways. For example, certain stages in life are high risk for substance abuse. Adolescents go through a stage in life where trying and learning new things is the norm, and this often includes experimentation with drugs. The risk increases if an adolescent is developmentally ahead of or behind peers (e.g., ahead or behind in the development of pubic hair, breasts for girls, or deeper voices for boys). Both girls and boys who develop early or late find drugs, particularly alcohol, to be useful in the transition from childhood to adulthood. Those who develop early tend to "hang out" with older peers who are more likely to be using. Those who develop early also use substances to fit in with the older kids. Teenagers who develop late often use alcohol and other drugs to make their peers think they are older and to feel older themselves. Almost all teenagers want to look or be older. Many believe drug use will help them. (Tobacco companies know this and advertise to take advantage of it.)

At the opposite end, older people are prime candidates for iatrogenic (induced inadvertently by a physician) and prescription drug abuse. They overuse and underuse. They mix drugs that should not be used together. They use each other's prescription drugs without the doctors' permission. Strangely enough, these two groups, adolescents and older adults, have a great deal in common. They are both going through major changes in their lives and they are both at risk for substance abuse as a result. The aging process is not easy for many people, and using chemicals to soften the blow is very common. Counselors who understand this can help their clients find other ways than using drugs to get through stages that are only natural in life. Therefore, an understanding of the stages of life and of the aging process will make this task easier for counselors.

Many alcoholism and drug treatment programs pay little, if any, attention to the past development of their clients ("What is past is past, and there is nothing we can do to change it, so why bring it up?"). If the past is brought up during treatment, it is usually only in the context of the recent past. Alcoholics Anonymous (A.A.) deals with the past in the eighth and ninth steps by suggesting that its members make a list of all the persons whom they have harmed, become willing to make amends to all of them, and then make direct amends to such people wherever possible, unless doing so would injure them or others. Although these steps deal with the past, and offer A.A. members an opportunity to rid themselves of possible guilt about previous actions, they focus mainly on past behavior with regard to drinking—which does not take human development into full consideration. The "drunk-a-log" is similarly deficient.

The drunk-a-log is often part of an A.A. meeting, where members tell how drinking led them down the path to dependency and how they have turned their lives around through A.A. Then they explain how they have learned to stay sober just one day at a time. This is fine as an attempt to remind the speaker and those listening of history, lest it repeat itself. Too often, though, this dialogue leads the listeners and the speaker to the conclusion that all of these problems began when alcohol or drugs entered the picture. Often, they assume that before alcohol and drugs, the speaker lived a normal, happy life, and if alcohol were removed, life would again be the proverbial bowl of cherries—but the very high rate of suicide for those recovering from chemical dependency suggests that this is not true. The number of persons with chemical dependency issues whose family histories include psychological, physical, and sexual abuse suggests that before alcohol or drugs, things were not that rosy.

In short, though each of us starts out much the same, at some time between the womb and the beginning of alcohol or drug use, we experience life events that have a direct effect on how we relate to our world. The more information the chemical dependency counselor has about these life events, the better the treatment plan can be—and the greater the chances are that the client will be successful in treatment.

Developmental Stages

Each major theory of counseling or psychotherapy embraces some form of developmental theory. Usually, this theory involves a rationale of how a person develops. This rationale is, in turn, related to some type of developmental dysfunction that the particular theory of psychotherapy is designed to treat. The first to theorize in this manner was Sigmund Freud. Freud's (1905) theory involved different stages of development, and posited that for those individuals who could not successfully complete these stages, the outcome was mental illness or deviant behavior.

Freud (1905) believed that every child goes through a sequence of developmental stages, each associated with a specific erogenous zone. He claimed that individuals passed through these stages on the path to a personality that is divided into three major parts: the id, the ego, and the superego. His stages of development were the oral stage, the anal stage, the phallic stage, the latency stage, and finally, the genital stage. Freud felt that each of these stages fulfilled a task in the development of a healthy personality. Freud's theories have had a great impact on how we view the development of personality today. One of the popular theories of psychotherapy, transactional analysis, uses personality divisions called the child, parent, and adult that closely parallel the id, ego, and superego of Freud.

This chapter will not present developmental theories. For a review of these, we suggest that the reader refer to a basic text on developmental psychology. Our aim is to suggest to the chemical dependency counselor that in order to provide the best treatment for chemical dependency, one should have an idea about how a person with alcohol or drug issues develops.

Chemical Dependency Development

Drinking alcohol or taking drugs is a behavior. The way one acts or behaves under the influence of drugs or alcohol is also a behavior. For each behavior, there is an antecedent or a reason. Although an individual's behavior may seem to be self-destructive, there is a reason, a "payoff," for this behavior. At the least, the behavior is leading that person in a direction that, for them, appears to be logical or the only direction available. Removing the alcohol or drugs is just a beginning; something therapeutic must happen to an individual before he or she will give up drugs or alcohol. Something must also assist individuals in making the choice to change negative or self-destructive behaviors.

Thus, to focus only on alcohol- or drug-taking behavior is a mistake. Self-help groups, including A.A., appear to have accepted this view. Of the 12 steps toward recovery from alcoholism, only one even mentions alcohol. The others deal with behaviors, emotions, attitudes, and changes regarding control of one's life. These are positive steps toward recovery that can be enhanced by using information regarding early personality development. Information that provides a key to the question "Why does this person behave the way he or she does?" will provide a direction for treatment. This includes what needs to change before the individual can behave in a more rational, self-fulfilling way. For many chemically dependent people, a change in behavior is brought about by a change in attitude. This change in attitude (sometimes known as therapeutic movement) is often brought about by one or more significant events in the person's life. (See the section "Emotional Stress or a History of Personal Trauma," later in this chapter.) When these events are manipulated or caused by the counselor, that is therapy. For example, if a person in a group experience becomes moved by the caring that the other group members show toward him and changes his behavior as a result of this experience, that is therapy. It is only common sense to believe that the more the counselor knows about what motivates a person with chemical dependency issues, the more accurately the counselor can set up these significant emotional events in order to bring about therapeutic change in thinking, feelings, and behavior.

Other Developmental Levels

Although early developmental theories include only the period from birth to early adulthood, it has become clear that humans continue to develop in many areas for most of their lives. Erikson's (1950) theory of psychosocial development runs from birth through old age, with eight stages altogether. Each of these stages is meaningful to the understanding of individuals as they progress through life. This can be best illustrated by reviewing a developmental stage and reflecting on how this information might be helpful to the chemical dependency counselor. For example, consider the important physical, emotional, and social characteristics of an adolescent male.

Physically, the adolescent male is in a state of rapid maturation. Some boys mature at an early age and some at a later age. Those who mature later are often not as self-confident and assured as those who mature earlier; however, those who mature later often become more sensitive and insightful than their early-maturing counterparts. There is likely to be a great deal of concern about appearance at this age, especially with regard to the opposite sex. The male sex drive is at a peak at the ages of 16 to 17. A strong sex drive and severely limited opportunities to satisfy it are sources of much concern to many young males.

Socially, the adolescent male comes increasingly under the influence of his peer group. Often there are conflicts between peer group and family values, which is another source of anxiety for the adolescent. Emotionally, the adolescent may be moody and unpredictable, partly because of biological changes associated with sexual maturation and partly because of confusion about identity. Adolescents are seldom intolerant and opinionated, partly because they may lack confidence and partly because of they lack experience as formal thinkers. In a search for a sense of identity, and in their efforts to become independent, many adolescents experience moments of confusion, anxiety, and anger. They may express their frustration by turning to alcohol or drugs or by otherwise rejecting established values. Adolescents also tend to emphasize the here-and-now over future consequences. They often look for immediate gratification rather than work toward some future goal. We now know that much of these changes are related to the belated development of their prefrontal cortex (i.e., their brain's "go" system overrides its "stop" system), which may increase youths' vulnerability to substance abuse and other risky behaviors (Bava & Tappert, 2010). It is important to note just how resilient and successful many adolescent males are, even during such a tumultuous time. Many contribute in positive ways in school, church, volunteer groups, and more. As a group, their strengths can include a sense of optimism, infectious vitality and a sense of fun, and a fresh perspective. As a group, they look much the same, but on further examination, each is very different.

Adolescents have a completely different set of problems than do adults. The goals for treatment may be the same, but the direction they take to reach the goals is dictated by the problems that they encounter on the way. For example, building self-image might be an appropriate goal. For the adult, this might be done through improved relationships with family members and improved performance on the job. For the adolescent, it might only be done through a peer group.

For a 45-year-old adult, the reality that alcohol intake is damaging his liver and that he might someday die as a result of this could be a motivating factor to give up drinking. This same news presented to the adolescent might have no effect whatsoever on his alcohol intake because he may believe he will live forever. Again, the more you know about the developmental factors of the individual you are working with, the more effective you can be in treatment planning and, thus, in treatment.

Family History and Genetics

Earlier in this chapter, the importance of development and how this relates to problems that clients experience later in life was discussed. No period of development is more critical to the development of the adult personality than early childhood. Almost without exception, personality theorists link major adult personality characteristics to certain categories of childhood experience (although there are exceptions to this contention). It seems reasonable to conclude, however, that if childhood experiences are so important in molding various personality attributes, the way one interacts with drugs and alcohol would be greatly influencing as well. There is nothing that has a greater impact on these early experiences than the family, and the family has a role in the treatment and prevention of chemical dependency problems.

Much of what goes on in families, particularly early on, determines the subsequent risk for substance abuse. The family is where a child develops a self-image. Children begin to feel good, bad, or indifferent about themselves. The family is where a child learns to make decisions, learns what sex should be like, and learns how to deal with anxiety and have relationships with others. All of these are important in the development of low or high risk for substance abuse. The family is also where children receive their genetic predisposition for substance abuse and where they develop values related to the use of mind-altering substances. The use or lack of use by parents and other relatives provides children with a model that they either follow or reject.

Two types of families influence the person with chemical dependency. First, and perhaps more critical to the development of the individual, is the family of origin. This family includes parents, relatives, or significant others who played a major role in a child's rearing. Attitudes and values about self and the world, as well as the use of alcohol and drugs, are mostly formed here, and thus play an important role in present behavior.

The second is the nuclear family. The nuclear family consists of those individuals with whom the person is living at the present time. This system is important because it may serve to create, maintain, or worsen problems that the person with chemical dependency is having at the time. The nuclear family is also important because it is a potential mechanism for positive change in the life of the person with chemical dependency.

Identifying Family Factors in the Development of Chemical Dependency

Three major theoretical areas of the etiology of chemical dependency include theories that are biologically or genetically based, theories that are psychological in nature (these include the theory that persons with chemical dependency have a distinct personality flaw that leads to chemical dependency), and theories that are sociocultural in nature (these propose that the largest determiner of drinking and drug use is the culture in which the person with chemical dependency lives).

Theories in each of these major areas are based to some degree on research findings and other empirical data. Evidence exists linking drug dependency or alcoholism with genetic factors, psychological factors, and sociocultural factors, but none of the research has established any one of these factors as the primary contributor to the etiology of chemical dependency. Most theorists believe that a combination of these factors causes one person to become chemically dependent and another person not to become so. One thing that is clear, and is becoming clearer as research in the area continues, is that the family has a major impact, perhaps *the* major impact, on the individual in each of these areas. The family influences all of the physiological and a great deal of the psychological and sociological development of the individual. The developmental foundation established early by the family reflects how a person relates to his or her environment, including his or her relationship with drugs and alcohol.

There is no conclusion from this that the family is the cause of chemical dependency. But it seems clear that the family cannot be ignored in regard to the etiology, treatment, or prevention of chemical dependency. To establish a clearer picture of the role the family plays in physiological, psychological, and sociological factors, it would be helpful to look at each factor from the perspective of the development of a risk level for chemical dependency. Remember that everyone is potentially at risk for problems with chemical dependency; however, some are at greater risk than others.

Meeting Interpersonal Needs Through Alcoholics Anonymous and Other Self-Help Groups

If the family is not available, the second best approach to treating chemical dependency is to provide a surrogate family to meet these needs: A.A. and other self-help groups serve this purpose for many. A problem may arise, however, if A.A. meets these needs at the expense of the real family (if it is intact). Many alcoholics have taken refuge at an A.A. meeting rather than working out unresolved family matters at home. When used properly, these groups are often very successful at reducing both psychological and sociological risk levels enough to allow individuals to seek family therapy to resolve family problems.

Sociologically, they provide a new social group with a new set of values with regard to drinking or using. Often, this means a change from a group where using or drinking to excess is not only acceptable but also encouraged, to a group where drinking or using in any fashion is not acceptable. This group, if it becomes a major influence on the individual, lowers the person's sociological risk level; if the individual maintains contact with the group and group members, he or she will continue to have a reduced sociological risk level.

Psychologically, people reduce their risk level if they respect and identify with the other members of the group whom they meet. They reduce their own feelings of hopelessness by seeing people who have had problems similar to theirs and who became better because they were able to stop using. There is some psychological relief in the knowledge that others in the world share similar problems; there is a feeling of acceptance that helps people feel better about themselves. Perhaps, most importantly, there is a feeling that by sharing experiences with other members, there is a chance that one could be helping other members stay sober. (For more on the benefits of groups, see Chapter 6.) This is carried even further when the member is asked to do 12-step work, which includes making house calls and home visits to individuals who are suffering from drug addiction or alcoholism and volunteering to share how he or she has been successful in maintaining sobriety. The 12-step call is a great esteem builder, and it serves to further reduce the psychological risk level by making the caller feel needed and useful.

Yet, risk reduction is best done through the family for several reasons. (Even if A.A. or other self-help groups are used in the beginning, the counselor should help clients work toward meeting their goals through the family.) The first reason is that the family is the logical place for these needs to be met. Second, the family needs help just as much as, or perhaps more than, the person with chemical dependency. By conducting family therapy, the counselor helps family members meet their own personal needs through the family system. This pays off not only for the person with chemical dependency but for the children in the family as well, by teaching them to meet their interpersonal needs through the family, thus reducing their risk of future problems.

Genetic Predispositions

A child's risk for alcoholism increases significantly when parents have alcoholism (Eaves & Sheperis, 2011; Molina, Donovan, & Belendiuk, 2010). The evidence is not as conclusive for other forms of drug abuse or addiction, but research has indicated a link between the generations of those who experience chemical dependency problems, just as research has indicated a link between the generations of those who experience depression and other mental disorders. Research has shown higher rates of alcoholism among relatives of alcoholics than in the population in general, with an intergenerational transmission risk as high as 50% (Molina et al., 2010). Although these findings indicate the involvement of genetic factors, they provide no details on *how* a predisposition to alcoholism is transmitted. One can assume that just as eye color or metabolism rates are passed on genetically, so is the *capacity* for drug or alcohol abuse. The chemical dependency counselor can determine the physiological risk level for a client by asking if parents or grandparents have had chemical dependency problems. If the answer is yes, it can be assumed that the person is physiologically at a higher risk of developing chemical dependency problems. However, it cannot be assumed that the person *will* have problems. Too many factors are involved to make that assumption.

The chemical dependency counselor can use information about parental problems with chemicals to let clients know that they are at increased risk and to establish the importance of reducing the risk levels in other areas, both psychological and social. Although physiological susceptibility can be established, environmental factors will still play a major role in the development of chemical dependency. The client can simply be told the following: "We don't know for sure what causes chemical dependency, but we do know that each of us reacts differently to drugs or alcohol based on our size, chemical makeup, and other genetically predisposed factors. Because your parents or grandparents had a problem, you are physically at increased risk to have such problems, as your children will be, too. If you have a problem now or if you think you will at some time choose to use drugs or alcohol, you must pay particular attention to any signs of impending problems, you must work to keep your risk levels low in the other two areas."

Sociological and Psychological Family-Based Risk Factors

The person who is sociologically at high risk is the one whose primary support system, most often the family, exposes that person to excessive chemical use, such as when a parent has a problem with alcoholism (Freshman, 2014). The person is at risk because the abuse of chemicals is an option for use as a coping mechanism, or it is an expected behavior. Groups such as Native Americans, Irish Catholics, and others have been identified as having high rates of alcoholism and other chemical dependency problems. The degree to which these social and cultural groups have influenced the individual is relevant to the sociological risk factor.

It is not uncommon for people who come from households that do not tolerate the use of one or more chemicals (e.g., a religious group with strong sanctions against the use of chemicals, commonly alcohol) to have difficulties as well. The message from the family, and usually the church, is clear: "Those who use are wicked. At the very least: They (users) have not chosen God's way." If these values are followed throughout life, and there is no use of drugs or alcohol, there can be no chemical dependency problem. But, if after becoming older, a person chooses to use alcohol or drugs, her or she will have a very difficult time not feeling guilty because of the messages received as a child. Problems are compounded by the fact that most drugs provide a temporary respite from guilt. The cycle becomes use, feel guilty, use more to relieve guilt, feel even more guilty, use even more. It is a difficult cycle to break. To complicate matters even further, the family of origin sometimes rejects the person because of the drug use, thus confirming the user's belief that he or she is truly bad and deserves to be punished. (For more on this, see the section "Religion," later in this chapter.)

In the abovementioned instance, there is not a clear distinction between a sociological risk and a psychological risk; in fact, these are often interrelated.

Such precision is not required, however, for understanding that the family has played a dramatic role in the development of the individual's risk level for chemical dependency problems. The psychological dynamics are there. One clear motivational factor in chemical use and abuse is to feel better. For reasons that are closely linked to the family, the person who becomes dependent on chemicals very often has a poor self-image, seeing him- or herself in relation to others ("I am not as good as my parents") or in relation to how one perceives one should be ("I have failed," "It is all my fault," "I haven't come close to living up to my potential, and I should"). Either way, the family of origin plays a vital role in these feelings. These factors have been explained in detail elsewhere, and for the counselor who is serious about providing a complete treatment program for clients, a highly recommended (although older) text is Lawson and Lawson (1998), *Alcoholism and the Family: A Guide to Treatment and Prevention*. It is sufficient to say that these factors determine how individuals feel about themselves—whether they feel in control of the world around them. If these feelings are essentially, "I am not OK" and "I do not have a great deal of control over things that happen around me or to me," these persons are psychologically at high risk to develop some form of chemical dependency problem.

One variable that remains constant is, of course, use. It is impossible to become chemically dependent if one does not use chemicals. This is not to say that it is impossible to have chemical dependency problems after one gives up the use of chemicals. On the contrary, very often the problems only begin when the person stops using. This is where the nuclear family becomes important: The family is a system, and if one or more members of that system have issues with chemical dependency, then the whole system suffers, not just the person who has an addiction. The system must be treated, and it is best treated as a unit. That does not translate to placing the person with chemical dependency in treatment while educating the family about the disease of chemical dependency and teaching them to live with, yet psychologically apart from, the person with chemical dependency. The family system, when functioning as a unit, is the place where family members should meet many of their needs (the need to be loved and the need for security, among others). If the family does not meet these needs, the system needs repair or redirection. When the family is intact, it is highly recommended that family therapy be used to restructure the family system so that all members are meeting appropriate needs through the family (see Chapter 7).

Gender and Sexual Functioning

Like human development, gender issues and human sexuality are often neglected in training programs for chemical dependency counselors. Consequently, many chemical dependency counselors feel ill-equipped to deal with their clients' sexual problems, and often these problems are neglected in the treatment plan. However, sexual problems rarely resolve themselves, and, if nothing else, it is the responsibility of the counselor to make an appropriate referral to a therapist trained to deal with problems of a sexual nature. This section of the chapter will discuss sexuality as it affects the person with chemical dependency and will suggest some prospects for treatment and referral.

Human sexuality is heavily intertwined in the development of each individual. The role that sex plays in establishing a positive self-image cannot be overstated. In turn, this variable also becomes critical to the treatment and rehabilitation of the person with chemical dependency. Very often, the person with chemical dependency has used drugs or alcohol to ease anxiety or conflicts surrounding the issue of sexuality. These conflicts can easily complicate the rehabilitation effort if they are not considered and dealt with as a primary part of treatment.

It has been suggested that the most appropriate way to deal with problems of a sexual nature is to consider the distinctive needs of women and men who are chemically dependent and to place them in gender-specific (same sex) therapy groups where issues may be best addressed (Eaves & Sheperis, 2011). Studies of addicted populations have found that certain characteristics peculiar to women who are chemically dependent should be addressed in treatment (Pape & Sarabia, 2014). For example, women are far more likely to have a history of sexual abuse. Much of it involves the family, and it many times happened in early childhood. Women who abuse drugs are more likely to be socially isolated than are men. They are more likely to be in an interpersonal relationship with an addicted partner. They are more concerned with interpersonal relationships than men, and they express many more issues about parenting and childcare. Given these differences, it is not surprising that the treatment needs of women may be better met in women-only treatment groups (Pape & Sarabia, 2014). Men also have issues of both a sexual and a non-sexual nature that women may not understand or relate to; these should also be dealt with in men-only groups. There may, however, be many things that men and women can teach each other about one another in a group setting. The choice of group membership criteria should be considered in relationship to the goals of the group (see Chapter 6); however, the impact of diversity should definitely be factored in to the decision.

Sex as a Source of Guilt

For the person who is chemically dependent, sex has often been instrumental in the establishment of a negative, rather than a positive, self-image. Guilt about sexual behavior is sometimes a primary motivation for drug- or alcohol-taking behavior. This guilt need not be connected to sexual behavior that occurred while the person was drinking or using; it might be sexual behavior that took place before such a period. For example, victims of childhood incest have many issues surrounding their sexuality that cause them guilt, great pain, conflict, and self-doubt. If incest is ignored as a factor by the chemical dependency counselor, the treatment for these individuals will be incomplete or altogether unsuccessful.

In other instances, sexual behavior that occurred during drinking or using may be a great source of guilt. The values regarding sex that a person has when sober are often violated when under the influence. Promiscuous sex, homosexuality, and incest are all potential guilt producers. It is the responsibility of the chemical dependency counselor to determine the client's primary sexual issues and to establish how these factors are involved with the drinking or drug-taking behavior. The counselor can then intervene therapeutically to help the client resolve these matters. If this is done successfully, sexual problems will no longer be a source of negative feelings for the client.

Obtaining the Sexual History

As is suggested in Chapter 5, assessment, or diagnosis, is the cornerstone of a successful treatment program, and a successful diagnosis is only complete with an accurate sexual history. To gain access to information of a very personal nature, it is critical to establish rapport between the counselor and the client. This rapport should be a natural part of a therapeutic counseling relationship. However, this may take time to establish, and the counselor should not rush to deal with sensitive subjects. Other, less threatening aspects of the client's history can be reviewed until the client is more comfortable with the counselor. With a subject such as sex, where values and feelings differ, it is only natural that some clients will be reluctant to bring up the subject, regardless of the quality of the client–counselor relationship. This does not mean that the counselor should not bring up the matter. If the client is reluctant to talk about sexual subjects, the counselor should discuss the importance of such issues with the client and model openness toward sex. This might be done with a certain amount of self-disclosure by the counselor about his or her own experiences, which may be more comfortable for the client if the counselor is the same gender.

With regard to the sexual history of the individual, the counselor needs to pay particular attention to issues surrounding patterns of dominance and control, dependency, intimacy, and childhood experiences—including parental attitudes toward sex. Dominance issues should be examined with regard to the client's present and past interpersonal relationships. Questions concerning who has control, the level of control (Is there over-control? When? How?), and what this does to the self-esteem of the parties involved should be considered.

Dependency issues should be examined with regard to who is dependent upon whom, when, and under what circumstances. Levels of intimacy should be determined, and the influence of childhood experiences on sexuality should be considered with regard to parents and siblings. How did family members relate to one another? Were they given opportunities for self-expression? What were, and are, the patterns of self-restraint that they developed? For people with chemical dependency issues, it is important to assess self-image and the role sex has played in the development of that self-image. It is also of interest to note how they see their sexual partners, whether spouses, boyfriends or girlfriends, or otherwise. What kind of image do they have of their sexual partners? What is their image of their relationships? After clients' relationships have been evaluated from the point of view of both parties, a more profound sexual history can be developed.

The sexual history should include an attempt to ascertain any specific dysfunction and a history of that dysfunction. It should also include the client's feelings with regard to the dysfunction. To complete the picture of the client's sexual background and how this background might be influencing current destructive behavior, a sexual history of the childhood, adolescent, and teenage years should be taken. Feelings regarding family, cultural, religious, and social influences should be explored. Premarital sexual experiences and feelings (first sexual experiences, first knowledge of sex, masturbation, and homosexuality) and courtship and marital history are also important.

Some additional areas to explore in a sexual history would be the details (onset, duration, circumstances) of a specific problem and how the client views the problem. It is also important to consider the possibility of HIV/AIDS. The client's physical and emotional condition, plus forewarnings of the dysfunction and associated symptoms, should also be considered.

Sexual problems have a variety of causes, both physiological and psychological. And, as noted earlier, these sexual problems are manifested in other psychological problems. It is not always clear how or to what degree each problem contributes to the other; either way, the important issue is the current affect and how it can be dealt with therapeutically.

Physiological and Psychological Sexual Dysfunction

Some possible psychological causes of sexual dysfunction include anxiety, religious orthodoxy, hypertension, lack of arousal in one's partner, inability to communicate sexual desires, lack of knowledge, relationship problems, and, of course, alcoholism and drug abuse. Additional possible physiological causes of sexual dysfunction include diabetes, arthritis, central nervous system damage, vaginal infection, endometriosis, irritation from vaginal foam or jellies, menopausal atrophy, mumps, cancer, dietary insufficiencies, and drug and alcohol use.

Some specific female dysfunctions that women report include the following:

• Not yet having had an orgasm
• Pain during intercourse (dyspareunia)

- An involuntary vaginal spasm preventing penile penetration (vaginismus)
- Absence of sexual feelings during intercourse
- Little or no sexual desire

Some specific male dysfunctions that men report include the following:

- Premature ejaculation (ejaculatio precox)
- Erection with delayed or no ejaculation (ejaculatio retardata)
- Inability to produce an erection (this may be called "impotence" and can occur as a primary or secondary dysfunction)
- Absence or diminution of sexual feelings during intercourse
- Little or no sexual desire

It is not necessary for a client to report even one of these problems for sex to be a major issue in chemical dependency. In fact, more often than not, the client will not report a specific problem. Sexual problems in a person with chemical dependency issues frequently revolve more around issues of guilt and self-image regarding prior sexual behavior and beliefs than around specific dysfunctions. The counselor should be aware, as well, that specific dysfunctions do occur and that they are often treatable.

Should You Refer the Client to a Sex Therapist?

Referring clients with sexual dysfunctions to a competent sex therapist or doing sex therapy themselves is an individual choice for chemical dependency counselors, and should be made keeping several factors in mind. First, what is the counselor's personal comfort level when it comes to dealing with sexual problems? Do the counselor's own values and personal experiences make it difficult to work on issues involving sex? Counselors who are not comfortable with their own sexuality cannot expect to be good sex therapists. Counselors should also consider their training; sex therapy is not something one does without proper training and instruction. There are many good books on the subject, and there are excellent workshops offered across the country on sex therapy.

The second factor to take into consideration is the availability of sex therapists in the community. In areas where quality sex therapists are widely available, the counselor may choose not to seek additional training in this area. If, however, there are no competent sex therapists available in the area, the extra effort expended on training in sex therapy will be well worth the effort. Clients will benefit from the counselor's additional skills, and the counselor's understanding of the role sexuality plays in chemical dependency will be increased. Even with additional training, however, there may be times when it is more beneficial to send the client to an intensive in-patient sexuality treatment program, such as the one established in St. Louis by Masters and Johnson (see Masters & Johnson, 1966).

The third factor to take into consideration is whether the chemical dependency counselor is willing to use marriage counseling to deal with the client's sexual problems. Sex between marital partners is often hampered by other issues in the relationship. For a relationship to thrive, it must have mutual understanding, trust, and acceptance. These qualities sometimes erode in a relationship when one member of the couple has alcohol or drug problems. The counselor who can assist in establishing a positive marital relationship will not only resolve many sexual issues but may also contribute to the resolution of a chemical dependency problem.

This book is not designed to train chemical dependency counselors as sex therapists or marriage counselors. Its purpose is to alert the counselor to potential problems that clients with chemical dependency issues may exhibit, and to direct the counselor to resources they can use to confront these problems. Marital and sexual problems are two of the complicating issues a chemical dependency counselor must confront, and they must be included to provide a complete treatment plan for clients.

To summarize the counselor's goals with regard to sexual problems: The counselor should uncover the client's sexual problems, freely examine the issues, and clarify problem areas. The counselor should also provide insights and interpretations as to how these problems are affecting a client's chemical dependency; provide emotional support, and reduce anxiety and hostility; and educate and give permission, when necessary, in an effort to reduce guilt and increase positive feelings of self-worth in the client.

Mental Health and Personality

Those who engage in substance use or abuse are a diverse group with regard to mental health. Some of them are mentally healthy except for the inappropriate use of drugs. Others suffer deeply from all manner of mental disorders, from clinical depression to anxiety or even schizophrenia. Counselors who work with those who have substance use disorders make three major mistakes regarding mental health issues and chemical dependency. First, they do not diagnose the mental illness and only focus on the drug abuse. This is usually because they believe that the symptoms of the mental health problem are only a result of the drug abuse. Second, they misdiagnose the mental illness because some of the symptoms of drug withdrawal are the same as the symptoms of mental illness. And, finally, they diagnose the mental illness and ignore the substance use. It is usually counselors who work primarily in the mental health area who make this third mistake.

So-called dually diagnosed patients are a complex group. It is difficult for even the most experienced and highly trained persons to sort out the symptoms caused by drug use or drug withdrawal from those of mental illness. The only accurate way is to make sure the patient is free of drugs, and has been for some time.

Another issue regarding a person with both mental health and substance abuse issues is that of treatment by psychotropic drugs. Some think that giving such a person any drug—even a prescription drug—is counterproductive. They feel it reinforces the idea that one cannot live happily without drugs. It is highly advisable for the chemical dependency (CD) counselor to have a solid background in pharmacology. This also includes a knowledge of drugs that are used to treat mental illness and a solid knowledge of mental illness, such as is usually found in an abnormal psychology course (see Chapter 9).

Although it is beyond the scope of this text to detail mental health issues, it is important to stress that the CD counselor who does not have a basic knowledge of mental illness will most assuredly make some tragic errors. For a review of this issue, see Nunes, Selzer, Levounis, and Davies (2010).

Closely related to mental health issues are issues of personality. The idea of an "addictive personality" has never really achieved favor among most chemical dependency counselors, but it is still accepted by some in the mental health field. Although each counseling approach has its own theory regarding personality constructs, all agree that much behavior is learned, and developmental events influence each individual's image of humankind. The degree of emphasis placed on prior learning varies from theory to theory. Whether this should be a central focus of CD counseling is a decision each individual counselor will need to make.

Personality can be defined as the way in which each person interacts with the world. This involves an awareness of who the individuals are in relation to others. What makes this difficult to understand and to track in individuals is that they all play different roles in different situations. Some personality characteristics that seem to be common to many people with chemical dependency issues include being manipulative, dependent, blaming, irresponsible, sensation seeking, and many others. There are those who believe that the pathological effects of mood-altering chemicals have an impact on personality functioning, particularly in the area of regression. Regression is a return to an earlier developmental stage of psychological functioning, or a shift to a less mature level of psychological defenses. Regression includes acting out, passive-aggressive behavior, and somatization (conversion of anxiety into physical symptoms), as opposed to the more mature mechanisms of suppression, humor, or anticipation (Vaillant, 1971).

Employment and Related Issues

Dr. William Glasser, founder of reality therapy, once said in a presentation on mental health that the two things people need to be in a state of good mental health are someone to love who loves them, and something to do that makes them feel worthwhile. The importance of feeling good about what one is doing has been almost absent as a treatment issue in most programs and individual treatment plans. Yet, if some thought is given to the issue, it is easy to see many cases where what the individual does on a daily basis relates directly to self-image and therefore to substance abuse. Some examples might include the following:

- A man retires from a job from which he derives great satisfaction and self-worth. With too much extra time on his hands and lowered self-esteem, because he is not contributing as he used to, he begins to drink too much or use too many prescription drugs. The fact that he may suffer from aches and pains that go with aging makes intoxication even more attractive.

- A woman who derives great pleasure from being a mother suddenly has an empty nest. She feels empty and useless, and she turns to drugs to dull this feeling.

- A young man who has never drunk alcohol or used drugs in his life because of his family's values against doing so goes to college or joins the military. The majority of his peers drink or use drugs because it is the "cool thing to do." He begins to emulate their behavior so he can fit in. He feels guilty about going against his family's values, so he uses even more to subdue the feelings of guilt.

In other situations, certain vocations are high risk for encouraging substance use. This may even be specific to a certain substances. Baseball players use snuff. Cowboys chew tobacco. Construction workers drink beer. Lawyers hang out with their peers in bars after work. Doctors and dentists have easy access to prescription drugs and are at risk of abusing them. Exterior painters have a break between jobs or when the weather is bad, so they drink. Sailors have long periods of work, and then they are off for long periods with little to do, so they drink. Those who are unemployed may spend their unemployment checks on drugs that will help them forget about their dilemma.

At the other end of the continuum are individuals who have high-paying jobs, such as actors or professional athletes. One might wonder why people with so much talent and money would ruin their lives by using drugs. It does not seem to make sense. In many cases, however, especially when these individuals go from being relatively poor to having literally millions of dollars seemingly overnight, there is a burden that goes with the wealth. It allows these people to have access to an unending supply of drugs. There are always those who will sell drugs, especially to those with a great deal of money. So if the person used drugs even a little before, it is tempting for them to use all they want, especially when it relieves them of the guilt they could easily feel about having so much when most of their friends and relatives have so little. They often ruminate on the questions, "Why was I born with this talent?" and "Why should I have all of this when most others do not?"

These conditions sound stereotypical and can all be viewed as just excuses to use, but they surely play a part in an individual's substance abuse problems, and they should be addressed in treatment. The issue is for patients to have something they are interested in, as either a vocation or an avocation, that gives them a sense of achievement or adds meaning to their lives. If they do not have this, permanent recovery from addiction will be difficult.

Racial and Cultural Affiliations

One's racial and cultural identity and affiliation have everything to do with self-image and, thus, chemical dependency. Race and culture affect behavior. They determine how well people fit into the world they live in. These identities make people politically strong or weak. They provide them with a feeling that they fit in, or that they do not. They give them their values. They teach them what is normal. They influence their views on gender and family. They are vitally important as an aspect of the treatment process.

However, the counselor and client must first understand these issues, and then acknowledge and accept them. These issues may not be the focus of substance abuse treatment, but they often offer a background from which the addiction can be understood. Counselors need to first address their own assumptions, beliefs, and biases regarding other races and cultures. It is not the job of the counselor to change the culture of a patient, although some counselors try. Rather, counselors should do all that they can to understand the relationship between the patient's racial and cultural background and the accompanying chemical dependency problems. As per the ethical guidelines discussed in Chapter 2, it is the counselors' responsibility to adapt their perspective to honor that of their clients.

All racial and cultural groups have their own set of issues, depending on setting and surroundings, as well as other differences, such as gender. A Black man in Kenya, Africa, likely has a different set of problems than a Black man in Alabama. A Native American woman on a reservation likely has a different set of problems than one living in an urban setting.

It is beyond the scope of this chapter to address the specific issues of Native Americans, Asians, African Americans, Hispanics, and other cultures and races. Native Americans alone represent over 400 different cultures. Each tribe is a culture unto itself. Asians and Hispanics come from many different cultures. It is imperative that the importance of these issues is stressed in the overall etiology and treatment of addiction.

Cross-cultural counseling cannot be separated from the broader sociopolitical environment. How therapy is rooted in and reflects the dominant values, beliefs, and biases of the larger society; how the racial and ethnic experience in the United States has influenced the worldview of the patient; and how counseling might represent cultural oppression are all issues to be addressed (Corey, 2012).

Is it possible for a counselor of one race or cultural background to truly understand what it is like for someone from an entirely different racial and ethnic background? And if the differences are vast, can the counselor accept the differences? Even if the counselor can do these things, will the patient ever be able to trust someone who is different from him or her? These issues are not unlike other issues in addictions counseling. Issues of whether someone without a history of substance abuse can really help someone with an addiction, or whether someone with alcohol issues can help someone with problems related to the use of cocaine, are issues that can be and should be discussed in treatment. Patients who can tell their counselors that they do not trust them and why have made progress. A patient who holds racial hostility or cultural issues inside will be more likely to relapse or not respond to treatment at all.

It is recommended that CD counselors take at least one course on race and culture, because a counselor with a few simple ideas about a specific race or culture may generalize them and falsely attribute these to individual patients. The most important issue, though, is the counselor's attitude. Being open and accepting and willing to learn from your clients will go a long way toward making up for a lack of knowledge about culture or race.

Sexual Orientation

It has become widely accepted, as witnessed by the increase in states legalizing gay marriage, that homosexuality is no more a choice than is being born with brown hair, and that it is our moral and ethical responsibility to support those who define their sexuality as other than heterosexual.

In a meeting of health and human services experts, Dr. Tony Papa, a professor in the psychology department at the University of Nevada, Reno, presented research on the health and social service needs of the local Lesbian, Gay, Bisexual, Transgendered, Queer (LGBTQ) community in Washoe County, with a population approaching 500,000. The statistics he presented were staggering in their portrayal of a severely marginalized subset of the population and the resulting harm that has been suffered as a result of ongoing discrimination and stigmatization. As to health concerns, the LGBTQ community reported less utilization of and access to needed medical and dental services. In regard to mental health concerns, Dr. Papa summarized the high levels of depression, ongoing suicide ideation, anxiety, and PTSD as "comparable to soldiers coming off the battlefield[s]" of Afghanistan and Iraq (T. Papa, personal communication, April 3, 2013).

Kathy Baldock, Executive Director of Canyonwalker Connections, and Kari Ramos, Project Director for the Nevada Coalition Against Sexual Violence, also described a population that faces unconscionable amounts of violence and ostracization from mainstream society. For example, gay youth are three times more likely to attempt suicide. Furthermore, 1 in 5 gay men, 1 in 3 lesbians, and 1 in 2 transgender individuals have been sexually assaulted (victims of sexual assault are 26 times more likely to abuse drugs). As evidenced by these high rates of violence and suicide rates, it is important to acknowledge the overlapping and compounded struggles that LGBTQ individuals face. It is estimated that approximately 10% of the population is LGBTQ. As Kari pointed out, "As social service providers, we wouldn't refuse any other 10% of the population, so why would we do this with LGBTQ individuals?" She went on to say, "Our responses say more about us than about the people we serve." For a county the size of Washoe, this would amount to almost 50,000 people not being afforded desperately needed services (K. Baldock & K. Ramos, personal communication, April 3, 2013).

The reason for presenting such a focused perspective on one county is to underline the impact of such stigmatization at a local level. This is by no means a rare example, but a reflection of similar statistics nationwide. (For an excellent discussion of these issues and other important considerations on working with people from the LGBTQ community, see Senreich & Vairo, 2014.)

To be effective in working with people from the LGBTQ community, counselors will need to examine and reconcile any stereotypes and prejudices they may have toward these individuals. It is important, too, for CD counselors to be fully aware of their "cultural" orientation as it relates to their clients' sexual orientation, and how it may influence their interactions, however subtly, with LGBTQ clients. Ideally, effective counselors will have taken the time to educate themselves on all points relevant to the LGBTQ community until they are conversant, fluent, and comfortable in providing needed counseling and supportive services.

Religion

Organized religion affects personal values, provides direction, defines meaning, and meets spiritual needs for many people. Religious beliefs can also affect an individual's risk for substance use or abuse. Some religions condone alcohol use and others do not. As mentioned earlier in this chapter, those who grow up in a religion that disapproves of alcohol use are at risk for problems if they choose to use alcohol. At the other end of the spectrum are some religions that use mind-altering drugs in a ceremonial fashion. Alcohol is often used in religious rituals, for instance, to represent the blood of Christ. Why should a CD counselor get involved in something as personal as religion?

If religious beliefs affect patients' self-image, their views on drug or alcohol use, or their beliefs in the spiritual meaning of life, they are important and should be addressed in treatment. Also, there have been abuses of religion as well as appropriate uses. Addictive behaviors are often related in some way (e.g., guilt) to religious beliefs. The CD counselor is not expected to be an expert in any one religion, and if counselors feel uncomfortable or inadequate dealing with such issues, they should refer their clients—perhaps to a minister or a priest or a rabbi. Religion is an important issue for many people, and it should not be overlooked in the overall treatment of chemical dependency or addiction.

Medical Problems

People with life-threatening medical problems or medical conditions that involve a great deal of pain are at risk to abuse drugs. A client's HIV/AIDS status is an important consideration for the chemical dependency counselor. Having unprotected sex while under the influence of a mind-altering substance or while using IV drugs are ways in which substance abusers can contract HIV/AIDS, not to mention a variety of other diseases (hepatitis, sexually transmitted diseases). The fear and anxiety that go with such conditions are eased by mind-altering drugs, whether prescription or illegal. In addition, alcohol is often used alone or in combination with drugs to alleviate pain or reduce anxiety. Although there may be some short-term relief, the client's physical problems are often worsened by this behavior. The CD counselor can assist patients who are in physical pain by recommending biofeedback, hypnosis, or pain clinics to help reduce the use of mind-numbing drugs to relieve pain. There are times, however, when the values of the CD counselor may be challenged when clients choose to use drugs to reduce suffering. For example, a counselor may not condone any use of marijuana, yet a patient may choose to use it to reduce the symptoms of chemotherapy.

Unfortunately, there are also other problems. Some doctors have been accused of inducing drug addiction in patients, and because of their fear of addictive drugs, some people are undermedicated for their pain, and as a result are suffering. Even so, as further detailed in Chapter 9, opioid pain relievers are amongst the most commonly prescribed drugs in the United States and are responsible for more overdose deaths than other, even illicit, drugs (Centers for Disease Control and Prevention, 2011).

Contrast this to the fact that in other countries, heroin and marijuana are medically available as pain relievers. In the United States, both substances remain illegal in the vast majority of states, even for cancer and AIDS patients, who might respond to these drugs better than to any other prescription drug now available. CD counselors can help resolve this social issue by educating themselves and the public not to overreact to heavy drug use or even addiction in those who are in pain or dying.

Other physical problems such as blindness, deafness, or muscular-skeletal disorders increase the risk of substance abuse. Each of these conditions has its own special set of problems. If a client has one or more of these conditions along with a chemical dependency problem, the counselor needs to understand what that person's specific issues are, how they may impact treatment, and how to adapt treatment to support such clients.

Exposure to the Criminal Justice System

Any discussion about criminal and deviant behavior must first begin with an understanding of the larger societal context within which such behaviors occur. To do otherwise might be to unjustly blame individuals for forces beyond their control. Consider, for example, the more than 300% increase of the numbers of prisoners from 1980 to 2004, from just over 300,000 state prisoners to 1.24 million (Vieraitis, Kovandzic, & Marvell, 2007). This, despite the fact that, according to the U.S. Census Bureau, the nation's population increased by only 20% during the same timeframe (U.S. Census, 2014).

This increase in the prison population coincided with the advent of President Reagan's War on Drugs, which began in 1980, when significant budget reallocations at the federal level dramatically increased the anti-drug budgets of the Federal Bureau of Investigation, Drug Enforcement Administration, and Department of Defense at the expense of federal investments for substance abuse treatment, prevention, and education (Alexander, 2012). This happened at the state budget level, as well, with expenditures for state prisons increasing 150% from 1986 to 2001, and with more prisons built between 1980 and 2000 than ever before in the history of the United States (Vieraitis et al., 2007). At the same time, stricter policies were adopted that sent offenders to prison for longer periods of time. Examples of these policies include so-called truth-in-sentencing laws that required offenders to serve a significant portion of their time, "three strikes laws" that required offenders to serve a significant period of time after three arrests, and "mandatory minimums," which again resulted in offenders serving a significant amount of time in prisons (Vieraitis et al., 2007). The result? More than 50% of the rise in state prisoners between 1985 and 2000 was because of drug offenses (Alexander, 2012). The vast majority of these offenses were for possession with no history of violence (Alexander, 2012).

The results of these and other shifts in policy and tactics have hit people of color especially hard. Although Whites, particularly White youth, have been found to have the highest rates of illicit drug use—with White students using cocaine and heroin at seven times the rate of Black students, and crack cocaine at an even greater rate—in seven states, as many as 90% of all prisoners serving time for drug offenses were African Americans (Alexander, 2012). In 2006, this unequal application of the laws resulted in 1 in 14 Black men being in prison, compared to 1 in 106 White men (Alexander, 2012).

Perhaps the harshest damage is done, however, once the prison terms have been served. Many ex-prisoners will forever carry the "felon" label, which means they can no longer participate in the electoral process, can be denied public benefits such as welfare and housing, and have difficulty finding an employer who will hire them (Vieraitis et al., 2007). The home communities to which these individuals return are also negatively impacted with greater neighborhood instability and disruption of family formation (Vieraitis et al., 2007). Is it any wonder, therefore, that prisons have been found to have criminogenic effects on those who have served time? In other words, prisoners are not less likely—but more likely—to commit crimes due to the time they served in prison (Vieraitis et al., 2007).

Aspiring chemical dependency counselors should keep in mind the historical and societal context of drug abuse and incarceration when working with clients who have had experiences with the criminal justice system and not overemphasize personal culpability that may better be attributed to society, because to do so would be to further perpetuate the harsh injustice of largely discriminatory practices.

This does not mean that counselors should not help clients learn and use strategies that will help them to negotiate these harsh realities, or to acquire new personal skills and knowledge for maintaining sobriety. Rather, these therapeutic interventions will resemble those delivered to non–criminal justice populations, but in the context of the information provided in the previous discussion.

Treatment programs in corrections settings, for example, can be integrated into the daily routines of inmates. Lessons of therapy can be reinforced and strengthened each day in the prison community by counselors, staff, and other inmates. Chemical dependency counselors can connect inmates with outside resources that will help them with their continued sobriety.

Counseling this population can be rewarding for the counselor, and substance abuse treatment as part of jail time makes a great deal of sense because it is very cost-effective in the long run for society. It costs only slightly more than no treatment at all, and it pays off in reduced recidivism rates, lower overall crime rates, and fewer behavior problems from inmates. Society has yet to see the full benefits of such treatment.

Emotional Stress or a History of Personal Trauma

It is not difficult for the counselor to identify negative emotions in chemically dependent persons. Patients in group or individual counseling often express sadness, grief, anger, fear, and rage. Positive emotions (e.g., joy, happiness, love, and caring) are usually less visible and often occur only as a sign that the patient is starting recovery. A goal of treatment is often to get clients to let go of, or change, highly charged negative emotions and replace them with positive emotions.

Anger is one of the most common emotions seen in individuals with substance abuse issues. Anger may or may not appear to be directed toward a specific person or event. In some cases, individuals with substance abuse issues may deny that this anger even exists. They may mask this emotion with another, such as sadness. Yet, they display repeated destructive, aggressive behavior toward others, usually while under the influence. A look into the developmental history of someone with an addiction might reveal a family background where anger and violence were not tolerated; thus, the only time it becomes acceptable to get angry or aggressive is while intoxicated. Then the person with an addiction has an excuse. Further examination might find that a great deal of unexpressed anger toward a parent or a sibling exists and that the issues involved therein have never been resolved. If this is the case, the therapist can help resolve the issue by bringing in the family or providing some type of substitute treatment, such as the "empty chair technique" (where the client addresses an empty chair, representing the person who is unable to attend therapy) for dealing with unresolved past issues. The therapist can also provide the client with alternative, positive ways of expressing anger. For some persons, just recognizing how past events have affected them is motivation enough to assist them in changing their feelings, thinking, and behavior.

Persons who come from families with alcoholism often have the types of difficulties described above. About 50% of people with alcoholism come from families with alcoholism present. What is not known is why only some of the children of parents with alcoholism develop alcoholism themselves and why others drink only moderately or choose not to drink at all. Of those who have problems with alcoholism, it is clear that their lives as children in families with alcoholism had a great deal to do with their own alcoholism. We know that modeling played a part in the development of their problem drinking. We also know that they may be at higher risk biologically or genetically. But most of all, we know that they were affected psychologically and emotionally. It is important to remember that not all children who grow up in families with alcoholism are damaged emotionally or will suffer from negative psychological conditions. As referenced in the section of the chapter discussing the adolescent male, all clients bring a blend of strengths and limitations learned as a result of their family relationships. Children from less-than-ideal family environments are no exception. Though risk factors may increase as a result of being in a family with alcohol and drug problems, they are also capable of learning successful strategies and developing strengths from the experience.

Stress and Psychological Factors

It has been the authors' clinical experience that psychological factors are very important in determining why and to what degree some people develop chemical dependency. People with drinking problems that come from homes with alcoholism generally do not like themselves, and they do not feel in control of what they see as their hostile environment. Furthermore, most, if not all, of their negative attitudes can be traced directly to their experiences as a child in a family with parents who drink. What is unfortunate is that many of their ideas and attitudes are erroneous and based on the sometimes-distorted view of the world that they had as children. For example, because of their parents' behavior they believed, and still believe, that their parents did not love them. Therefore, they see themselves as unlovable. After all, if one's own parents do not love them, who will? This is seemingly logical reasoning, but a child has no understanding of the complexities of alcoholism and other addiction and the behavior connected with it. To the child, the behavior is clear and the message is clear: Because my parents treat me as they do, I must be unloved and unwanted. At the very least, the message is confusing: "Daddy loves me but Daddy has a disease?" For a child, and even for many adults, a disease does not excuse past or future behavior. A parent missing a birthday or missing Christmas is a disappointment to a child, disease or no disease. And if the child resents the parent who drinks for his or her neglectful behavior, then telling the child not to drink because the parent has a disease only makes the child feel guilty about natural feelings. For the child, the only real option is to have the parent demonstrate his or her love through consistent loving behavior.

For adults who grew up in a family with alcoholism, an understanding of their parents' behavior—and the connection to why they are now behaving the way they do—could change some of their own destructive behavior. Many people with alcoholism do not make a connection between their own behavior and that of their parents. They have also given little, if any, thought as to why their parents behaved the way they did and to the impact that their grandparents had on their parents. It is a common belief that all people have a set of choices and are free to make whatever choice they want. The reality is that long before they make many choices, they are programmed to make one choice over another, and their choices are not always in their own best interest. However, if they know how they have been programmed, they can override their programming and make choices that are truly in their best interest. Hence, adults who grew up as children of alcoholics should re-examine the issue of their self-worth. Given additional information and evidence (i.e., people who care about them, past successes, parents who perhaps are now sober and can express love to them), they can decide that they need to re-assess their feelings of worthlessness and examine how they could make new decisions regarding their future behavior. For them, this might mean remaining sober and allowing themselves to enjoy life.

In most instances, it is possible to trace the antecedent of a behavior and to develop patterns of past behavior. It is also possible to predict, with some degree of accuracy, which future behavior will be based on past behavior. It is almost impossible, however, to do this without a knowledge of each person's developmental history. This should also include a history of past trauma. As mentioned, the family is often a source of this trauma, though not always. Veterans of the Vietnam War, for example, often live with the trauma not only of the war but also of an unpopular war. This has been similarly true of veterans returning from Afghanistan and Iraq, as evidenced by higher suicide risk (Schoenbuam et al., 2014). After risking their lives and seeing many of their friends killed, it is no wonder that this group is at high risk for substance problems. However, substance abuse is not the only issue that should be addressed in therapy. The trauma must be dealt with, perhaps even before the substance abuse. Patients will be unlikely to give up drugs unless they have resolved the issues of the war.

For women (and some men), a likely source of trauma will be sexual violence. Up to one-third of women are expected to be sexually assaulted, and in more than 50% of cases, by someone known to them (Luce, Schrager, & Gilchrist, 2010). Individuals at particularly high risk include adolescent girls, women, and children during times of war, and women serving in the military (Luce et al., 2010). Many women will have difficulties successfully addressing any substance abuse issues until this trauma is directly addressed, as in the case of a patient of the authors who had been horrifically and repeatedly sexually abused as a child and teen. A known trigger for her to use was the anxiety she felt in reaction to the frequent nightmares she experienced in which she relived the sexual trauma. It wasn't until counseling directly addressed this issue that her substance use declined dramatically.

A trauma may also be caused by a random event that changes lives forever. A patient of the authors, who was a cocaine abuser (and a heavy alcohol user when he could not get cocaine), had been to in-patient treatment four different times. During the initial interview, it was revealed that at age 18, while he was in high school, this now 28-year-old young man had been driving with a friend when an accident occurred. The friend was not only killed, he was decapitated in full view of the patient. Further inquiry revealed that although this patient was still feeling a great deal of guilt over this incident, not one of the treatment programs had even asked him about it. It was very unlikely that this individual would be able to give up drugs unless this issue was resolved, or at least addressed.

Because of the many similarities among persons who are chemically dependent, it is easy for a chemical dependency counselor to believe that each client is basically like the others. There are, however, far more differences among chemically dependent persons than there are similarities. The knowledge of these differences often separates a counselor who is mostly effective from one who is mostly ineffective.

Drugs of Choice

The drug, or drugs, that an individual chooses to use or the type of addiction is another consideration that the counselor will use in designing an appropriate treatment plan. There are some differences that need to be considered. For example, a cocaine or stimulant user may present very differently than an alcohol or depressant user—the effects of heavy stimulant use include symptoms of paranoia and agitation that may not be seen in depressant use. Of course, the fact that a cocaine user had to break the law to use and an alcohol user did not have to will play a part in this. It is beyond the scope of this text to detail each addiction or drug, and their similarities and differences; however, Chapter 5 provides additional information on this. We also suggest that chemical dependency counselors take a course in pharmacology and be aware of the different effects and side effects of drugs, as well as psychotropic medications (further discussed in Chapter 9).

Other Addictions

Though there is much conversation, both casual and professional, around non–substance-related addictions, there is only one—gambling—that is formally recognized as an addictive disorder in the DSM-5. Gambling Disorder contains nine criteria, including "needs to gamble increasing amounts of money in order to achieve the desired excitement" and "lies to conceal the extent of involvement with gambling," of which at least four must be met within a 12-month period in order to be diagnosed. Eating disorders are addressed in a different section of the DSM-5, though the DSM's authors acknowledge similarities with substance-use disorders, such as craving and compulsion (American Psychiatric Association, 2013).

What about other addictions? Some people develop addictive behaviors around things as varied as sex (including masturbation and online porn), exercise, candy and soft drinks, fast food, social media, video games, shopping, and more. While not formally diagnosable, these different process addictions likely share many similarities with substance use disorders.

Substance abuse counselors who are tempted to treat such disorders and process addictions should be cautioned. Though similarities there may be, there are also significant differences. The concept of abstinence, for example, is not really useful in the treatment of eating disorders or possible process addictions relating to sex, shopping, or exercise. As well, the treatment of eating disorders and other addictions involves knowledge of specific issues and treatment options. In some states, substance abuse counselors will need additional credentialing, demonstrating the additional training they have received in these areas, or they will be considered to be practicing outside of their field.

Summary

The chemical dependency counselor who has a knowledge of diversity issues, skills in identifying these issues and treating resulting problems, the ability to treat the family as a system, and the willingness to look at society's role in all of this will find the field of chemical dependency treatment rewarding and a continual challenge. Counselors who do not possess this knowledge or these skills will be constantly perplexed by a client with chemical dependency issues and might believe the client was not ready for treatment. They will be unable or unwilling to see that it was not the client who was not ready for treatment, but that they lacked the skills to identify appropriate treatment plans. Meanwhile, the counselor with an understanding based on knowledge in these and other areas that make each client diverse will be able and willing to take the appropriate responsibility for what happens in treatment and to make adjustments as necessary to provide a successful treatment plan.

References

Alexander, M. (2012). *The New Jim Crow*. New York: New Press.

American Psychiatric Association. (2013). *Diagnostic and statistical manual of mental disorders: Fifth edition*. Arlington, VA: Author.

Bava, G., & Tapert, S. F. (2010). Adolescent brain development and the risk for alcohol and other drug problems. *Neuropsychology Review, 20,* 398–413.

Centers for Disease Control and Prevention. (2011). *Policy impact: Prescription painkiller overdoses.* Rockville, Maryland: Author.

Corey, G. (2012). *Theory and practice of group counseling*. Belmont, CA: Brooks/Cole.

Eaves, S. H., & Sheperis, C. J. (2011). Group work with adult populations. In B. T. Erford (Ed.), *Group work processes and applications* (pp. 263–276). Upper Saddle River, NJ: Pearson.

Erikson, E. (1950). *Childhood and society.* New York: W. W. Norton.

Farkas, K. J. (2014). Assessment and treatment of older adults with substance use disorders. In S. L. Straussner (Ed.), *Clinical work with substance abusing clients* (pp. 421–441). New York: Guilford Press.

Freshman, A. (2014). Assessment and treatment of adolescents with substance use disorders. In S. L. Straussner (Ed.), *Clinical work with substance abusing clients* (pp. 395–420). New York: Guilford Press.

Freud, S. (1905). *Three essays on the theory of sexuality.* S.E., 7.

Gant, L. M. (2014). Assessment and treatment of drug-using individuals with HIV/AIDS. In S. L. Straussner (Ed.), *Clinical work with substance abusing clients* (pp. 495–519). New York: Guilford Press.

Gladding, S. T. (2009). *Counseling: A comprehensive profession*. Upper Saddle River, NJ: Pearson.

Lawson, A., & Lawson, G. (1998). *Alcoholism and the family: A guide to treatment and prevention* (2nd ed.). Austin, TX: PRO-ED.

Lawson, G., & Lawson A. (Eds.). (2011). *Alcoholism and substance abuse in diverse populations* (2nd ed.). Austin, TX: PRO-ED.

Luce, H., Schrager, S., & Gilchrist, V. (2010). Sexual assault of women. *American Family Physician, 81*(4), 489–495.

Masters, W., & Johnson, V. (1966). *Human sexual response*. Boston: Little, Brown.

Molina, B. S. G., Donovan, J. E., & Belendiuk, K. A. (2010). Familial loading for alcoholism and offspring behavior: Mediating and moderating influences. *Alcoholism: Clinical and Experimental Research, 34*(11), 1972–1984.

Nunes, E. V., Selzer, J., Levounis, P., & Davies, C. A. (Eds.). (2010). *Substance dependence and co-occurring psychiatric disorders*. Kingston, NJ: Civic Research Institute.

Pape, P. A., & Sarabia, S. E. (2014). Assessment and treatment of women with substance use disorders. In S. L. Straussner (Ed.), *Clinical work with substance abusing clients* (pp. 442–465). New York: Guilford Press.

Schoenbaum, M., Kessler R. C., Gilman S. E., Colpe, L. J., Heeringa, S. G., Stein, M. B., Ursano, R. J., & Cox, K. L. (2014). Predictors of suicide and accident death in the Army Study to Assess Risk and Resilience in Servicemembers (Army STARRS): Results From the Army Study to Assess Risk and Resilience in Servicemembers (Army STARRS). *Journal of the American Medical Association Psychiatry, 71*(5), 493–503.

Senreich, E., & Vairo, E. (2014). Assessment and treatment of lesbian, gay, and bisexual clients with substance use disorders. In S. L. Straussner (Ed.), *Clinical work with substance abusing clients* (pp. 466–494). New York: Guilford Press.

U.S. Census Bureau. (2014). 1980s estimates files available at the national, state, and county levels of geography. Retrieved from http://www.census.gov/popest/data/historical/index.html

Vaillant, G. E. (1971). Theoretical hierarchy of adaptive ego mechanisms. *Archives of General Psychiatry, 24*, 107–118.

Vieraitis, L. M., Kovandzic, T. V., & Marvell, T. B. (2007). The criminogenic effects of imprisonment: Evidence from panel data, 1974–2002. *Criminology and Public Policy, 6*(3), 589–622.

CHAPTER 9

Psychopharmacology and the Chemical Dependency Counselor

CHAPTER OBJECTIVES

- Understand the basic arguments for and against the use of medications for treating psychological disorders and alleviating psychological symptoms
- Realize that medications are not a panacea and are only one of many tools to be considered and incorporated into treatment for the benefit of the client
- Identify and recognize the different classes of drugs and what they are used for
- Understand when the use of such drugs may be of benefit
- Describe the specific role that substance abuse counselors have vis-à-vis psychopharmacology

Great advances have been made in better understanding the neurobiology of addiction, and the "medicalization" of the treatment of various mental health disorders has become increasingly common. It is for these reasons that those who aspire to be substance abuse counselors and wish to work effectively with their clients must familiarize themselves with the different medications available for treating a variety of addictions directly. Additionally, it is important to have some basic understanding of the different drugs available to treat a variety of mental health disorders. There exists, too, a healthy amount of resistance toward and skepticism about this increased medicalization and development of additional pharmaceuticals. It will be helpful for substance abuse counselors to be familiar with the context of this debate.

This chapter has a few specific purposes in mind: one, to make sure that aspiring substance abuse counselors understand the concerns of those who argue in favor of the use of psychotropic medications and the concerns of those who are not necessarily opposed to the use of medication but are opposed to mainstream attitudes regarding medication; two, to help aspiring substance abuse counselors acquire a basic framework for understanding the different classes of drugs available; and finally, to help them understand their role in supporting clients and their utilization of psychopharmacology services.

What Chemical Dependency Counselors Need to Know About Psychopharmacology

According to "Comorbidity: Addiction and Other Mental Illnesses," a research report published by the National Institute on Drug Abuse in 2008 and revised in 2010:

> Many people who regularly abuse drugs are also diagnosed with mental disorders and vice versa. The high prevalence of this comorbidity has been documented in multiple national population surveys since the 1980s. Data show that persons diagnosed with mood or anxiety disorders are about *twice as likely* to suffer also from a drug use disorder (abuse or dependence) compared with respondents in general. The same is true for those diagnosed with an antisocial syndrome, such as antisocial personality or conduct disorder. Similarly, persons diagnosed with drug disorders are roughly twice as likely to suffer also from mood and anxiety disorders. (p. 2)

And, from "2009 National Survey on Drug Use and Health: Mental Health Findings":

> Among the 20.8 million adults with a past year substance use disorder, *42.8 percent* (8.9 million adults) *had a co-occurring mental illness* in 2009. In comparison, among adults without a substance use disorder, 17.6 percent had any mental illness. (Substance Abuse and Mental Health Services Administration, 2010, p. 35)

It seems likely, then, that substance use counselors will come into contact with clients who have a co-occurring disorder. Just as likely, counselors will come into contact with clients who are using, or may benefit from using, medications to treat these disorders and/or their addictions directly.

According to a report that reviewed the prescription drug claims of more than two million Americans to assess the use of a variety of psychotropic drugs between 2001 and 2010, more than 1 in 5 Americans and more than 1 in 4 women used such drugs in 2010 (Medco Health Solutions, 2011). If, as was previously reported, persons who are suffering from a drug use disorder are twice as likely as the general population to have a mental health disorder, it is reasonable to assume that the percentage of such persons using medications to treat psychological and behavioral disorders will also be higher. This means that substance abuse counselors should not be surprised to see as many as 40% to 50% of their clients utilizing such prescriptions!

Whether this is a good or bad thing is debatable and beyond the scope of this chapter. It will be instructive, though, to look at some of the factors behind the increase of the use of psychotropic medications. It will be up to readers to form their own opinions about the utility and efficacy of such medications, and will likely involve additional research outside the bounds of this chapter. Whatever conclusions readers ultimately draw, it will be helpful to be familiar with the larger context of this conversation.

One possibility for the higher rates of usage may be due to a decline in stigma associated with the use of such drugs, such that more patients are self-identifying and seeking, or are at least more comfortable with, such remedies (Horgan, 2012). If this is indeed the case, then perhaps we can take comfort that the rates of use are increasing for the right reasons.

Unfortunately, the majority of prescriptions for psychotropic medications are written not by trained psychiatrists but by general practitioners who have limited training in treating psychological or behavioral disorders. Indeed, as many as 4 out of 5 prescriptions written for psychotropic medications are not written by psychiatrists. This is happening at the same time that the percentage of patients receiving psychotherapy has fallen, which may be related not to efficacy rates, but to market forces. Specifically, clinician reimbursement rates for psychotherapy fell and thus patients had higher out-of-pocket costs related to the use of psychotherapy (Smith, 2012).

A study by the Yale School of Management (King & Essick, 2013) found that the use of antidepressants, stimulants, and antipsychotics varied widely across geographic regions. For example, the use of antidepressants ranged from less than 1% of residents to more than 40% of residents, depending on where they lived in the United States. This study also found that the utilization of psychotropic medications rose with increased access to health care, insurance coverage, and pharmaceutical marketing efforts.

Finally, there is much debate as to whether the possible benefits conferred by psychotropic medications are worth the many well-documented risks and side effects of taking such medications. The list of side effects should be carefully considered alongside the possible benefits that such medications provide. A more extensive list of risks for specific classes of psychotropic medications will be provided in detail later in this chapter. Still, a sampling of such risks will prove instructive: drowsiness, dizziness, rapid heartbeat, tremors, nausea, sexual problems, sleeplessness or drowsiness, constipation, seizures, hallucinations, changes in weight, liver damage, and nightmares (National Institutes of Health, 2008).

Research indicates that non-drug therapies and strategies can be as effective as medications for achieving therapeutic goals. In the treatment of depression, for example, cognitive behavioral therapy, exercise, light therapy, and lifestyle changes (e.g., diet, sleep) have all been found to be effective and/ or helpful in reducing feelings and symptoms associated with depression. It will be helpful for substance abuse counselors, then, to be familiar with all such strategies to best support those clients struggling with depression, as well as for treating other co-occurring disorders.

Future Directions of Research

It is hoped that future research will result in psychotropic medications that are better able to alleviate unwanted symptoms while reducing and/or even eliminating possible side effects. As an example, the Research Domain Criteria project, launched by the National Institute of Mental Health, has as its goal the transformation of diagnosis by "incorporating genetics, imaging, cognitive science, and other levels of information" (Insel, 2013). This project hopes to identify relevant biomarkers and to collect the "genetic, imaging, physiologic, and cognitive data to see how [it] cluster[s] and how these clusters relate to treatment response."

The National Academy of Sciences has developed an effort with a goal of "precision medicine" that would utilize "genomic, epigenomic, exposure, and other data to define individual patterns of disease, potentially leading to better individual treatment" (Insel, 2011). As a reference point for how transformative such a shift in thinking this represents, this National Academy of Sciences report references how the treatment of cancer has been "revolutionized by the application of molecular biology." Instead of utilizing the less precise and traditional diagnostic labels such as "kidney cancer" or "lung cancer," doctors are now looking for particular genetic mutations specific to tumors. When specific "driver mutations" are identified, medications can be developed to specifically target and block the growth of related cancerous tumors (Insel, 2011).

Because the National Institute of Mental Health is the largest source of mental health research funding in the United States (Clark, 2010), the announcement of the Research Domain Criteria project and its stated aims represents a significant and potent paradigmatic shift in thinking about and conceptualizing mental health disorders (Lane, 2013). It is possible that this shift in thinking may lead to discoveries that could lead to a "precision medicine"–based approach. It will likely take years—if not decades—of ongoing and continuing research before it is possible to know whether psychological disorders will ever be able to be treated as definitively as many physical disorders are at the present time.

Who Can Prescribe Medications

If a client or patient is to receive medications for the treatment of a mental health disorder or substance use disorder, he or she will need to visit a medical professional who has the ability to write prescriptions. The list of medical professionals who can prescribe medications includes physicians, physician assistants, and nurse practitioners. It is advisable and preferable, however, to refer clients only to those medical professionals—psychiatrists and psychiatric nurse practitioners—who have had specific training and education in mental health disorders, as they are generally in a better position to manipulate the prescription-administration process such that clients experience relief from troubling symptoms while minimizing unwanted side effects.

After conducting an evaluation and considering a patient's symptoms, a medical professional will generally consult a list of possible drugs for treating those particular symptoms and, based largely on their experience treating previous patients with such drugs, will make a choice as to which prescriptions to write and at what dosage levels. Because not all patients respond equally to such medications, the medical professional is generally limited to a few options for optimizing the patient's response: (a) A medication's dosage level can be adjusted upward or downward; (b) a different medication can be selected; and (c) a medication can be taken in conjunction with other medications. From our personal and professional experience in working with clients, we have seen success from all three of these strategies being used singularly and together. As well, we have witnessed clients for whom none of these strategies appeared to work.

Some drugs are meant only for short-term relief, whereas others may be prescribed for years, depending on what a client is dealing with. When discontinuing the use of a medication, it is important to do so under the supervision of a medical professional, as serious side effects can be experienced if the use of such drugs is discontinued too abruptly.

Classes of Drugs

More on each particular class of drugs is provided in further detail below. Those used to treat pain and addictions are considered last. Unless otherwise specifically referenced, the text consulted as a reference in describing how each of these drug categories works is *Basic and Clinical Pharmacology* (Katzung, 2007).

Antidepressants

As per the *Diagnostic and Statistical Manual of Mental Disorders–Fifth Edition* (DSM-V), the possible causes of depression are thought to be multifactorial, with symptoms ranging from poor concentration to feelings of hopelessness (American Psychiatric Association, 2013). Antidepressants generally work by affecting the amount and accessibility of the neurotransmitters serotonin, norepinephrine, and dopamine (Food and Drug Administration [FDA],

2009). As well, it may take several weeks before the full therapeutic effects of such drugs are experienced. These are also sometimes used to help reduce anxiety for some patients.

There are different classifications of antidepressants:

- **Selective Serotonin Reuptake Inhibitors (SSRIs)**—These antidepressants work by blocking the reabsorption—or reuptake—of serotonin. They tend to have fewer side effects than some of the other classifications. Examples of SSRIs include:

Brand Name	Generic Name
Celexa	Citalopram
Lexapro	Escitalopram
Paxil	Paroxetine
Prozac	Fluoxetine
Zoloft	Sertraline

- **Serotonin and Norepinephrine Reuptake Inhibitors (SNRIs)**—These antidepressants work by blocking the reuptake of both serotonin and norepinephrine. Side effects can include increased blood pressure, dry mouth, nausea, and constipation. Examples of SNRIs include:

Brand Name	Generic Name
Cymbalta	Duloxetine
Effexor	Venlafaxine
Pristiq	Desvenlafaxine

- **Atypical Antidepressants**—Medications in this category are called "atypicals" because they don't fit well into any of the other classifications. Some can be sedating and are sometimes prescribed as sleep aids; others (Wellbutrin) may help some people quit smoking. These generally have fewer side effects. Examples of atypicals include:

Brand Name	Generic Name
Oleptro	Trazodone
Remeron	Mirtazapine
Wellbutrin	Bupriopion

- **Tricyclics**—These were first discovered in the 1960s and can still be effective for some. They are associated with a wide range of side effects including dry mouth, constipation, blurred vision, urinary difficulties, weight gain, and more. Examples of tricyclics include:

Brand Name	Generic Name
Anafranil	Clomipramine
Elavil	Amitriptyline
Norpramin	Desipramine
Pamelor	Nortriptyline
Sinequan	Doxepin

- **Monoamine oxidase inhibitors (MAOIs)**—As indicated, these medications inhibit action of the MAO enzyme. These are often used as a last resort because of the seriousness of related side effects, including dizziness, stomach upset, twitching muscles, sleep problems, and death related to high blood pressure. Examples of MAOIs include:

Brand Name	Generic Name
Emsam	Selegiline
Marplan	Isocarboxazid
Nardil	Phenelzine
Parnate	Tranylcypromine

For all classifications of antidepressants, the risk of suicide must constantly be monitored. Patients, particularly those younger than 25, may notice an increase in suicidal ideation within the first few weeks of beginning an antidepressant (FDA, 2009). Research has shown that antidepressants may work better for those with more severe bouts of depression and/or in combination with talk therapy (NIMH, 2013b).

Anxiolytics (Anti-Anxiety Drugs)

There are many different anxiety disorders, including agoraphobia, obsessive-compulsive disorder, post-traumatic stress disorder, and generalized anxiety disorder, to list a few (American Psychiatric Association, 2013). Unlike antidepressants, the different classifications of anxiolytics have differing mechanisms for reducing anxiety and/or its symptoms.

The different classifications of anxiolytics include the following:

- **Benzodiazepines**—While benzodiazepines are highly effective, they have a generally short half-life. As well, habituation and physical dependency generally develop quickly. There are relatively few side effects, but withdrawal symptoms are possible if patients quit abruptly, and anxiety can rebound.

Brand Name	Generic Name
Ativan	Lorazepam
Klonopin	Clonazepam
Librium	Chlordiazepoxide
Valium	Diazepam
Xanax	Alprazolam

- **Beta-Blockers**—These drugs are used to help alleviate the physical symptoms that occur with particular anxiety disorders.

Brand Name	Generic Name
Inderal	Propranolol
Tenormin	Atenolol

- **Others**—These are drugs that don't fit neatly in the previous categories and include antihistamines known for creating mild sedative effects.

Brand Name	Generic Name
Benadryl	Diphenhydramine
Buspar	Buspirone
Equanil	Meprobamate
Neurontin	Gabapentin
Vistaril	Hydroxyzine

Research has supported psychotherapy, specifically cognitive behavioral therapy, to be as effective in treating anxiety disorders as medications. One of the benefits of utilizing psychotherapy is the avoidance of side effects associated with utilizing anxiolytics. Another benefit is that psychotherapy tends to be longer lasting since patients learn coping skills that actually help to reduce anxiety, whereas medications require ongoing use to accomplish the same effect. As with depression, the best results seem to be those that involve both psychotherapy and medications together (Schiffman, 2011).

Mood Stabilizers

Mood stabilizers are medications used to help manage symptoms of bipolar disorder, a mental health disorder noted for abrupt and dramatic swings in mood and energy, from experiencing a manic episode with feelings of uncontainable and unmanageable energy to depressive episodes with feelings of sadness and hopelessness (NIMH, 2013b). Because the use of mood stabilizers affects liver, kidney, and thyroid functioning, an electrocardiogram may be required and regular blood tests are utilized to help ensure the proper therapeutic dose (Texas State University Counseling Center, 2013).

Examples of mood stabilizers include:

Brand Name	Generic Name
Lithium Carbonate	Lithium
Depakote	Valproic Acid
Tegretol	Carbamazepine
Valium	Diazepam
Xanax	Alprazolam

Side effects of lithium include restlessness, indigestion, joint/muscle pain, and brittle nails and hair. Side effects associated with other mood stabilizers include drowsiness, dizziness, diarrhea, constipation, headache, and heartburn (NIMH, 2013a).

Psychostimulants

These medications are generally prescribed for hyperactivity, attention-deficit disorder, narcolepsy, and some depressive conditions. Psychostimulants work by increasing the amount of available norepinephrine and help with increased alertness, wakefulness, and concentration.

Examples of psychostimulants include:

Brand Name	Generic Name
Adderall	Amphetamine
Cylert	Pemoline
Dexedrine	Dextroamphetamine
Ritalin	Methylphenidate

Anti-Psychotics

Anti-psychotic medications, also referred to as "neuroleptics" (major tranquilizers), are utilized to treat disordered or psychotic thinking primarily for people who have schizophrenia and severe bipolar disorder. They are considered to be dopamine antagonists because they work largely by blocking dopamine production. It is because of this dopamine blocking that one of the side effects includes Parkinsonian-like symptoms and tardive dyskinesia, which is an often permanent disorder noted by facial tics and involuntary muscle movements and tremors; additional medications may be given to address these side effects (Katzung, 2007).

Examples of anti-psychotics include:

Brand Name	Generic Name
Haldol	Haloperidol
Loxitane	Loxapine
Moban	Molindone
Prolixin	Fluphenazine
Thorazine	Chlorpromazine

Pain Management

It is helpful, as well, to be familiar with drugs used for pain management, particularly opioid pain relievers with a high potential for abuse and dependency. This is because they are amongst the most commonly prescribed drugs in the United States and because these prescription painkillers are responsible for more overdose deaths than other, even illicit, drugs (Centers for Disease Control and Prevention, 2011).

Examples of opioid pain relievers include:

- Codeine
- Fentanyl
- Hydrocodone
- Morphine
- Oxycodone
- Percocet
- Vicodin

Drugs Used to Treat Addictions

The drugs most commonly used to treat addictions are listed and described below. Though currently limited, research continues apace to identify specific targeting sites for the development of new medications that will, hopefully, one day have the capacity to stop drug cravings.

- **Alcohol**—There are three drugs in the United States that have been approved specifically to address alcohol dependence. **Disulfiram** (Antabuse) is an aversion drug that causes uncomfortable side effects when a person taking the drug also uses alcohol. **Naltrexone** (Revia) and **Acamprosate** (Campral) are both opioid antagonists and are prescribed to help patients' alcohol cravings (*New York Times*, 2013).

- **Nicotine**—Drugs used to treat nicotine addiction include **nicotine replacement products**, which include patches applied to the skin, gum, lozenges, sprays, and inhalers. All of these provide a predetermined dose of nicotine when used. Non-nicotine medications include bupropion (Zyban) and varenicline (Chantix). **Bupropion** is an antidepressant drug that mimics nicotine in that it increases levels of dopamine and norepinephrine. **Varenicline** blocks nicotine receptors in the brain, thus decreasing withdrawal symptoms and the feelings of pleasure associated with using nicotine.

- **Opioids**—There are three main medication options for treating opioid addiction. The longest used is **methadone**, which is a slower acting opioid agonist and is taken orally so as to further reduce the rate of absorption associated with other routes of administration. It is typically taken on a daily basis and only available through specifically approved treatment providers. **Buprenorphine** (Subutex, Suboxone) is a partial opioid agonist and provides users relief from cravings without the euphoric high or harmful side effects associated with other opioids. **Naltrexone** (Depade, Revia) is an opioid antagonist and is available in an oral form that must be taken daily, or in a form that is injected once a month.

Summary

Unless substance abuse counselors have had the requisite training and have the needed credentials, it is not generally within their scope of practice to prescribe medications. As the previous pages have hopefully illustrated, it is nonetheless incumbent upon substance abuse counselors to develop a familiarity with the medications that have been thus far discussed, as well as the mental health disorders, in the case of psychotropics, for which they are prescribed. It is imperative that substance abuse counselors not consider the use of such medications to be in violation of a client's sobriety as it is vitally important to co-treat the substance use disorder and mental health disorder concurrently.

Substance abuse counselors will be most helpful in being a source of support for the client as relates to their use of medications. This will involve the sundry case management activities in which substance abuse counselors are well versed and may include helping to identify providers, set appointments, sort through information, be a sounding board, and more. Whenever possible, it will be helpful for substance abuse counselors to work in concert with those prescribing such medications. In this way, a well-informed substance abuse counselor will be in a position to best support clients utilizing a variety of medications on their path to sobriety.

References

American Psychiatric Association. (2013). *Diagnostic and statistical manual of mental disorders* (5th ed.). Arlington, VA: Author.

Centers for Disease Control and Prevention. (2011). *Policy impact: Prescription painkiller overdoses.* Rockville, Maryland: Author.

Clark, J. (2010, May). Funding your future: Four keys to tapping into the National Institutes of Health research dollars. *Monitor on Psychology, 41*(5), 60.

Food and Drug Administration. (2009). *FDA consumer health information: Understanding antidepressant medications.* Silver Spring, MD: Author.

Horgan, J. (2012). *Are psychiatric medications making us sicker?* Retrieved from http://blogs.scientificamerican.com/cross-check/2012/03/05/are-psychiatric-medications-making-us-sicker/

Insel, T. (2011). *Director's posts about NIMH: Improving diagnosis through precision medicine.* Retrieved from www.nimh.nih.gov

Insel, T. (2013). *Director's posts about NIMH: Transforming diagnosis.* Retrieved from www.nimh.nih.gov

Katzung, B. (2007). *Basic and clinical pharmacology.* New York: McGraw Hill.

King, M., & Essick, C. (2013, March). The geography of antidepressant, antipsychotic, and stimulant utilization in the United States. *Health and Place, 20,* pp. 32–38.

Lane, C. (2013). *Side effects: The NIMH withdraws support for DSM-5.* Retrieved from www.psychologytoday.com/blog/side-effects

Medco Health Solutions. (2011). *America's state of mind report.* New Jersey: Franklin Lakes.

National Institute of Mental Health. (2013a). *Bipolar disorder.* Retrieved from www.nimh.nih.gov/health/topics/bipolar-disorder/index.shtml

National Institute of Mental Health. (2013b). *What is depression?* Retrieved from http://www.nimh.nih.gov/health/topics/depression/index.shtml

National Institute on Drug Abuse. (2010). *NIDA research report series: Comborbidity: Addiction and other mental illnesses.* NIH Publication No. 10-5571. Rockville, MD: Author.

National Institutes of Health. (2008). *Mental health medications.* NIH Publication No. 08-3929. Rockville, MD.

New York Times. (2013). *Alcoholism in-depth report.* Retrieved from http://www.nytimes.com/health/guides/disease/alcoholism/print.html

Schiffman, J. (2011). Anti-anxiety medications explained: What you need to know about the medications used to treat anxiety. *Psychology Today.* Retrieved from http://www.psychologytoday.com/blog/anxiety-help/201111/anti-anxiety-medications-explained

Smith, B. (2012, June). Inappropriate prescribing: Research shows that all too often, Americans are taking medications that may or may not work or may be inappropriate for their mental health problems. *American Psychological Association, 43*(6), 36.

Substance Abuse and Mental Health Services Administration. (2010). *Results from the 2009 National Survey on Drug Use and Health: Mental Health Findings.* (Office of Applied Studies, NSDUH Series H-39, HHS Publication No. SMA 10-4609). Rockville, MD: Author.

Texas State University Counseling Center. (2013). *Psychotropic medications.* Retrieved from www.counseling.txstate.edu/resources/shoreview/bro/psychmed.html

CHAPTER 10

Aftercare and Relapse Prevention

CHAPTER OBJECTIVES

- Define aftercare and relapse prevention
- Examine how several different treatment programs provide aftercare and relapse prevention
- Examine what the research on aftercare indicates about its effectiveness
- Examine the relapse prevention models of both Marlatt and Gordon, and Gorski
- Identify Marlatt and Gordon's specific and global relapse prevention strategies
- Examine the outline of Gorski's Developmental Model of Recovery
- Outline the basic principles and procedures of relapse prevention employing the Gorski model
- Examine the research on relapse prevention and the factors that have an impact on relapse
- Identify characteristics of people with alcoholism who are relapsing and non-relapsing
- Examine the role of self-efficacy in relapse prevention

This chapter, unlike the others in this book, focuses on what happens to those with substance abuse problems after they have completed primary treatment. While usually thought of as following treatment, both aftercare and relapse prevention actually begin with primary treatment when the person decides to stop or reduce the use of a mood-altering substance. For example, one can see the typical 12-step program as being designed to provide aftercare and to prevent relapse, and both of these goals are built upon the first step of Alcoholics Anonymous (A.A.). However, aftercare and relapse prevention have specific aims that are somewhat different from the aims of primary care. For this reason, it is important to define what is meant by *primary care, aftercare,* and *relapse prevention.*

Primary care has been defined in different ways by different people. The Institute of Medicine's (1990) special report on alcohol problems provided some of the more widely accepted definitions in the substance abuse field. The authors of this report define *primary care* as follows:

> the application of therapeutic activities to help the individual reduce alcohol consumption [could read *drug use* also] and

attain a higher level of physical, psychological, and social functioning while in either independent living or in a sheltered living
environment. (Primary care includes both brief intervention and
intensive intervention.) (p. 65)

The Institute of Medicine's (1990) report defined several other subphases
of treatment that will not be included here. However, it is necessary to include
one additional subphase outside our discussion because some people may define this type of treatment as aftercare. What this report calls *extended care-
stabilization* is defined as "the consolidation of gains achieved in primary care
through continued participation in treatment and supportive activities while
in either independent living or in a transitional supportive, sheltered living
environment" (p. 65).

Aftercare is defined by this same report as "the continued provision of some
therapeutic input to maintain the gain in functioning achieved through intensive intervention and stabilization while in either independent living or in
transitional or long-term supportive, sheltered living environment" (p. 66). (It
is important to note that there seems to be some overlap between this definition and the one given for earlier extended care and the one that follows for
relapse prevention.)

Relapse prevention, according to the Institute of Medicine's (1990) report,
is defined as follows:

the continued provision of therapeutic activities to avoid the
return to prior patterns of drinking [or drug use] and to maintain
the gains in functioning achieved through brief intervention or
intensive intervention and stabilization while in either independent living or in a transitional or long-term supportive, sheltered
living environment. (p. 66)

What these definitions illustrate is that treatment phases overlap. For example, it is often difficult to know where aftercare ends and relapse prevention
begins. The Institute of Medicine's report attempted to break down treatment
into three major phases. The first is *acute intervention* and includes emergency
treatment and detoxification. The second phase is *rehabilitation*, which sub-
sumes the attempts to get patients to change their drinking behavior. Individuals may have to learn new ways of living and thinking during this phase and
develop some new coping skills. The third stage is *maintenance and extended
care* (which is seen as an extension of primary care) and *aftercare*. However,
aftercare is used by the Institute to describe patients' long-term efforts to maintain the changes they have made in formal treatment.

These various ways of dividing up the phases of treatment may be quite artificial because patients may actually get the first so-called formal treatment in a particular area of their lives only when they are in aftercare, or the first day of formal treatment may play a critical role in aftercare. Thus, as noted earlier, treatment may not always occur in precisely arranged stages or phases. However, for the purposes of this chapter, each of the treatment phases will be discussed as if they were clearly separate.

This chapter focuses on aftercare and relapse prevention. First to be described and evaluated will be aftercare. Then relapse prevention, which is one of the major issues confronted in aftercare, will be discussed. This chapter will include some examples of aftercare and relapse prevention programs, descriptions of procedures and instruments used in these programs, and any research available that supports and/or argues against the effectiveness of aftercare and relapse prevention.

Aftercare

Getting a stable definition of *aftercare* has been difficult. The way it has been defined has changed over time and is partially dependent on who is proposing the definition. For example, aftercare, as originally defined by the Joint Commission on Accreditation of Healthcare Organizations (1983) included all the services provided for the patient following his or her discharge from the treatment agency. It is worth remembering that in the early 1980s, the Minnesota Model, a 28-day intensive inpatient treatment program based on Alcoholics Anonymous's 12 steps, was in vogue. Aftercare was seen as any services that helped recovering persons deal with the abrupt transition from an intense treatment program to life in the everyday world.

We will compare and contrast three current programs that provide treatment that extends beyond what one might call primary care. Two of these programs are built on the Minnesota Model, but they differ in the degree to which they use psychosocial treatment. A major portion of the difference is the use of clinical psychologists and/or a psychological approach. The third program is based on a developmental model. In the developmental model, the 12-step program of A.A. is not employed as a central component of treatment philosophy or as a main focus of treatment. Because of these differences and because of the differing populations that they serve, the three programs have different treatments following primary care. Economic factors, such as what type of aftercare third-party payers will fund, are also important.

Aftercare: Three Examples

Valley Hope is a chemical dependency program located in several midwestern and southwestern states. Treatment facilities managed by the Valley Hope

Association in Norton, Kansas, can be found in Kansas, Nebraska, Missouri, Oklahoma, Texas, Colorado, and Arizona. This is a non-profit organization that has been very successful, as demonstrated by its growth from one agency in Norton, Kansas, to 18 treatment facilities in seven states. All of Valley Hope's treatment centers share a common philosophy. Much of the philosophy is based on the Minnesota Model and the use of A.A.'s 12 steps. Valley Hope has at least two treatment facilities in each of the seven states it serves, with at least one providing residential and one providing outpatient services.

As might be expected from a program that is concerned with the continuum of care, Valley Hope also offers an aftercare program, referred to as "continuing care" by Valley Hope. The aftercare program may be obtained as part of the primary care treatment or may be purchased separately. Aftercare consists of weekly group sessions for as long as a client needs. For those unable to attend in person, another option exists: Support is available through an online platform that allows 24-hour access.

Another view of how Valley Hope is hoping to make treatment more accessible in all its forms to all those who need assistance, including those in various stages of aftercare, is given in the Winter 2013 edition of the organization's newsletter, *Coffee Cup*. This view was written by Dr. Ken Grogoire, Valley Hope's CEO and President. Gregoire is careful to note that Valley Hope provides "real outpatient treatment not just aftercare which we now call continuing care to denote that what happens after residential treatment is real treatment too." He goes on to describe the Open House for Valley Hope's recently renovated facility in Overland Park, Kansas:

> [The newly renovated facility] looks new, feels new and even smells new. We have a Coffee Shop that looks like a Starbuck's coffee shop [with] computer stations, a big screen TV, café tables and chairs and very comfy lounge chairs. Patients can be in treatment at their kitchen table or at our Coffee Shop in our online treatment program. If they are having a bad day and just want safe company they can drop in, have a cup of coffee and hang out, watch a ball game, or play cards or do homework. Around the corner from the Coffee Shop is the office where our physician sees patients . . . yes, that's right our physician…having a physician provide support and treatment for our patients in outpatient treatment is new for us . . ."

The future of aftercare, as Dr. Gregoire suggests, is on-demand aftercare services that feel less clinical and more personable and are accessible in a variety of formats, whether in-person or online.

The **Bryan Independence Center**, located in Lincoln, Nebraska, has been in place since the beginning of the 1970s. It sees addiction as a chronic, potentially relapsing condition and is truly a Minnesota Model program since it was established by trainers from the Johnson Institute in Minnesota. Historically, the Bryan Independence Center has depended heavily on third-party payments and is now part of Bryan Health, which might best be described as a network of medical providers, including doctors and hospitals. Today, treatment is seen as a continuum of care that includes inpatient and partial care for both adults and adolescents, as well as intensive outpatient care.

Depending on the clients' needs, movement through each level of treatment has variable lengths of stay, with 23 days being the average length of stay in residential treatment. Physicians are incorporated into treatment as needed. All of the different levels of service are provided through a multidisciplinary team of providers, including counselors, nurses, teachers, spiritual counselors, mental health technicians, psychiatrists, and mental health practitioners. There is an adherence to a "drop-down" model of treatment to de-intensify care as appropriate and warranted. Services provided include, but are not limited to, youth-specific treatment, family workshops, various support groups, and a chemical dependency intervention nurse. At present, the Bryan Independence Center offers two aftercare support groups that are facilitated by alumni and free to those who have completed treatment through the organization.

For more about these services and how the Bryan Independence Center attempts to customize treatment to each individual, visit their website at www.bryanhealth.com. The Bryan Independence Center's program is trying to find a way to meet patients' treatment needs by providing a program that is flexible, customer oriented, and sensitive to the current managed care reimbursement system. They have begun an extensive renovation and construction project estimated for completion in Fall 2014 that, according to artists' renderings, will have the same effect on the aesthetics of the treatment experience as did Valley Hope's reimagining of its "coffee shop" to feel more like a modern Starbucks.

CenterPointe (formerly the **Lincoln Lancaster Drug Projects**) is not an A.A. or 12-step-based program. Instead, it is based on a biopsychosocial model: a holistic approach that attempts to combine all other models excepting the moral model. The individual and the application of the holistic approach are the focus of this treatment center. The holistic approach assumes that biological events affect psychological functioning, that psychological functioning affects social functioning, and vice versa.

This holistic approach, as indicated, requires an understanding of a person in hir or her entirety. Without looking at the whole person, all the problems or all the possible resources that could be used to assist recovery cannot be recognized. The treatment of the whole person means treating several presenting problems at the same time. This approach has led to the agency's treating dual-diagnosis clients (i.e., clients with co-existing substance abuse and mental health problems), with neither disorder being primary. Because of the nature of the clients' histories (many are homeless, many have limited resources, and many have dual mental health diagnoses), the treatment is often longer than in most substance abuse centers. Treatment runs as long as 6 to 8 months for clients in their "Co-occurring Residential Treatment" program.

For more about CenterPointe and the variety of services it provides, visit their website at www.centerpointe.org. As for aftercare services, CenterPointe provides case management and crisis/relapse prevention services as part of its "Recovery Support" services to help support its clients to live independently.

See Table 10.1 for a comparison of the three programs just described.

The three program descriptions in Table 10.1 point out that the way in which aftercare is incorporated into treatment varies in important ways across different alcohol treatment programs. These differing aftercare programs make it difficult to compare the effectiveness of aftercare in general and its specific effects in particular in the overall recovery rate of persons who have been treated for alcohol and drug problems. One way to resolve whether these varying aftercare programs are effective is to utilize research findings on aftercare. Such research should help clarify the effectiveness of aftercare in alcohol and drug treatment.

Table 10.1
Comparison of Three Treatment Programs

	Valley Hope	Bryan Independence Center	CenterPointe
Provides Continuum of Services	Yes	Yes	Yes
Clients Served	Individuals 16 and older	Adults and adolescents	Low income, dual diagnosis
Facilities	18 stand-alone sites in seven states	Associated with a hospital	10 sites plus housing units
Aftercare Offered	Yes, in weekly group sessions; time frame is open-ended; also incorporate online support	Yes, facilitated by alumni and free to those who've completed treatment	Yes, through case management and crisis/relapse prevention services
Integrated Care	Holistic and individualized	Holistic and individualized	Holistic and individualized
Website	valleyhope.org	bryanhealth.com	centerpointe.org

Research on Aftercare

There is a great deal of research that has been done on aftercare. However, there is what can be called a natural confound between participation in aftercare and the degree of investment in what Littrell (1991) calls the "packaged treatment program" (p. 191) that precedes aftercare. A confound is where two factors that could conceivably account for the outcome of a research study co-occur and make it difficult to establish causality. In the case of aftercare, it is the motivation that the client initially brings to treatment that may (with or without the treatment offered in aftercare) affect outcome. The higher the motivation, the more likely clients are to do well in treatment and the more likely they are to attend aftercare. Thus, clients' choices to attend and to complete aftercare treatment may be heavily influenced by the level of motivation and desire for change with which they leave the prepackaged program. Despite this possible confound, several studies have looked at the rate of participation in aftercare treatment in terms of the percentage of people who participated and how much they participated.

It should be first noted that participation rates in aftercare have historically been low. In one study, only 66% of 122 patients attended aftercare following an intense treatment program and only 28% attended more than three sessions (Pokorny, Miller, Kanas, & Valles, as cited in Littrell, 1991). Other programs' attendance rates at aftercare have been even lower. Of 90 Veterans Administration patients who completed an 8-week inpatient treatment program, only about one-third attended one aftercare session. Only 9% attended more than four sessions (Pratt, Linn, Carmichael, & Webb, as cited in Littrell, 1991). The perception of the ward by a person with alcoholism was a predictor of aftercare attendance, as cited in Littrell (1991). Littrell reports that the mean number of aftercare sessions attended in most studies is about three.

Studies that allow a causal statement to be made usually involve random assignment to an aftercare treatment, no follow-up treatment, and/or a differing treatment like a telephone aftercare service that has patients call in. The findings from these studies are that aftercare has no effect. That is, these more carefully controlled studies fail to support the prediction that aftercare will produce a more positive outcome than no aftercare and/or a lower level of aftercare. This might mean that *when allowed to choose aftercare,* those patients who are most invested in staying sober attend, and those less interested in remaining sober do not. An alternative hypothesis is that those patients who are most likely to comply with program recommendations are the ones who attend aftercare. Littrell (1991) suggests, from her review of the literature, that compliance is a personality factor that is positively associated with outcome in those with alcoholism.

In another important study by Connors, Tarbox, and Faillance (1992), male and female problem drinkers participated in an 8-week drinking-reduction program. Following this program, they were randomly assigned to either a 6-month group aftercare program, a telephone aftercare program, or no aftercare. Regardless of aftercare program, the majority of patients (64%) reduced their drinking following treatment. As the authors of this study note: "Aftercare, at least as operationalized in this study, did not moderate treatment outcome" (p. 471).

In a more recent study, Kaminer, Burleson, and Burke (2008) divided a group of 144 subjects into three aftercare groups. One group was placed in a five-session in-person aftercare group, another was provided with a brief telephone intervention, and a third was asked to not participate in aftercare for 3 months following treatment. The findings from this study illustrate some of the difficulties in understanding the results of aftercare studies. Though the researchers found the active aftercare groups to record fewer drinking days and fewer heavy drinking days compared to those in the no-aftercare group, all three groups had lesser rates of abstinence (i.e., more use) at the end of aftercare than immediately after treatment.

Burleson, Kaminer, and Burke (2012) followed up their earlier study with 121 subjects looking at the effects of aftercare at the end of aftercare, and 3 months, 6 months, and 12 months post-aftercare. Their results mirror their previous findings, with the active aftercare groups recording less use relative to the no-aftercare group, but all three groups recording more drinking occasions per month and increased numbers of drinks consumed per occasion at 3-month, 6-month, and 12-month follow-up compared to immediately at the end of aftercare.

What to make of all this? Well, for one thing, a review of the literature demonstrates little to no consensus as to what aftercare should look like. How long should it last? How many sessions? How frequently? In group or individually? In person or telephonically? Are different aftercare supports more appropriate for certain individuals or groups?

It will be no surprise to the reader, then, given the current lack of specificity as to what "aftercare" actually entails that research seems to support the contention that aftercare has little differential impact on treatment outcome when proper experimental controls are included. This does not necessarily mean that individuals who attend aftercare do not receive many benefits from aftercare programs. It does mean that whatever clients obtain from this extended-care experience cannot be demonstrated to have an impact under appropriate experimental conditions, or at least not enough impact to influence treatment outcome. It may be that when more precise diagnostic instruments are developed, the matching of patients with addictions to the appropriate postcare conditions may demonstrate a significant role for aftercare. It is important that the patients who are most likely to gain from this type of extended care be assigned to this longer-term treatment.

Relapse Prevention

Because alcohol and drug abuse are seen as *relapsing conditions,* one of the key factors in keeping a person drug free is minimizing the danger of relapse. Three approaches to relapse prevention will be discussed in this section. The first one (Marlatt & Gordon, 1985), the Relapse Prevention (RP) model, is possibly the best known (Lewis, 2014). It is a biopsychosocial model based on learning principles and some limited research by various investigators. Marlatt and Gordon took a social learning approach to relapse prevention, and Marlatt and his associates have been a major influence in the substance abuse field through their research on relapse prevention. (A discussion of research findings will follow the presentation of the two relapse models.)

The second approach (Witkiewitz & Marlatt, 2004), the Dynamic Model of Relapse, is an adaptation of Marlatt's Relapse Prevention model. In order to better account for the relapse process in all its complexity, the Dynamic Model of Relapse became a non-linear model set against a backdrop of high-risk situations (also known as "contextual factors"). It tries to account for all of the different factors contained within individuals and their environments to improve upon the RP model for fully explaining why and how relapse occurs.

The third approach (Gorski & Miller, 1986), known as "Gorski's Developmental Model of Recovery" or the "CENAPS Model of Relapse Prevention," is also a biopsychosocial one; the principles have been simplified and described with less learning-based, psychological jargon than has Marlatt and Gordon's approach. Also, Gorski's model is based on the 12 steps used by most of the Minnesota Model treatment centers.

Relapse Prevention: Marlatt and Gordon

Relapse and relapse prevention can be viewed from several perspectives. Marlatt and Gordon (1985) reviewed some of those perspectives in order to clarify the reasons why approaches to relapse prevention can vary depending on the philosophy on which they are based. For example, the paradox of control in the disease model (which is the base for the Minnesota Model and most other models of treatment in this country) is that those with alcoholism are told that alcohol problems originate from physiological factors that lead them to lose control of their drinking. They are told they must abstain, but the paradox is that abstaining is a *form of control.* Marlatt and Gordon said, in fact, that the individual can only maintain control if he or she abstains. To relapse is to lose control.

One of the problems of this disease-model approach is that while it absolves those with alcoholism from blame for their abusive drinking, it can potentially make them see themselves as helpless to change it. Some research suggests that if people are told that their drinking is genetic (and by implication that they can do little about it), they feel that they can do less about the problem than people who are given a social learning explanation.

Of course, in both of these models, the disease model and the social learning model, clients benefit from knowing that they are predisposed to a drinking problem, and, thus, they remain vigilant (Marlatt & Gordon, 1985). The disease model is successful if it can teach those that abuse alcohol what Wallace (1978) calls an "esoteric belief" (i.e., abusive drinkers are convinced that they are sick, that they are suffering from a medically recognized illness, and that they are no longer capable of drinking without losing control). According to Marlatt and Gordon, teaching this esoteric belief does not seem to be very effective in preventing relapse. Some research suggests that only 10% of those with alcoholism in various treatment programs manage to abstain for as long as 2 years. Relapse may be the turning point where disease theory may fail (Marlatt & Gordon, 1985). Acceptance of the A.A. position that you are always just one drink away from being a drunk means even a one-drink lapse can precipitate a total, uncontrollable relapse. Thus, in the disease model, just one lapse is tied to the expectancy that you have total failure.

Another way of seeing drinking problems is as an addiction—as nothing more than an acquired habit pattern. From the social learning perspective, addictive behaviors are viewed as overlearned habits that can be analyzed and modified in the same manner as other habits (Marlatt & Gordon, 1985). Using this conceptual perspective, Marlatt (1985a) outlined the relapse process.

Marlatt's (1985a) overview of relapse factors that contribute to slips will be followed by a more extensive discussion of these factors. First, Marlatt was careful to specify that his description of relapse applies to those people who have chosen voluntarily to abstain from the addictive behavior.

In this model, individuals are assumed to experience perceived self-control while they are maintaining abstinence. The longer persons can maintain abstinence or control over the addictive behavior, the greater their perception of self-efficacy. (Self-efficacy is defined as, "the individual's expectation concerning the capacity to cope with an impending situation or task. A feeling of confidence in one's abilities to cope with high risk situations is associated with an increased perception of self-efficacy—a kind of 'I know I can handle it' feeling" [Marlatt, 1985a, p. 40].)

Perceived control continues until the individual is exposed to a high-risk situation. (Any situation that is a risk to the person's sense of self-control is defined as high risk.) By looking at a number of relapse episodes from a variety of addiction problems (problem drinking, heroin addiction, compulsive gambling, and overeating), researchers arrived at three categories of high-risk behaviors that are closely related to relapse. The first of these three categories is *negative emotional states* (35% of all relapses occur during this type of state). The person in this state is seen as experiencing negative (and unpleasant) affects. These emotions can include frustration, anger, anxiety, depression, or boredom, which occur at or before the relapse event occurs. The source of these emotional upsets is intrapersonal.

When another person or a group of people are the source of relapse, another category of high-risk behaviors, *interpersonal conflict* (accounting for 16% of relapses), is involved. Interpersonal conflict precipitators of relapse include negative, conflictual interaction such as with the marital partner, with friendship relations, or with family members or employers. Arguments with other people and confrontations at work or in social situations would be other interpersonal conflicts that could potentially contribute to relapse.

When the individual is placed under *social pressure,* it means that pressure is being placed on a person with an addiction to engage in the addictive behavior by another person or group of people. This third relapse-precipitating factor accounts for 20% of all relapses. Marlatt (1985a) presented a more detailed and more finely honed analysis of the three factors and their influence on relapse.

From their analysis of relapse episodes, Marlatt and Gordon (1985) concluded that there were more similarities than differences across various types of addictions. In other words, the three high-risk situations are involved in similar ways among relapses from cigarette smoking, gambling, overeating, heroin, and alcohol.

The level of self-efficacy determines how effectively individuals can cope with these high-risk situations. Positive coping responses in the high-risk situations outlined above increase self-efficacy, as well as increase future self-coping responses in high-risk situations. However, positive expectations about the use of alcohol (or other addictions) compete with these positive coping responses. Therefore, those with addictions are at risk for violating their abstinence from the substance they have previously abused. If substance abusers do consume a drug while in a high-risk situation, then another cognitive process, the abstinence violation effect (AVE), occurs. The AVE has both a cognitive and an affective component in reaction to substance consumption (e.g., alcohol). These components are aroused by the knowledge that substance abusers have violated their commitment to abstinence from ethyl alcohol. The AVE includes (1) a sense of guilt or failure and (2) persons re-categorizing themselves as "drinking" rather than as abstinent persons (McCrady, 1989).

The following is a summary of Marlatt and Gordon's (1985) model of relapse prevention.

- Telling persons how to deal with a relapse is viewed by some professionals as indicating to those with alcoholism that they will relapse, and this leads to a self-fulfilling prophecy. Marlatt (1985b) pointed out that fire drills and lifeboat drills are conducted for ship passengers to prevent disasters should the worst happen. The same could be argued for alcohol relapse prevention. How to deal with a relapse should be seen as part of an ongoing treatment program.

- Involving clients in working out their relapse-prevention program is emphasized. The overall goal is to increase their awareness of the choices that they have in dealing with their problem. There is also a focus on developing individualized coping skills and self-control abilities. All of these factors contribute to a sense of mastery and self-efficacy. The teaching of these skills is done gradually, at a pace that allows mastery without clients' being overwhelmed by too much too soon. Thus, the sense of mastery also helps build self-efficacy.

- Marlatt utilized two types of intervention strategies to prevent relapses: specific intervention strategies and global self-control strategies. Specific intervention strategies are procedures directed at immediate precipitants of relapse. Global self-control strategies are designed to help modify clients' lifestyles and to deal with covert threats to relapse. The procedures used in both strategies can be subsumed under the categories of skill training, cognitive reframing, and lifestyle intervention.

- Skill training involves learning both cognitive and behavioral responses to deal with high-risk situations. Cognitive reframing techniques have several uses. They help the client see the habit-change process as a learning experience, they help in introducing coping imagery to deal with urges and cravings, and they help in restructuring how clients see the initial relapse. This latter use involves coping with AVE. This effect is a sense of failure and guilt, or the feeling that everything gained in recovery is lost as a result of a drinking slip.

- An examination of the specific intervention and global self-control strategies suggested by Marlatt gives a clearer picture of how relapse prevention techniques are operationalized. Specific intervention strategies involve teaching clients to recognize the high-risk situations that may trigger a relapse. These must be individualized because the risks are different for each person. It is important for clients to recognize as early as possible in a chain of behaviors that the behaviors are leading them closer to high-risk situations that may trigger a relapse. The earlier that individuals are aware of the risks, the sooner they can intervene by using coping skills and by using these cues as both warning signals and reminders to engage in alternative or remedial actions. Clients should be taught to monitor their reactions, check their sense of competency, and use relapses and descriptions of previous relapses to alert themselves to modify their behavior. They should be taught relaxation, stress management, and efficacy-enhancing imagery as coping responses. In the face of decreased self-efficacy and the perception of a positive outcome from drinking (alcohol will make them feel better), efficacy-enhancing imagery again helps. Education about the immediate positive and the long-term negative delayed effects of alcohol use may also be beneficial. Two other procedures that help clients limit the impact of relapse are (1) contracting with them that should they drink, they will limit alcohol's use and (2) using a reminder card that tells them what procedures to follow if they slip.

- Another training device sometimes used to anticipate relapse is "programmed relapse." That is, letting clients drink in the presence of the counselor so they discover that they can go back on the wagon after this programmed slip. To deal with AVE, cognitive restructuring is involved. Clients are taught to see the slip as a mistake and not as a total failure. They learn to attribute blame to the situation and not to themselves. These examples are not exhaustive, but give some of the major preparations for preventing and limiting relapse with these risk sources.

- Global self-control strategies help clients establish a broader framework for resisting relapse. To deal with lifestyle imbalances, clients are trained to develop a balanced daily lifestyle and to utilize positive addictions such as jogging or meditation. To deal with the client's desires for indulgences, substitute indulgences such as recreational activities or massage. Global self-control strategies that are used to deal with urges and craving for alcohol include coping imagery, stimulus control techniques, labeling, and detaching oneself from the feeling state (that is, recognizing that the urge to drink will occur and that it will eventually pass). Individuals must deal with rationalization and denial by becoming aware of these defenses and by treating them as aids to alert themselves about drinking risks. To deal with high-risk situations, those with alcoholism should make up relapse "road maps" that show where risks are likely to occur and how to avoid those situations. Avoidance strategies can then be used (Rivers, 1994, pp. 152–153).

The above quote suggests some ways of using relapse prevention strategies that are primarily based on clinical work in the area of relapse prevention. Unlike many areas in the alcohol field, quite a bit of research has been conducted on Marlatt's and his colleagues' paradigm of prevention. This research will be reviewed following the summary of the next two relapse prevention models.

Dynamic Model of Relapse

In order to better account for the complexity inherent in relapse prevention, Witkiewitz and Marlatt reformulated Marlatt's and Gordon's (1985) model and named it the Dynamic Model of Relapse (Witkiewitz & Marlatt, 2004). Research found that Marlatt's and Gordon's model appeared to have efficacy when applied to a wide variety of issues, including depression, obesity, and panic disorder. It was also found to be effective in working with people with addictions, particularly to alcohol. Though research supported components of

Marlatt's and Gordon's model, there was criticism about a lack of findings in support of the model as a whole (Witkietwitz & Marlatt, 2004).

One of the biggest changes incorporated by Witkiewitz and Marlatt's (2004) Dynamic Model of Relapse was to move from a linear to a non-linear model to acknowledge the myriad processes thought to be at play, both independently and together, in the process of relapse, something the word *dynamic* attempts to capture in the title. The Dynamic Model of Relapse presupposes the contribution of two important influences: tonic and phasic.

Tonic processes are thought to be more stable and fixed variables that individuals carry with them (such as genetic predisposition, family history, personality, and sensitivity to medications and drugs). These are known as "distal risks." Tonic processes also include "cognitive processes" (such as belief in oneself [i.e., self-efficacy], personal beliefs about addiction and relapse, expectations related to drug use, and physical withdrawal). Tonic processes are thought to be responsible for determining susceptibility to relapse.

Phasic responses, on the other hand, are thought to be more variable (such as changes in mood, physical well-being, cravings, and motivation, to name but a few). These variables are assumed to vary depending on the situation and over the course of time. Other phasic processes, which are also thought to be tonic processes, include coping behaviors, cognitive processes, and affective states. "Thus, tonic processes can determine who is vulnerable for relapse, phasic processes determine when relapse occurs" (Hendershot, Witkietwitz, George, & Marlatt, 2011, p. 4).

The interplay between phasic and tonic processes is reflected in Figure 10.1. As can be seen, both the phasic and tonic processes are set against a backdrop of high-risk situations. These are the contextual factors that must be considered any time when putting together a relapse prevention plan.

As described earlier, Witkiewitz and Marlatt's (2004) Dynamic Model of Relapse is not linear and instead "predicts feedback loops among hypothesized constructs" (Hendershot et al., 2011, p. 5). For example, someone who has historically experienced severe withdrawals may lose motivation for discontinuing use in order to forestall experiencing such symptoms. Or, a person who has been abstinent from alcohol for quite some time finds an unexpected drink thrust into her hands at a wedding and, not wanting to make a scene or draw attention away from the newly married couple, finds her motivation for continued abstinence wavering. One of the better summaries of the Dynamic Model of Relapse is provided by Lewis (2014):

> The . . . components of the dynamic model might appear as
> if it is a linear progression from distal risks to substance use.
> In reality, however, the dynamic model shows relapse as a
> multidimensional, nonlinear process with many overlapping
> components. (p. 156)

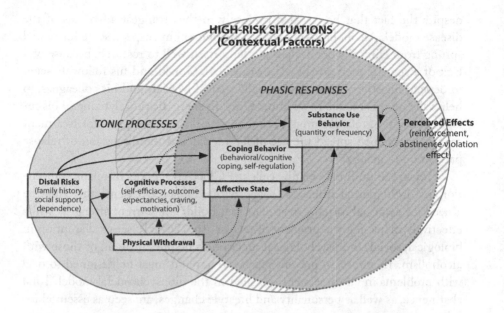

Figure 10.1. Revised cognitive-behavioral model of relapse. Note. From "Relapse prevention for alcohol and drug problems: That was Zen, this is Tao," by K. Witkiewitz and G. A. Marlatt, 2004, *American Psychologist,* 59. Available from http://www.substanceabusepolicy.com/content/6/1/17

Gorski's Model of Relapse Prevention

While Marlatt and his colleagues developed their model of relapse prevention around laboratory and clinically based research, Gorski's work—also known as the CENAPS Model of Relapse Prevention—seems to have been generated from clinical work and observations. His own description on how his model was developed is given in several places, but one of the best summaries is in a book by Gorski and Miller (1986) entitled *Staying Sober: A Guide for Relapse Prevention.* Gorski's work on developing procedures to prevent relapse of substance abusers began when he was exclusively assigned to a group of relapse-prone patients. He found that while they knew the A.A. principles well, they somehow could not put the principles to work in their lives. Following the Minnesota Model, he developed a model of relapse prevention that is tied very closely to A.A.'s 12 steps and to treatment approaches that are typical for most U.S. alcohol and drug treatment programs.

An important aspect of Gorski's model of relapse prevention is that he perceives recovery as a developmentally based disorder and uses that model to help monitor where the client–patient is at any given time in terms of the relapse process. He sees his model as being based in a biopsychosocial model despite the fact that he has tied it closely to the strongest advocates of the disease model, Alcoholics Anonymous. As one might suspect, since his model sprung from clinical work, it does not lend itself well to research, because of a lack of a specific methodology (Lewis, 2014). Gorski and his followers seem to depend on others' research, especially that of Marlatt and his colleagues, to help validate this model. In addition, Gorski's energetic proselytizing of his relapse prevention model through numerous workshops designed for treatment centers has helped spread the use of his model and the discussion of relapse prevention in general.

Gorski has outlined what he calls the CENAPS model of relapse prevention in a 1990 journal article. He suggests that for some patients, there may be a need for a special form of treatment that builds "on current strengths while effectively managing the problem of relapse" (p. 126). He sees a disruption in biological, social, and psychological function to be present in all of those with alcoholism. Therefore, to prevent relapse, treatment must be designed to deal with problems in all three areas specified in the biopsychosocial model. Total abstinence, as well as personality and lifestyle changes, are seen as essential for full recovery.

In what he calls the developmental model of recovery (DMR), he suggests that there are six stages that persons who are addicted to alcohol usually go through on their way to recovering from a substance abuse disorder. As these are described, paraphrasing Gorski's description given in 1989, it is interesting to note how traditional 12-step programming is built into the developmental process.

In **Stage 1: Transition**, patients discover that they have a problem with alcohol. However, they initially believe that they can deal with this problem by simply learning to control the use of the substance. This stage ends when they learn that they are unable to control their use and are powerless over the substance being used. While individuals do not know why they are out of control or how to be sober, they now know that they must stop using the substance if they want to turn their lives around.

In **Stage 2: Stabilization**, those with addictions are aware that they have a problem with alcohol and drugs but are unable to stop their abuse of the substance. At this point, they have to deal with postacute withdrawal syndrome, including being shaky and confused. In this stage, those with alcoholism must learn "to stay away from one drink (or one dose of drugs) one day at a time" (Gorski, 1989, p. 6).

In **Stage 3: Early Recovery**, those with addictions must make internal changes. As the physical craving for the drug is relieved, they learn to be comfortable with abstinence. It is a time of both expanding their knowledge about the addiction and learning how to cope with daily problems without the addictive substance(s).

In **Stage 4: Middle Recovery,** those with addictions learn how to put balance back in their lives. Relationships with people must be mended and significant relationships must be re-evaluated. The role of a career in their lives must be assessed. If there are areas of discontent and unhappiness, they must personally acknowledge these, and actions must be taken to change things. If someone close to them has been harmed by their actions, they must take responsibility and attempt to repair the damage.

In **Stage 5: Late Recovery,** the focus is on ineffective patterns of living that have been learned in childhood. Since so many of those with addictions report coming from dysfunctional families, they may not have learned how to be happy and how to deal with concerns like intimacy and affection when relating to others. Late recovery ends when recovering persons have accomplished the following three things.

1. We recognize the problems we have as adults that were caused by growing up in a dysfunctional family.
2. We learn how to recover from the unresolved pain that was caused by growing up in a dysfunctional family.
3. We learn how to solve current problems in spite of the obstacles caused by how we were raised. (Gorski, 1989, p. 7)

In **Stage 6: Maintenance,** those with alcohol and drug problems learn that their addiction is for life. They realize that they can never again use alcohol and drugs. There is also a recognition that for the rest of their lives they must practice a daily recovery program to avoid addictive thinking. They also realize that they must continue to grow as people.

These developmental stages are important because the factors emphasized in developing a relapse prevention program for a person in Stage 1 would differ dramatically from the planning of a relapse prevention program for someone who is in Stage 6. Therefore, the developmental model of relapse, postulated by Gorski, is important for planning relapse prevention techniques. The intervention needed is thought to be tied to where the person is in terms of the six-stage model outlined above.

The CENAPS model of relapse prevention views abstinence from alcohol and other mood-altering drugs as the most effective goal for all chemical dependency treatment. However, this is not the exclusive goal. Improvement in biopsychosocial functioning is also an important aspect of the approach. According to Gorski (1990):

> The CENAPS Model integrates recent advances from the medical, psychological, and social sciences. It consists of a theoretical model, educational materials, therapy procedures, and self-help methods. The treatment and self-help approaches are directed

toward three areas: assessment, recovery planning, and relapse
prevention planning. (p. 125)

As a result of the multidimensional nature of the relapse prevention program, the CENAPS model programs organize themselves around three basic
components—a stabilization and assessment program, a primary recovery program, and a relapse prevention program. The *stabilization and assessment program* is early in treatment and relapse prevention and provides detoxification
and psychosocial stabilization. Here the patients are evaluated for placement in
primary care or in a relapse prevention program. Self-assessment, professional
diagnosis of disease stage and type of disease, stage of recovery, and the kind of
relapse warning signs that are present are included in the evaluation.

In the *primary recovery program*, Gorski indicates that the patient (and
therapist) should recognize that addiction is a biopsychosocial disease. They
should also understand that the addictive disease will require lifelong abstinence from mind-altering drugs, and the development (and use) of an active
recovery program to maintain abstinence. During primary care, other problems (e.g., personality, vocational, family, social, marital) that can interfere
with sobriety should be treated. It is here that those in recovery begin working
through the developmental model of recovery (DMR) by beginning at the
transition stage; patients have decided that they have a problem and need a life
change (i.e., that they must deal with their substance abuse problem). During
the stabilization stage, patients deal with acute and postacute withdrawal and
with threatening life issues that may be immediate threats to sobriety.

Early stage is a stage where a deeper understanding of the recovery process
is gained and more profound understanding of drug dependence is developed.
Management of problems and feelings without the use of alcohol or drugs is
also begun during this stage. It is in the middle recovery stage that lifestyle
changes are made and/or lifestyles are repaired. The need to develop a balanced
lifestyle, one of the chronic problems of recovering people (see Chapter 11), is
emphasized during this stage. During late recovery, the next-to-last stage, patients move to work on broader psychological issues that may cause either discomfort or pain during the recovery process. The final stage, the maintenance
stage, is the lifelong process of growing and developing, making transitions in
life, and confronting the possibility of relapse. It is the latter issue that adds
extra work to the lives of those in recovery. Everyone moves through life and
deals with the issues as outlined for this stage by Gorski. However, for recovering persons, maintaining sobriety through these transitions is something they
must have as a lifelong constant. They must always work on *relapse prevention*,
the third component in a CENAPS model program. The reader should keep in
mind that Gorski sees his relapse model as tied to a DMR; therefore, dealing
with each stage in a successful way ultimately affects relapse prevention.

Basic Principles and Procedures of Relapse Prevention

An elaborate discussion of Gorski's model is beyond the scope of this chapter. The reader is referred to original sources (Gorski, 1988a, 1988b, 1989, 1990; Gorski & Miller, 1986) for a more complete presentation of the procedures used at each stage. However, a presentation of the principles of this model and brief examples of procedures related to them will be outlined below. It should be noted here that this summary is based almost entirely on Gorski's 1990 article outlining the model, and it is a succinct description of his position.

Principle 1: Self-Regulation

"The risk of relapse will decrease as the patient's capacity to self-regulate their thinking, feeling, memory, judgment and behavior increases" (Gorski, 1990, pp. 128–129).

Relapse Prevention Procedure 1: Stabilization

One of the basic measures of whether patients have mastered this stage is whether or not they can carry out the basic tasks of everyday living. One must provide seclusion from drug use (i.e., provide a drug-free environment). Treatment personnel must also help patients deal with the way that they justify the use of alcohol or drugs (e.g., "I am not ever going to get well anyway, so why shouldn't I drink?"). Patients must be reminded over and over about the past disasters that have accompanied their substance use and abuse. At the same time, they must be provided with ways of coping with immediate threats to sobriety and decisions about what can be done if they should use chemicals. Having a plan to work with is very important during this early stage of recovery. Not noted by Gorski, but important just the same, is the need to return some type of structure to the often chaotic lives of those with chemical dependency issues.

Principle 2: Integration

"The risk of relapse will decrease as the level of conscious understanding and acceptance of situations and events that led to past relapses increases" (Gorski, 1990, p. 129).

Relapse Prevention Procedure 2: Integration

Relapse prevention is built on the patients' self-assessment. Here, careful exploration of presenting problems helps to establish where there are relapse risks. The therapist can identify immediate problems that could lead to relapse and provide interventions that will reduce the risk. Once the immediate relapse-threatening issues are ascertained and appropriate interventions are provided, the second type of self-assessment is undertaken. This is a careful exploration of their life history. What were things like in grade school, high school, and college? What are patients' lifelong friendships and romantic relationships like? One of the goals of reconstructing a life history is to find self-defeating behaviors that are threats to relapse. Other goals include building rapport and relationships between therapist and patient, as well as between patient and therapy group. The third goal is to resolve the pain associated with painful memories. The final step in the procedure is to carefully reconstruct a relapse history for patients. This history includes a so-called recovery-relapse calendar that shows the date of recovery and relapse. This calendar helps reinforce the past number and severity of relapses and the dangers that persons with addictions face during recovery.

Principle 3: Understanding
"The risk of relapse will decrease as the understanding of the general factors that cause relapse increases" (Gorski, 1990, p. 130).

Relapse Prevention Procedure 3: Understanding
The task here is to provide accurate information to a person with an addiction about what contributes to relapse. Gorski is very precise about what he believes is the best procedure to follow in providing this education. The education process should incorporate a minimum number of lectures, since he sees this as the poorest way to communicate effectively with recovering substance abusers. According to Gorski (1990):

> The recommended format for a relapse education session is the following: (1) introduction and pretest (15 minutes); (2) educational presentation-lecture, film, or videotape (30 minutes); (3) educational exercise conducted in dyads or small groups (15 minutes); (4) large-group discussion (15 minutes); and (5) session posttest and review of correct answers (15 minutes). (p. 130)

Principle 4: Self-Knowledge
"The risk of relapse will decrease as the patient's ability to recognize personal relapse warning signs increases" (Gorski, 1990, p. 130).

Relapse Prevention Procedure 4: Warning Sign Identification
In group, a warning-signs list for relapse is reviewed by all group members. The initial step for all group members (each member develops his or her own warning list) is to select five warning signs that they feel are representative of them from a composite list. The group members then take their lists and, during warning-sign-analysis time, individually present examples of how each of the warning signs preceded relapse in the past. Both the therapist and group members listen to these warning signs, and try to detect hidden warning signs that the patient is not aware of. Through this process, each patient, the therapist, and the entire group move toward a final warning list for the patient. The

final warning-signs list has two types of warning signs: those stemming from core addiction issues and those arising from core psychological issues. Core psychological issues cause pain and discomfort but do not, says Gorski, lead the patient directly to relapse. It is the addictive thinking that does that (i.e., the core addictive warning signs.)

Principle 5: Coping Skills

"The risk of relapse will decrease as the ability to manage relapse warning signs increases" (Gorski, 1990, p. 131).

Relapse Prevention Procedure 5: Warning Sign Prevention

Gorski feels that the better those with addictions are able to manage warning signs, the better they will be at managing threats to relapse. He advocates the use of mental rehearsal, role playing, and therapeutic assignments. Management training takes place at three levels. At the first level, patients deal with situational-behavioral issues. They are taught to avoid situations that arouse warning signs and to change behavior patterns should these situations appear. The second level is cognitive-affective. Patients must be trained to challenge irrational thoughts and be instructed on how to deal with overwhelming and/ or unmanageable feelings. The "self-talk" that one uses must be modified. Patients learn how to use imagery and to deal with such imagery. The third level, the core-issue level, is where patients are taught to recognize core addictive and psychological concerns that produce warning signs that they are at risk for relapse. For example, Gorski sees patients' core beliefs that they must be better than everyone else as being driven at the core level by low self-esteem. It is the low self-esteem that is behind the irrational thinking that they must be best at everything. Low self-esteem underlies the unmanageable feeling that they must always prove themselves, and the associated self-defeating behavior. They really do not deserve success, so why not make a fool of themselves while drinking? (These concrete examples are ours, not Gorski's.)

Principle 6: Change

"The risk of relapse will decrease as the use of daily inventory techniques designed to identify relapse warning signs increase" (Gorski, 1990, p. 132).

Relapse Prevention Procedure 6: Inventory Training

Patients are taught to monitor how well they are keeping to a relapse prevention program. This daily inventory is an ongoing check on the emergence of relapse warning signs. There is a morning planning inventory to plan the day (e.g., identifying three recovery goals for the day), and in the evening, individuals complete an inventory to review their progress and to detect any problems (e.g., patients review their warning-signs list and check to see if they have completed assigned duties).

Principle 7: Awareness
"The risk of relapse will decrease as the use of daily inventory techniques designed to identify relapse warning signs increases" (Gorski, 1990, p. 132).

Relapse Prevention Procedure 7: Inventory Training
Here Gorski suggests that patients susceptible to relapse keep two daily inventories to help monitor compliance with individual recovery programs. The morning inventory helps persons check for possible relapse warning signs that might arise on any given day. In the morning, a patient might be asked to identify three primary recovery goals and to create a "to-do" list. An evening inventory is employed to review progress and to assess possible problems. The evening inventory is used to review how well the recovering person has completed his or her required recovery activities.

Principle 8: Significant Others
"The risk of relapse will decrease as the responsible involvement of significant others in recovery from co-dependency and in [the] relapse planning process increases" (Gorski, 1990, p. 132).

Relapse Prevention Procedure 8: Involvement of Others
Gorski is adamant about the involvement of significant others with the patient. This support helps increase the effectiveness of the relapse program. The more psychologically and socially well-adjusted the people are around the addicted person, the more effective they can be in relapse prevention. Gorski and others have developed a protocol to be used by significant others who work with the patient on relapse prevention.

Principle 9: Maintenance
"The risk of relapse decreases if the relapse prevention plan is regularly updated during the first three years of sobriety" (Gorski, 1990, p. 132).

Relapse Prevention Procedure 9: Relapse Prevention Plan Updating
Gorski calls for a monthly updating of the patient's relapse plan for the first 3 months, quarterly updates for the rest of the year, and semiannual updates for the next 2 years. Thereafter, the relapse plan should be done annually. He warns that while the largest number of relapses occur during the first 6 months following primary treatment, relapse warning signs constantly change as the person's life changes. He also notes that less than one-quarter of the variables that cause relapse can be detected in initial treatment.

   This brief outline of the three different views of relapse prevention suggests that all are incomplete. In the case of Marlatt and Gordon, there is less clear-cut operationalization of just what is needed and how this learning-based relapse prevention program can be tied to existing programs. In many cases, existing U.S. alcohol and drug treatment programs have a disease orientation. The

Dynamic Model of Relapse may be an improvement, but suffers from a similar lack of specificity and predictability, limiting its clinical application for now. On the other hand, Gorski has his relapse prevention model tied closely to the Minnesota Model and the 12 steps of Alcoholics Anonymous. His model is definitely close to the majority of existing programs and thus is readily usable by them. Unfortunately, Gorski's model has not been supported by research studies to evaluate its effectiveness with patients (Chatav & Stuart, 2009). For this reason, relapse prevention programs are still often being conducted for the most part on the basis of clinical observations and are being evaluated by the same means. In the next section, we review what research says about relapse prevention. Most of this research is based on Marlatt and Gordon's approach. Because of its relative newness and complexity, there is less research available on the Dynamic Model of Relapse. There is little research, as well, currently available on the Gorski model.

Research on Relapse Prevention

Before we dive into the research on relapse prevention, it is worth taking the time to step back and acknowledge that other chronic medical conditions—like being overweight, having allergies, or having diabetes—are not viewed the same as are addictive behaviors. This may seem like an obvious statement, but think about it for a moment. If someone regains some or all of the weight he or she lost, experiences a return of allergic symptoms, or suffers a drop or rise in blood sugar, one rarely hears the word *relapse* in explaining what has happened. It is understood that such variations are expected in the management of chronic medical conditions. It is our contention that a similar approach would benefit the treatment of those with addictive behaviors. In their textbook *Treating Addiction*, Miller, Forcehimes, and Zweben (2011) felt so strongly about this that they utilized the word "maintenance" as a replacement for the word *relapse*.

Not to belabor the point, but Miller, Walters, and Bennett (as cited in Miller et al., 2011) examined 8,389 cases treated for alcohol use disorders and found strong evidence in support of treatment for reducing severity of alcohol use. Though only about one-quarter of people remained abstinent in the year following treatment, days abstinent from alcohol increased 128% and alcohol consumption decreased 87% for the remaining three-quarters. These impressive results came about in response to a single episode of addiction treatment! As Miller et al. (2011) suggest, a similar pattern of decrease in high blood pressure or high blood sugars would be viewed as treatment success.

Still, in large part because the word *relapse* has such a storied history in the treatment of addictions, we are not as comfortable completely abandoning it as Miller et al. (2011) have done. They may be correct that the concept of relapse provides little helpful clinical utility, but it is important to be familiar with not only the strengths and shortcomings of the three primary theoretical relapse prevention models, but also the research on relapse prevention for what it can teach us about treating addictions.

Research suggests (Miller, Walters, & Bennett, as cited in Miller et al., 2011) that most people will relapse in the first few months following treatment. However, many of these relapsers reinstate abstinence following a loss of sobriety. Miller, Walters, and Bennett (as cited in Miller et al., 2011) reported, as already indicated, an increase of 128% in days abstinent in the year following completion of treatment.

In terms of establishing factors that precipitate relapse, Hendershot et al. (2011) have suggested that negative emotions—also referred to as "negative affect"—are strongly related to relapsing behavior. Positive mood, as well, has been found to be related to the use of alcohol. Other factors thought to play a role include (a) self-efficacy (essentially a person's belief in whether he or she can be successful in a particular situation) and (b) self-control and coping responses. Hendershot et al. (2011) have summarized the research reported on these and other factors as precipitants of relapse.

Negative emotions, which Marlatt (1985a) found to be a precipitant in 59% of relapses by those with alcoholism, can be either intrapersonal or interpersonal. *Intrapersonal* negative emotions include feelings like frustration, free-floating anger, fear, sadness, loneliness, and so forth. These feelings accounted for 38% of the precipitants of relapses in Marlatt's research. Negative emotions resulting from *interpersonal* conflict were responsible for 18% of the relapses. Included here were feelings associated with a lack of appreciation from others, guilt feelings, and perceptions of being accused unjustly. Feeling bad physically (negative physical state) accounted for 3% of relapse precipitants. Marlatt's research of relapse precipitants has been complemented by others. Shiffman and Waters (as cited in Hendershot et al., 2011) found rising levels of negative affect in the hours preceding a lapse. Witkiewitz and Villarroel (as cited in Hendershot et al., 2011) found past and current negative affect to be significantly related to drinking rates.

Negative emotions can also be seen as being aroused by external stressors. Rosenberg's (1983) research on a sample of those in recovery from alcoholism found those who experienced more negative life changes and fewer positive life changes had a higher probability of relapse. An earlier study by Hore (1971) found that the overall sample of subjects studied demonstrated no relationship between negative life events and relapse. However, he did find a subset of those with alcoholism for whom the experiences of negative life events led to relapse and suggested that this subset may be more sensitive to life events.

Others have also suggested an interaction between history of alcoholism and stress in the environment. For example, if the drinking has disrupted the relationships of those with alcoholism with their family, and then some negative event occurs involving the family, there is likely to be relapse. Littrell

(1991), in her summary statement regarding negative emotions, indicates that "stress can be a factor in precipitating or increasing drinking, but there are individual personality differences, and the sources of stress may make a difference" (p. 93).

Littrell (1991) also reviewed the research on social pressure, the second leading cause of relapse in Marlatt's (1985a) research. She notes that social pressure can be direct, as when a friend encourages you to take a drink, or indirect, as when the people around you model drinking as the appropriate behavior in which to engage. The flipside of social pressure would likely incorporate both a person's belief in his or her ability to remain sober ("self-efficacy") and his or her development of adequate coping responses. Though the research on the contributions of self-efficacy and self-control is complex and not conclusive (Witkiewitz et al., 2011), a study by Muraven (as cited in Witkiewitz et al., 2011) found that research participants who practiced small acts of self-control over the course of 2 weeks had significantly longer periods until relapse.

The test of personal control as a cause of relapse, interestingly enough, accounted for 11% of relapses in Marlatt's (1985a) study. Relapsers seemed to be testing whether they could control their drinking or avoid the negative consequences of alcohol use of this specific drinking occasion. One of Marlatt's surprising findings was that only 3% of relapsers reported their lapses as due to interpersonal positive emotions (none reported intrapersonal positive emotions as a cause of relapse). Research by Tennen, Affleck, and Kranzler (as cited in Hendershot et al., 2011) suggested that positive emotions may play an important role in precipitating relapse. Intuitively, a major role for positive emotions in precipitating relapse would make sense, because so much occurs around individuals' having a good time with people they have not seen for some time or around holiday celebrations. Good feelings toward others are often present, and alcohol is associated with having a good time. Littrell (1991) cites additional research that supported the importance of positive emotions in precipitating relapse. She notes that some people stay sober because of the fear arousal of the long-term consequences of drinking. Having a pleasurable and good time tends to undermine this fear type of motivation for staying sober. If a person does not have some other type of motivation, like pride in being sober, then when a pleasurable event occurs in his or her life, he or she may turn to drinking, because drinking is one of the few activities that has been previously associated with positive events in the person's life.

Though cravings and urges were present in 11% of relapses for those with alcoholism in the Marlatt (1985a) study, there is some concern that there may be internal and external cues for cravings and developing a "drug urge" (Baker, Morse, & Sherman, 1987). This view is reflected in the update of Marlatt's model, the Dynamic Model of Relapse, in which internal and external factors are operationalized as being contributors to relapse, not cravings and urges per se (Witkiewitz & Marlatt, 2004).

The above discussion of the research on precipitants of relapse should be understood in the light of what Littrell calls "unanswered questions." For example, does the drinker's pattern of drinking prior to starting the recovery process suggest future precipitants of relapse? Do people who drink in a bad mood also have high potential for drinking when alone or under stress? Those whose drinking occurred most often in convivial situations might be more likely to relapse in a pleasurable party atmosphere or after having some type of personal success. At present, these guesses are still at the hypothesis stage and need additional research before they can be established as principles for relapse management.

The finding that those with problems related to the use of alcohol differ from other drinkers in terms of the expectations that they hold about what alcohol will do for them is another issue of importance. Shiffman, Balabanis, and Paty (as cited in Hendershot et al., 2011) found, for example, that a positive relationship has been demonstrated between likelihood of lapses and positive outcome expectancies for smoking.

Expectancy—also referred to as "outcome expectancies"—has become a major concept in the substance abuse treatment field. Research supports the conclusion of outcome expectancies having a mediating effect on personality factors, genetic variations, and negative affect (Hendershot et al., 2011). The operationalization of the expectancy concept by Brown, Christiansen, and Goldman (1987) is perhaps the most widely researched. In their review, they define expectancy as follows:

> Expectancy refers to an intervening variable of a cognitive nature . . . the term expectancy, rather than attitude or belief is usually involved when the author refers to the anticipation of a systematic relationship between events/objects in some upcoming situation. The relationship is understood to be of an if-then variety; if a certain object is registered then a certain event is expected to follow. (Brown et al., 1987, as cited in Carle, 1993, p. 1)

Research has been examining the cognitive processes referred to in the above quote and has convincingly demonstrated a relationship between these processes and relapse, whether involving the use of alcohol, tobacco, or heroin (Hendershot et al., 2011). These expectancies seem to have a bearing on relapse risk. For example, Brown (1985) found that alcohol expectancies enhanced the prediction of drinking outcome at 1 year following treatment (Carle, 1993).

Another unanswered question is whether planned relapses differ from impulsive ones. Some individuals may feel that they cannot continue their sobriety and that they are pressured daily to drink. When these individuals do drink, they may fully expect disastrous, long-range consequences, yet they simply feel that they can no longer maintain their "white knuckle" sobriety. Still others plan their relapses, believing that they are "alcoholics," but also believing that they will drink for a short time and then return to sobriety or to normal drinking and escape the difficulties of long-term destructive drinking. These two diverse thoughts may lead to differing outcomes when relapse occurs. It is probable that cognitions about relapse differ in more subtle ways and that these subtle differences may have an effect on the accuracy of predicting a relapse in a particular person's case.

Yet another question is how much genetic variability may influence a person's ability to discontinue use or prevent relapse, not only for pharmacological interventions but also for psychosocial interventions. In regard to pharmacological interventions (i.e., Antabuse, nicotine replacement, bupropion), genetic variability can account for how well such drugs are metabolized and how well patients respond to them (Hendershot et al., 2011). In regard to psychosocial interventions, genetic variability has been found to be related to increased likelihood of relapse, increased likelihood of heavy drinking, and response to treatment (Hendershot et al., 2011).

A final unanswered question is whether the core motivation for ceasing to use an addictive substance is related to relapse. If a person quits substance abuse for health reasons, will he or she be more likely to relapse when the person feels good? Persons who quit drinking to please their family may be more vulnerable to relapse when they feel that family members have treated them unfairly. One way to understand the importance of these factors is to look at the characteristics of people with alcoholism who are relapsing and non-relapsing.

Characteristics of People With Alcoholism Who Are Relapsing and Non-relapsing

Witkiewitz and Marlatt (2004) outlined some of the major factors that determine resistance to and risk for relapse. One of the factors determining relapses is the degree of self-efficacy about staying sober that the person has. Hendershot et al. (2011) define *self-efficacy* as "the perceived ability to enact a given behavior in a specified context" (p. 6).

The difficulty is: How do you measure self-efficacy? What factors in these measurements predict relapsing and non-relapsing individuals? Littrell's (1991) review of the literature suggests that individuals in treatment are themselves good predictors of whether they are going to relapse or not. They also can predict the situations in which they are likely to relapse (Chapman & Huygens, 1988; Condiotte & Lichtenstein, 1981; DiClemente, 1981; McIntyre, Lichtenstein, & Mermelstein, 1983). How individuals see themselves in relation to dealing with substance abuse use and dealing with temptation also appears to be important to Littrell (1991). In summarizing those factors that describe people who successfully deal with relapse, she stated:

> Feelings of self-efficacy, a propensity to use positive self-reinforcement and positive images (offering themselves thoughts of the benefits of sobriety, and experiencing pride in accomplishment when maintaining sobriety), and the permission of strong coping skills were recognized as important. (p. 105)

When one looks more closely at the characteristics of those with alcoholism who are relapsing and non-relapsing, it is clear that multiple differences between the two groups have been found. For example, people who believe that they can achieve the goal of sobriety tend to be more likely to achieve the goal. Littrell (1991) cites Donovan and O'Leary's 1983 study that divided those with alcoholism on their subjective estimate of whether they would succumb to pressure to drink. Those who reported that they would be highly likely to give in to pressure to drink reported drinking in a more chronic and obsessive fashion, said they used more external resources to cease drinking, reported higher rates of loss of control when they did drink, and had more physical, psychosocial, and psychological damage as a result of drinking. In addition, those who saw their sobriety as being the result of chance or the result of fate were more likely to relapse.

Another factor is the degree of motivation that persons have toward their own ability to manage their recovery. The less motivated the person is about achieving sobriety, the more likely the person is to stay in treatment for a shorter period of time and to be discharged prematurely for violation of treatment-program rules. One of the danger signals for persons who may not do well in treatment is for them to say, particularly early in treatment, that they now believe that they will be able to easily handle their treatment in the future. It does seem to be necessary for persons in treatment to have some doubts, some sense of a real struggle before them, in order to maximize the impact of their treatment.

How does this match up with feelings of self-efficacy? In general, those people with higher levels of self-efficacy are better able to prevent relapse (Witkiewitz & Marlatt, 2004). However, persons who develop skills for dealing with threats to relapse are the ones who seem to do better (Miller et al., 2011). Those people who simply have faith that they will not relapse do more poorly. In addition, coping skills of non-relapsers, both behavioral and cognitive, are employed in greater number and diversity than by those individuals who relapse. The effective use of these skills may build self-esteem and may lead to greater use of the tools to stay sober. People who do better in terms of relapse do not shower themselves with self-recriminations; instead, they are able to see themselves as doing something positive, as coping and as acting as good role models for others. In fact, having a positive attitude toward life in general is associated with positive outcome (i.e., a reduction in relapse).

What recovering persons must always deal with is their cognitive appreciation of what the addictive substance does for them. One of the important cognitive factors is expectancies about what the drug will do. It should be no surprise, for example, that "youthful drinking [and, by implication adult drinking] is influenced by the modeling of alcohol consumption; the creation of specific expectations of the benefits of drinking via media portrayals of sexual prowess, power, and success and by social reinforcement from peer groups" (Monti, Abrams, Kadden, & Cooney, 1989, p. 6).

All of these factors add up to the fact that non-relapsers must make, over time, considerable lifestyle changes. They need to develop a life interest that takes the place of the time formerly spent drinking. Whether it is just having the activity alone or perhaps a more global change (now perceiving oneself as a runner, not a drinker) that helps is still unknown (Littrell, 1991). In addition, social support from one's family is associated with better outcomes (Miller et al., 2011). Of course, there is always a possible confound with the severity of the drinking history of the recovering person and the amount of social support that a family may be willing to give.

While there are clear indications in the literature about what may determine a relapse, what is still unknown is how best to intervene with those people who are potential relapsers. Just exactly how do we intervene with someone who is not motivated to recover? How does one teach relapse prevention skills to someone who still has positive feelings toward using the abused substance? These things await more research. We need better measurement tools, better intervention strategies, and more outcome research to evaluate the effectiveness of treatment and relapse prevention. It is also probable that ongoing assessment of using potential will be needed to fully exploit both aftercare and relapse prevention strategies. These two areas of substance abuse rehabilitation—aftercare and relapse prevention—seem to loom prominently in the future intervention and treatment of substance abuse problems.

References

Baker, T. B., Morse, E., & Sherman, J. E. (1987). The motivation to use drugs: A psychological analysis of drug urges. In P. C. Rivers (Ed.), *Alcohol and addictive behavior* (Vol. 34), Nebraska Symposium on Motivation (pp. 257–323). Lincoln, NE: University of Nebraska Press.

Brown, S. A. (1985). Reinforcement expectancies and alcoholism treatment outcome after a one year follow-up. *Journal of Studies on Alcohol, 46*, 304–308.

Brown, S. A., Christiansen, B. A., & Goldman, M. A. (1987). The alcohol expectancy questionnaire: An instrument for the assessment of adolescent and adult alcohol expectancies. *Journal of Studies on Alcohol, 48,* 483–491.

Burleson, J. A., Kaminer, Y., & Burke, M. A. (2012). Twelve-month follow-up of aftercare for adolescents with alcohol use disorders. *Journal of Substance Abuse Treatment, 42*(1), 78–86.

Carle, D. (1993). *Predicting drinking patterns of college students: The AEQ vs. the AEQ-A.* Unpublished doctoral dissertation, Department of Psychology, University of Nebraska, Lincoln.

Chapman, P. L. H., & Huygens, I. (1988). An evaluation of three treatment programmes for alcoholism: An experimental study with 6- and 18-month follow-ups. *British Journal of Addictions, 83,* 67–81.

Chatav, Y., & Stuart, G. (2009). Cenaps model. In G. Fisher, & N. Roget (Eds.), *Encyclopedia of substance abuse prevention, treatment, & recovery* (pp. 157–158). Thousand Oaks, CA: SAGE.

Condiotte, M. M., & Lichtenstein, E. (1981). Self-efficacy and relapse in smoking cessation programs. *Journal of Consulting and Clinical Psychology, 49,* 648–658.

Connors, G. J., Tarbox, A. R., & Faillance, L. A. (1992). Achieving and maintaining gains among problems drinkers: Process and outcome results. *Behavior Therapy, 23,* 449–474.

DiClemente, C. C. (1981). Self-efficacy and smoking cessation maintenance: A preliminary report. *Cognitive Therapy and Research, 5,* 175–187.

Gorski, T. T. (1988a). *Do family of origin problems cause chemical dependence? Exploring the relationship between chemical dependence and codependence.* Independence, MO: Independence Press.

Gorski, T. T. (1988b). *The staying sober workbook: Instruction manual.* Independence, MO: Independence Press.

Gorski, T. T. (1989). *Passages through recovery: An action plan for preventing relapse.* Minneapolis: Hazelden Foundation.

Gorski, T. T. (1990). The Cenaps Model of relapse prevention. *Journal of Psychoactive Drugs, 22,* 125–133.

Gorski, T. T., & Miller, M. (1986). *Staying sober: A guide for relapse prevention.* Independence, MO: Independence Press.

Hendershot, C. S., Witkiewitz, K., George, W. H., & Marlatt, G. A. (2011). Relapse prevention for addictive behaviors. *Substance Abuse Treatment, Prevention, and Policy, 6*(7), 1–17.

Hore, B. D. (1971). Life events and alcoholic relapse. *British Journal of Addictions, 66,* 83–88.

Institute of Medicine. (1990). *Broadening the base of treatment for alcohol problems.* Washington, DC: National Academy Press.

Joint Commission on the Accreditation of Healthcare Organizations. (1983). *Consolidated standards manual for child, adolescent and adult psychiatric, alcoholism and drug abuse facilities.* Chicago: Author.

Kaminer, Y., Burleson, J. A., & Burke, R. H. (2008). Efficacy of outpatient aftercare for adolescents with alcohol use disorders: A randomized controlled study. *Journal of the American Academy of Child and Adolescent Psychiatry, 47*(12), 1405–1412.

Lewis, T. F. (2014). *Substance abuse and addiction treatment: Practical application of counseling theory.* Upper Saddle River, NJ: Pearson.

Littrell, J. (1991). *Understanding and treating alcoholism: Volume 1.* Hillsdale, NJ: Lawrence Erlbaum.

Marlatt, G. A. (1985a). Relapse prevention: Theoretical rationale and overview of the model. In G. A. Marlatt, & J. R. Gordon (Eds.), *Relapse prevention* (pp. 3–70). New York: Guilford Press.

Marlatt, G. A. (1985b). Situational determinants of relapse and skill training. In G. A. Marlatt & J. R. Gordon (Eds.), *Relapse prevention* (pp. 71–127). New York: Guilford Press.

Marlatt, G. A., & Gordon, J. R. (Eds.) (1985). *Relapse prevention.* New York: Guilford Press.

McCrady, B. S. (1989). Extending relapse models to couples. *Addictive Behaviors, 14,* 69–74.

McIntyre, K. O., Lichtenstein, E., & Mermelstein, R. J. (1983). Self-efficacy and relapse in smoking cessation: A replication and extension. *Journal of Consulting and Clinical Psychology,* 51, 632–633.

Miller, W. R., Forcehimes, A. A., & Zweben, A. (2011). *Treating addiction: A guide for professionals.* New York: Guildford Press.

Monti, P. M., Abrams, D. B., Kadden, R. M., & Cooney, N. L. (1989). *Treating alcohol dependence.* New York: Guilford Press.

Rivers, P. C. (1994). *Alcohol and human behavior: Theory, research and practice.* Englewood Cliffs, NJ: Prentice Hall.

Rosenberg, H. (1983). Relapsed versus non-relapsed alcohol abusers: Coping skills, life events and social support. *Addictive Behaviors, 8,* 183–186.

Valley Hope Association. (2013, Winter). *Coffee cup.* Norton, KS: Author.

Wallace, J. (1978). Working with the preferred defense structure of the recovering alcoholic. In S. Zimberg, J. Wallace, & S. B. Blume (Eds.), *Practical approaches to alcoholism psychotherapy* (pp. 19–29). New York: Plenum.

Witkiewitz, K., & Marlatt, G. A. (2004). Relapse prevention for alcohol and drug problems: That was Zen, this is Tao. *American Psychologist, 59,* 224–235.

CHAPTER 11

Counseling Those Reluctant to Recover

CHAPTER OBJECTIVES

- Examine the reasons people don't respond to treatment
- Examine the principles of effective treatment
- Examine the counselor's role in this lack of response
- Give examples of what counselors can do with resistant clients or patients

Treatment of chemical dependency is often thought to go something like this: The chemically dependent person either seeks treatment on his or her own or is encouraged to go to treatment by a significant other, such as an employer, a wife, or a judge. The patient speaks to a counselor, who helps him or her to discover that the use of chemicals or addictive behavior is at the root of most of their problems in life. The patient is encouraged to seek support in a self-help group and to give up the use of chemicals and/or the general dependence on addictive behaviors totally and for life. Many of these individuals are able to do so. Some have one or two relapses along the way, but then are able to remain clean and sober or to stop their addictive behaviors. A significant number of people are able to do this on their own without the use of a treatment professional (Straussner, 2014; Walters, 2000).

Why Don't People Change?

Then there are those who, despite encouragement and help from treatment professionals, seem unable or unwilling to change. Treatment professionals have terms to describe these individuals, terms like *treatment resistant* or *constitutionally unable to change*. Some treatment professionals may believe that the reason these individuals don't change is that they have not yet "hit bottom." That is another way of saying they have not experienced enough pain as a result of their use or behavior to motivate them to change. However, it is easy to blame the client or patient for his or her lack of success in treatment. Senator Harold Hughes, a leader in the push to provide treatment for alcoholics, often noted that alcoholism is the only disorder in which the patient is blamed when treatment fails. White (1998) believes that the approach of blaming patients protects the service provider (counselor) at the expense of the addicted client and his or her family. He also believes that this can mask broader social policy failures.

In this chapter, we will assume that everyone has the potential to change. And, we will assume that those who don't change after a particular treatment need a different treatment, not more pain in their life. We will also assume that those who don't change do not just need more of the same treatment. Some people do finally change after having more of the same treatment, such as the person who goes to A.A. many times while still drinking before choosing to be abstinent. Other people won't respond to certain types of treatments but may respond to others, just as one type of cancer might respond best to radiation while another type of cancer might respond better to chemotherapy. The hard part is to know which type of addiction or substance abuse responds to which type of treatment.

Some people are able to give up the use of their chemical of choice but do not change their destructive behavior. Sometimes such a person will be labeled a "dry drunk." Again, this implies a defect in the individual, rather than a problem with the quality of treatment he or she has received. In reality, a dry drunk is a victim of insignificant and ineffective treatment for the specific problems that he or she has. Very few individuals with addiction problems can just give up their addictions and become happy, fully functioning adults as a result. Most often, there are multiple issues that need to be addressed. Plus, resistance to change is a human condition; all humans resist change at some level. However, it is perplexing when an addict needs to change yet, despite encouragement from others, he or she doesn't. This is especially difficult to understand for people who have been through the process and have changed. If others would just see the world as they do, these people reason, they would change, too. Many people working in this field fall into this category.

Before we go further, let us examine the elements of effective treatment. If these elements were present in more treatment programs, there would be far fewer reluctant-to-change individuals in treatment.

The Principles of Effective Treatment

There are many paths to recovery, but some principles of effective treatment have stood the test of time and research. These principles have been compiled and presented by the National Institute on Drug Abuse in National Institutes of Health (NIH) publication No. 12-4180, which is available online. In brief, the 13 principles of effective treatment are as follows:

Principle 1: Addiction is a complex but treatable disease that affects brain function and behavior—Addictive behaviors are very complex and, as discussed elsewhere in this book, they involve complex brain-based changes that can persist long after the cessation of drug use. These changes in brain functioning and structure may account for the heightened risk of relapse that many experience.

Much of what is offered as treatment today is very basic. Programs are designed with approaches that have worked with people in the past. These therapeutic interventions have been shown to be effective through research or clinical experience or, perhaps, both. It is assumed that because these approaches have worked for one set of individuals, they will work for everyone. This is a false assumption. Chemotherapy works for some individuals with some types of cancer. Others respond to radiation or surgery or some combination of these. If a cancer patient does not respond and dies, we do not blame the patient. We assume that the doctors were not able to find a treatment approach that worked for that patient. In chemical dependency (CD) treatment, however, we assume that the patient did not do what *he or she* needed to do to recover. It is wrong to look at it this way—and yet it is also right.

People do need to take responsibility for their lives, their illnesses, and their behaviors. It is a wise doctor who counsels cancer patients to take charge of their illness and to find out all they can about it; to speak with others who have had the same illness and who have recovered from it; to ask them what they did and how they did it; to research new treatment approaches and alternative approaches; and to make changes in lifestyle that may make existing treatments more effective. If a doctor suggests that a patient do these things, but they don't do them, it might be assumed that this patient is unmotivated to recover. This might be a faulty assumption. The patient could just be paralyzed with fear and feeling helpless. He or she may want to recover more than anything and may want to live, but just doesn't have the knowledge to do everything possible to live. Or, the patient may in fact want to die, and may indeed be reluctant to recover.

The same could be true for CD patients or those with addictive disorders. They may want to recover and just don't know how to access the help they need, or they may be reluctant to recover because they would just as soon be dead and they know their drug use will help them get there. Either way, the counselor can play a major role. In the first case, the counselor can help the patient access the necessary treatment. In the second case, the counselor can help the individual find new reasons for living.

Either way, the process is likely to take time—more for some than for others. The dynamics of all human behavior are complex. The dynamics of addiction are perhaps even more complex than most other behaviors. However, a counselor who understands this, is patient, and gives the addict credit for the ability to get better if he or she chooses to will be successful in most cases. The counselor who chooses to use only one approach and to blame the individual for an inability to get better will have many clients/patients who appear unmotivated to recover.

Principle 2: No single treatment is appropriate for all individuals—
Counselors like to believe that they can help all their patients or clients. There

is a personal investment in the counseling they do with patients and in the type of treatment they provide. It is only natural for counselors to believe very strongly that what they do will work, if the patients will just take advantage of therapy and treatment as it is offered. Patients who do, it is believed, will get better and be able to make necessary changes. In reality, many counselors can't agree among themselves or with their patients about what it is that needs to change, or how change takes place. Some counselors still believe that confrontation is the way to facilitate change. Others believe that love and understanding are what is needed. Again, what is real is that each person is motivated to change in his or her own special way. Change takes place for each person when each person is motivated to change and when each person has some idea of how he or she should look after the change process. To be motivated to change, each person must like what change looks like.

Counselors who are flexible and adjust to each patient according to the patient's needs are the most successful in helping the change process. A flexible counselor will recognize that each patient changes in a different way, but that there are only three main things that can change for an individual: behaviors, thoughts or cognitions, and emotional reactions or feelings—all of which are connected and all of which must ultimately change if the individual is to sustain change. For example, drug taking is a behavior based on, in large part, thoughts and feelings the user has related to the use. If someone who uses drugs changes his or her drug-taking behavior only because of external motivating factors (e.g., an employer, the law, family pressure) and stops using drugs for a while, it is very likely that he or she will return to drug use unless he or she is also able to change the way he or she thinks and feels about drugs.

Each person is likely to change these three things at different rates and in different orders. Some people are more motivated by thoughts, and others, by feelings. It is part of the counselor's job to assess which of these areas is the most important for each client or patient. When these areas have not been assessed and addressed by the counselor, the patient may seem reluctant to recover and may be more resistant to treatment. For example, a smoker may not change smoking behavior until the individual changes his or her thinking about smoking. A heroin addict may not be able to change his or her thinking about heroin use until that person changes drug-using behavior first. In the case of the smoker, the behavior change is not as important as in the heroin user's case, where changing the heroin-using behavior is most important.

Another area that is not often addressed in treatment—but should be— is the patient's purpose for drug use. As Muller and Schuman (2011) have pointed out, people use drugs for different reasons, including to reduce anxiety and to increase sensation. The sensation seeker is likely to use drugs that stimulate. Someone with high anxiety is likely to use depressant drugs. A primary goal of treatment for the patient with anxiety would be to help him or her learn ways to reduce anxiety without drugs. A treatment goal for the sensation seeker would be to help him or her find ways to experience the sensations he or she is looking for without using drugs, perhaps through something like skydiving.

It is easy to see how patients with different needs could seem treatment resistant if they were all treated the same. A patient with anxiety may not need sensation-seeking activities. In fact, he or she may resist them. A sensation-seeking person may not want or need to learn how to reduce anxiety and may resist such an effort; thus, becoming a resistant client.

One of the treatment dynamics that produces more treatment-resistant patients than any other is the handling of *denial*. Denial is seen as a useful concept for the counselor because it becomes a way to corner patients who say that they do not have the problem the counselor believes they have. Often this happens when a client resists a label such as "alcoholic," or, when he or she does not believe in a treatment, such as giving up alcohol totally for life. Counselors recognize denial as a symptom of the disorder, so patients cannot escape a diagnosis; they must either accept it or exhibit one of the primary features of the disorder—denial—thus lending creditability to the diagnosis. No one really wins this debate, and the patient often leaves without receiving help because he or she won't accept a label or a diagnosis and treatment plan that the counselor offers. This is sometimes related to the debate about whether addiction is a disease; the patient believes one thing, and the counselor believes another.

When a counselor gets into a power struggle with a patient and the patient is labeled as "treatment resistant," there is nothing therapeutic that happens in that relationship. The degree that denial is experienced in a counseling context is directly related to the choices that a counselor makes in how she or he chooses to relate to the client (Miller & Rollnick, 2013). A better reaction to such a patient would be for the counselor to refer the individual to a person or program that is more in line with that individual's thinking. There are more programs available today. Some are listed in the appendix of websites at the end of this book.

Not everyone sees addiction the same way. As noted throughout the chapters of this book, there are a plethora of alternatives to the traditional disease approach to addictions and to 12-step self-help involvement used to treat it. If counselors are to be effective with resistant patients, they need to know what alternative treatments are available. They must know what theories those treatments are based on even if they don't believe in those approaches. And, they must be willing to refer patients to those treatment options when necessary for the best interests of the patients.

Principle 3: Treatment needs to be readily available—Treatment for chemical dependency has been negatively affected by a number of factors, including inadequate funding, Health Maintenance Organizatons (HMOs), and Preferred Provider Organizations (PPOs). It is much more difficult today for many individuals to get the treatment they need than it has been in the past, especially if those individuals have limited means. The more difficult it is to access treatment, the easier it becomes for those with addictions to not seek treatment. This sets the individual up to seem reluctant and to wait until the problem has compounded before he or she seeks treatment. Counselors and therapists can help by offering creative ways to provide treatment for those who need it. That might mean something like offering group therapy sessions with half the group able to pay and half not able to pay. The point is that one major way to deal with a reluctant patient or client is to make treatment readily available.

Many programs, as currently designed, do the exact opposite of this. Intentionally or unintentionally, they have rules or policies that benefit the highly motivated and eliminate those who are not. This is understandable if resources are limited. It is natural to want to help those most likely to benefit from the treatment. The fact is, many people who should be motivated to stop destructive behaviors or addictions are not. The payoff for their drug use or behavior is too great. That does not mean that they cannot be or will never be motivated. It means that the person who motivates them will need to be creative and persistent, and will need to have an understanding of the dynamics of their addictions. They will need an understanding of what motivates a person to want to continue doing something that is destructive.

Principle 4: Effective treatment attends to multiple needs of the individual, not just to his or her drug use—What one person needs in treatment is not necessarily what everyone needs. There are some common needs, which were discussed earlier in this book. And most everyone needs hope and encouragement. However, it is true to a large degree that different people need different things in treatment. The following case is an example of a patient whose needs were not met in treatment.

This particular patient was seen in therapy by this author after he had been through three treatment programs. Two of these were inpatient and one was an outpatient program. After months in treatment programs and after many hours of therapy, he was still using both cocaine and alcohol. He was in his late 20s with a history of substance abuse since high school. He had attended many self-help meetings, which he was encouraged to do by treatment staff. That had not seemed to help.

As is my normal procedure, I asked the patient if there had been any significant events in his life that he felt I should know about. It was disclosed that he had been in an auto accident in high school, during which he was driving while intoxicated. Further disclosure revealed that his best friend was not only killed in the accident but also decapitated, an event this patient was witness to. The patient was only slightly injured as a result of the accident. However, emotionally, I believe that he had been severely impacted. It was surprising when the patient disclosed that this issue had *never* been addressed in treatment. This is a case in which the focus had been on stopping the patient's drug use—an approach that would fail until the issue of his friend's death was addressed and dealt with in therapy.

Drugs were serving two purposes in this patient's life: first, to help numb his guilt feelings, and second, as a sort of suicide-by-the-payment-plan. In this case, the need to deal with the death of a friend was more important than the need to address the drug use. There was very little chance he would give up his drug use until the death was dealt with. After dealing with the accident, other issues around his relationship with his father also needed to be addressed, and, as in Principle 8 below, the treatment plan needed to be adjusted as it progressed.

Principle 5: Remaining in treatment for an adequate period of time is critical for treatment effectiveness—The focus on brief therapy brought on by managed care has not necessarily been good for those with addictions. Most addictive behaviors or substance abuse problems develop over time. They are deeply rooted in the psychological, emotional, and even social areas of patients' lives. They take time to address in therapy. There are few, if any, quick fixes in the treatment of addictions. If a therapist tries to end therapy before the patient is ready, and the patient relapses, the therapist may respond by labeling the patient "resistant" or "reluctant to recover," rather than taking responsibility for ending therapy before it should have been ended. A therapist must take the necessary time with a patient to deal with the issues that need to be addressed.

Principle 6: Behavioral therapies (including individual, family, or group counseling) are the most commonly used forms of drug abuse treatment—For the very reasons listed above, it is important to offer individual or group therapy. Patients deserve to benefit from behavioral interventions that may support them in a variety of ways, including increasing their motivation to change, providing motivational incentives to maintain sobriety, teaching effective drug resistance and problem-solving skills, offering fun and engaging activities that don't involve drugs, and increasing their ability to have satisfying relationships. The patient, as well, needs to have time and a place to deal with his or her issues, or, put another way, the dynamics of his or her addictive behavior. This is especially true for the "reluctant to recover." The benefits and aspects of both individual and group therapy have been discussed earlier in this book. It is important in this chapter to point out that, often, those who do not respond to treatment have had too little treatment or inappropriate treatment or both. Here again, it is easy to blame the client for not responding to what is offered, rather than examining what was offered in the way of therapy. A group that is designed only to do "step work" may or may not deal with the specific issues of individual group members. Also, a counselor who has a predetermined idea about what all clients need to do to get sober may not get the response he or she wants or expects from all clients. People are different, and they have different motivations for using drugs. They have different motivations for stopping drug use. It is the counselor's job to find out what motivates each individual, and not to lump all addicts and abusers into the same group. It is fine to point out similarities between group members, but their differences must be explored as well.

Principle 7: Medications are an important element of treatment for many patients, especially when combined with counseling and other behavioral therapies—Too often during the treatment process, clients are told that the only way to live life is drug free. This includes even psychotropic drugs utilized in the treatment of mental health disorders. As drug counselors and therapists in other fields who treat patients with chemical dependency get more training and education in dual diagnosis and psychopharmacology, this will most likely change. In fact, it has already improved, with many licensed mental health professionals now required to have a course in psychopharmacology. In most areas of the country, programs that had problems with their clients or with patients using any and all drugs in the past have loosened up on that stance. This could be because of the new focus on dual-diagnosis patients, as discussed earlier. Perhaps the people who run and design programs are beginning to understand that there are times when psychotropic medications are necessary—maybe even before the addictive behaviors can be addressed in treatment.

There is no doubt that some people who are labeled or thought to be "reluctant to recover" are just undermedicated with the appropriate psychotropic medication. During the 45 years of this author's clinical experience, quite a number of individuals have been able to attribute their eventual sobriety after many failed attempts to psychotropic medications. Yet this is a difficult situation because it is hard to differentiate the symptoms of use and withdrawal from the symptoms of a mental or psychological problem. Is a client or patient depressed and then does he or she use alcohol? Or, did alcohol and the behaviors that resulted from alcohol use cause the depression? Questions such as these need to be addressed and answered during the course of treatment, especially with those reluctant to recover.

One last note on this principle. It presupposes that chemical dependency counselors will be fluent and open to recognizing the positive benefits of utilizing pharmacological interventions for directly treating those with addictions. For opioid addiction, this would include methadone, buprenorphine, and naltrexone. For treating alcohol dependence, acamprosate, disulfiram (Antabuse), and naltrexone have been approved. There are a variety of options for treating nicotine addiction, including patches, gum, lollipops, lozenges, and sprays, as well as certain oral medications including burpropion and varenicline. These were all discussed in Chapter 9.

Principle 8: An individual's treatment and services plan must be assessed continually and modified as necessary to ensure that the plan meets his or her changing needs—Unfortunately, many treatment programs across the country offer only "McTreatment"; that is, everyone gets the same program. This usually includes step work, individual therapy, group therapy, and education regarding the "disease" of addiction. No attention is paid to each patient's special needs. This "McTreatment" works for some people; otherwise it would not continue to be used. However, those who have low motivation to change are often the ones who don't respond to "McTreatment." They need something different that may involve different forms of treatment (including medication, as just discussed in the previous principle) and referral and/or case management to many other needs related to employment, parenting, housing, and more. That is why it is important to understand the dynamics of the addiction or addictive behavior of each individual. Chapter 8 offers some of the issues that must be continually assessed during treatment.

Principle 9: Many drug-addicted individuals also have other mental disorders—There is a problem in addition to the one of many CD counselors not knowing enough about when or why psychotropic drugs may be necessary for those they treat. There is the additional problem of the mental health practitioner who has an insufficient knowledge of chemical dependency and the dynamics of addiction. This has been addressed somewhat in some states by requiring a course on the subject in all graduate programs in which students are studying to become licensed mental health professionals. However, one course, no matter how good it is, seems insufficient to prepare anyone to work with alcoholics and addicts. This most certainly is not enough training to understand the complexities of addictive behaviors and chemical dependency.

This means that either mental health workers need to learn a great deal more about addiction or CD counselors need to learn a great deal more about mental disorders and their treatment, including psychopharmacology. Or, treatment programs need to hire people from both fields, people who can get along and agree on what is best for the patient. Until such an integrated approach to treatment becomes standardized, we will continue to have patients caught in the middle who have been labeled reluctant to recover.

Principle 10: Medically assisted detoxification is only the first stage of addiction treatment and by itself does little to change long-term drug abuse—There was frustration among the medical professionals in the beginning phases of the development of treatment approaches to chemical dependency. Emergency room physicians and staff often worked long and hard to help an alcoholic or addict detox only to have him or her return to drinking or using. Doctors and nurses who worked in emergency rooms became resentful and even reluctant to treat those alcoholics and addicts who seemed not to heed medical advice and who also seemed bent on self-destruction. This was because they saw addiction in terms of the medical complications of detoxi-fication, not as a complex disorder with many interlaced dynamics (Lawson & Lawson, 1998). There are few in either the medical or CD fields who still believe detox is sufficient treatment for alcoholics or addicts. However, due to managed care and cutbacks on inpatient treatment dollars, many people receive only detox. Then, of course, they are likely to be seen as unmotivated to recover when they predictably need future help.

Principle 11: Treatment does not need to be voluntary to be effective—Because of the limited number of treatment beds available in the United States, it has become accepted procedure for treatment programs to ask potential cus-tomers to show some sign of a strong motivation before they are admitted to treatment. This might be in the form of a few weeks of sobriety or something like remaining sober while on the waiting list to get into the program. This has certainly increased the success rates for these programs and those who are ad-mitted to them, but it has done little for those with low motivation to recover who have a difficult time meeting the criteria set by such programs.

Motivation can come in many forms, depending on the situation. Many communities have had success with "Drug Courts." These are courts with judges who are trained in working with addictions. They know the treatment programs in the community that are available, and they have staff that can evaluate individuals with addictions and can recommend which treatment program would be best for each person. Upon sentencing, usually for a drug-related crime, the person is given a choice of treatment or jail. Most choose treatment over jail. Treatment is not voluntary, but many of these individuals recover during this time. However, these programs vary in effectiveness. It is thought that the most successful ones will likely be those that address all of the issues that people with addictions bring to treatment, not just addiction. It would seem that programs that only addressed issues of addiction would have a high number of participants who remain unmotivated to recover or who re-turned to using after the program was over.

Principle 12: Drug use during treatment must be monitored continu-ously, as lapses during treatment do occur—Part of the reason for the success of the Drug Courts is that they routinely test the participants for drug use. The threat of jail for a positive drug test is very motivating for most participants. These tests are fairly inexpensive and can be used by any counselor who has reason to believe their counselee might be using drugs and lying about it. The threat of a drug test is motivation enough for most individuals to keep them from using drugs.

It may, however, be diagnostic of an individual with low motivation to re-cover when someone who knows he or she is going to be tested for drugs uses anyway. When famous sports figures or actors who have everything to lose are caught on a drug test using drugs, most people, including most CD counselors, shake their heads in disbelief and make statements like, "I can't believe they were so stupid." Or "Why would anyone blow a multi-million dollar contract just to get high?" Although this type of behavior is difficult to understand, it is best viewed as treatment failure rather than as an opportunity to blame the individual. The treatment failed to identify and address the motivating factors behind the individual's drug use. This approach does not let the individual drug user off the hook regarding responsibility for his or her behavior, but it accepts that there must be some powerful underlying reasons that drugs are more important to this individual than they would be to most people.

At some point, each individual has to take responsibility for his or her own self-destructive behavior. But, until they are motivated to do so, it is unlikely they will. It is exactly those patients/clients who do not respond to traditional CD treatment who need special understanding and alternative forms of treatments and motivations. What they do not need is to be told they are hopeless and will never be able to change their behavior. What they do need is someone who is willing to work with them to help them understand the dynamics behind their destructive behavior—destructive behavior that is so obvious to others, yet not to them.

Principle 13: Treatment programs should test patients for the presence of HIV/AIDS, Hepatitis B and C, tuberculosis, and other infectious diseases, as well as provide targeted risk-reduction counseling, linking patients to treatment if necessary—In some cases, individuals have low motivation to recover when they have a fatal disease or a chronic illness. The idea that "they are going to die anyway so why not continue to use drugs" is difficult to address. This type of individual needs special treatment. In other cases, individuals who have diseases such as HIV or AIDS and do not know it are subjecting others to the disease. Drug users are at high risk for such diseases. That is why it is important for drug treatment programs to assess for such diseases. Counseling can help those who engage in high-risk behaviors, and it can help those people who are ill to manage their illness. Such counseling should focus specifically on what clients can do to reduce their risks from infection and how to avoid engaging in high-risk behaviors. Access to and support for medical treatments (i.e., HIV testing available on-site, drugs proven effective for combatting HIV) is also important.

The Counselor's Role in a Patient's Lack of Response to Treatment

It is the counselor who is in charge of and responsible for therapy, not the patient. The patient is responsible for his or her recovery and choices, which will either lead toward or away from that recovery. But part of the counselor's responsibility is to let the patient know the choices that are available and the possible consequences of each choice, including good choices and bad choices. It is also important for the counselor to know as much as he or she can about what has motivated the patient's choices in the past. This includes giving credit to the patient for all of his or her decisions, good and bad, even when they seemed good at the time and they ultimately turned out to be negative. In the beginning phases of drug use, and perhaps for a long time, drugs were working for the individual. They were meeting the individual's needs in some way. Perhaps drug use still works for the individual. Drugs do what they were designed to do. They alter consciousness, change feelings, dull pain, enhance joy, energize, depress, and do a variety of other seemingly positive things. If they did not work for the individual, they would not be a problem. Few people, if any, abuse lettuce. There is no war on lettuce. Lettuce does not work as drugs do.

When a counselor chooses to ignore the positive aspects of drugs in the life of the user, he or she is discounting the reality of that individual. Discounting someone's reality is not a good way to begin to build a therapeutic relationship. Truth and honesty are a much better basis for such a relationship. It would not be truthful to claim that everything a person who used drugs got from drug use was negative. If that were true, why would the person use? If the counselor does not recognize and acknowledge the positive aspect of drug use, he or she forces the client to react by taking a polarized position on the positive aspects of drug use to counteract all of the negatives brought up by the counselor. Why should the patient admit to only the negative aspect? That would make him or her seem foolish for using in the first place. Even if patients don't verbalize polarization in therapy, it is a dynamic that is set up, and they will often act out their side of the issue by using drugs during or shortly after treatment. If both patient and counselor agree that drug use has had and will only have negative effects, and the patient is willing to make choices based on that belief, therapy is not really necessary. An adversarial relationship is not usually therapeutic. Rather than taking sides, it is more therapeutic for the counselor and counselee to agree on both the negative and positive aspects of drug use. Then it becomes easier for clients with low motivation to recover to realistically examine how drugs have negatively impacted their life, as well as to see the positive things they got from drugs. And, it becomes easier for them to make the choice to not use drugs in the future. Unless, perhaps, the positive aspects truly do outweigh the negative aspects. This might be the case with an AIDS patient who is smoking marijuana to allow himself to take medication and to maintain an appetite. If this is the case, the counselor cannot deny it. However, the counselor can point out potential negatives, such as being arrested and having to live the last few months of one's life in jail. Patients have low motivation to recover when all they can see are the positive aspects of drug use. They become even more unmotivated when their counselor fails to see the positive side of drug use, and the patient continues to focus on the positive in order to convince the counselor that the patient is right. It is the counselor, not the patient, who can change this dynamic. It does no one any good to blame the patient for being resistant to treatment.

This is only one dynamic where the counselor can play a role to make the patient more resistant or less resistant to treatment. The point is that there are many dynamics between the patient and the counselor, and that it is the counselor who needs to figure out what the dynamics are and how to use them in the best interests of the patient.

Dos and Don'ts of Working With Individuals Unmotivated to Recover

The things that help unmotivated individuals to move toward recovery are the same things that help most people with chemical dependency. However, in most cases, those who have been labeled "unmotivated," "resistant," or "reluctant" have not been offered the individualized help they need. They have been offered McTreatment, which is a program that may or may not work for most people. But, they are not like most people. If they were, they might respond to traditional treatment. Perhaps there should be two types of CD counselors: those who do what is traditional and what works for "most" people and those who work with those who seem resistant. Here is a list of dos and don'ts for working with those unmotivated to recover:

Dos

- Do examine the positive aspects of a patient's drug use
- Do explore other ways to meet the needs that drugs once met
- Do give credit for having the ability to choose to recover if he or she wants
- Do look at family issues that may influence the way one thinks and feels
- Do help the patient understand the dynamics of his or her addictive behavior
- Do give hope for his or her recovery
- Do make sure your reality is real
- Do give a choice of self-help recovery groups, including none at all
- Do give choices and discuss the possible outcomes of each choice
- Do teach patients to be better choosers

Don'ts

- Don't continue doing what is not working
- Don't get into a power struggle over the patient's use of drugs
- Don't be afraid to confront the patient with reality (see reality dos above)

- Don't force the patient to go to a specific meeting with no alternative
- Don't be afraid to refer the patient to someone else
- Don't forget to rule out psychological and emotional problems
- Don't forget to evaluate for PTSD (see Chapter 8)
- Don't counsel the patient not to use psychotropic medications, if prescribed
- Don't give up on the patient

Counselors would be wise, as a final note, to keep the above suggestions in mind even when working with those motivated to recover.

Summary

The theme of this chapter is that it is the counselor, not the client or patient, who should bear the primary responsibility for treatment failure. Some readers may feel that the responsibility for recovery cannot be born by the counselor without taking responsibility away from the client or patient. Both the client and the counselor share some responsibility. However, it is the counselor who is getting paid. When the counselor seeks to blame the client without recognizing his or her own role in the treatment failure, it is a bit like the man searching for his keys under the street lamp, not because he lost them there but because the light is better there. The light may be better with the focus on the patient's failure, but to find answers regarding treatment failure, the counselor may need to look in the darkness of his or her own failures: failures to identify what motivates the patient to continue using drugs and failures to appropriately address these issues during treatment.

Addictive behavior is hard to understand. Treatment and the process of change are equally difficult to grasp. However, the counselor who looks at both sides of the equation—his role and the client's role—will be at a distinct advantage over the counselor who only sees one side.

References

Lawson, A., & Lawson, G. (1998). *Alcoholism and the family: A guide to treatment and prevention* (2nd ed.). Austin, TX: PRO-ED.

Miller, W. R., & Rollnick, S. (2013). *Motivational interviewing: Helping people change* (3rd Ed.). New York: Guilford Press.

Muller, C. P., & Schumann, G. (2011). Drugs as instruments: A new framework for non-addictive pshcyoactive drug use. *Behavioral and Brain Sciences, 34,* 293–347.

NIH Publication No. 12-4180. (2012). Principles of drug addiction treatment: A research-based guide. Retrieved from http://www.drugabuse.gov/publications/principles-drug-addiction-treatment-research-based-guide-third-edition/principles-effective-treatment

Straussner, S. L. (2014). Assessment and treatment of clients with substance use disorders. In S. L. Straussner (Ed.), *Clinical work with substance-abusing clients* (pp. 3–38). New York: Guilford Press.

Walters, G. D. (2000). Spontaneous remission from alcohol, tobacco, and other drug abuse: Seeking quantitative answers to qualitative questions. *American Journal of Drug Abuse, 26*(3), 443–460.

White, W. L. (1998). *Slaying the dragon: The history of addiction treatment and recovery in America.* Bloomington, IL: Chestnut Health, Systems/Lighthouse Institute.

CHAPTER 12

Harm Reduction:
A (Relatively) New Concept of Care

CHAPTER OBJECTIVES

- Introduce and define the concept of harm reduction
- Examine interventions that reduce the consequences of drinking
- Present examples of harm reduction and their role in prevention and treatment
- Introduce the concept of server training as a harm-reduction strategy
- Review the Alcohol Skills Training Program (ASTP) and its potential effectiveness in harm reduction
- Introduce the concepts of the "Wheel of Change" and Motivational Interviewing

A great many people who abuse alcohol and drugs suffer serious problems. They frequently have social, legal, financial, and psychological difficulties that require extensive use of society's resources.

An even greater number of people who use alcohol and drugs do not suffer serious problems. While many of these drinkers and drug users reduce or stop their intake of chemicals when they reach a critical period in their lives (see Zucker, 1987), these individuals may respond to less lengthy interventions and less expensive treatment if their use is addressed during a period when they are in danger of suffering serious problems. Both chronic abusers and those going through a window of risk can potentially be reached by a relatively new approach called "harm reduction." Harm reduction has been slow to gain acceptance in the United States. It has been used effectively in Scotland, England, Canada, and other countries. Many of these countries have produced outcome studies that indicate a reduction of problems with drug and alcohol abuse, as well as reductions in numbers of drug abusers and social users. Other outcome studies are planned or in progress worldwide. Studies suggest that alcohol use and abuse can be reduced with a minimal 3-hour intervention employing the Alcohol Skills Training Program (ASTP).

This chapter outlines the history of harm reduction and presents overviews of two programs for reducing risk in alcohol and drug users. The two harm-avoidance approaches include the Server Training Program in Oregon, and the ASTP groups utilized at the University of Nebraska–Lincoln. The Server Training Program is directed toward individuals or groups who serve alcohol to patrons. The ASTP groups are structured, brief process/tasks with college students who have alcohol-related offenses.

Harm Reduction Described

The concept of harm reduction was introduced to the United States alcohol and drug community by Marlatt in 1966 (as cited in Inciard & Harrison, 1999). Marlatt wrote a paper describing what harm reduction was, how it developed, and how it worked. He predicted that harm reduction was coming to the United States. At about the same time, several other writers described the concept and its goals.

Single (1996) outlined the history of harm reduction in a comprehensive review article. He noted that the concept of harm reduction could be traced back to a vocal group of public health specialists who were grappling with the serious health risks of AIDS. In the face of zero tolerance for drug use by legal authorities, these public health professionals decided to deal with the problem from a different perspective. They developed multiple prevention measures aimed directly at reducing the spread of the HIV epidemic. Those measures included exchanging old needles/syringes for new ones and providing bleach kits to clean addicts' used needles. These interventions emphasized the reduction of the harmful effects of drug use, but did not focus on eliminating the use of the drug by the addict. These efforts came to be labeled "harm reduction" or "harm minimization."

While abstinence might be the ultimate goal, these harm-reduction approaches can be utilized even if drug abstinence cannot be achieved. Harm-reduction approaches have been established in England, The Netherlands, and other parts of Europe. They are also in place in Australia. Harm reduction is still, unfortunately, less common in North America, although it appears better established in Canada. As but one example of the barriers to the implementation of harm-reduction strategies in the United States, a ban on federal funding for needle exchange programs was not lifted until 2009 (Marlatt & Witkiewitz, 2010).

Marlatt and Witkiewitz (2010), in a comprehensive review of the literature, documented the many ways in which harm-reduction strategies have been employed and the research that supports their efficacy. One of the most encouraging aspects of harm-reduction programs that comes out of evaluation studies (e.g., Donoghoe, Stimson, Dolen, & Alldritte, 1989; Riley, 1993), is that the programs have been able to reduce the spread of AIDS (and other diseases) without increasing drug use in the general population. Indeed, safe injection facilities in more than a half-dozen countries that provide drug users a place where they can inject their own drugs with clean equipment and under medical supervision have been linked to an increase in utilization of detox and other addiction treatment services (Marlatt & Witkiewitz, 2010). Despite its success, or maybe because of it, Single (1996) suggests that the harm-reduction approach is at a choice point: Harm reduction lacks a clear, generally agreed-upon definition. *Harm reduction* is currently applied to both licit and illicit drugs and interventions, which go beyond needle replacement. For example, the term has been applied to alcohol-prevention programs. Dr. Alan Leshner, the former director of the National Institute of Drug Abuse, has suggested that the term *harm reduction* be dropped altogether due to its association with—Leshner would probably even go so far as to use the words "legitimization of"—illicit drugs (Marlatt & Witkiewitz, 2010).

In the alcohol-prevention field, a harm-reduction emphasis has historically been placed on reducing accessibility and reducing consumption. Efforts at harm reduction with alcohol include programs that limit off-premises sales, hold servers responsible for serving intoxicated persons, place limits on advertising, and increase the fines and jail time for driving while intoxicated. Taxing alcoholic beverages also plays a role in availability and amount consumed. Additional efforts include training medical personnel to utilize brief interventions and housing those who are homeless and have alcohol problems without requiring that they cease drinking.

Harm reduction in the alcohol field focuses on decreasing the risk and severity of destructive effects of alcohol use. This is often done without reducing alcohol consumption. Conventional prevention measures have primarily stressed the negative effects of alcohol. "Generally the message for all drinking is unequivocal: Drinking less is better" (Single, 1996, p. 240). The message given through harm-reduction programs is to avoid problems when one drinks. As Single (1996) puts it, "[Harm reduction] focuses on decreasing the risk and severity of harmful consequences arising from alcohol consumption without necessarily decreasing the level of consumption itself" (p. 240).

Single (1996), as well as Marlatt and Witkiewitz (2010), outlines several examples of a harm-reduction approach to alcohol prevention and treatment. They also consider the issue of controlled drinking and factors favoring harm reduction as a prevention approach. A brief review of examples and evaluation of controlled drinking and positive aspects of the harm-reduction approach follow. After this review, the Server Training Program and ASTP Groups will be detailed as examples of programs that follow the harm-reduction model.

Examples of Harm-Reduction Approaches in Prevention of Intoxication

Interventions That Directly/Indirectly Reduce Consequences of Intoxication (Single)

There are a number of interventions that directly or indirectly reduce the consequences of intoxication. One example is the invention of special glassware that breaks into small beadlike pieces when broken. This reduces harm when a fight breaks out in a saloon. Other helpful interior changes in places where alcohol is served include padding the furniture and compartmentalizing space in pubs and taverns. These modifications reduce injury should an altercation occur. Other changes protect individuals from drinking and driving. Programs exist in the United States that provide a person to drive the intoxicated drinker home, as well as someone else to drive the drinker's car home. Other U.S. programs provide safe transportation on New Year's Eve, a night when many indulge in alcohol to toast the new year. Reduction of harm also includes things not tied directly to lessening the negative effects of alcohol, such as air bags in cars. Air bags reduce deaths and the severity of injuries suffered by drunken drivers and their victims. It is important to note that all of these programs are aimed at reducing the harmful effects of alcohol, not at reducing drinking.

Reducing Alcohol Content in Beverages (Single)

Low alcohol content (light beers, low-alcohol wines, light spirits) can reduce alcohol intake without reducing the overall volume of consumption. Such beverages maintain the liquor industry's profitability and serve the public health of the country at the same time. There are programs that increase the availability of alcohol to people who were known to be at risk for drinking alcohol obtained from dangerous sources (e.g., shoe polish). Special store hours make alcohol available so that these abusive drinkers do not poison themselves with less potable alcohol. The goal of programs like this is completely at odds with an abstinence-based approach, but it is consistent with a harm-reduction approach.

Controlled Drinking (Single)

Some alcohol treatment agencies do not require their clients to quit using alcohol. Instead, clients are asked to work on being "controlled drinkers." This approach is diametrically opposed to 12-step-model approaches that advocate strict abstinence. However, such controlled drinking programs are often dealing with different clients. The controlled drinking approach may be dealing with drinkers who are alcohol abusers but not alcohol dependent. They may also be drinkers who are in a "developmentally limited" stage of drinking (Zucker, 1987). Total abstinence is not an acceptable goal for these drinkers, but more-controlled drinking may be. Thus, controlled drinking appears to be an important option to reduce drinking in the subset of abusive drinkers. It may be difficult or impossible to convince these drinkers that they are addicted to alcohol. However, they may accept that they can and should drink more responsibly and safely. A broader view of this type of user is presented later in the chapter when the ASTP program is outlined.

Housing First (Marlatt & Witkiewitz)

Because there is an incredible cost incurred by the public for responding to those who are homeless and have alcohol dependency issues (and, not infrequently, mental illness as well), some municipalities have begun providing stable housing to such individuals with no expectation that such individuals abstain from drinking. Research indicates that such individuals experience increased stability, decreased use of alcohol, and decreased intoxication. Just as importantly, the cost of providing such a program was more than 60% less of the costs (i.e., law enforcement, emergency room utilization) that would have been incurred had they continued to be homeless.

SBIRT (Marlatt & Witkiewitz)

Because so many people with drug and alcohol problems interface with the medical system at some point in their lives—one study found that more than 1 in 5 trauma patients "screened positive for substance use, risky behavior, abuse, or dependency at the time of admission" (Madras, Compton, Avula, Stegbauer, & Clark, as cited in Marlatt & Witkiewitz, 2010)—a brief intervention utilizing a motivational interviewing approach has been developed for use by those in medical settings. The Screening, Brief Intervention, and Referral to Treatment model (also known as SBIRT) helps medical professionals, as its name suggests, to broach the subject of alcohol and drug use, enhance motivation for healthful change, and refer patients to appropriate substance abuse treatment services. "The preponderance of evidence [suggests] that even a brief intervention in a medical setting can result in significant reductions in alcohol use, reinjury, and other adverse consequences" (Marlatt & Witkiewitz, 2010, p. 599).

Factors Favoring Harm Reduction as a Prevention Approach

Political leaders from the governments of Canada, France, Germany, Italy, Japan, Russia, the United Kingdom, and the United States—also knows as the "Group of 8"—issued a report from a summit indicating that "it is essential to focus on prevention of the main risk factors such as harmful use of alcohol and tobacco, physical inactivity, unhealthy diets, as well as harmful environmental conditions" (G8 Health Experts, as cited by Marlatt & Witkietwitz, 2010, p. 593). Single (1996) emphasizes that, in the alcohol field, harm reduction is a "part of a distinct trend toward prevention measures aimed at minimizing the negative consequences of drinking rather than decreasing drinking" (p. 241). This is not to say that demand reduction efforts aren't important. Indeed, they are powerful tools that can have powerful effects. Canada's requirement that alcohol drinks be sold at a minimum price suggests that a 10% increase in the average minimum price for alcohol would result in an

8% decrease in consumption, a 9% drop in hospital admissions, and a 32% drop in "wholly" alcohol-caused deaths (Stockwell & Thomas, 2013). Single suggests that the trend toward minimizing negative consequences of drinking, as opposed to decreasing drinking, will continue as the public becomes more aware of evidence about the potential benefits of more moderate alcohol consumption. He points out that widespread media attention has been given to the beneficial effects of moderate drinking.

Another factor favoring harm reduction as a preventive approach is the empirical support for a national focus on drinking "occasions." It has been established that a number of heavy drinking occasions are related to health problems, family conflict, vocational problems, financial difficulties, and alcohol-based difficulties with the legal system. The number of heavy drinking occasions shows a higher relationship to the above problems than does level of alcohol consumption. Some drinkers, for example, consume a small amount of alcohol but have a significant number of times when they consume five or more drinks at one sitting. If light drinkers drink five or more drinks at one sitting, they have a greater chance of having drinking-related problems than do heavy drinkers who rarely or never drink in an immoderate fashion. Of course, over the long haul, heavy drinkers are at risk for the chronic health problems associated with heavy drinking.

It might be possible to reduce heavy drinking occasions among all drinkers via server training, improved enforcement of licensing requirements, and provision of preventive education, such as advertising, to make drinking and driving and being intoxicated socially unacceptable (Single, 1996). Programs might also be directed at heavy drinkers so they receive the attention they need. Research about bringing such programs directly to the people—whether school-based, college-based, computer-based, in medical settings, and in the workplace—has demonstrated the efficacy of such approaches, with savings estimated at up to $102 for every dollar invested in such programs (Marlatt & Witkiewitz, 2010). But, Single says, other drinking types cannot be ignored since the findings indicate that it may be most efficient to target preventive education to the general population. This is because people who consume alcohol at levels associated with alcohol dependence contribute substantially to levels of alcohol problems (Single, 1996).

Given the research data now in hand, the most conservative approach to prevention through harm reduction would be to aim for light to moderate drinking with all users of alcohol. This might be possible by establishing the pattern of moderate drinking as the national norm. Research in university settings (Larimer & Cronce, as cited in Marlatt & Witkiewitz, 2010) has suggested that communicating norms in a college setting is more effective than educational interventions alone. This might work nationwide if a temperate drinking norm could be established for all segments of the population. Heavier drinking would then be socially unacceptable.

Server Training as an Example of Harm Reduction

Training programs directed toward bartenders and others who sell alcohol to patrons is an example of harm reduction. Most of these training programs are aimed at increasing moderate drinking (and so, reducing heavy drinking). Servers are instructed to recognize and gradually cease sales to intoxicated patrons. They are taught to replace what the intoxicated person is drinking with a beverage that has a lower alcohol content. Owners and servers are directed to avoid "Happy Hours" and other volume discounts of alcohol. They are asked to monitor entrances and to consistently "card" individuals who appear underage. They are also told to make sure that the intoxicated person has a safe way home.

Single (1996) describes server training as an attempt to reduce drinking-associated consequences without generally restricting drinking or lowering the profits of licensed establishments. Evaluations of server-training programs show that establishments that have server-intervention programs in place tend to attract more customers and increase profitability. The server-training program utilized in the state of Oregon (also in California and other states) provides a detailed overview of this type of harm reduction.

The training program manual *Alcohol Server Education* (Oregon Liquor Control Commission, 2010) for server training includes a history of alcoholic beverages, intervention techniques for dealing with visibly intoxicated persons, a review of applicable laws, alcohol and minors, etc. A section on "Visibly Intoxicated Persons" is especially important to people in alcohol prevention and treatment. The manual lays out "50 Likely Signs of Visible Intoxication," which clearly pinpoint those patrons who should not be served additional alcoholic beverages. Included are the following areas and signs:

Appearance

1. Bloodshot, glassy, or watery eyes
2. Flushed face
3. Droopy eyelids
4. Blank stare or dazed look
5. Twitching or body tremors
6. Disheveled clothing

Speech

7. Thick, slurred speech
8. Loud, noisy speech
9. Speaking loudly, then quietly
10. Rambling train of thought
11. Unusually fast or slow talking
12. Slow response to questions or comments

13. Repetitive statements

14. Bravado, boasting

15. Making irrational statements

Attitude

16. Annoying other guests and employees

17. Argumentative

18. Aggressive or belligerent

19. Obnoxious or mean

20. Inappropriate sexual advances

21. Overly friendly to other guests or employees

22. Boisterous

Behavior

23. Swaying, staggering, or stumbling

24. Unable to sit straight

25. Careless with money

26. Difficulty making change

27. Restless

28. Depressed or sullen

29. Crying or moody

30. Extreme or sudden change in behavior

31. Overly animated or entertaining

32. Crude, inappropriate speech or gestures

33. Drowsiness or falling asleep

34. Lack of focus and eye contact

35. Difficulty standing up

36. Unusual walk

37. Can't find mouth with glass

38. Falling down or falling off of chair

39. Difficulty lighting cigarettes

40. Lighting more than one cigarette

41. Clumsy

42. Difficulty remembering

43. Spilling drinks

44. Disoriented

45. Agitated, anxious
46. Grinding teeth
47. Vomiting

Other

48. Odor of alcohol, marijuana, or chemicals
49. Excessive perspiration
50. Repeated trips to restroom or outside area

Training that makes the server aware of the level of functioning of a customer ensures that access to alcohol will be reduced or cut off entirely if the customer is drinking too much. In making sure that the customer does not become intoxicated, server-training programs will help reduce fighting, driving while intoxicated (and the resulting car crashes), and falls and other accidents that can be life threatening to the customer and the people around him or her. These preventive techniques also increase sales for the establishments offering these approaches (Single, 1996).

Alcohol Skills Training Program (ASTP) Groups as an Example of Harm Reduction

The ASTP groups are an example of a harm-reduction approach to alcohol use and abuse problems for college students. The University of Nebraska–Lincoln (UNL) utilizes ASTP groups as a harm-reduction method to provide intervention for students with alcohol-related problems. These groups have been described by an in-house paper by Merriwether (1997) as well as in a dissertation by Potts (2002).

As is true in many universities, UNL has major problems with underage drinking and drinking in residence halls. Students are referred to the ASTP groups for those offenses, as are students arrested for minor in consumption (MIC) or for minor in possession (MIP; University of Nebraska–Lincoln, 2014). Prior to the availability of the ASTP groups, students were treated by a 20-hour-plus alcohol education program. Participants showed a very high relapse rate following that program.

In order to combat abusive drinking more effectively, the university Student Health Center recently contracted with the Department of Psychology training clinic to provide intervention for people adjudicated for alcohol abuse and associated behaviors at the university. The training clinic intervention consists of the ASTP groups. The groups are based on Motivational Interviewing (MI) strategies. The training that group facilitators receive is summarized by Potts (2002), as well as the BASICS Training Manual (see Dimeff, Baer,

Kivlahan, & Marlatt, 1999). The ASTP groups are structured, very focused, and relatively brief procedures made up of two sessions of about $1\frac{1}{2}$ to 2 hours each. The entire thrust of the ASTP groups is to promote a more moderate, and therefore safer, use of alcohol. The ASTP groups have, in large measure, replaced the education program as an intervention for adjudicated students.

The ASTP groups focus on (1) alcohol education with a harm-reduction approach and (2) creating a discrepancy between the student's drinking behavior and his or her goal(s) in life. The usual techniques of Motivational Interviewing are utilized to maximize the impact of these groups and to create a discrepancy. Readiness for change as proposed by Prochaska, Norcross, and DiClemente (1994) is used as a stages-of-change model. This model proposes that an individual's behavioral change entails progression through six stages: precontemplation, contemplation, preparation, action, maintenance, and recycle/relapse.

Stage I: Precontemplation—Persons at this stage lack awareness of the negative consequences they have suffered and are suffering. These are individuals whom alcohol treatment agencies may have classified as "in denial" in the past. These drinkers see no problems or reasons for change.

Stage II: Contemplation—This is where the drinkers are aware that a problem exists, but are still ambivalent about whether their problems are great enough to warrant change on their parts. They are not sure if they want to change even if they do perceive a problem. They are, in a word, ambivalent to change. They think about change but are not quite committed to making modifications in their behavior.

Stage III: Preparation—This stage begins when ambivalence to change moves to a desire to make changes in drinking behavior. People in this stage begin to make plans, establish goals, and identify the means to reach these goals.

Stage IV: Action—This stage requires more energy, commitment, and skills, because the alcohol-abusing person needs to try out new behaviors and new ways to cope. Individuals in this stage are "implementing the change plan...and actively trying to change" (Miller, Forcehimes, & Zweben, 2011, p. 111).

Stage V: Maintenance—Persons are dealing with developing new coping behaviors and goals and planning ahead for possible relapses.

Stage VI: Relapse—Here individuals have suffered a slip or a relapse back to old behaviors or drinking patterns. This stage need not be seen as a failure, but may be used to build drinkers' self-confidence so that they can make a slip then resume a commitment to a life that is alcohol free.

These six stages are referred to as the "Wheel of Change." Using this wheel makes it easier to understand the presence or absence of substance abusers' motivation to change their use patterns. It is possible to measure where a person is in the stages of change with this wheel. This knowledge helps the facilitator in two specific ways: It reduces the facilitator's frustration about resistance to change and allows him or her to know which approaches are best to use at a particular level of change.

Anticipating that clients may be at different points on the Wheel of Change makes it easier to deal with group members' ambivalence when it occurs. It allows the group leader to "roll with resistance" rather than to confront the resistance. Following this type of intervention usually reduces defensiveness and denial. The reduction of these obstacles to change occurs not just in the group member discussing these issues. It also works to reassure all the group members that they will not be heavily confronted by group leaders. So, using the Wheel of Change reduces defensiveness in all group members and assists in open and honest communication.

The stages-of-change model illustrates the differences between group members who may be at different points on the Wheel of Change. Group leaders can expedite sharing of levels of change by group members by asking them the "whys" of their behavior. Asking someone in the preparation stage about what got him or her to think about making changes in drinking behavior may get the preparation stage client to talk about things that a person in the precontemplation stage is just beginning to consider.

In addition to the stages-of-change model, a second important factor in the ASTP group is Motivational Interviewing (MI). Motivational Interviewing consists of therapeutic techniques drawn from procedures used in the helping professions, including Rogers and Dymond's (1954) client-centered approach and cognitive-behavioral therapy. It has been known for years that the confrontational approach used in many alcohol-treatment approaches is, at a minimum, ineffective. At its worst, confrontation is harmful in the treatment of alcohol problems. Heavy confrontation techniques were once used extensively in alcohol-treatment programs. They have been a long-standing issue for some in the alcohol-treatment field (e.g., Landfield & Rivers, 1975). The incorporation of less-aggressive confrontation meets the needs of many in the treatment field.

MI has two major goals. The first is to help people to build a commitment toward change. The second is to help them make a change, eventually. The technique focuses on reducing ambivalence and removing barriers to change by drawing most heavily on the client-centered perspective.

MI is designed to meet people in the stage of change they occupy at a given time. The strategy followed to do this in the ASTP groups is to create a discrepancy between the student drinkers' personal goals and their current use (and abuse) of alcohol. The goal is for the facilitators to get the person (or persons, in the case of groups) to objectively evaluate how they drink and what the consequences of their drinking are. Consistent with Landfield and Rivers's

(1975) work in groups, MI posits that when individuals are allowed to look at their drinking objectively, without becoming defensive, then facilitators and student drinkers do not become involved in a power struggle. Without a power struggle, students are free to come to their own conclusions about their drinking behavior.

Five basic principles used in implementing the ASTP groups are as follows:

Principle 1: Express Empathy—The emphasis here is on building rapport and relationships between the group facilitators and group members. By expressing empathy for them, the group leaders let the group members know that they understand them. Empathy is expressed in various ways, including acceptance of persons where they are, reflective listening, and understanding the students' ambivalence toward changing their drinking behavior.

Principle 2: Develop a Discrepancy—In this case, facilitators attempt to develop a discord between the participants' present behavior and his or her greater life goals. Because it is hard to allow individualized goals in the ASTP groups, these goals must be established initially at the group level. Most groups agree that their broad goal is to increase what they find positive about drinking and to minimize their negative findings. Following these discussions, maximizing life goals and minimizing alcohol's effects on those goals are reviewed by facilitators and group members.

Principle 3: Avoid Argumentation—Some group members are defensive initially, and sometimes they are hostile in the ASTP groups. Group leaders attempt to avoid increasing defensiveness by keeping interactions at a non-judgmental discussion of drinking and its consequences. The facilitators' goal is to provide a safe and supportive setting where group members can openly discuss concerns about drinking. The best way for a facilitator to avoid argumentation is to accept that there are negative and positive consequences of drinking. Facilitators build a safe place for members to talk openly about the risky behaviors they may engage in by focusing on both positive and negative effects of drinking, without trying to convince or pressure members to change (Merriwether, 1997).

Principle 4: Roll With Resistance—Following MI principles, facilitators must assume that any change in behavior is up to the group member. It is expected and openly acknowledged that group members will be reluctant and ambivalent about change. Asking group members what they think about an issue leads them to self-disclose. This approach allows group leaders to work around a group member's resistance without argumentation.

Principle 5: Support Self-Efficacy—This concept can be specifically defined: "Self efficacy is concerned with judgments about how well one can organize and execute courses of action required to deal with prospective situations that contain many ambiguous, unpredictable and often stressful elements" (Bandura, 1981, pp. 200–201). ASTP facilitators help build a sense of self-efficacy by assisting members in building confidence about their drinking decisions, and then by telling them that they can stick to the goals or changes they choose to make. Goals and changes may include generating options and tools to explain their change in drinking behavior to peers. Supporting self-efficacy is crucial.

It is also important to provide some "alcohol education" to group members, because many of them are unaware of alcohol's potential effects and dangers. Typically, this is done using the Socratic method. Examples of topics covered include (1) how alcohol gets into the drinker's system (it first enters the stomach, some alcohol enters the bloodstream through the stomach wall, and the rest enters the bloodstream through the small intestine); (2) influences on rate of absorption (higher concentrations of alcohol are absorbed faster, whiskey shots are absorbed faster than beer, there is slower absorption when food is in the stomach, faster absorption occurs for people who weigh less, faster absorption occurs for people who drink fast); and (3) how alcohol leaves the drinker's system (90% is removed from the blood by oxidation in the liver, alcohol is broken down into a toxic chemical (acetylaldehyde), then into CO_2 and water; the 10% not oxidized by the liver is expelled through sweat, breath, or urine).

The rate of oxidation is also discussed. An example of a question that might be asked in this area is "Have any of you ever tried to sober up someone who was intoxicated?" Members are asked what was effective. Facilitators point out that a healthy liver can oxidize about one drink per hour and that not much can influence oxidation rates—this is why things like cold showers and vomiting fail to help the drunken person sober up. All these types of educational points are made with ample opportunities for group members to ask questions.

Blood alcohol levels and recognition of their impact are discussed in the first of the $2\frac{1}{2}$-hour sessions. *Blood alcohol level* (BAL) is first defined, and the legal limit is established (0.08% in Nebraska). Factors that influence alcohol level, such as quantity consumed, speed of consumption, weight of the drinker, and gender, are reviewed.

The behavioral effects of BALs are also explained. This is done via discussion and a handout sheet. For example, light and moderate drinkers experience effects at a BAL of .02%. At .04%, most people feel relaxed. At a BAL of .06%, drinkers' judgment is somewhat impaired and drinkers are less rational about their capabilities. At .08%, there is definite impairment of muscle coordination and driving skills. There is increased risk of nausea and slurred speech. At a BAL of .10%, there is clear deterioration of reaction time and control. This is the BAL where it is illegal to operate a motor vehicle in most states. At a BAL of .15%, balance and movement are impaired and there is the risk of blackouts and accidents. At a BAL of 0.30%, many people lose consciousness and there is a risk of death. At a BAL of .45%, breathing stops and death occurs.

After making the ASTP group members aware of the behaviors and dangers associated with BALs, the facilitator discusses the advantages of monitoring drinking. The following rationale is provided. After people engage in a particular behavior for weeks, months, or years, they may become less and less aware that they are carrying out that behavior. For example, a person may drive to work without thinking about it. The same pattern can occur in relation to drinking. Drinkers may not be aware of how much alcohol they drink or how quickly they consume the alcohol. One way drinkers become more aware of how often, how much, and how fast they drink is to monitor drinking behavior. This requires drinkers to pay close attention to drinking as it happens and to keep track of it as they go. Consistent with the non-confrontational methods utilized in the ASTP groups, this information is delivered in a non-judgmental fashion. Group members are asked to monitor the next week's drinking and bring the results to the second session.

Additional questions and information about tolerance and drinking enable the group members to better understand some of the signs of addiction. For example, "Over time a person has to drink more and more to feel the same effect, to feel drunk." Or, "When they drink the same amount of alcohol, they feel less drunk than they ought to." (The quoted material here and what follows is taken from a summary outline developed by the University of Nebraska-Lincoln's faculty and students, based on information that can be found in Dimeff et al., 1999. Summary information is provided as well from Potts, 2002.) The reader is encouraged to read the cited material for more information.)

This glimpse of the initial session of the ASTP group should allow the reader to see that both Motivational Interviewing and educational approaches are melded together. The assignment for self-monitoring will allow the group members to be confronted by their own drinking quantities and frequencies. Potentially, these data can create a discrepancy that may motivate group members to consider a change in drinking behavior.

An overview of the ASTP groups' second session provides the reader another view of the impact of the process. Session two usually opens with feedback and discussion about alcohol, including group members' thoughts about the self-monitoring exercise. The information gathered on the assessment instruments completed in session one have been summarized and are handed back. Questions, thoughts, and comments are solicited. Some members are obviously surprised by the amount they drink. Others say the information is wrong (even though they provided the information on which the summaries are based). Some members say that the information is presented incorrectly. But, the majority are usually surprised by the magnitude of their drinking. (Remember that the members in these groups have been referred by the University Judicial system for alcohol infractions and/or have been picked up by local police and charged with an alcohol violation.)

MI principles are used and the facilitators roll with resistance. This strategy is effective because some members who are confronted are at a stage of change where they are open to using the information. These members make statements that they are surprised—and sometimes shocked—by their level of alcohol use. This starts a group discussion of drinking levels. The biphasic effect of alcohol (a moderate amount of alcohol makes you feel good, but there are decreasing positive feelings as blood alcohol level goes higher) is elaborated. Students are asked if they notice any changes in alcohol's effects over the course of an evening when they are consuming alcohol. They are asked, "How do you feel after the first drink? The second? The eighth?" Once the members give their responses to these questions, the biphasic curve is drawn on a chalkboard. It is pointed out that most drinkers usually feel good after one or two drinks. However, as they continue to consume more and more alcohol, the "good feeling" does not increase but is reduced.

Group members learn that, as blood alcohol levels fall, there is a depressant effect. The myth that if drinkers just drink more alcohol they will feel good again is just a myth. In reality, there is a point of diminishing returns. This level for most people is around a BAL of .05%. Group members learn that if they want to maximize their pleasurable feelings from alcohol, they should learn to drink so that their blood alcohol levels are about .05% and no higher.

Teaching the biphasic effect is consistent with a harm-reduction approach. It should be noted again that this approach does not promote abstaining. Instead, the approach attempts to show group members how to get the most pleasure out of alcohol without placing themselves at risk for injury, social problems, family problems, and so forth. The entire thrust of the ASTP groups is to promote a more moderate and, therefore, safer use of alcohol. It is important to note that this approach is not appropriate for someone who may have more serious alcohol problems.

The group members are given forms to complete that ask them for information on details of their alcohol use. They are told that the details they give will be used to build a profile summary for them. Thus, they need to be as accurate as possible to obtain an accurate summary profile of their drinking. This procedure allows for a comprehensive evaluation of the group member's drinking. Some examples of the questions on which summary profiles are based include the following:

1. What is the maximum amount of alcohol you have consumed in a single sitting in the past month?

2. On the occasion that you drank the most in the last month, how many *hours* did you spend drinking on that occasion?

3. On a given evening during the past month how much alcohol did you consume?

4. On a given weekend during the past month, how many *hours* did you spend drinking? Please estimate.

Information is also gathered on family history of alcoholism, history of high blood alcohol levels, legal problems, and multiple Driving While Intoxicated (DWI) arrests and/or Minor in Possession (MIP) charges. These converging sources, which may suggest heavy drinking and alcohol abuse, are used to assess whether the group member should be referred to other programs for additional assessment and possible treatment. Extremely abusive drinkers are not thought to be suited for a harm-reduction approach. They are referred for additional assessment and treatment.

Studies evaluating the effectiveness of ASTP groups elsewhere have found that such interventions have resulted in program participants reducing their drinking and experiencing fewer consequences related to the use of alcohol (Hernandez et al., 2006; LaBrie, Pedersen, Lamb, & Quinlan, 2007). The MI principles on which this program is based have been found to be "effective with a wide range of behaviors, including those related to unhealthy life styles, addictive behaviors, and unsafe sex practices" (Hanson & El-Bassel, 2014, p. 152).

Uniting Harm Reduction and Traditional Treatment

One of the political issues faced by the harm-reduction approach is that it does not advocate abstinence from drug use. In the case of alcohol, harm reduction recommends procedures for increasing the "highs" of alcohol use. A major strength of the approach is that it is designed to reach drinkers who are not now targets of prevention and intervention by the caregiving systems in the United States. The actions of these "social drinkers" add considerable risk to themselves and others at certain points in their drinking careers.

Alcohol and drug treatment programs need to find ways to intervene earlier in abusive drinking and using cycles. Earlier intervention would help prevent problems in the much more numerous population of social drinkers and "recreational" drug users. The psychological, physical, legal, and economic impact these individuals have on society, their families, and themselves would be reduced by earlier intervention. A harm-reduction approach reaches those who abuse alcohol and/or drugs in their window of risk, as well as reaching the most pathological alcohol and drug users, offering both groups intervention and treatment.

CASE STUDY OF WORKING WITH A CLIENT
UTILIZING A HARM-REDUCTION APPROACH

The case of a client that one of the authors worked with will demonstrate how a harm-reduction approach can be utilized in the context of traditional treatment. "Tony" showed up at our office in rural Nevada having walked to our building from his home a mile away with the heavy smell of alcohol on his breath, asking if he could speak with a counselor. Through the course of meeting with Tony, a man who was 40 but looked 60, I learned that he knew his health had been seriously compromised by his drinking, that his liver was close to failing, and that he was now getting sick almost immediately after drinking any alcohol. He was convinced that he would die shortly if he couldn't find a way to stop drinking but that traditional treatment—several stints in local in-patient facilities (detox)—hadn't worked. Would I be willing to meet with him once a week so that he could at least have someone to talk to and, if possible, find a different way to reduce his drinking?

Tony attended our meetings dependably. Even though he typically had alcohol on his breath from drinking earlier in the day, he talked achingly of the pain and shame of being in the throes of alcoholism. Deeply religious, he felt that he was dishonoring God's work by not more fully living up to his potential. He had lost a job he very much enjoyed as a construction worker due to sneaking drinks at work. His limited income was being spent primarily on alcohol with very little left over for food or other necessities. He had very few friends as he would drink in isolation and spent most days in an alcoholic haze when he was out. He was tired of feeling lonely, unfulfilled, scared, and as though he were morally bankrupt.

Throughout our sessions, I utilized a Motivational Interviewing approach by rolling with resistance (i.e., Tony was not open to beginning with abstention from alcohol, as he didn't think it possible), expressing empathy (i.e., it was not hard for me to understand how hard Tony's life was), developing discrepancy (i.e., noting, when appropriate, the difference between where Tony was and were he wanted to be), and supporting self-efficacy (i.e., finding times in Tony's life where he had been successful and pulling those forward into the present). We continued to probe, plant seeds, and find ways that Tony might be able to approach a reduction in his drinking.

Tony eventually expressed willingness and began setting goals for reducing his drinking. He had successes and he had lapses and relapses. He utilized A.A. because he felt it was supportive and helpful. With each lapse and relapse, we identified additional triggers (whether emotional, social, or otherwise) around which we developed strategies. The periods of time between his lapses and relapses increased. The length of time spent in a relapse decreased. The amount of alcohol consumed decreased. More importantly, he felt happier than he had in a long time and felt as though he might finally able to be successful in his fight against alcoholism. After 3 months of sobriety, he decided he didn't need to see me anymore and went his own way.

About 2 years later, Tony came back to my office to say hello. During the course of our conversation, he filled me in on how his sobriety had gone. He had managed another few months of sobriety before again relapsing into drinking for another 9 months or so. Utilizing A.A. and the techniques we had discussed in counseling, he was able to re-establish sobriety. At the time of our meeting, he had been sober for over 15 months, the longest period of sobriety he'd ever had. He was gainfully employed and had followed up on needed medical care. He felt satisfied, happy, and pleased with how he was living his life.

References

Bandura, A. (1981). Self-referent thought: A developmental analysis of self-efficacy. In J. H. Flavell & I. Ross (Eds.), *Social cognitive development: Frontiers and possible futures* (pp. 200–239). Cambridge: Cambridge University Press.

Dimeff, L. A., Baer, J. S., Kivlahan, D. R. & Marlatt, G. A. (1999). *Brief alcohol screening and intervention for college students (basics): A harm reduction approach.* New York: Guilford Press.

Donoghoe, M. C., Stimson, G., Dolen, K., & Alldritte, L. (1989). Changes in HIV risk behavior in exchange schemes in England and Scotland. *AIDS, 3,* 267–272.

Hanson, M., & El-Bassel, N. (2014). Motivating clients with substance use disorders through the helping process. In S. L. A. Straussner's (Ed.), *Clinical work with substance-abusing clients* (pp. 141–164). New York: Guilford Press.

Hernandez, D. V., Skewes, M. C., Resor, M. R., Villanueva, M. R., Hanson, B. S., & Blume, A. W. (2006). A pilot test of an alcohol skills training programme for Mexican-American college students. *International Journal of Drug Policy, 17,* 320–328.

Inciard, J., & Harrison, L. (Eds.). (1999). *Harm reduction: National and international perspectives.* New York: Sage.

LaBrie, J. W., Pedersen, E. R., Lamb, T. F., & Quinlan, T. (2007). A campus-based motivational enhancement group intervention reduces problematic drinking in freshmen male college students. *Addictive Behaviors, 32,* 889–901.

Landfield, A. W. & Rivers, P. C. (1975). An introduction to interpersonal transaction and rotating dyads. *Psychotherapy: Theory, Research and Practice, 12,* 366–374.

Marlatt, G. A. (1996). Harm reduction: Come as you are. *Addictive Behaviors, 21,* 779–788.

Marlatt, G. A., & Witkiewitz, K. (2010). Update on harm-reduction policy and intervention research. *Annual Review of Clinical Psychology, 6,* 591–606.

Merriwether, K. (1997). *Alcohol skills training groups: A departure from Yalom's traditional group psychotherapy.* Unpublished paper, Department of Psychology, University of Nebraska-Lincoln, Lincoln, Nebraska.

Miller, W. R., Forcehimes, A. A., & Zweben, A. (2011). *Treating addiction: A guide for professionals.* New York: Guildford Press.

Oregon Liquor Control Commission. (2010). *Alcohol server education: Online training manual.* Retrieved from https://www.olccclass.com/Resources/Workbook

Potts, K. A. F. (January 1, 2002). Efficacy of the alcohol skills training program: A brief group intervention for high -risk college student drinkers. *ETD collection for University of Nebraska–Lincoln.* Paper AAI3055270.

Prochaska, J. O., Norcross, J. C., & DiClemente, C. C. (1994). *Changing for good: A revolutionary six-stage program for overcoming bad habits and moving your life forward.* New York: Avon Books.

Riley, D. (1993). *The harm reduction model: Pragmatic approaches to drug use from the area between intolerance and neglect.* Ottawa: Canadian Center on Substance Abuse.

Rogers, C., & Dymond, R. (1954). *Psychotherapy and personality change.* Chicago: University of Chicago Press.

Single, E. (1996). Harm Reduction as an alcohol-prevention strategy. *Alcohol, Health & Research World, 20,* 239–243.

Stockwell, T., & Thomas, G. (2013). Is alcohol too cheap in the UK? The case for setting a minimum unit price for alcohol. *Institute of Alcohol Studies Report.* Retrieved from: http://www.ias.org.uk/uploads/pdf/News%20stories/iasreport-thomas-stockwell-april2013.pdf

University of Nebraska-Lincoln. (2012). *Step-by-step process of the behavioral, alcohol an drug intervention plan*. Retrieved from http://housing.unl.edu/contracts/pdf/ InterventionPlan.pdf

Zucker, R. (1987). The four alcoholisms: A developmental account of the etiologic process. In P. Rivers (Ed.), *Alcohol and addictive behavior* (Vol. 34, pp. 27–83). Nebraska Symposium on Motivation. Lincoln: University of Nebraska Press.

CHAPTER 13

Treatments That Work: Evidence-Based Therapies

CHAPTER OBJECTIVES

- Examine the variety of evidence-based practices available to treatment providers
- Review the research supporting evidence-based practices
- Consider how best to match clients with treatment options
- Review the characteristics associated with effective therapists
- Examine how best to determine treatment duration and length
- Examine how best to determine the quality of a program

In the early days of medicine, "surgery" was a rather rudimentary affair. Because the role of bacteria was not well understood in the prevention of infection, very few surgeons washed their hands or sterilized their equipment, much less gave any thought to the cleanliness of the room in which they were operating (Hollingham, 2008). This, not surprisingly, resulted in a high casualty rate from post-operative infections (Hollingham, 2008). If patients survived both the surgery and any infection they acquired afterward, they were surely severely traumatized by what they had just gone through since they were fully awake when they were cut into and/or a limb was cut off (Hollingham, 2008; Seah, 2001). Not that surviving from surgery was a sure thing, as many of the first surgeons killed more of their patients through questionable practices than they saved—with procedures such as "trephination," wherein holes were literally drilled through the skull to drain away blood and the "bad humors" thought to be responsible for the patient's illness (Hollingham, 2010; Seah, 2001). It is a wonder that the medical field survived such inauspicious beginnings and has developed into something much more humane and helpful.

Whether through accidental discovery or dedicated research, medicine has taken notice of and embraced what works so that, by now, there are commonly accepted best practices that are used nearly uniformly. We expect all medical personnel, for example, to wash their hands when meeting a patient. Any instruments or equipment utilized through a course of surgery is expected to be cleaned and sanitized before being used on another patient. Anesthesia has been developed to help patients more comfortably make it through what would otherwise be horrifyingly painful procedures, bordering on human torture if experienced while fully awake. Brain signals are even monitored while a patient is under the influence of anesthesia to ensure that the part of him or her that is conscious of pain is not registering it (Besser, 2013). "Questionable" and invasive interventions have been phased out in favor of less invasive and more successful procedures—such as arthroscopic surgery, wherein small holes are utilized instead of a deep, long slice through the skin to make necessary repairs (as is now frequently done with a variety of surgeries, including those for the knee and shoulder). You hear very few, if any voices, arguing that these advancements are not, in fact, improvements over the early days of doing surgery. We would hazard a guess that nearly anyone faced with a surgery would not elect the conditions associated with those early days. So why is it so hard for professionals in addictions treatment to do the same?

The early days of substance abuse counseling involved not much more than intuition and a lot of guesswork. Since so much of the literature and thinking about "alcoholics" and "drug addicts" was pejorative, the treatment modalities tended to, with the benefit of hindsight across the decades, be conceived of and delivered with similar disdain. As but one example, alcoholics were judged to be morally inferior while those with other chronic health conditions—for example, asthma, allergies, diabetes, and high blood pressure—were not. This lack of respect led practitioners to consider interventions that now seem less than respectful, chief among them the notion of needing to break through a patient's denial through harshly confrontational techniques that make those utilized by the CIA in recent years look mild in comparison (White, 1998).

In recent years, "evidence-based treatment" has become increasingly common as different modalities, when examined under the microscope of properly applied research methodology, have been found to have scientifically supported utility in addressing and treating chemical dependency. These are rather varied and range from family interventions to pharmacological to behavioral to cognitive-behavioral and more. We will be examining some of these different modalities in this chapter, including the research that supports them. As well, we will consider the research on matching patients with the different treatment modalities as a way of optimizing treatment success, revisit therapist characteristics thought to be crucial in supporting such success, and examine how treatment settings can support or detract from a client's success.

Before we continue, though, we would be remiss if we didn't acknowledge the understandable resistance to evidence-based treatment. We believe that this resistance is not due to the different therapies found to be evidence-based but to the various processes—political, economic—that seem to make for an uneven playing field for therapies that seem equally if not more impactful, but not yet found to be evidence-based. Those programs and therapies with the requisite capital, social and otherwise, are able to proceed. In a perfect world, the process of authenticating a therapeutic approach as evidence-based would be more democratized and accessible to all.

What we are not saying is that non–evidence-based therapies have no value. It has been our own personal and professional experience, in fact, that tells us just how contextually rich and powerful such therapies can be as vehicles for client engagement, motivation, and treatment. While they may they not have the necessary accumulation of capital, it is also true that current research methodology, techniques, and tools may not be sophisticated or sensitive enough to describe or account for what may very well be sound and effective therapies.

With such resistance and criticisms noted, it seems as foolish to turn a blind eye to the directions in which research points us as it would be to ignore the decades of accumulated wisdom responsible for generating more humane and successful surgical interventions. As professionals in the chemical dependency field, it is our requisite duty and responsibility to stay abreast of and be open to developments in the ways in which we work with the clients so that we can be maximally effective. It is not up to research to conform to what we think to be true, but for us to remain adaptable enough to incorporate the newest technologies, philosophies, and approaches as we endeavor to help clients address problems related to the use of drugs and alcohol. It is in this spirit, then, that we begin by looking at some of the treatment approaches that have thus far been identified as evidence-based. Since we have already discussed the evidence supporting pharmacological interventions and harm reduction, the following discussion focuses only on psychosocial practices.

A Sampling of Psychosocial Evidence-Based Practices

Due to space limitations, this section can only highlight a sampling of some of the more prominent psychosocial evidence-based practices. If the reader is interested in reviewing all of the more than 330 interventions that have thus far been determined to be evidence-based, she or he is encouraged to visit SAMHSA's National Registry of Evidence-Based Programs and Practices at www.nrepp.samhsa.gov.

Motivational Interviewing

Motivational Interviewing (MI) differs from the other practices that follow in that it isn't concerned so much with how people change, but with what makes them want to change, and what practitioners can do to directly enhance this desire so that patients more quickly and readily engage in healthier behaviors. If the other approaches are the "cake," then MI is the "icing," a way in which therapy can be delivered. As touched upon previously in Chapter 12, MI utilizes the transtheoretical model of change put forward by Prochaska, Norcross, and

Diclemente (1994) as a way of conceptualizing the different stages of change that clients may be in and through which they may pass.

Motivational Interviewing utilizes different acronyms to help practitioners and students remember its basic tenets. One that was already introduced in Chapter 12 was REDS, which referred to *rolling with resistance*, *expressing empathy*, *developing discrepancy*, and *supporting self-efficacy*. Another that is helpful for remembering basic skills that are at the heart of MI is OARS:

- **Open-ended questions**—These are questions that require more than a "yes" or "no" to answer and give the client an opportunity to elaborate about his or her concerns.

- **Affirmations**—Because so many clients considering being substance-free have doubts as to their abilities to be successful, affirmations are deployed as way to increase their self-efficacy.

- **Reflections**—A variety of reflections are utilized around both literal and emotional content as a way of helping clients to "hear" their thoughts and concerns spoken aloud by someone else, thereby gaining additional perspective. A "double-sided" reflection is one in which a counselor attempts to capture a client's ambivalence: "On the one hand, you really enjoy the way that alcohol relaxes you, and yet, on the other hand, you've just earned two DUIs."

- **Summaries**—Summaries might be thought of as "long-range reflections" in the sense that they are also utilized to help clients "hear" their thoughts and concerns spoken aloud by the counselor. The purpose of a summary, though, is to highlight patterns and themes for the client to consider: "So far I've heard that you have many and very strong reasons for wanting to quit using, including the loss of your job, the breakup of your marriage, running out of money, feeling lonely and scared, and knowing this isn't the life you want to lead."

The skills outlined, when utilized skillfully and in the context of a collaborative relationship, are deployed to help clients engage in change talk. A bit like being a butcher and putting one's thumb on the scale, these skills are deliberately and purposefully, but not too forcefully, used to tip the scales in the balance of change. The different types of change talk are captured in the acronym DARN:

- **Desire**—Essentially, why would clients want to make a change?
- **Ability**—These are statements clients make that speak to their ability to make a change.
- **Reasons**—As the term suggests, these will be statements that speak to what reasons clients may have for making a change.
- **Need**—Finally, and again as the term suggests, why do clients need to make a change?

Throughout it all, MI counselors are reminded to remember the acronym RULE:

- **Resisting the righting reflex**—It seems we all have a natural desire when helping another person to want to fix them, offer advice, or act in other ways that can have the opposite effect of what we are intending. Better to recognize this impulse and resist it.

- **Understanding the client's own motivations**—This seems simple yet it is amazing how many counselors make assumptions about a specific client's use. Without understanding the specifics about the motivations for their use, it will be next-to-impossible to tailor treatment interventions and develop strategies to successfully address these motivations.

- **Listen with empathy**—As discussed in Chapter 4, empathy is considered to be a core condition for effective counseling.

- **Empower the client**—It is important, as has been discussed in previous chapters, that clients believe they have the wherewithal to change.

Motivational Enhancement Therapy

Motivational Enhancement Therapy (MET) utilizes motivational interviewing over a relatively brief period of time, say two to four sessions, in order to enhance a client's motivation for engaging in treatment. One way in which this is done is by restructuring the intake/assessment process in which clients must participate in order to access services. At many agencies, perhaps the majority, much of the time is taken up with filling out forms, taking assessments, and making sure all of the required questions have been asked and boxes checked. This runs the risk of seeming deeply impersonal and irrelevant to the clients, and missing a vital and opportune moment for connecting with clients when they are at, perhaps, one of the more accessible and influential moments for strengthening their desire to make a positive change in their lives. An agency using MET would likely have a very different intake/assessment process. Instead of taking just one session, the intake/assessment might take up to four sessions. This would allow counselors to not have to start with questions about paperwork, but to have the time to directly address the motivations clients bring to the treatment center, and to utilize motivational interviewing techniques to enhance this motivation.

Brief Interventions

As was touched upon in Chapter 12, brief interventions are often conducted in non-traditional treatment settings utilizing a motivational interviewing style and techniques. Brief interventions are typically one to four visits of varying length, from 10 minutes to more than an hour (Miller, Forcehimes, & Zweben, 2011).

Cognitive Behavioral Therapy

The crux of cognitive behavioral therapy (CBT) and treatment approaches that incorporate its principles is that it is geared toward achieving desired changes in behavior by changing the underlying thought processes associated with maintaining the undesired behaviors into those that will support the new desired changes. The utilization of such an approach means that the counselor, when teaching such concepts, is in the role of coach or teacher and is actively directing and facilitating the content to be taught. As applies to substance abuse treatment, there are three specific approaches of interest:

- **Social Skills Training**—These skills often center on helping clients learn to be assertive in their communications with others—neither aggressive nor passive. Associated with these skills would be explicit work around developing refusal skills (i.e., practicing how to say "no").

- **Self-Control Training**—These skills are those associated with learning how to manage desires to use. This might involve such things as "thinking the first drink through" or "urge surfing" to reduce the intensity of feelings associated with certain cognitions so that other non-using strategies can be implemented.

- **Stress Management Training**—As the name implies, these skills are those needed to proactively and healthfully manage stress. Not only would clients review active interventions for reducing stress, but they also would increase awareness of, and learn how to manage, cognitions associated with stress.

While working with a client with any of the above CBT approaches, a clinician will likely uncover "unwritten rules" that have previously stopped clients from progressing further; for example, a client learns he or she can't say "no" because of being concerned with rejection and hurting the other person's feelings. As part of this work, a clinician can help a client to examine this underlying belief, to see if it really holds true, and to offer other, more adaptive beliefs; for example, after working on this belief for a while, a client may adopt a belief wherein he or she realizes that a person who won't accept their "no" doesn't really have his or her best interests at heart. Such a realization may obviate a client's concerns about rejection.

Community Reinforcement Approach

The Community Reinforcement Approach (CRA) is a treatment modality that is directed toward the goal of making sobriety more rewarding than using or drinking. It does so in a very structured way by utilizing a functional analysis to examine all of the antecedents of using (i.e., With whom were you using? Where were you using? What were you thinking prior to using?), the specific circumstances of using (i.e., What time were you drinking? Where were you drinking? How much were you drinking?), and the consequences of using—both positive and negative. Positive consequences tend to be experienced in the short term and can be related to perceived positive changes in the client's affect (i.e., less stressed, more relaxed) and other motivations (i.e., having fun with friends). Negative consequences (e.g., not being able to pay a bill because a client spent it at the bar) tend to be experienced in the long term. By doing a functional analysis, certain patterns will often present themselves around which strategies for increasing the likelihood of sobriety can be developed.

As but one example of how effective this can be, the author worked with a client who wanted to quit using alcohol. We discussed a variety of issues that could be contributing to the client's condition, ensured that the client's motivation remained engaged, and commiserated with mutual hand-wringing when the client invariably and inexplicably lapsed into drinking during the week. After 2 or 3 months of this and being no closer to helping the client toward his goal, we took the time to do a full functional analysis of his drinking behavior. What we saw hit us like a load of bricks: The one and only time at which he was at risk for drinking was immediately after he got off work. More specifically, on the 30-minute drive home from work! The reason for this was that, as the client explained, he worked in construction. After work, he would often be hot and thirsty and want something cold to drink, both to refresh himself but also as a reward for a hard day's work. To satisfy these desires, he would stop at a particular corner store and pick up cold beer, which he would then proceed to drink at home.

It was readily apparent that the focus of our counseling had been too broad, and it became laser-focused after seeing the results of the client's functional analysis. All at once, or so it seemed, instead of trying to conquer some vague and unapproachable foe, we had a problem that was both articulable and manageable. We both felt invigorated by this renewed focus and set to the task at hand: What could the client do to make other choices that would minimize the likelihood of his drinking beer immediately after work?

I can't say that we were immediately successful after this newfound information. In fact, our first few ideas were downright failures. One, for example, was for the client to walk into the convenience store and buy something cold that wasn't alcoholic. In hindsight, it seems obvious that this would fail for a variety of reasons, but it was the client's suggestion, one he was willing to try and one from which he and we learned through its implementation that whatever strategy we developed would have to minimize the likelihood of his needing or wanting to stop by the corner store.

Here is the strategy we ultimately came up with that significantly reduced his drinking of alcohol. When the client and his wife went shopping for groceries over the weekend, he would select a variety of non-alcoholic cold drinks (i.e., sports drinks, soft drinks, and iced teas and coffees). He would put a selection of these non-alcoholic drinks into a cooler that he would fill with ice and keep in his car. This meant that after work he could reach into his cooler and pull out a cold non-alcoholic drink that felt both refreshing and rewarding. This seemingly and achingly simple strategy virtually addressed the client's problems with alcohol overnight.

It isn't always—in fact, it is rarely—this easy or simple. The example above, though, is offered as an illustration of the Community Reinforcement Approach.

Contingency Management

Contingency Management (CM) raises more debate than any of the other approaches amongst students of this author's university class for it can seem as though clients are being rewarded for what they "should" be doing anyway. In essence, contingency management is the offering of rewards to clients for continued sobriety. This can be done in a variety of ways, including the well-known "step" system wherein clients earn privileges when in residential treatment for progress they have made and for "good" behavior. Another way in which CM can be utilized is to give clients who submit a clean urinalysis the opportunity to select a tab or piece of paper out of a box or bowl. Some of the pieces of paper might be simple "Atta Boys!" or "Atta Girls!" with motivational sayings. Others might be redeemable for smaller prizes, while still others could be redeemable for larger and more sought-after items (e.g., a music player, tablet computer).

Family Therapy

There are a variety of approaches that engage at least some part of the family system, four of which are described in further detail below, much of which comes from SAMHSA's (2006) National Registry of Evidence-Based Programs and Practices (NREPP):

- **Behavioral Couple Therapy (BCT)**—As it indicates, this is work that is extensively done with both the identified patients and intimate partners with the following assumptions in mind: (1) Intimate partners can play a role in helping to make abstinence rewarding, and (2) relapse risk can be minimized by helping to reduce relationship stress. According to SAMHSA's (2006) NREPP:

    In BCT: The therapist works with both the person who is abusing substances and his or her partner to build a relationship that supports abstinence. Program components include a recovery or sobriety contract between the partners and therapist; activities and assignments designed to increase positive feelings, shared activities, and constructive communication;

and relapse prevention planning. Partners generally attend 15–20 hour-long sessions over 5–6 months. A typical session follows this sequence: (1) the therapist asks about any substance use since the last session; (2) the couple discusses compliance with the recovery contract; (3) the couple presents and discusses homework assigned at the last session; (4) the couple discusses any relationship problems since the last session; (5) the therapist presents new material; and (6) the therapist assigns new homework.

- **Brief Strategic Family Therapy (BSFT)**—This therapy is a brief therapy—meaning that it is typically delivered in as few as 8 sessions, with the average being 12 to 16 and no more than 24—that works with the family system around three specific goals: (1) to minimize maladaptive behavior problems in adolescents related to drug and alcohol use and other at-risk behaviors; (2) to improve adolescent success in such areas as school attendance and performance; and (3) to improve overall family functioning. This last goal is accomplished primarily through strengthening the parents' abilities to provide effective and positive guidance, oversight, and engagement in the lives of their children. BSFT has been designed so that it can be conducted in a variety of settings, including the family's home.

- **Multidimensional Family Therapy (MDFT)**—This therapy is often utilized when working with adolescents who have substance abuse and/ or co-occurring disorders, and their families, in an outpatient or day treatment setting. It is similar to BSFT in that it is typically delivered across 12 to 16 sessions. It is similar to the Matrix Model below, in that it is a manualized set of interventions with the goals of assisting youth in increasing the effectiveness of their coping and problem-solving skills so that better decisions are made, and assisting family functioning to minimize the likelihood that an adolescent will experience problems related to substance abuse.

- **Community Reinforcement and Family Therapy (CRAFT)**—As its name implies, this approach incorporates elements from CRA in the context of working from a family systems perspective. The CRAFT approach was developed to work with concerned others (i.e., parents, spouses) of family members with drug and alcohol issues. Through working with a therapist, the concerned others would learn how to disengage from unproductive communication and relational patterns. Whereas previously they might have carried their passed-out spouse to bed, they would instead leave them on the floor of the living room to experience the shame of being questioned by the children as to why they were not in bed. Or, instead of lying to an employer for a spouse on the phone, the concerned other would either hand the phone directly to the client or tell the employer the truth (i.e., "The reason Dan can't come to the phone right now is because he is passed out"). At the same time, the concerned others would learn communication skills and other strategies learned in counseling to make sobriety more rewarding than using.

Matrix Model (for Stimulant Abuse)

The Matrix Model consists of a manualized set of interventions found to be effective for working with clients who have issues around the use of stimulants such as methamphetamine. These interventions are offered in an intensive outpatient group setting and incorporate elements from many of the previously described approaches, including skills building, cognitive restructuring, refusal skills, stress management, functional analysis, and more. The manual is available for free and can be accessed from the Substance Abuse and Mental Health Services Administration online store at www.store.samhsa.gov.

12-Step Treatment Approaches

As the name implies, these are treatment approaches that incorporated the 12 steps as identified in Alcoholics Anonymous. It has been the authors' experience that the majority of programs that incorporate the 12 steps do so in ways that aren't optimally effective (i.e., they are utilized in a haphazard or overly dogmatic manner).

One example of an evidence-based approach to utilizing the 12 steps is the program "Twelve Step Facilitation Therapy" (as identified in NREPP, 2014). It is administered over 12 to 15 sessions and is considered to be "brief, structured, and manual-driven." There are two goals of therapy. Acceptance is the first, the idea that only complete abstinence from alcohol and other drugs is needed. The second is surrender, which relates to a "willingness" to utilize 12-step programs as a tool for sobriety.

Effectiveness of Treatment Modalities

Studies relevant to a particular treatment modality are reviewed as part of the process of being listed as an effective treatment modality on the National Registry of Evidence-Based Programs and Practices. In the interest of space and as an example of the research supporting each evidence-based practice, below are highlights from the studies for three of the therapies reviewed in the previous section. Readers are encouraged, if they would like to review the research associated with other evidence-based practices, to visit www.nrepp .samhsa.gov.

- **Motivational Interviewing**—Motivational interviewing has been associated with reduced alcohol consumption both with respect to quantity and quality (Baer, Kivhlahan, Blume, McKnight, & Marlatt, 2001; Marlatt et al., 1998; Senft, Polen, Freeborn, & Hollis, 1997), decreased negative consequences/problems associated with the use of alcohol (Baer et al., 2001; Marlatt et al., 1998; Monti et al., 1999), decreased drinking and driving and fewer alcohol-related injuries (Monti et al., 1999), increased abstinence from cocaine and opiates (Bernstein et al., 2005), and better retention in treatment (Carroll et al., 2006).

- **Brief Strategic Family Therapy (BSFT)**—Brief Strategic Family Therapy has been associated with increased engagement in therapy (Coatsworth, Santisteban, McBride, & Szapocznik, 2001), decreased conduct problems and socialized aggression (Santisteban et al., 2003), decreased substance use (Nickel et al., 2006; Santisteban et al., 2003), and better family functioning (Santisteban et al., 2003; Szapocznik et al., 1989).

- **Matrix Model**—The Matrix Model has been associated with increased treatment retention, increased treatment completion, and decreased drug use during treatment (Rawson et al., 1995; Rawson, et al., 2004).

Additionally, in a meta-analysis of four studies that examined the effectiveness of 15 different psychosocial approaches, 7 of the top 8 included those listed earlier in this chapter (Finney, Wilbourne, & Moos, 2007), with social skills training being ranked as most effective followed by, in decreasing order: self-control training, brief motivational counseling, behavioral marital therapy, community reinforcement, stress management training, and cognitive therapy.

Matching Patients to Effective Treatments

Just as not all patients going to urgent care have a broken bone and therefore don't need a cast, not all of those with addictions need the same type of treatment. A painkiller might be best for someone walking into an urgent care with pain, an antibiotic for someone with a bacterial infection, and an x-ray for someone who might have a broken foot. It makes similar intuitive sense that people with addictions will respond differently to the various treatment modalities possible, and that it would be helpful to have some sort of organizing system that would help clinicians be able to make informed decisions about matching patients to the most effective treatment options for them.

One approach for organizing client information so that it informs the matching of clients to treatment levels is known as the *ASAM Patient Placement Criteria for the Treatment of Substance-Related Disorders* that has been developed by the American Society of Addiction Medicine (Mee-Lee, 2013). This approach assesses client functioning and presentation across six dimensions; these were identified and discussed in Chapter 5. After each of these dimensions has been rated according to what level of risk is present, clinicians then make a determination as to which level of care to place a client in. These four levels are as follows:

- **Level I: Outpatient Treatment**—This level of care is for those clients generally needing 9 hours or less per week of outpatient services. It may be helpful for a wide variety of clients, from those "stepping down" from more intensive levels of care to those who present as "resistant" and need time in a less restrictive environment in order to enhance and strengthen their commitment to treatment.

- **Level II: Intensive Outpatient / Partial Hospitalization**—This level of care may generally consist of up to 20 hours per week of outpatient services. This additional time provides additional structure and exposure to treatment for clients who need it. As well, this level of care may work well for those clients who have job, family, or other obligations around which they need to fit time for treatment.

- **Level III: Residential / Inpatient Treatment**—This level of care is for those clients who would benefit from a 24-hour structured program to support their treatment and sobriety. This level of care may be particularly helpful for those who feel as though they need to be removed from toxic environments and/or need a "clean slate" in order to have a running start at sobriety.

- **Level IV: Medically Managed Intensive Inpatient Treatment**—This level of care is reserved for those with the most acute detoxification, intoxication, medical, and/or mental health needs and need access to the full services of a hospital in order to be kept safe and healthy. It is not uncommon for clients entering treatment to be triaged and stabilized for a few days at this level of care before being discharged directly into Level III care.

It is best for counselors to think of these different levels of care as fluid, not static. When clients improve, they are hopefully "stepped-down" to the next lower level of care (i.e., from inpatient to intensive outpatient (IOP) and from IOP to outpatient) before being discharged into (hopefully) some form of aftercare program. When clients deteriorate, conversely, clients are "stepped-up" to the appropriate next higher level of care so that they may be stabilized and their needs addressed. If treatment is akin to medicine, we are trying to match the appropriate "dosage" to the needs of a client.

While it makes intuitive sense to match clients to the appropriate level and kind of treatment, the research has been less than conclusive about the importance of doing so. As but one example, the largest study done to date in regard to treatment matching—Project MATCH—randomly assigned patients to three quite different treatment modalities and compared outcomes.

One of the three was a 12-step facilitated therapy, another was a brief stint of Motivational Enhancement Therapy, and the third was a cognitive-behavioral–based therapy. Offered as outpatient treatment or aftercare, all three therapies produced strong and roughly equivalent outcomes, with robust gains reported even 3 years post-treatment. On only one measure was there a significant difference, with patients in the 12-step facilitated therapy reporting a rate of abstinence that was 10% higher (Miller et al., 2011).

What does this mean? Does it mean that we should just throw a dart at a dartboard to determine what level of care or type of treatment in which to place a patient? No. Most likely it means that we haven't yet asked the right questions and/or developed sensitive enough research methodologies and technologies with which to capture the right information. What the research does seem to point to is the importance of individual differences among clients and developing better clinical awareness of how these differences may affect client success in treatment. Miller and colleagues (2011) specifically note these differences in support of this point:

- Clients whose social networks did not support sobriety did better in the 12-step facilitated approach at the 3-year follow-up. The thinking is that A.A. and similar groups offered new social networks that supported abstinence and sobriety that helped to counter the negative effects of the non-supportive social networks.

- Clients who presented as "resistant" to change (i.e., they were angrier and/or had low motivation to change) did better with Motivational Enhancement Therapy. This makes sense because this is exactly what MET was designed to do—decrease resistance and increase the motivation of clients for change.

- Twelve-step facilitated therapy seemed to be a better fit for clients with less severe psychological dysfunction.

- In aftercare, clients with less severe alcohol dependence did better with CBT; those with more severe alcohol dependence did better with 12-step facilitated therapy.

Therapist Characteristics

Chapter 1 reviewed the research that discussed characteristics thought to make for effective therapists. A not completely inclusive list of these characteristics is abbreviated below to refresh the reader's memory. Effective addictions-specialized counselors are those who:

- Have positive believes about the clients they serve
- View their clients as generally trustworthy, capable, dependable, and friendly

- Hold a positive view of themselves and have confidence in their abilities as helpers
- Demonstrate congruence, empathy, and positive regard
- Have a capacity for tolerating ambiguity
- Are able to establish good social relationships in general, not just with clients
- Are anxious and sensitive to the expectations of others
- Can be patient and non-aggressive in relationships
- Are concerned about social progress
- Have a solid identity
- Appreciate themselves and their strengths
- Are open to change
- Learn from their mistakes and are willing to admit them
- Are authentic, sincere, and honest
- Have a sense of humor
- Live in the present
- Appreciate the influence of culture
- Have a sincere interest in others
- Derive meaning from their work
- Maintain healthy boundaries
- Are understanding and caring
- Are good listeners
- Hold non-stigmatizing attitudes toward their clients
- Have an openness and willingness to celebrate diversity
- Demonstrate an active interest in helping their clients
- Keep their clients' charts and notes current and organized with a sufficient amount of detail
- Anticipate problems and discuss potential strategies with clients
- Are well organized
- Have therapeutic optimism
- Understand and abide by professional and personal ethics and values
- Have a sense of humor
- View themselves as role models
- Learn to be direct as needed
- Become familiar with 12-step work
- Develop appropriate conceptualizations of addiction
- Have advanced training and keep up with the increasing complexity of addiction

- Are open to new treatments
- Have an ability to manage increasing complex interventions

This list is not exhaustive, and the reader is invited to revisit Chapters 1 and 4 to review the qualities and skills that make for an effective counselor. As relates to evidence-based practices, the last four in the list may be the most relevant.

As new knowledge and research continues to be done, it will surely effect how we view addiction. Indeed, cutting edge brain-imaging and genetic research has already answered many questions about addiction while raising many more. The way in which we as professionals conceptualize addiction may very well need to change as new techniques for conducting research and new technologies are developed. One of the biggest shifts for many professionals with at least 20 years of experience has been to move from a confrontational to a collaborative style of engaging with a client.

In order to keep up with all of these changes, addictions professionals will need to have the perspective that learning never ends. A college degree is just the first step, and the hard-earned knowledge that came with that degree will expire if regular investments in ongoing learning are not made. This means taking the time to attend conferences, enroll in ongoing classes, belong to and read a counseling association's publications, keep up on the research, and more.

Flexibility, then, will also be required of counselors to not become so attached to what they think they know based on research that is now outdated that they miss the implications from future developments for shifting their counseling practice. New treatments, treatments combining several elements of already-known approaches in novel ways, and new technologies will require an adaptability for counselors to be able to learn and incorporate so that they can remain optimally effective for the sake of their clients' success.

With the implementation of evidence-based therapies, all of the above are necessary requisites plus at least one more important skill: an ability to manage increasingly complex interventions. Many of the evidence-based therapies are manualized, which implies that particular steps must be taken in particular sequence to remain true to the program design as tested. For many, if not all, it will not be enough to be familiar with a program design's underlying concepts; it will be necessary to obtain training specific to delivering and implementing an evidence-based therapy.

Duration and Amount of Treatment

Research has consistently supported the idea of keeping people in treatment for as long as possible, as better outcomes have been associated with longer periods of treatment. This is consistent with the understanding of addiction as a chronic disease that will need ongoing management and intervention.

The difficulty associated with this research, though, is wondering what reasons might account for the research findings. Perhaps quantity has been more important than quality with the treatment approaches available at the time of research. Perhaps "treatment" as referred to in the research hasn't been so rigidly defined and actually entails activities better described as "aftercare." People with diabetes, for example, "self-treat" at home on a daily basis in order to manage healthy blood sugar levels; this doesn't mean, though, that such patients are in treatment. These are but two examples of how it is difficult to come to agreement with the idea that the longer one is treatment the better the outcome. Miller and colleagues (2011) make this point in relation to treatment duration:

> There are then perhaps two broad service delivery lessons to be learned from the brief intervention literature. One is that we may overestimate the level of service that many clients need. There is a natural tendency for behavioral health professionals to assume that more is better in terms of our services . . . A second broad take-home message is to adjust service delivery to clients' needs. For a certain proportion, a briefer motivational intervention is sufficient, increasing the availability of more intensive services for others who need them. (p. 151)

Another confounding variable is what constitutes "success." Because the perception of addictions treatment is often so overlaid with pejorative societal judgments, it is easy to overlook and dismiss what would otherwise be considered a runaway success if considered from the perspective of any other chronic disease. As first discussed in an earlier chapter, Miller, Walters, and Bennett (as cited in Miller et al., 2011) examined over 8,000 cases of treatment consisting of only one episode. From this one intervention, 24% of those treated completely abstained in the year following. The remaining 76% increased days abstinent by 128% and decreased alcohol consumption relative to pretreatment levels by 87%.

The previous point on what constitutes "success" is similar to a related point in that the purpose of an evidence-based therapy must be evaluated and may differ from that of other evidence-based therapies. Many are designed to substantially resolve the issues clients have around their substance abuse. Others are designed with a different goal in mind. In the case of Motivational Enhancement Therapy, for example, it is to increase the commitment of clients to engage in further and more substantive treatments. Another way of putting this is that the goal of MET is not treatment per se, but to get clients ready for treatment.

A final note on treatment duration is that different evidence-based approaches require different lengths and frequencies of administration in order to be consistent with the program design supported by research. As previously noted earlier in this chapter, some of the briefer therapies might conceivably and effectively be delivered in as few as eight sessions. Compare this to the Matrix Model, which has been designed to be delivered over the course of a calendar year. Future and current pharmacological approaches—methadone, for one—may require ongoing treatment compliance for certain patients and clients to be successful.

Treatment Settings

How, then, might be we able to ascertain which programs are of a sufficiently high quality in deciding where best to place clients? What treatment setting factors (e.g., staffing ratio, comprehensiveness of services offered) might be associated with better outcomes? Might we find some answers somewhere that could point us in the right direction?

These are all great questions. In the real world, the most common answer is provided in the form of organization-wide licensing and/or accreditation. Just as licensing for individual clinicians indicates the realization of minimum standards (i.e., base level of education reached, certain number of hours supervised, requisite trainings obtained), so is accreditation thought to serve a similar purpose for organizations. Two of the most common in the treatment of addictions are those offered by the Joint Commission on Accreditation of Healthcare Organizations (JCAHO) and the Council for Accreditation of Rehabilitation Facilities (CARF). In order to obtain either of these accreditations, organizations must ensure that certain targeted processes—risk management, strategic planning, business practices, clinical practices, client care—are provided for at a threshold determined to be acceptable by the accrediting bodies. These accreditations may be sought for a variety of reasons, including to help an agency stand apart from others without the accreditations and to obtain funding from a funder who requires such accreditation. Ostensibly such accreditations signal to the world at large that services provided within the accredited organization are of a high quality and standard.

The research, unfortunately, is rather thin regarding how it is possible to make distinctions regarding the quality of treatment provided amongst service providers. In a comprehensive review of the literature available at the time, Wells et al. (2007) found little empirical evidence that linked accreditation with the quality of care provided in substance abuse treatment practice. In their own analysis of over 1,000 outpatient substance abuse treatment facilities, Wells et al. (2007) looked at whether accreditation was associated with certain desirable treatment practices. Specifically, they looked at the *comprehensiveness* of services provided and *sufficiency* of time for treatment, as each of these elements is specifically listed in the National Institutes of Health's

(2012) *Principles of Drug Addiction Treatment*. The results were equivocal, to say the least. No associations between accreditation were found with staffing ratios. JCAHO accreditation was found to be more highly related with clients receiving physical examinations and mental health care, probably because such facilities so accredited are hospitals. Associations for treatment sufficiency and accreditation were negative. Another review of the data on the same 1,000+ outpatient substance abuse programs revealed declines in client care as relates to the NIH's principles of effective treatment. These included a decrease in clients receiving medical and social services that had not been reversed, a leveling off and/or decrease of HIV-prevention efforts, a decrease in services available to women, and a limiting of treatment duration and intensity in response to managed care demands (D'Aunno, 2006).

In the absence of any apparently objective or reliable measure of treatment setting quality, the following advice is offered to aspiring counselors:

• Pay attention to your community's "grapevine" regarding what programs are considered to be of high quality. Those programs considered to be of high quality will oftentimes be associated with more clients reporting satisfactory treatment experiences and through the opinions of other treatment professionals.

• How an agency is run oftentimes says more about the quality of an organization's programs than what specifically is offered. Do clinicians who work for a particular organization get enough time to do necessary paperwork and sundry tasks, or are they worked to the point of exhaustion and burnout? Are reports professionally put together? Is confidentiality respected? Is supervision regularly provided? Does the facility have a good feeling?

• Higher-quality programs seem to do a better job of addressing the needs of their clients, not just the substance abuse issues. How well does the program attend to all the myriad needs clients bring to counseling: housing, employment, childcare? Does the program actively link clients to needed vocational and other needed services?

• Does the staff speak respectfully about the clients it serves? Those associated with more effective programs tend to hold the clients they serve in high regard and do not speak in demeaning terms or tone about their clients.

• Are evidence-based practices utilized? An agency striving to provide the best quality service available should be able to describe the evidence-based practices being utilized by its therapists.

• Do staff have adequate training? An agency that values education and training will be an agency that encourages its staff to engage in ongoing learning and to pursue advanced degrees.

- Effective organizations oftentimes have a clear mission statement, a statement of values, and perhaps even annual goals derived from a strategic plan.

- Staff at effective organizations oftentimes are encouraged to work collaboratively with personnel both inside and outside the organization.

Summary

It would not be surprising if this chapter was experienced as frustrating. While there is solid research supporting the various evidence-based therapies that were reviewed, as well as for characteristics of effective therapists, there seemed to be little definitive agreement or guidance provided by the literature regarding other important aspects of treatment, such as setting, length, amount, or matching of treatment. What, then, is an aspiring chemical dependency counselor to do? Hopefully by now, the end of this chapter and near the end of this book, the answers have become clear.

It will be important to stay abreast of developments in the field, to receive adequate and competent supervision, to develop a network of colleagues for consultation around ethical and legal issues, to receive ongoing training on developing therapies, to astutely pay attention to what your clients are telling you, to stay current on what services are offered in the community and which are worth referring to, to trust your own intuition and judgment, and more. It has been our honor through the pages of this book to try to help you along your way and make your journey a little easier, perhaps, than were our own journeys. We are thankful and humbled to whatever degree we may have succeeded. Finally, we wish you the best of luck and can't wait to see what contributions you make in the provision of addictions services.

References

Baer, J. S., Kivlahan, D. R., Blume, A. W., McKnight, P., & Marlatt, G. A. (2001). Brief intervention for heavy-drinking college students: Four-year follow-up and natural history. *American Journal of Public Health, 91*(8), 1310–1316.

Bernstein, J., Bernstein, E., Tassiopoulos, K., Heeren, T., Levenson, S., & Hingson, R. (2005). Brief motivational intervention at a clinic visit reduces cocaine and heroin use. *Drug and Alcohol Dependence, 77*(1), 49–59.

Besser, R. (2013). *New brain monitor aims to alert doctors when patients wake during surgery.* Retrieved on July 13, 2014, from http://abcnews.go.com/blogs/health/2013/01/17/new-brain-monitor-aims-to-alert-doctors-when-patients-wake-during-surgery.

Carroll, K. M., Ball, S. A., Nich, C., Martino, S., Frankforter, T. L., Farentinos, C., et al. (2006). Motivational interviewing to improve treatment engagement and outcome in individuals seeking treatment for substance abuse: A multisite effectiveness study. *Drug and Alcohol Dependence, 81*(3), 301–312.

Coatsworth, J. D., Santisteban, D. A., McBride, C. K., & Szapocznik, J. (2001). Brief Strategic Family Therapy versus community control: Engagement, retention, and an exploration of the moderating role of adolescent symptom severity. *Family Process, 40*(3), 313–332.

D'Aunno, T. (2006). The role of organization and management in substance abuse treatment: Review and roadmap. *Journal of Substance Abuse Treatment, 31*(3), 221–233.

Finney, J. W., Wilbourne, P. L., & Moos, R. H. (2007). Psychosocial treatments for substance use disorders. In P. E. Nathan & J. M. Gorman (Eds.) *A guide to treatments that work* (3rd ed.). New York: Oxford University Press.

Hollingham, R. (2008). *Blood and guts: A history of surgery.* New York: St. Martin's Press.

Marlatt, G. A., Baer, J. S., Kivlahan, D. R., Dimeff, L. A., Larimer, M. E., Quigley, L. A., et al. (1998). Screening and brief intervention for high-risk college student drinkers: Results from a 2-year follow-up assessment. *Journal of Consulting and Clinical Psychology, 66*(4), 604–615.

Mee-Lee, D. (Ed.). (2013). *The ASAM Criteria: Treatment criteria for addictive, substance-related, and co-occurring conditions.* Chevy Chase, MD: American Society of Addiction Medicine.

Miller, W. R., Forcehimes, A. A., & Zweben, A. (2011). *Treating addiction: A guide for professionals.* New York: Guilford Press.

Monti, P. M., Colby, S. M., Barnett, N. P., Spirito, A., Rohsenow, D. J., Myers, M., et al. (1999). Brief intervention for harm reduction with alcohol-positive older adolescents in a hospital emergency department. *Journal of Consulting and Clinical Psychology, 67*(6), 989–994.

National Institutes of Health, National Institute on Drug Abuse. (2012). *Principles of drug addiction treatment: A research-based guide* (NIH Publication No. 12-4180). Retrieved from http://www.drugabuse.gov/publications/principles-drug-addiction-treatment-research-based-guide-third-edition/principles-effective-treatment

Nickel, M., Luley, J., Krawczyk, J., Nickel, C., Widermann, C., Lahmann, C., et al. (2006). Bullying girls—Changes after Brief Strategic Family Therapy: A randomized, prospective, controlled trial with one-year follow-up. *Psychotherapy and Psychosomatics, 75*(1), 47–55.

Prochaska, J. O., Norcross, J. C., & DiClemente, C. C. (1994). *Changing for good: A revolutionary six-stage program for overcoming bad habits and moving your life forward.* New York: Avon Books.

Rawson, R. A., Marinelli-Casey, P., Anglin, M. D., Dickow, A., Frazier, Y., Gallagher, C., et al. (2004). A multi-site comparison of psychosocial approaches for the treatment of methamphetamine dependence. *Addiction, 99,* 708–717.

Rawson, R. A., Shoptaw, S. J., Obert, J. L., McCann, M. J., Hasson, A. L., Marinelli-Casey, P. J., et al. (1995). An intensive outpatient approach for cocaine abuse treatment: The Matrix model. *Journal of Substance Abuse Treatment, 12,* 117–127.

Santisteban, D. A., Coatsworth, J. D., Perez-Vidal, A., Kurtines, W. M., Schwartz, S., LaPerriere, A., et al. (2003). The efficacy of Brief Strategic Family Therapy in modifying Hispanic adolescent behavior problems and substance use. *Journal of Family Psychology, 17*(1), 121–133.

Seah, R. (2001). The history of surgery: A thoughtful glance. *The Lancet, 357*, 1808.

Senft, R. A., Polen, M. R., Freeborn, D. K., & Hollis, J. F. (1997). Brief intervention in a primary care setting for hazardous drinkers. *American Journal of Preventive Medicine, 13*(6), 464–470.

Substance Abuse and Mental Health Services Administration. (2006, October). *Behavioral couples therapy for alcoholism and drug abuse.* Retrieved from SAMHSA's National Registry of Evidence-Based Programs and Practices available at http://www.nrepp.samhsa.gov/ViewIntervention.aspx?id=134

Szapocznik, J., Rio, A., Murray, E., Cohen, R., Scopetta, M., Rivas-Vazquez, A., et al. (1989). Structural family versus psychodynamic child therapy for problematic Hispanic boys. *Journal of Consulting and Clinical Psychology, 57*(5), 571–578.

Wells, R., Lemak, C. H., Alexander, J. A., Nahra, T. A., Ye, Y., & Campbell, C. I. (2007). Do licensing and accreditation matter in outpatient substance abuse treatment programs? *Journal of Substance Abuse Treatment, 33*(1), 43–50.

White, W. (1998). *Slaying the dragon: The history of addiction treatment and recovery in America.* Normal, IL: Chestnut Health Systems.

CHAPTER 14

How to Survive in a Chemical Dependency Agency

CHAPTER OBJECTIVES

- Examine general problems that occur in social service agencies
- Examine the roles inter- and intra-agency conflict play in agency effectiveness
- Identify the demands of early job adjustment in chemical dependency agencies
- Examine the importance of maintaining communication with outside agencies
- Explore ways to live with the demands of long-range counselor adjustment
- Explore ways to avoid burnout
- Examine the importance that job choice plays in counselor survival in chemical dependency agencies
- Examine the need to adjust to changing job demands and roles as the field adjusts to managed care and other professional changes

Each year, new counselors enter the drug and alcohol treatment field. Each counselor has survived some selection process, some type of training experience, and other stress-related activity. However, many will discover that the field of chemical dependency counseling is filled with experiences that they did not anticipate and for which they were poorly trained. Most addictions counselor training programs give little attention to the types of system-level problems that exist in all agencies, and they spend a minimal amount of time dealing with the system issues peculiar to substance abuse treatment agencies.

As a result of the failure to deal with these issues and to help prepare the counselor for the adjustment needed to work effectively within a given job setting, many counselors experience anxiety; frustration, and anger as they attempt to adjust to their jobs. While most of these counselors survive the process of adjustment from the idealism of training to the reality of the job place, many are unaware that the frustrations, anxieties, and self-doubts that they experience are also occurring in their colleagues, and thus, they lose a valuable opportunity to share their feelings with others. As for those who do not survive the intensity and work demands of the chemical dependency workplace, some leave without doubting that the job change was the correct vocational decision for them. Some leave because they cannot deal with the ambiguity or the mixed messages so frequently given in caregiving systems. Others leave with anger and, due to their frustration, display hostility toward the system. Still others leave with the feeling that they have failed in some basic and personal way, both as a human being and as a professional.

Survival is defined here as the ability to adjust to job demands without being overwhelmed by stress (i.e., avoiding burnout). It is of course possible to survive in an agency by simply becoming less involved with clients and disengaging from the agency (i.e., by suffering burnout). This latter condition is defined as existence.

This chapter addresses some of the problems and raises issues that the author has observed in his work as a staff member, an outside consultant, and a trainer of personnel in the substance abuse treatment field. This chapter will focus on issues common to most social service agencies (e.g., dealing with internal staff relations and roles), as well as those specific to substance abuse treatment agencies (e.g., dealing with the potential problems that can develop between staff members who are themselves recovering from chemical dependency, referred to here as "recovering counselors") and staff members who are not (referred to here as "non-recovering counselors"). Counselors should be aware that many of the specific issues that they will confront may be ignored or treated too briefly in this chapter. A complete coverage of all the possible issues that substance abuse counselors will confront in the job place is clearly beyond the scope of this chapter. However, it is hoped that some of the issues raised here will be helpful to counselors by making more public and explicit issues that were previously experienced but not articulated. Making these issues a labeled part of the experience of counselors makes it possible for much of the frustration, anxiety, and anger generated by these experiences to be shared with colleagues and dealt with as real staff-maintenance issues. This awareness will improve counselors' morale and help them focus on the job of providing better services to their clients.

Some Initial Considerations

This chapter deals with issues applicable to most social service agencies and some that are specifically relevant to the drug and alcohol service system. We shall first turn to a consideration of problem issues that are applicable to most service agencies, including those in the substance abuse field.

One of the things that you, as a counselor, may not be initially aware of is that like your clients, the agency you work in has its own ability to adjust and meet its problems or to behave in irrational and destructive ways. There are several reasons why social service agencies may have more problems than agencies not dealing with the personal problems of people. These considerations are discussed next.

Daily Demands of Clients

Frequently, clients attempt to set one staff member against another, either to get something they want or to vent unresolved hostility. Because clients may have dealt with many agencies in the past, not infrequently they have developed a highly manipulative style of dealing with such agencies. For example, they may have found that being demanding or extremely dependent is an effective tactic for dealing with bureaucracies. They may have also learned that setting one counselor against another can keep the pressure off them when they enter treatment. It is possible for counselors to react negatively to these behaviors, rather than to see them as a part of the clients' problems. In an agency where there is not adequate communication among staff members, these problems can escalate and lead to deterioration in staff relations.

Communication Breakdowns

Client demands can cause problems when there is poor communication in an agency. In fact, like a marriage relationship, an agency rapidly begins to show serious difficulties when there is a breakdown in communication. While breakdowns in communication frequently occur, they are usually corrected if the basic structure and process of communication are in place. However, we are talking here about chronic problems in communication. These may occur as vertical communication problems (e.g., a supervisor with a counselor) or as horizontal problems (e.g., between two counselors doing the same type job). Left unchecked, these problems can develop into distrust, with the result that communication exists only in smaller cliques, and a type of war can break out between these cliques. Regardless of the pattern, the efficiency of the agency is seriously affected, and the functioning of the agency can be distorted in drastic ways. Like a family, agencies will adjust to communication breakdowns and may well continue to function for considerable periods of time. However, both work efficiency and the morale of many of the agency's workers are lowered when these negative adjustments are made.

Emotional Involvement With Clients

One of the factors that is involved in most social service agencies is the need for counselors to become emotionally involved with clients. Emotional invest-ment in individuals is a characteristic usually found in the effective caregiver. However, when a caregiver invests himself in a client, there is a potential that the client will disappoint or frustrate the caregiver. This frustration can lead to a drop in the self-esteem and general morale of the staff member, which is par-ticularly true in the substance abuse field, where chemical dependency counsel-ors work with clients who show a pattern of frequent relapse. Therefore, work-ing with these clients can be particularly frustrating to new counselors, who are already concerned about their ability to become competent counselors. In this situation, new counselors are constantly seeing clients relapse and asking themselves if they are doing all they can for their clients. In many cases, novice counselors blame the failure on themselves and, consequently, suffer self-doubt and a loss of self-esteem. An interesting consequence of emotional investment and caring is that, generally speaking, the counselor who is able to empathize with the client, and project warmth and concern, is usually the most effective counselor. In other words, being concerned and caring leads to more effective treatment in most caregiving situations. However, it is not uncommon for the most committed and caring counselors to suffer counselor burnout. Conversely, many of the people who are not emotionally invested in their clients may well be survivors in the agency but at the cost to the clients. (Many counselors may be people who had originally been very caring but, due to disillusionment, have become cynical and less caring about their clients.) Another danger for substance abuse workers is that they may vent all of their job frustrations on the client, who is the most visible source of their frustrations. Therefore, a balance between the ability to emotionally invest in a client and to maintain some emotional distance is basic to survival in caregiving agencies.

Ambiguity of Tasks

Another issue faced by staff in social service agencies is the general ambiguity of the tasks that they are asked to perform. Few therapists, for example, can ever say that their counseling was the major factor (or sometimes, even a minor factor) in a given client's recovery. In fact, a counselor who does carry out a specific intervention will only know if the intervention led to a positive outcome by waiting to see how the client changes. Frequently these delays between intervention and outcome are quite lengthy, and even very effective therapists can feel they have done little to help the client.

Conflict Between Recovering and Non-recovering Staff

One of the most important differences between substance abuse agencies and other caregiving agencies is that in many, perhaps most, chemical dependency agencies, both recovering and non-recovering personnel are employed. There are very few caregiving systems, outside the substance abuse field, where people who are recovering from the problem become therapists. While many agencies manage the relationships among people with differing entrance credentials quite well, some agencies do not spend enough time or energy dealing with the potential problems that may ensue, some of which are discussed below.

Staff Motivation

Recovering staff in chemical dependency agencies are frequently suspicious of the motivation of the non-recovering staff, particularly in alcohol and drug agencies. For example, those in recovery may wonder why a person who has not suffered through an alcohol problem would care anything about the welfare of those who have. (Many of those with alcoholism, despite their own recovery, still view those with active alcoholism in a moralistic way. They assume that other people also have this viewpoint.) And while they seldom voice their concerns to the non-recovering counselors, the recovering counselors frequently wonder if the non-recovering counselors are working in the agency simply because the jobs were available, or if they plan to "rip off the agency by drawing their pay and doing little to earn it." In some cases, they may see the non-recovering counselor as a con artist who is trying to gain control of the agency (i.e., become the head of the agency). In general, recovering staff may see non-recovering staff as less dedicated than they are and may resent their equal or superior status in the agency.

Education Differential

Recovering staff can sometimes be threatened by the fact that the non-recovering staff have more training. Because many recovering counselors enter the addictions treatment field through on-the-job-training or workshop experiences, they do not receive the academic credentials that go with formal education. Many of these counselors are extremely sensitive about their lack of formal education and seem to fear that, someday, the better-educated, non-recovering counselors will reveal the recovering counselors' ignorance to the world in one fell swoop of intellectual ambush. Obviously, this fear makes the counselor who is recovering very cautious and circumspect in his dealings with the better-educated, non-recovering counselor. While this attitude may seem quite irrational to the casual observer, it is better understood when one remembers the problems with self-esteem and lowered self-worth that many of those with addictions must struggle with for an extended period of their life following the achievement of sobriety.

A regrettable consequence of these first two points of friction is that although the recovering counselor has much to offer the non-addicted counselor, because of the suspiciousness and hostility generated between the two groups, a beneficial exchange between them may not be possible. It is also true that the degreed counselor may have skills and points of view that might benefit the recovering counselor. Unfortunately, the frequent antagonism between the two camps may not allow for constructive dialogue—a dialogue that might eventually lead to better care for both types of counselors' clients.

Formation of Cliques

The non-recovering counselor may resent the in-group cliquishness of the recovering counselors. The fact that the recovering counselors have a built-in bond of Alcoholics Anonymous (A.A.) association and some experiences that they perceive as shared can make the non-recovering counselor feel excluded. Another aspect of this same issue is that the non-recovering staff member may see recovering staff members as exercising a reverse sort of snobbery. That is, the recovering counselor may insist that the only way one can really understand someone with an addiction is by being one and that, as a result, the non-recovering counselor can never really be effective.

Differing Attitudes Toward Alcoholism

There may be differences in the way the recovering and non-recovering counselors view alcoholism. In many cases, the recovering counselor will see alcohol problems in less-differentiated ways than the academically trained counselor who, through education, has been exposed to widely differing models of alcoholism. For example, on the one hand, the recovering counselor may see addiction as an either/or issue (i.e., either you have an addiction or you don't). The notion of alcoholism as a disease may have been fundamental in the recovering counselor's training history, and close ties with the philosophy of A.A. may be seen as the sole basis for treatment.

On the other hand, the academically trained counselors may have been exposed, through university training, to a multicausal model of addiction and may see differing types of interventions as appropriate where there are differing developmental histories for the alcohol and drug abuse. It goes without saying that these differing approaches can frequently become the basis for a communication breakdown and neither group really appreciates that a major part of the problem is in the model that they are using to treat alcoholism and addiction.

Academic vs. Craft Training

Another difference exists in the source and philosophy of training for the degreed professional and the recovering alcoholic counselor. Kalb and Propper (1976) have characterized the differences between these two types of substance abuse professionals as science versus craft training, respectively. On the one hand, the scientist-professional background of the degreed counselors usually means not only that they have learned their caregiving skills experientially, as an apprentice to a skilled counselor, but also that through didactic training, they have been exposed to the teachings of many others regarding alcohol problems. In this type of training, counselors will normally be exposed to a wide range of differing viewpoints and are encouraged to exercise independence in establishing their concepts of the issues. The ability to engage in original, independent thinking and to critically evaluate the work of one's teachers and peers is the highest calling of the scientist-professional model.

On the other hand, craftspeople obtain their qualifying skill or knowledge primarily through observing and experiencing the actual tasks required under the tutelage of a master craftsperson. The knowledge that they acquire is a product of the experiences of their teacher, and the acquisition of the craftsperson's skills is demonstrated by the ability to consistently replicate the performance of the master craftsperson. In mastering these skills, only limited elaborations of style are allowed, and critical examination of the traditions of the craft are actively discouraged. In fact, shared agreement on the traditions of the craft is the criterion for loyalty in a craft-like organization.

In the past, paraprofessional preparation in the chemical dependency treatment field has primarily followed the craft model. Trainees are usually indoctrinated in the philosophy and principles (the 12 steps) of A.A. by trainers who are themselves recovering from alcoholism and who have used this approach in their own recovery. These students are expected to emulate their teachers' thinking and actions. Their goal is to one day be like their teachers and teach others what they have learned. As a result, most paraprofessionals in the addictions treatment field are committed to traditional concepts and are resistant to alternative views of addictions. The steadfast refusal to question their own premises, despite conflicting evidence, helps to create and maintain an intense loyalty and unity among these recovering counselors. While this problem between the recovering and non-recovering counselors has been an ongoing one, it could become more severe in the next few years as more drug and alcohol counselors complete training in more formal settings and are exposed to competing models of drug and alcohol use and abuse.

Appropriate Modeling Behavior vs. Emotional Catharsis

The non-recovering counselor may sometimes view the recovering counselor as having as many psychotherapy needs as the clients he or she is trying to help. Of course, lay counselors may very well tie their recovery to helping other people, particularly since twelfth-stepping is a tenet of A.A. Frequently there is a close tie between the treatment philosophy of an alcohol treatment program and the philosophy of A.A. Therefore, recovering counselors may use their own histories with drug and alcohol abuse extensively to teach other patients how they managed their personal recoveries. There is, of course, a fine line between illustrating appropriate recovery behavior and experiencing some emotional catharsis that may be useful to the mental health of the recovering counselor. It is also probable (and possibly necessary, in order to appropriately model the desired behavior) that the recovering counselor will use a group or individual session to deal with his or her own personal problems. It is imperative, however, that counselors, whether recovering or non-recovering, remember that they are there to help the people in treatment, not themselves. Whenever a counselor's problems become the predominant, ongoing focus of treatment, then the concern of fellow counselors is justified, and it may be necessary to intervene, in some way, to find outside therapy for the counselor having difficulty.[1]

---

1 The reader is referred to Knauert and Davidson (1979) and to Wegscheider (1981). The latter author has generated a checklist so that people working with substance abusers can evaluate their own levels of adjustment at a given point in time. Wegscheider (1981, pp. 248–253) has introduced what she has labeled "the whole person inventory." This inventory covers both personal and job-related issues and may be helpful to counselors who are experiencing difficulty.

Addictions Counselors and Other Mental Health Professionals

Problems for new addictions counselors may be especially pronounced when it becomes necessary for them to work with people from other disciplines. It may be particularly difficult, for example, for those substance abuse counselors working in mental health agencies. There one must relate to disciplines such as psychology, psychiatry, and social work, which have different ideological and philosophical training histories. Bridging the gap to form a collegial relationship may be very difficult for the substance abuse counselor, for a number of reasons. First, the philosophical and ideological differences among the above training disciplines are great, and these differences are even more pronounced between the substance abuse counselors and these professions. For example, the center of client motivation for most mental health professionals is in the client (i.e., the client must want to change before therapy can be effectively instituted). In working with those who have issues related to the use of alcohol and drugs, considerable external coercion may be used to get persons to enter treatment and to get them involved in the initial stages of treatment. Second, many mental health personnel view individuals who are working with those who have addictions as paraprofessionals. As Kalb and Propper (1976) have noted, the paraprofessional has operated as an adjunct to, and under the supervision of, the professional in mental health settings. The paraprofessional in the addictions field, however, has been a teacher or colleague rather than a student. These differences in expectations about roles add to communication difficulties. Finally, a considerable amount of hostility toward, and avoidance of treatment of, those with addictions has historically been present in all of these disciplines. Many of them see those with addictions as a lower level of client, and may see the addictions counselor, regardless of level of training, as a person who is competent only to deal with these hopeless clients. Many mental health agencies insist on both physical and administrative separation of the two caregiving systems. Frequently, less-than-ideal communication is often maintained between these two groups, and considerable resentment and hostility can develop.

As noted above, this is not an exhaustive list of the potential problems that may exist between recovering and non-recovering counselors. It is hoped, however, that it will alert drug and alcohol counselors to some of these issues and lead to the issues being discussed among staff members.

Inter-agency Conflict

Because the alcohol field began as a grassroots movement, primarily through A.A. and the National Council on Alcohol,[2] it has developed as a highly

---

2   A fact frequently overlooked by the alcohol field is that the field actually had considerable professional-scientific input at its inception and that the founder of the National Council, Marty Mann, actually received considerable support from Jellinek and his group at Yale (see Jellinek, 1960/2012).

personalized, very politicized system. In particular, there has been a major concern with protecting one's turf against competing agencies, both in and out of the chemical dependency field. Part of this paranoia is historically justified, since drug and alcohol treatment has traditionally been underfunded. Individuals in the field have had to fight for scarce resources with other caregiving systems (e.g., mental health agencies) and even with competing substance abuse treatment agencies. As a result, not only has the system developed some paranoia toward agencies outside the chemical dependency field, but also within the field one agency may become suspicious of other agencies that might be competing with it for patients. With this view of internal and external agencies as threats to their survival, drug and alcohol agencies are frequently susceptible to rumor, internal fantasy generation, and the distortion of facts. While all of these problems can be present in human service agencies generally, the degree of severity seems to be greater in the drug and alcohol field. Of course, this means that some forum for open discussion of the issues and some mechanism for resolution of differences must be rigorously maintained. When clear channels of communication are not maintained, then chemical dependency agencies can engage in very destructive behaviors.

Inter-agency Conflict and Client Care

None of the above issues would be of much importance if they had little bearing on the care of clients. However, relationships within and between agencies can directly and indirectly affect the quality of care provided to the clients of these agencies. We will consider only a few of the more important consequences of disrupted internal and external agency relationships. The main point to remember here is that agency functioning is not an abstract event, unrelated to day-to-day client care. As we shall see, there are rather direct tie-ins between some of the above issues and the quality of client care provided by an agency.

One example of the direct impact of problems among agencies is that the appropriate referral of clients can be disrupted. For example, if you do not have good relations with a long-term care agency and a client discharged from your treatment center needs this care, the probability of adequate referral is lowered. The reader could doubtless supply many other illustrations of how poor relationships with other agencies can potentially affect client care, ranging from referral to aftercare.

Indirect effects of internal and external agency conflict are more difficult to observe (and frequently more difficult to correct). However, if you concentrate on a given agency, you can readily see how many of the indirect effects discussed here are operating in that agency. Whenever there is internal or external strife surrounding an agency, the amount of emotional energy left to caregivers to do their daily counseling is reduced (and thus their effectiveness is reduced). In addition, the frustration, anger, and anxiety felt by the counselors are communicated to the clients under their care. Therefore, in agencies where staff are spending considerable time and energy dealing with internal or external conflict, clients receive less effective treatment. The clients frequently begin to show acting-out behavior in response to the caregiver's emotional reactions being transmitted to them. This trickle-down effect usually occurs about 2 weeks following the initiation of the caregiver's conflict and for the same amount of time following the resolution of the conflict.

These problems indicate that the frequently held notion that inter- and intra-agency planning meetings are a waste of valuable treatment time is not necessarily accurate. The provision of a structure (e.g., regularly scheduled meetings) to discuss issues, and the existence of an ongoing process (an openness and honesty between staff members in communication) are important for substance abuse agencies. Ensuring open communication can lead to more effective treatment of clients and a reduction of acting-out behavior on the part of the people in treatment.

Early Job Adjustment in an Agency

Most counselors would agree that drug and alcohol agencies are not unchanging, static organizations. However, one of the things that caregivers frequently overlook is the fact that they themselves also change in a number of ways in the course of their careers. The ability to manage psychological and philosophical adjustments is crucial to survival in caregiving agencies. In this section, we shall examine some of the adjustments that caregivers entering an agency may need to make over a period of time. We will also suggest some strategies that can be helpful in dealing with these issues. A cautionary note: The sequence of adjustments described here is typical, but may not occur for all counselors in all settings. The timing of each of the following phases is also highly variable, both across settings and for caregivers in the same setting. Therefore, the phases described should not be perceived as automatic procedures that will be experienced by all alcohol counselors or all caregivers.

The Honeymoon Period

Part of the problem new counselors face is that they simply do not know the agency very well. Another problem is that the new counselor may approach the job in an idealized way. If we were to have an organizational chart of the agency drawn from the new counselor's perspective, we would expect that much of the agency would be left out, and the counselor's role in the agency would be much larger than it would be from the perspective of an objective observer. The new counselors' egocentric behavior is initially reinforced, since in the early days and weeks, people in the agency usually welcome them in and attempt to be very supportive. Additionally, the counselors are, ideally, not yet swamped with a heavy caseload and have time to interact with their new colleagues. None of this is necessarily maladaptive since we would hope that a new counselor would enter the job with enthusiasm and excitement. However, this period, sometimes called the "honeymoon" period, is not generally characteristic of the experiences that counselors will encounter once they become fully involved with their job in the agency.

One reason for highlighting the honeymoon period is that some counselors early on suffer severe doubts about whether they have chosen the right job or right career because of the contrast between this period and the emotional letdown that they experience following it. After the honeymoon period, some counselors may feel that they have chosen the wrong job or the wrong career. While these feelings may be correct, leaving the agency at this point may be a serious mistake simply because the counselor may not have enough information on which to base a rational decision. The point for counselors to remember if they suffer some early disillusionment within the first 3 to 6 months is that other very competent, committed, and dedicated counselors in the same agency may have had the same feelings and stayed with the job until the initial adjustments were made.

Mastering Routine Tasks

Several other adjustment phases in caregiving agencies have been described (Sarata, 1979). These phases are usually filled with ambivalence and uncertainty for the caregiver. We will call the first of these phases "mastering standard operating procedures." This stage usually overlaps the honeymoon period described above. In mastering procedures, the counselor is preoccupied with learning things such as the clerical demands of the agency (e.g., how to fill out the necessary forms correctly, how to get progress notes typed up, and how to complete the procedures for setting up an interview with the family). Many counselors may experience this period as a time when there are an overwhelming number of things to learn. Many fear that they will never learn it all. Generally, counselors at this point in this phase are so busy with the nitty-gritty functions of the agency that they have relatively little concern about their comparative job performance. To their disappointment, new counselors discover that a portion of the work they will be doing is routine, monotonous, and uninteresting. The boring routine of learning the right forms to use, the appropriate channels through which to get things done, and so forth, may be tasks that the new counselors did not anticipate. In addition, they learn that their general training in counseling did not provide many of the technical details needed in their new job. Close relationships with a more experienced counselor or their supervisors are needed for them to handle the adjustments in this phase. However, novice counselors must be mature enough (and assertive enough) to seek out this technical advice and support in order to reduce the stress of this period.

Comparing Work Attitudes and Philosophies

In the third phase, counselors may begin to compare their work attitudes and philosophies with those of co-workers and superiors. Each interaction seems to provide an opportunity for the new workers to compare their ideas to those of relevant others in the job place. While some counselors may be concerned with what supervisors think, more often counselors are interested in what their fellow counselors are thinking and doing. The sharing of experiences with fellow counselors is important because new chemical dependency counselors face what has been called the "crisis of competence" (Cherniss, 1980). The comparison of their performance with those of their peers allows feedback about the relative quality of their performance. Being able to share experiences and receive support from their peers provides several benefits for the neophyte counselors. First, colleagues can offer the neophyte counselors a sympathetic ear when they want to talk about work problems, resulting in an emotional release of tension and anxiety. Second, a better perspective and understanding of the problem is frequently possible after sharing job problems with colleagues. Third, supportive colleagues are particularly important when the novice counselors find themselves in conflict with administrators or agency policy. Fourth, colleagues also offer a readily available resource for the large amount of technical information that must be acquired. Fifth, colleagues offer feedback on one's performance, feedback that is important for the feeling of professional competence. Finally, colleagues can help the new counselor confirm or disconfirm his perception of his performance on the job.

Self-Doubts About the Caregiver Role

Eventually, the fourth phase of early job adjustment is reached. This phase involves a preoccupation by the caregivers with their fitness for, or commitment to, the caregiver role. Counselors may begin to examine how far their clients have progressed and to question whether or not they are doing an effective job. Counselors may also begin to reflect on the stresses and satisfactions experienced in the job. The paramount question that seems to be asked during this phase is, Are the job and I suited for each other? Moving to another agency is one way to resolve the uncertainties of this issue. However, the counselor should be aware that working through the above phases and learning to pace oneself seem to be necessary adjustment procedures for assuming the caregiving role.

The above adjustments are frequently experienced by the counselor in a lonely, internal struggle. It is frequently lonely because caregivers find it difficult to request assistance for themselves and often relegate their own cares and concerns to another time. It is important, then, for counselors to seek out peer and supervisor support as they progress through these phases. The question "Should I share my concerns with others in the agency?" is one that must be answered by counselors based on their perception that other staff will be supportive and on their own ability to be open. If the counselor does decide to risk asking for support, a potential long-range advantage is that, even if specific questions are not answered, the counselor has built a network of support that can be utilized in the future.

An awareness of the above phases should be helpful in two ways to new counselors entering an addictions agency.

1. Like their clients, it is better if counselors have some preliminary understanding of some of the things they may experience. Daily adjustment requires the ability to label and understand experiences. If neophyte counselors are aware that the above experiences are relatively common, they are less likely to be hesitant in sharing their experiences with co-workers. In particular, if other counselors at the same level are present, it may encourage the counselors to form a minisupport and discussion group. Support from peers may be readily available in the agency.

2. If a particular job situation is not going well, an awareness of the existence of ongoing workplace adjustments may allow the counselor to more readily put things in perspective. For example, when the above phases are being worked through, the occurrence of a frustrating event can have a heavier impact on the counselor's morale. An awareness that experiences may have a greater impact on people when they are already feeling perplexed and confused (something counselors tell their clients all the time) can be helpful in maintaining a more objective and long-range perspective. Both of these points can be useful in surviving the initial adjustments necessary in the workplace.

Communication Issues Within an Agency

One of the factors frequently overlooked in assessing the quality of care provided to clients in a drug and alcohol agency (or any caregiving agency) is the degree to which an agency communicates internally and externally. This section focuses on internal agency communication; external communication (communication with other agencies) will be considered in the following section.

Open Communication

One of the most obvious advantages of open communication within an agency is that if counselors talk to each other, then clients are likely to get better and more appropriate care. This function is frequently (but certainly not always) appreciated by drug and alcohol caregivers and can be seen in daily staffing meetings, where lively discussions of client progress and what types of interventions may be needed occur. What is often ignored is that adequate communication regarding clients requires clear communication among staff in that agency.

This staff communication network frequently involves a highly personalized series of interactions. When these personalized interactions are characterized by openness, sensitivity to other colleagues, candor, and trust, then the agency is more likely to perform well such tasks as evaluating client progress and planning treatment. However, when the communication network is characterized by defensiveness, insensitivity, dishonesty, and mistrust, even basic client evaluation and treatment planning sessions become distorted by the overall breakdown in communication within the agency. The breakdowns can occur for a number of reasons. Some examples include the following: competition for what may be considered a more ideal job assignment; distance that may be created because co-workers have little in common in terms of outside interests; or a situation in which one person may be perceived as the favorite of the supervisor and the rest of the counselors scapegoat that person. Whatever the reason, jealousy, envy, or simple lack of interest can create communication gulfs in an agency (Cherniss, 1980).

As implied above, the lack of sensitivity on the part of counselors toward colleagues can lead to defensive behavior and to closing down communication between counselors and their colleagues. Much of what has previously been discussed would apply in the area of defensive behavior; however, one additional point should be made. All people have vulnerable points. If they are attacked at these points, they will overreact and behave in irrational ways. Counselors should become aware of these vulnerabilities in their colleagues and avoid arousing defensiveness whenever possible. If they do, however, make a fellow counselor defensive, counselors should remember that their colleague is likely to behave in an irrational manner. Frequently, it is better to apologize for making the person angry and then to try another tack in communicating with the individual about the issue.

Personal Insensitivity and Communication

Personal insensitivity within an agency can have a powerful impact on communication. There will be times when counselors do not get the support and concern they need from their fellow counselors, simply because the other counselors are so preoccupied with their own job responsibilities. Also, it is frequently forgotten (or overlooked) that it is the small, sensitive things that count in day-to-day interaction. Being human and humane with colleagues can reduce emotional and psychological distance and make communication both easier and more open. Since counselors are human, they tend to talk more to the people who are sensitive to their needs and to become more defensive (and so, less communicative) toward those people who are not sensitive to their needs. A common error for counselors is to attend so much to the needs of their clients that they ignore entirely the needs of their peers. Counselors frequently show sensitivity, warmth, care, and concern with their clients, then leave the counseling session and greet their colleagues as if they had been trained in the Attila the Hun School of Therapy. Again, the empathy and warmth shown to patients is not transferred to counselors' interactions with colleagues.

Areas of Potential Insensitivity

One area of potential insensitivity comes out of the differing training histories of the personnel typically employed in an alcohol agency. The degreed, professional counselor may be insensitive to factors such as the role that A.A. plays in the lay counselor's life. Professional counselors may, in the beginning, be insensitive to the fact that for people using A.A. as a support group, an attack on A.A.'s principles is similar to an attack on a person's religion (i.e., they are touching on an area that is a central value for these people). New counselors will quickly be made aware that for the recovering counselor, the strengths and weaknesses of using A.A. as a support group is not a topic for academic discussion. Obviously, an early encounter of this type can lead to anger, defensiveness, and less effective communication between the two groups.

Recovering counselors, on the other hand, sometimes are insensitive toward non-recovering counselors. For example, the recovering counselor may make caustic remarks about the degreed counselors' lack of a true understanding of the problem they are trying to treat. Attempts to belittle the utility of education also reflect insensitivity and defensiveness on the part of the recovering counselor when such comments are directed at their academically trained peers. These patterns of interaction affect the degree and level of communication and lead to the formation of cliques within an agency.

Communication Structures

In order to better understand communication breakdown, counselors need to understand or make explicit some factors that are so much taken for granted that they are never really looked at closely. To begin with, there are format and form issues involved in communication within any agency. For example, setting up daily meetings implies that some format has been provided within which communication can occur.

New counselors must learn the format of communication in their agency. This structure can vary from highly formal meetings, with someone acting as chairperson, to a casual hallway meeting system where things are decided in a very informal way. In some cases, a highly formal system may be set up, but this system is not really involved in how things get communicated (e.g., things may be communicated and decisions consensually agreed upon prior to the formal meeting). The issue is not which one of the above formats is most effective (both can be effective or ineffective), but rather which one or which combination is used in the agency. When counselors first enter an agency, part of the honeymoon period described earlier should be spent studying how things are communicated and how tasks are accomplished in the agency. If counselors are initially aware that two systems of communication and decision making can co-exist, they may be less frustrated when they discover that issues that they bring to the more formal session are not extensively debated or considered before a decision is made.

The Communication Process

In addition to understanding the structure of communication, it is also important to recognize and monitor the process of communication. As noted earlier, if people in the agency are basically honest, open, sensitive, and supportive toward their colleagues, then there is likely to be a relatively free and easy exchange of information. If the members of an agency cannot talk to one another, then the best series of structured meetings will not lead to effective communication. While the structure of communication patterns may provide the vehicle for communication to occur, open, trusting communication with colleagues will determine whether the communication patterns will be clear and effective.

In some agencies, disagreements are avoided or played down in order to maintain a surface harmony. Inevitably, this results in distorting the process of communicating, and dealing with some issues among counselors is avoided at all cost. For example, feelings toward one staff member may be so intense that some or all of the counselors avoid confronting that staff member about issues where there is disagreement. Again, not only communication processes, but also decision-making procedures, can be distorted.

Communication Breakdown and Mistrust

Mistrust in an agency is frequently a byproduct of a breakdown in communication, but, obviously, it also can contribute to communication problems once it is present. Sometimes mistrust occurs because an individual has dealt with personal confidences in a destructive manner. At other times an individual (or the agency hierarchy) has not followed through on promises or supported staff members in the agency when a difficult issue is being dealt with. Mistrust is a threat to the fabric of intra-agency communication and, once established, can seriously erode the quality of staff interaction. The question that is sometimes asked is, Can anyone be trusted or is everyone out for Number One?

Mistrust, like communication, can either be vertical or horizontal, or it can be present at all levels when the entire agency has problems with trust. When there are problems throughout the agency, an easy way out is to make some outside threat a greater problem than the problems that need to be dealt with internally. While such a strategy may be effective for a short period of time, it does not provide a long-term solution. Like the marriage relationship, relationships within agencies can only be assured by continually dealing with issues as they arise. As with other communication issues, a common mistake is believing that only a single intervention is required to deal with mistrust. An agency maintenance issue can be dealt with routinely where communication and trust levels are high, but becomes difficult to deal with when they are not. Some strategies that seem to be helpful here include the following:

- Keep messages between counselors and their peers clear, and deal with interpersonal problems as they occur, rather than putting them off. Reducing ambiguity in communication with peers is an important goal in this respect.

- Remember that personal fantasy and rumor are like gas on a burning fire when trust is an issue. Counselors should attempt to confirm or disconfirm rumors as soon as they hear them. They should also check out their fantasies of what is going on in the agency; it is remarkable how easily messages can become distorted. If counselors would like to confirm this, they should try passing a verbal message through 10 or more people (at a party, for instance). Usually even a simple message will show some dramatic change. Another way to confirm that multiple modes of communication work better is to write the message down and pass it both in written and verbal form, which should result in a significant reduction in the distortion of the message. A similar issue occurs in counselors' anticipation of what is going to happen when they fantasize about what is occurring in an agency: These fantasies are usually partially, or entirely, wrong.

- If counselors are not physically located in the same facility, they should remember that they may have difficulty managing communication with their colleagues. Here you may have to create some method of maintaining contact with your co-workers. Some possible solutions might include having coffee once a day in the central agency or having lunch with fellow counselors once a week, or more if counselors are located in the field rather than in a central office. The practical side of regular contact is that it allows counselors to deal with ongoing problems in the agency. Of more central importance is the fact that physical and psychological distance is reduced between counselors and their peers through regular contact. If people see and talk to one another on a daily basis, there is less likelihood that mistrust will become a problem. It should again be noted that colleagues provide a powerful support system for new counselors. Without the moral support of colleagues, many new counselors would not make an active effort to resolve their job-related difficulties and could withdraw into mindless conformity.

- Remember, there is a need to provide internal support for communication. Counselors should be aware that they have the most control over their own behavior. They should make every attempt to deal openly and honestly with their peers. Also, they should remember that overcoming mistrust can take time and, in an agency where there are problems, they may not receive much reinforcement for their attempts to deal with issues in a clear and straightforward manner. That will be particularly true when issues of peer insensitivity and defensiveness co-exist in an agency; this is not an uncommon occurrence where mistrust is an issue.

A common failure in dealing with communication process issues is to assume that a one-time intervention that results in better communication is all that needs to be done. However, the same breakdowns in communication are likely to recur in an agency. Counselors should be aware that ongoing sessions devoted to specific breakdowns in communication may be necessary. They should not conclude, simply because there is decay in the communication process over a period of time following an intervention, that what they tried was ineffective or that repairing the communication pattern is hopeless. Rather, the problem should be viewed as a maintenance issue in which previously successful interventions can be utilized again.

Communicating With Supervisors

No matter what one's position is as a newcomer to an agency, a counselor will need to manage effective communication with people superior (and subordinate) to him or her in rank or status. One factor that may directly affect a counselor's survival is how he or she deals with people in positions of authority (i.e., supervisors). It is interesting that counselors can sometimes deal so effectively with clients and yet be very ineffective in using identical principles when they interact with their supervisors.

It is helpful for counselors to become aware of their own personal feelings and reactions to authority. Frequently, counselors react to supervisors on the basis of long-held emotional reactions to authority figures. When they have a disagreement with a superior, the first question they should ask themselves is how much of this is their own emotional response to an authority figure. A good rule of thumb is that counselors should never confront a superior when angry and out of control (even if they are right), because they may not present their ideas as clearly and precisely as they would like. If counselors are angry but are under control and can verbally express their anger (and their reason for it), their ideas are more likely to be well received. One thing that might be helpful to counselors when communicating something they feel strongly about is to ask themselves how they would feel if someone attacked them personally when complaining about some of their actions. One should not forget that people in positions of power are also feeling human beings. Counselors might also ask themselves if their motive is simply to let off steam, or if they really want to communicate with the person.

A common error in communication is for counselors to avoid interaction with their supervisor. It is almost as if counselors feel that the best way to manage their situation is to blend into the woodwork. If counselors get to know the supervisor as a person, the tendency and need to maintain distance are usually lessened and communication is improved.

Supervisors as a Factor in New Counselor Survival

Supervisors are critical to the initial development and continuing survival of chemical dependency counselors. Some specific ways that supervisors can aid in the development of competence in novice caregivers are outlined below. These include the following:

- Supervisors can provide technical suggestions and advice that can increase the counselors' effectiveness.
- Supervisors provide feedback to the new counselors; positive feedback can help alleviate anxiety, while negative feedback delivered constructively can help the counselor correct weaknesses.
- When the supervisor is readily available to the new counselor for consultation, the counselor feels less alone and isolated, and the fear of harming a client through ineptitude is decreased.
- Supervisors provide a reference point for the new counselor (e.g., if the new counselor sees the case in the same way as the supervisor, then the counselor is reassured that his own competence in understanding a case is adequate).

In general, for the new professional, a supportive, but discreet, supervisor has been found to be associated with positive career development (i.e., positive survival; Cherniss, 1980).

Interacting With Support Personnel

Regardless of their status in the agency, counselors will probably find someone with lower status than themselves with whom they must interact. For example, how will they, as entering counselors, deal with clerical personnel? Obviously, they will want to be sensitive to secretarial needs and will want to promote as much productivity as possible. One rule of thumb is to adopt a style of interaction with subordinates with which they can be comfortable. If counselors are easygoing individuals, it is likely that a brusque, business-like style with administrative assistants will be difficult to maintain. If counselors try to assume roles that are not consistent with their usual style of interaction, then typically they will under- or overplay them. Remember, a wide variety of approaches work in communicating with people. This can be confirmed by observing the different styles that fellow counselors use in interacting with people.

Cutting Through the Bureaucracy

One area that frequently seems to be overlooked is the general insensitivity of bureaucracies toward people. One result is that the professional role that the counselor has been trained for may be difficult to carry out in the face of bureaucratic demands. For example, bureaucrats may see what is needed from a different point of view than the counselors do; this is particularly true in the area of professional autonomy. The irrational and sometimes destructive rules and policies of chemical dependency agencies may be a major source of frustration and stress for novice counselors. The new counselors find that one of their tasks is to mediate between bureaucratic demands and client demands. Frequently, drug and alcohol counselors personalize some of the bureaucratic indifference that can occur in care agencies. This can lead counselors to assume that what is occurring is a personal vendetta directed toward them. In point of fact, what is occurring may be totally unknown to the person (or persons) who could correct it, and it will remain that way unless counselors initiate action to open communication and resolve the problem. Frequently, counselors find that the person responsible is just as eager to have the problem corrected as they are. In other words, counselors should check out perceived injustices to see if they are simply oversights.

The solution to another problem in communicating with the bureaucracy is also in the hands of the counselor. As noted above, many counselors find that keeping charts up to date, writing treatment plans, and so forth, is unexciting and boring. Counselors may do these tasks but gripe incessantly about doing them, or resist doing them at all. It may well be that this lack of response to the bureaucracy by counselors can lead to poorer care for their clients and more work for their colleagues. What can be overlooked is that these bureaucratic tasks, as onerous as they are, do help maintain communication within an agency and can ensure better care for the client.

In fairness, it should be noted that general griping about the bureaucracy is characteristic of care agencies. In fact, if not taken to extremes, this griping can allow anger and frustration to be expressed toward a non-reactive source. However, when the griping includes passive resistance or active sabotage of the system, then a vital communication link is threatened.

The importance of establishing open, positive communication with colleagues cannot be over-emphasized for new counselors. The role of a novice counselor is psychologically stressful and can be emotionally demanding even when the new counselors have open access to their more experienced peers and can depend on their advice and support. Without this support, the adjustment is infinitely more difficult.

If counselors could always rely on working out problems with colleagues, the world of work would be a happier place. However, the reality of life is that despite their strong efforts to communicate with peers, there will be some colleagues with whom counselors simply cannot communicate. At this point, they have to attempt to find ways to go around these colleagues and to do their job in spite of them. That is, they may have to live with these so-called problem colleagues if they choose to stay in the agency. One question the counselor may have to answer is, Can I work out a way to live with this person, or must I leave the agency for my own peace of mind? Another way of phrasing the question would be, Do I like what I'm doing well enough to put up with working with this person? In other cases, one will encounter colleagues who are already burned out and who have very negative attitudes toward the job. For new counselors, these negative attitudes can be extremely contagious, causing them to quickly lose their enthusiasm and drive for the job. Therefore, avoiding contact with such colleagues is essential for new counselors, particularly during the first months on the job.

Maintaining Communication With Outside Agencies

The practical importance of maintaining open and effective liaisons with other agencies, in terms of meeting the needs of clients, has already been demonstrated. The lack of adequate communication with other agencies also affects the overall morale and functioning of the entire agency and its personnel. Many of the same factors that apply to intra-agency communication also apply here. For example, openness, sensitivity to colleagues, candor, and trust are as necessary for inter-agency communication as they are for intra-agency communication. When the communication network is characterized by negative factors such as mistrust and insensitivity, poor communication will exist among the agencies in a community.

The establishment of positive inter-agency communication requires effort at several levels. For example, Rivers, Sarata, and Book (1974) have pointed out the potential role that chemical dependency agency secretaries can play in maintaining inter-agency communication. It is important for counselors to understand that adequate communication involves many levels. (They may sometimes assume that communicating with outside agencies is the responsibility of their superiors.) Counselors' actions can add to or detract from, in significant ways, how well agencies may communicate. Another issue is that since interactions among some agencies may be very infrequent, the perception that one agency has of another may be based on the quality of interaction an agency had with a specific counselor.

As in intra-agency communication, it is critical that what is to be communicated is specified as clearly as possible. To reduce inter-agency ambiguity, it is necessary that the agency's intra-agency communication be firmly established and operating properly—a necessary but not sufficient condition for effectively communicating with outside agencies.

Some of the same factors that make intra-agency communication difficult are also problematic in inter-agency communication. The only difference is that inter-agency problems may occur more often and require more effort to deal with than the communication problems within a single agency. There is one built-in problem in inter-agency communication: distance, both physical and psychological. If the physical locations of agencies are close, some natural communication might occur through various staff members who bump into each other in the parking lot, and so forth. However, these casual interactions are not as likely when agencies and their staffs are physically located in various parts of town. This physical distance can retard the development of close personal relationships among the various staffs. When these close personal relationships are not present, then it is possible for rumor and fantasy to increase drastically and for many imagined slights to occur. These negative fantasies can interfere with inter-agency functioning.

Distance as a Factor in Inter-agency Communication

When groups of people are separated from each other, they attempt to maintain order in their perception of an outside group by filling in any missing blanks. Frequently, when they do not know the people in the outside group, they fill in these missing blanks in a negative fashion (i.e., they imagine the worst thing that these people could do to them and their agency and proceed to make it fact). An illustration of how rapidly suspicion, paranoia, and negative fantasy in fellow professionals can be provoked is given in an exercise that was conducted with a group of professionals who were midway through a year-long training program.

The group was initially broken into two subgroups. The exercise required one subgroup to learn an anagram task and then to teach it to the second subgroup. The subgroup that was to teach the task remained on the first floor and, like many community agencies, became totally focused on mastering the task. The members of the second subgroup were sent out of the room, with no explanation of their role or what was to be expected of them, except that the first group would teach them a task and that they were to remain in an upstairs room for about 2 hours. Shortly after reaching the second floor, the subgroup to be trained began to wonder what was going to happen to them. Then they began to wonder if, perhaps, the first subgroup would not try to present the material in such a way as to confuse them and to make them appear silly. As time passed (the first subgroup continued to be totally involved in learning the anagram task), the second subgroup's fantasies about being humiliated became more real. To deal with the anticipated humiliation, they established a password that, when called out, would signal the entire group to leave the building and abandon the training exercise. After 2 hours, the second group was brought back to the first floor for training by the first group. The waiting group's initial reaction was so defensive that someone in the first group eventually thought to ask what was going on. Once the fantasies of the second subgroup were shared with the first group, an attempt was made to deal with their fears. Considerable time and energy were needed to dissipate the suspiciousness and anxiety of the second group by members of the first group.

What is amazing about this situation is that the people in the two subgroups were well acquainted with one another and had formed close working relationships over the previous 6 months of training. They also had regular group meetings, where problems could be worked out. Despite the apparent closeness, separation for a short time—in a situation where one group had been given ambiguous information about the intentions of the other group—produced immediate paranoid fantasies. Following the completion of the exercise, it was pointed out that the first group could have kept the second group in the room while the first group learned the task, and that this not only would have reduced the destructive fantasies of the second group but also would have facilitated the teaching and learning of the task.

Two things are apparent from this exercise. First, if well-acquainted colleagues can become suspicious of one another's motives within a 2-hour period, separated by only a single floor in the same building, imagine the possible difficulties that can arise among agencies separated by several miles and without close working relationships. Second, if the first group had involved the second group in the task from the beginning, all of the problems could have been avoided. When one agency is planning policies that may affect another agency, bringing the second agency in to the planning process from the beginning may significantly reduce the fantasies held by personnel in the second agency.

Dealing With Inter-agency Fantasy and Rumor

Another problem created by distance and inadequate communication patterns is rumor. While the need to check out intra-agency rumors is important, the need to deal constructively with rumors concerning outside agencies is imperative. This is particularly so when these rumors consist of possible negative actions by the outside agency. (Unfortunately, these types of rumors are most frequently negative in nature.) As is the case with intra-agency communication, there is a strong need to confront these inter-agency fantasies and rumors and to build channels of communication that assure that they can be dealt with quickly. Some principles that are potentially helpful in dealing with these problems are outlined below.

Maintaining an Avenue of Communication

In every community, it is necessary to maintain some vehicle of communication among agencies. A coordinating committee (with representatives from all local chemical dependency agencies) that meets regularly is essential. Not only do the meetings allow for people to deal with ongoing practical issues, but they also offer the opportunity to establish a network of people who can check out rumors and fantasies between meetings, quickly and definitively. Delay in dealing with these problems only allows them wider circulation and therefore makes them more "real." Not being as definitive as possible when debunking these erroneous communications gives credence to such rumors and fantasies.

Unambiguous Communication

An agency has the same responsibility to communicate clearly and with minimum ambiguity with other agencies as do individuals. Whenever agencies are dealing with issues and announcements that could draw strong reactions from another agency (e.g., because it is potentially threatening to that agency), it is wise to use multilevel channels of communication. Do not just send a memo! One possible approach might be to first go and talk with an agency representative, discuss the proposed issue at some length, and ask for feedback. Whenever possible, incorporate any suggestions and ask the agency or agencies affected if they would like a representative to come to discuss the issue at a staff meeting. While this may not be necessary with minor issues, the time spent may be less than that needed to resolve poorly communicated messages later. Also, it leaves a given agency with better, not worse, communication links with other agencies.

Long-Range Counselor Job Adjustment: Dealing With Ethical Issues

While new counselors may be overwhelmed with the adjustments necessary to manage a new job in a seemingly brief period of time, they may also be making adjustments to long-term problems of the profession. For example, the new counselor may enter the agency with considerable eagerness to change its policies and procedures and effect rapid and drastic change. The young counselor may see his enemy as the entrenched bureaucracy. One of the adjustments that young counselors must make over time is the transition from neophyte to member of the establishment. While this transition may not seem important to new counselors initially, most counselors will eventually face adjustment to the increased job demands and responsibilities of the experienced counselor (i.e., they will be faced with the responsibility for setting and maintaining the policies of the agency). In brief, every counselor will eventually become part of the establishment.

In the process of surviving in the agency to reach the point of being a part of the establishment, counselors must learn to pace themselves, to cope with the ethical dilemmas confronted in the job place, and to avoid job burnout. A consideration of some of the ethical issues that counselors may face will be presented first. Finally, a discussion of job burnout will be presented and steps that may reduce burnout will be outlined.

Dealing With Unethical Behavior in an Agency

As a drug and alcohol counselor, you will be entering a caregiving area where problems with appropriate ethical behavior abound. It is not true that drug and alcohol counselors are more, or less, ethical than other caregivers; however, they will face as many ethical issues as counselors in the mental health field, and the guidelines provided for them are not infrequently less well defined than those of mental health professionals.

In order for new counselors to manage their own ethical behavior, it is frequently necessary for them to consult counselors more experienced than themselves. Neophyte counselors should never hesitate to ask about an ethical issue, and most professional counselors will continue to seek advice about ethical dilemmas throughout their careers. While concern for following proper ethics should be a central value for counselors, it also has practical survival implications. Every year, one of the major reasons that a significant number of counselors are dismissed from alcohol and drug agencies is that they are judged to have behaved unethically.

It would be impossible to specify all the possible ethical dilemmas that counselors could encounter in their work. To do so would require a listing so lengthy that Google would be needed just to search through it. This section will cover only some of the more obvious potential ethical problems.

Propriety in the Client-Counselor Relationship

A key factor for counselors to consider, when dealing with clients, is that, in the treatment situation, the counselor has considerable power over a person who may be very vulnerable emotionally. Whenever counselors are in a power relationship in a professional setting, they should provide safeguards for themselves and their clients so that this power is not deliberately, or inadvertently, misused. One of the best safeguards is to be alert to the power relationship. Counselors should ask themselves if their actions are likely to be interpreted as taking advantage of the client. Of course, counselors are frequently attempting to get their clients to try new behaviors—to do something that the clients do not choose to do (i.e., to change). Counselors often use the relationship they have with clients to get things accomplished. Most of these interventions are both appropriate and necessary. However, there will be times when counselors' actions toward clients could be seen as questionable. A brief discussion of some of the ethical issues that are most problematic for chemical dependency counselors follows.

Dating a current or former client—It is surprising how many chemical dependency couselors violate this taboo. Most fail to remember that the relationship begins in an unequal power relationship and that this power differential can place the client at a strong disadvantage. Dating a former client seems to be less of an ethical issue until it is remembered that the relationship began with this same power differential while the client was in a vulnerable and impressionable position. Therefore, posttreatment dating has some of the same problems that exist in dating a client in active treatment.

Sexual intercourse with a current or former client—This represents the epitome of taking advantage of the unequal power relationship, and of the client's vulnerability. It is by far most frequent with a male counselor and a female client. Many drug and alcohol counselors see this action as grounds for dismissal from the agency.

Failing to maintain the confidentiality of a client—This is a shady area and one that is sometimes more difficult for chemical dependency counselors than it is for some other caregivers. In many settings, considerable treatment is done by volunteer counselors, and personal data are shared in a casual and open manner. While this atmosphere may be helpful in treatment, it opens up the possibility that information shared by a counselor about a client may be revealed unthinkingly by one of these volunteer counselors. Also, there are frequent visitors to chemical dependency settings, and counselors must be careful about who is within hearing distance when discussing a client. A related problem occurs when information about the client has to be shared with outside agencies. Frequently, law-enforcement authorities or the client's employer may request a report on the client's progress and possible prognosis; making the judgment of just what should be included in these reports must be done very carefully. Here, the seeking of advice from more experienced counselors and finding out how the reports will be used are important steps.

Sharing information with family and friends—While the client may frequently give blanket permission to share information, the counselor may still have to make judgments as to how much information is shared and how it is presented.

There are several other less dramatic examples of unethical behavior: not assuming professional responsibility for clients and not maintaining adequate supervision for oneself is one example; another is misrepresenting one's credentials to an agency in order to gain employment.

The preceding ethical dilemmas are based on the individual actions of a counselor. Frequently, however, the agency in which a counselor is employed may have a supervisor who is engaging in actions that are unethical or not in the best interests of clients or staff. For example, supervisors in an agency may attempt to use their positions to seek sexual favors from subordinates. Or, an agency may not systematically obtain its clients' permission before releasing information. In many states, the latter action would be a violation of state law (in addition to violating federal regulations).

Of course, there will be other situations that are not so clear-cut. In many cases, the counselor will have to make more subtle decisions. When agency policies or actions do not agree with one's perception of correct procedure, it would seem wise to think of these problems as lying on a continuum. For example, counselors might want to see problems of agency procedure improved, but allow their supervisors to deal with such problems. A second point on the continuum might be, "I hold the agency responsible, and I intend to document what is happening." A final point on the continuum might be, "These are actions I can't be a party to, and if I cannot get them changed, I must resign. These actions violate my professional (or personal) ethics and values." In other words, some actions by an agency involve minor borderline violations; others are more serious and may need to be monitored carefully by counselors; still others are so clearly beyond the pale that counselors can only opt for leaving the agency if things are not changed.

Resolving Ethical Problems

In terms of proceeding to deal with these issues, counselors might discuss their concerns on the first level with colleagues, soliciting their opinion, and perhaps even talk to their supervisors about the changes that they perceive are needed. This approach might lead to the elimination of agency policies that the counselors find annoying; of course, it is possible that the counselors will simply have to live with the issue. On the second level, the problems are more acute, and documenting of the issues should occur after the counselors have approached their supervisors and pointed out the problem. If no solution is provided, the counselors verbally (or in writing) should inform superiors that they will be documenting events because they view the issue as an ethical problem for the agency and as one that causes the counselors considerable concern. On the final level, it is assumed that the counselor has gone through the steps described above and, in addition, has met with trusted colleagues inside and outside the agency prior to deciding to leave. Leaving an agency because of unethical practices is sometimes the only thing that can be done; however, the counselor should remember that leaving the agency usually means losing powerful leverage in getting unethical actions and policies changed.

Long-Range Counselor Survival: Job Adjustment and Avoiding Burnout

Modifying Work Goals

Over the span of their careers, social service workers change in the way they approach their jobs. A study of professional workers in several social service agencies found the following changes in new professionals:

- Professionals modified the work goals they had set out to accomplish. The modification was frequently in the direction of accepting more modest goals in terms of job accomplishment.

- There was a strong tendency for professionals to reduce their level of personal involvement in the job. Physical and emotional withdrawal from clients was a common occurrence. This reduced investment in clients was accomplished by reducing the role of work in their lives and increasing fulfillment in their lives outside the workplace.

- There was a tendency for new professionals to shift responsibility for failure from themselves to things outside themselves (e.g., they blamed the clients or the system for failures on the job).

- Over time, young professionals became less idealistic, less trusting, and more conservative in their attitudes toward clients and people in general.

- There was increased concern about self-protection and enhancing their own lives (e.g., gratification of their own needs at work became more important). Also, there was increased concern about salaries and maintaining freedom of action in the job place (Cherniss, 1980).

Reality Shock

These changes were described as occurring because of reality shock. Most of the professionals discussed had little experiential or internship training and thus entered their jobs with idealistic expectations that were not based on the realistic demands of the job. Most chemical dependency counselors do have considerable experiential training before taking their first job; however, while the proportion of the training occurring in real-life settings is high, most chemical dependency counselors spend much less absolute time in training than did the professionals in the above study. In other words, while the experiential training certainly helps to insulate chemical dependency counselors against some of the stresses suffered by these professionals, it is probably still insufficient to prevent many of these same changes from occurring in the lives of substance abuse counselors. In fact, some degree of change in job perception and attitudes toward work in the direction of the changes noted above is probably normal and to be expected. These changes may be necessary for counselors to survive in the workplace. However, when pressures in the workplace are extreme, there is the danger that chemical dependency counselors may experience job burnout.

Counselor Vulnerability to Burnout

Burnout has been described as a frequently occurring event in the lives of those counselors working with people with chemical dependency. Oser, Biebel, Pullen, and Harp (2013) noted, for example, that a person working in the role of drug and alcohol counselor is extremely vulnerable to burnout and that he or she is affected in the following ways:

- Social service work is psychologically fatiguing or stressful.
- Service providers experience and exhibit an identifiable pattern of burnout reactions.

- Behaviors associated with burnout reduce the individual's effectiveness with clients; indeed, burnout can cause the service provider to act in ways that are harmful to clients.

The effects of burnout are potentially harmful not only to clients, but also to the counselor's job performance, job satisfaction, and morale. Thus, burnout can play a crucial role in determining whether the counselor survives in the chemical dependency agency. It is important to first examine the characteristics of burnout that addictions counselors have experienced and reported. The ways these same counselors describe the recognition of burnout in their colleagues is secondarily important. As the following findings indicate, both perspectives are important, because one's perception of burnout changes drastically depending upon whether it is being experienced personally or is being viewed in another person.

Personal Responses to Burnout

Sarata (1982) presents a list of the personal responses to burnout given by participants in a burnout workshop for alcohol counselors (see Table 14.1). The response reported by the largest percentage of counselors was that of being drained, exhausted, and tired of listening and thinking so hard. The fact that burnout can affect self-esteem is reflected in the counselors' reports of feeling helpless, incompetent, and overwhelmed.

A chemical dependency counselor would be wise to become well acquainted with the types of experiences reported by Sarata's (1982) substance abuse treatment counselors. These warning signs can be used to alert counselors that they either need to spend some time away from their jobs or increase their involvement in the maintenance strategies and behaviors that are outlined below. Sarata found that 65% of the counselors involved in his workshop were at a point when they should examine their lives for some possible change; 7% of the counselors were clearly experiencing burnout. These findings suggest that chemical dependency counselors need to spend more time monitoring their job reactions and taking corrective action where needed.

Burnout as Viewed by Others

Table 14.2 presents the ways in which burnout was observed in others. As Table 14.2 shows, counselors suffering burnout are perceived as reacting in ways that are destructive to inter-agency communication; they behave in ways that can affect the morale of the people around them; and their style of dealing with their clients becomes drastically counter-therapeutic. If these descriptions are accurate (they do agree with the authors' observations), they stand as evidence that people who have been outstanding counselors and colleagues can show extreme deterioration as a result of not maintaining themselves on the job. Of course, one should remember that things occurring at home and in the counselor's personal life can be the cause of many of the behaviors linked to burnout;

in other cases, the strain of the job is reflected in the person's home life. Not infrequently, there is an interaction between what is going on at work and the reaction of people at home. However, in some cases, the person will report feeling better and more relaxed away from work and then report headaches, anger, and frustration shortly after arriving at the workplace. Such dramatic changes may reflect burnout or extreme dissatisfaction with the job, or both.

Maintaining Peak Counselor Efficiency: Avoiding Burnout

At this point, it is important to outline some ways in which chemical dependency counselors may maintain themselves at peak work performance, as well as point out some of the traps that many chemical dependency counselors fall into in the workplace.

Table 14.1
Phrases Used by Alcoholism Counselors to Describe Their Burnout Experiences

Respondents (N = 93)	Responses (N = 348)	Type of Phrase
71%	19%	Drained, exhausted (e.g., "tired of thinking so hard and listening so intently")
45%	12%	Helpless, incompetent, overwhelmed (e.g., "the faster I worked, the behinder I got")
34%	9%	Angry (e.g., "wanting to lash out")
30%	8%	Depressed
30%	8%	Anxious, fearful (e.g., "scared for self and clients")
26%	7%	Emotionally troubled, volatile (e.g., "losing control of self, uptight")
26%	7%	Irritable
17%	4%	Frustrated (e.g., "about what I failed to accomplish")
16%	4%	Alone (e.g., "dumped upon and unsupported")
16%	4%	Wanting to escape (e.g., "hoping clients don't show, dreaming about my vacation")
12%	3%	Resentful (e.g., "everyone is making demands")
10%	3%	Misunderstood and/or sorry for self
10%	3%	Uncaring
7%	2%	Caring too much (e.g., "taking cases home")
	6%	Other (e.g., "rigid, controlling, critical of others, having tunnel vision")

Note. From *Burnout Workshops for Alcoholism Counselors*, by P. B. V. Sarata, 1982. Unpublished paper.

Maintaining a Life Outside the Agency

Many counselors feel that a measure of devotion to their job is the fact that they are totally committed to it. Counselors should be acutely aware that they need to discriminate between values directed toward work, and values directed toward other things in life. Both are important in maintaining long-range peak performance on the job. For example, maintaining relationships with family and friends can give counselors a time-out from the job place, allowing them to get needed emotional support and psychological repair following a bad day at the office. A counselor's failure to maintain an outside life may not have drastic effects on counselor performance in the short run, but grave risks are run if the counselor remains totally involved over a long period of time (e.g., several years). For one thing, the necessary network to emotionally support the counselor once he or she experiences burnout simply will not be there when it is needed (e.g., family and friends will be more distant and less readily available when the counselor needs their support). With individuals who have not practiced personal maintenance, it may be necessary to leave the alcohol or drug field for several years in order to recharge their batteries—a practice common to chemical dependency counselors who simply do not, or cannot, work without making the job their total life commitment.

Making a more qualified commitment to the drug and alcohol field is particularly difficult for those counselors who are themselves in recovery. For example, it is frequently difficult for recovering counselors to discriminate among the job, the work needed for A.A. maintenance, and maintaining close relationships with friends (many of whom are in recovery themselves). In this situation, there is generally considerable mutual support. However, there is also the tendency to get into a pattern where one talks shop constantly, and the arena of one's life is drastically narrowed. Thus, the very necessary distractions of doing other things and not obsessively dwelling on job-related issues are lost.

Modeling a Balanced Life

While the above adjustments are important for preventing burnout, there are some other issues that are just as crucial. Drug and alcohol counselors, like all caregivers, are modelers of appropriate behavior for their clients. In fact, modeling is emphasized by recovering counselors, and they will frequently point out similarities between their history and personality and those of clients. In some cases, counselors give specific advice about methods and procedures that clients can use to deal with their alcohol or drug problems from the perspective of "This is the way I managed it and so can you." However, when recovering counselors also model a life that is filled with little but work, they are modeling behavior that the large majority of people would see as inappropriate. In other words, the counselor who maintains a balanced life presents a healthier model for the client to emulate. This notion of a healthy, balanced life as a useful tool

Table 14.2

**Phrases Used by Alcoholism Counselors to Describe Indicators
of Burnout Among Coworkers**

Respondents (N = 93)	Responses (N = 298)	Type of Indicator
45%	16%	Withdrawn, isolated, silent, shuts office door, won't discuss work with others
35%	11%	Complaining, bitches about everything
32%	10%	Spaced-out, can't follow conversation, only half listening, forgetful
20%	7%	Avoids work, absent, clock watching, does personal errands, tardy
19%	7%	Critical of others, blames co-workers, scolds clients, terminates problem cases
16%	6%	Depressed, loss of confidence, perseverates about mistakes, turns every conversation to pessimistic side
16%	5%	Procrastination, does only enough to get through each day
13%	5%	Loss of objectivity, gets overinvolved with clients, misreads clients
12%	4%	Emotionally flat, flat affect, lacks enthusiasm, loss of concern
12%	4%	Emotionally volatile, paranoid, screams, throws things
10%	4%	Physical problems
10%	4%	Very busy, hassled, too busy for anything
	15%	Other (e.g., inflexible, tunnel vision, poor hygiene, smokes too much)

Note. From *Burnout Workshops for Alcoholism Counselors*, by P. B. V. Sarata, 1982. Unpublished paper.

in caregiving has frequently been under-estimated by substance abuse counselors. Many recovering counselors seem to turn their obsession with drugs and alcohol into an obsession with work; they become workaholics.

Dealing With Excessive Agency Work Demands

Recovering counselors (and many non-recovering counselors) are extremely dedicated and committed to the alcohol field and to the clients they serve. Frequently, chemical dependency agencies take advantage of these dedicated counselors. They are the ones who are persuaded to spend extra hours at the facility and who can be counted on to volunteer for the many extra services needed by the agency. Often the supervisor will involve the dedicated counselor in additional tasks simply because the supervisor is not alert to the possible consequences of his actions. Yet other supervisors are unscrupulous in their use of people or are eager to find a quick and simple solution. Whatever the reason, the counselor should be alert to the possibility of being used, since it increases the risk of early job burnout.

Maintaining a Reasonable Caseload

The heavier the workload, the greater the tendency for counselors to suffer burnout. It has been pointed out that it is not simply the long hours that create burnout; rather, it seems to be the increased direct contact with clients (Cherniss, 1980). Since intense involvement with clients is characteristic of the substance abuse field, counselors should be particularly wary here. A heavier client workload is manageable if there are frequent time-outs from client contact; another way of saying this is that the quality of workload, as well as the amount of time spent with clients, affects the burnout rate.

Another quality-of-workload factor is the scope of client contact (i.e., the range of problems addressed by a professional working with a particular client and the extent to which the counselor sees the client in different kinds of situations). For example, counselors may never have the opportunity to follow up on their successful cases; thus, they only see those clients who are re-admitted for treatment. Therefore, counselors only receive negative feedback from populations who typically experience high relapse rates (e.g., a detox unit) and receive almost no feedback about the people they have helped, because all their time is spent meeting the needs of their so-called failures. For this reason, establishing some sort of follow-up system for successful cases may be a useful strategy, not only to better evaluate effectiveness, but also to help prevent burnout. In brief, counselors will deal more effectively with job stress when they are exposed to the full range of clients' lives—from detoxification to long-range recovery.

Ambiguous Agency Goals and Objectives

A factor that seems to affect a new professional's burnout rate (and one that is present in some substance abuse agencies) is a lack of clarity about agency goals and expectations (Cherniss, 1980). When the guidelines that counselors are expected to follow are changed from week to week, counselors, who are still uncertain about their competence, face an additional stress in the job place. When counselors survive the initial stress created by a lack of structure, they may, with more experience and confidence, exploit this ambiguity. For example, in an unstructured situation, it may be possible to secure more advantageous working conditions for counselors and better services for their clients. However, in the initial stages, the ambiguity or conflict in goals only increases the new counselors' sense of helplessness.

Maintaining a Reasonable Job Perspective

Frequently, counselors fail to maintain a reasonable perspective regarding their own job and the agency in which they work. The ability to maintain an awareness of one's own limitations, the limitations of the agency where one works, and the limitations of the substance abuse field in general is crucial to chemical dependency counselors. In order to obtain a realistic perspective on these factors, the chemical dependency counselor may need to do several things. For example, counselors should attend outside conferences and communicate with other agencies in and out of the substance abuse field as often as possible. If counselors do not maintain contact with other agencies, they begin to see the way their agency does things as the only way to approach the treatment of substance abuse, which causes an egocentric approach to treatment—a particular problem in the substance abuse field.

Maintaining Contact With Other Professionals

The author has been at several conventions where different groups described approximately the same type of program as new and innovative. None of the groups were aware that the other groups had similar programs (and similar problems), so an opportunity to compare how specific problems could be dealt with was lost. This tendency to become self-centered and self-satisfied can lead to a selective gathering of information and a failure to appreciate other ways of doing the job.

Being open to new information and seeking it out are important in preventing burnout. One of the things that seems to work to prevent burnout is to explore new and different ways of thinking about the job. Maintaining in-service training programs and attending outside workshops and various other outside training experiences are ways of insulating against burnout and the consequent drop in the quality of care for clients. A penny-wise-and-pound-foolish stance by an agency is to fail to subsidize attendance at these training experiences and to insist that all of the counselor's time be spent with clients. The result of this lack of professional stimulation is that counselors become less motivated and show many of the signs of burnout noted above. An indirect benefit of having counselors involved in outside training experiences is that they become more open to other points of view (and to other agencies), thus improving communication possibilities with other community agencies. They also keep up with new ideas and innovations in the field much better.

Staff Support Groups

There are some additional strategies that may help to prevent burnout. These methods of dealing with job burnout are somewhat more dependent on the existing structure, policies, and attitudes of an agency than those noted above. One strategy is for newer counselors to develop a staff support group. These groups provide opportunities to regularly discuss and analyze burnout experiences with others who are working in similar situations, which tends to reduce burnout and its effects. In support groups, counselors from the same agency or from different agencies come together, usually on a regular basis, to talk about their work experiences. There is usually no formal leader and as little structure as possible. Typically, counselors share job-related satisfactions, frustrations, and uncertainties. Those with specific problems can present them to the group and receive concrete suggestions. There is also an atmosphere of acceptance and concern by group members. The danger here is that these groups can turn into "bitch" sessions. A genuine effort must be made to go beyond simply sharing emotions to suggesting new attitudes and strategies for dealing with problems. A real danger is that the group can become dominated by members who have already burned out. Since the attitudes that are associated with burnout are highly contagious, especially where a high degree of burnout already exists in an agency, the forming of a support group from existing staff may be counterproductive for the less experienced counselors.

Rotating Workloads

Another strategy that is designed to provide variety for counselors in the workplace is to rotate counselors' workloads. For example, taking a turn at performing the intake sessions in an agency offers an opportunity for relief from ongoing routine. One chemical dependency intake-and-referral agency asked each counselor to spend one day each month visiting clients who have been referred for inpatient treatment (and their agencies). These visits improved communication with outside agencies and provided some variety for the drug and alcohol counselors. Another possible adjustment is to make sure that counselors see a variety of clients. In some drug and alcohol agencies, new counselors may initially be assigned more revolving-door clients because these clients are seen as less rewarding by the rest of the staff. While many of those with addictions issues recover, the success rate is usually low, further placing stress on new counselors who may already be struggling with feelings of self-doubt about their competence.

Performance Feedback

Still another procedure to help reduce the burnout rate is to increase performance feedback for new counselors. Many agencies are casual about feedback, and the new counselor must be assertive enough to ask for it. (This is sometimes difficult for counselors to do when they are already unsure of their ability.) Feedback is particularly important during the first six months of the job and should be given frequently.

One way that an inexperienced counselor can obtain feedback is to work with a more experienced counselor in seeing one or more clients. For example, the new counselor might work with an experienced counselor on a family case or a marital problem or co-lead a group with another counselor. These experiences are instructive and a chance to gain some estimate of one's performance relative to that of a more experienced counselor in the agency. This procedure also helps reduce the new counselor's social isolation in the agency.

Finally, factors that are not under the counselors' control may reduce or speed up burnout. For example, burnout is less likely for those counselors working in agencies with clear and consistent goals. Defining clear and consistent goals is, unfortunately, a task that is difficult for many substance abuse agencies. New counselors should be aware of this job stress and realize that it may have a severe impact on them. They should also be aware that changing this may be beyond their control; learning to live with the ambiguity or leaving the agency may be the only choices they have. An associated issue is that the agency should have realistic goals. Many agencies have grandiose notions about their missions. Administrators in these agencies may demand that counselors carry 40 clients per week in individual counseling, maintain liaison with local agencies, and keep all records and charts up to date. Unfortunately, these high work demands cannot be met, and it is precisely those dedicated and committed counselors who hate cutting corners and doing shoddy work who suffer the most (i.e., they are the staff most likely to burn out in their attempt to keep up with the unrealistic work demands).

As this discussion shows, burnout is indeed a very serious problem for substance abuse agencies. However, the points outlined above should allow the chemical dependency counselor to avoid many of the problems associated with burnout. In the final analysis, it may be necessary for some people to work at other jobs periodically in order to regain the motivation and drive to work effectively in the alcohol or drug field.

Job Selection: A Critical Choice in Counselor Survival

Taking a job is a difficult experience under the best of circumstances, especially for a new counselor. Whether the job applicant is a newly trained counselor or very experienced, he or she will be making choices about whether to take a job with incomplete knowledge of how a given agency functions. Knowledge about the agency may be so scarce that the counselor may not even know what questions to ask. In some cases, counselors may feel that they should not ask too many questions since that might make them appear too pushy to the potential employer.

In the author's experience, most agencies are impressed by an applicant who is able to ask informed and appropriate questions about a position. Most interpret such questions as reflecting interest in their agency and as coming from an applicant who will be a thoughtful, knowledgeable, and invested employee. Of course, the major issue here is how questions are asked about the job. On the one hand, applicants who are insensitive to the needs of the inter-viewer, or are too blunt in posing questions, may do themselves considerable harm. On the other hand, most agency employers will respond positively to well-thought-out questions that reflect some knowledge of the agency and a genuine interest in learning more about the job.

Finding Out About Your Potential Employer

Getting to be an informed job applicant does require some effort, but it will usually pay off in better job selection. Some of the procedures for getting pre-pared to ask sensible questions about the job are discussed below.

Read as Much About the Agency as Possible

Frequently, agencies will have websites and put out pamphlets to describe their mission, types of clients served, and so forth. While these websites and pam-phlets are frequently idealized descriptions of the agency and therefore should be accepted with caution, they do give the counselor an idea of how, ideally, the agency sees itself functioning. They can also allow the counselor, in conjunc-tion with information gathered through other sources, to find out how well the agency has met its idealized goals. If there is minimal overlap between how the agency sees itself and how it seems to function, it would be important to ask, in the interview, what the agency does, how it functions, and what its mission is (to see if these inconsistencies can be resolved). An agency that has gross in-consistencies between its mission statement and what it actually does may be an agency in considerable turmoil—and it may be a tough place in which to work.

Find Out as Much as You Can About the Agency
From Other Community Agencies

Information from other agencies must be used with caution. The intense po-liticization of the drug and alcohol field can produce some distortion in one agency's views of another agency (because of vested interests), and this factor must be weighed when very negative impressions of a given agency are being expressed. Coordinating groups made up of local alcohol and drug counselors who deal with several chemical dependency agencies in the community may provide some important feedback. In any case, it would be wise to ask several agencies, in an informal way, how they see the prospective employing agency. As noted below, an agency that maintains clear and open communication with other agencies is likely to be more efficient and create less frustration for its employees. Less conflict with outside agencies means that counselors will have more resources available to do their job and will be less likely to suffer burnout.

How the Agency Fits Into the Overall Community System

Another factor that job applicants are likely to overlook is how the agency fits into the overall service delivery system in a community. For example, what need is the agency meeting in the community, and is it likely that the need will continue to be a high priority for the community? The reality of all job situations is that they are more likely to continue if they are perceived as needed by the people who provide the funding. Therefore, establishing whether the agency plays an important role in the continuum of care (in the opinion of coordinating agencies and other agencies in the community) may give the counselor a sense of job security potential for the agency. In this same vein, it might be important to ask outside sources (and try to glean from the written information on the agency) what the future role of the agency is likely to be. Not infrequently, agencies can make drastic changes in role and function, and counselors who thought they were taking a job in an agency with one mission suddenly find that they are in an agency with another mission altogether. Also, even if the counselors have worked in agencies with the same explicit role and function, they cannot take for granted that they know what the new agency does. It is wise to treat each new job situation as one in which the counselor goes through considerable data collection prior to the interview, regardless of how much the counselor thinks he knows about the agency. Both the counselor and his future employer will benefit from this approach.[3]

Agency Overseeing Authority

A question that may initially escape the counselor (but that may prove to be important once employment is undertaken) is, To whom does the agency answer in terms of ultimate responsibility? Is it the city council, county commissioners, a state agency, a board of directors, or some other group? If possible, you should also try to find out how actively the overseeing body is involved in agency decisions and day-to-day administration. Generally speaking, overseeing authorities are responsible for setting policy, while supervisory personnel in the agency are responsible for day-to-day decisions on how the work is done (i.e., how the policies are to be implemented). A rule of thumb is that overseeing authorities should not be involved in program administration because they are not as aware of how the agency functions as are the on-site administrators. When the overseeing agency is heavily involved, it frequently means that the agency has serious internal problems. For example, it may mean that the board has lost confidence in the administrative head of the agency. It could also mean that the governing board is composed of people who will not allow the agency to function without their steady input. Or, it could mean there have been serious blowups within the agency or between the agency and the community at large. None of these things bode well for a counselor and will most surely increase the job stress under which the counselor must work.

---

3   The author is indebted to Phillip Tegler, Director of Directions, an employee assistance program, for suggestions about things that counselors should inquire about prior to taking a job at an agency. Mr. Tegler is a former staff member of the survival skills program, Southeast Community College, Lincoln, Nebraska.

Basic Personality Types in Caregiving Agencies

In addition to what you find out about the agency, it is important to have an awareness of who you are and what you want from a job, before you proceed with the interview. While there are several ways to answer this type of question, one way may be to look closely at what your primary needs are. Cherniss (1980) outlined four basic types of people whom he found working in human service agencies. While any general description of caregivers is bound to be an oversimplification, these career orientations may be helpful to counselors in outlining their own primary needs.

Social Activists

These individuals want to do more in their daily work than provide help to a given client. Personal security and status seem to mean very little to these people: Their primary objective is to bring about some type of social and institutional change that would better the lives of the people they seek to help. In brief, these individuals seem to be concerned with social values and wish to work with people who share their ideology and commitment to social change. In the chemical dependency field, there are many people seeking to change the way the system delivers services or meets the needs of clients with chemical dependency. Many of them are frustrated because they have entered agencies where it is difficult to be involved with or bring about these system changes. The types of agencies in the chemical dependency field that are most apt to accomplish these goals are not likely to be direct-service agencies; instead, they are likely to be state agencies, coordinating and advocacy groups such as the local alcohol and drug councils, or alcohol and drug foundation groups.

Careerists

Cherniss (1980) sees the individuals in this group as seeking success as it is conventionally defined. Prestige, respectability, and financial security are what is important to careerists. These individuals want to make a good impression on colleagues, supervisors, and anyone else who might control their career advancement. While the chemical dependency field frequently disparages people who seek career advancement, these individuals usually are sympathetic, caring, and helpful to the clients they serve, and they provide a high level of service—it is just that their primary goal is to secure recognition and advancement. If career and job advancement are important to counselors, then they should find out which opportunities exist in the agency for advancement and whether a job there can be a solid preparation for seeking a better job in another agency. The use of a job to advance one's career may initially seem distasteful to some counselors, but careful career planning may mean that they get to where they want to go in a more efficient and better-prepared manner.

Artisans

To these individuals, the issues of career advancement and financial success are less important than the intrinsic quality of their work. Professional service and growth are also important to these service givers. They wish to perform well, according to their own internal standards. Cherniss (1980) sees the individuals in this group as the most individualistic. They tend to value autonomy and independence more highly than do social activists or careerists, they tend to be less competitive than individuals in these other groups, and they like working with people who know more than they do because they can learn from them. Cherniss found that artisans will tend to leave a job (even when seen as successful by the agency that employs them) simply because the job is no longer stimulating and challenging. Those who feel that this description fits them should be concerned about things like the ability to work independently with minimal constraints from supervisors. Individuals such as these would probably prefer an agency that stresses the individual professional responsibility and authority of the counselor; they would also like to be in an agency with stimulating personnel from whom they can learn. Frequently, these attributes are found in agencies that are trying a new approach to treatment or are trying to deal with chemical dependency issues in a new way. These individuals would be very unhappy in an agency where there were severe bureaucratic barriers and demands and where there is a rigid authoritarian chain of command in terms of supervision.

Self-Investors

Self-investors are more involved in their life outside work than in their careers. These individuals are not motivated by work-related concerns. In general, they seek interesting work that is moderately challenging but that does not demand too much of them. They also desire pleasant, friendly co-workers and supervisors. If your job is not going to be the central part of your life, you may want an agency that is less demanding in terms of workload. You might also seek a place where the people seem to get along well with one another and value their interaction with one another very highly. While some people might view this role as inferior to some of the others mentioned, it may be realistic for many counselors. For example, if a man or woman has a major investment in maintaining the family, such a job may be the most appropriate choice. It should be noted that Cherniss (1980) found that people with this career orientation were committed to maintaining an adequate performance level and that they would work extremely hard to bring their work level up to an acceptable standard.

Cherniss (1980) has been careful to point out that most people are really a mixture of all four of these types. In fact, he has a fifth category called a "mixed type" that combines qualities of the other four types. At the very least, a consideration of these types of career orientations should allow counselors to come up with their own set of job requirements: requirements that will fit their specific needs. Such a procedure should help clarify exactly what the counselor may want from a job and lead to his or her asking appropriate questions in the job interview.

The Job Interview

If you are well prepared and have an understanding of the things you want to ask, you can obtain a considerable amount of important information from a job interview. For example, you will want to get as precise a job description as possible from the person who is responsible for hiring you. You may want to know who will supervise you and to whom you will answer in the agency. It may be important to ask about where you will be housed, office availability, and so forth. It goes without saying that you should also ask about salary and the possibility of raises. All of these questions are relevant and important; however, there may be other issues that are even more important.

Orientation Period

Find out if the agency usually has an orientation period where the new counselor can become acquainted with the agency and the job, which will provide the means and the time for new employees to learn the tasks that will allow them to do their job more easily and effectively. Cherniss (1980) found that if counselors were dropped into a new job without orientation or a chance to get their feet on the ground, they were less likely to have a positive attitude toward the job and more likely to suffer burnout.

Workload Demands

Try to establish the workload demands that the agency expects. Generally speaking, the greater the workload, the greater the probability for burnout. Even a heavy workload can be managed, though, if there are frequent opportunities for time-outs from face-to-face contact with clients. It is also important to determine the range of client contact available. Being responsible for a variety of different clients and being able to follow the same client through the system can help prevent burnout.

Degree of Job Stimulation

It is important to determine the amount of intellectual stimulation, challenge, and variety in the job. These factors will determine whether a counselor suffers burnout: The more of these characteristics that are present in the job, the less likely it is that the counselor will suffer burnout.

Degree of Job Freedom

Try to find out how much freedom you will have on the job because rigid bureaucratic control of a counselor's actions in the job place can lead to more rapid burnout. (This may be an important thing to find out about an agency during the interview. For example, psychiatric hospitals usually have more rigid bureaucratic control than does an outpatient alcohol treatment center.) If freedom to do the job your way and on your own schedule is important to you, it would be especially wise to ask current employees about the amount of autonomy that they feel they have.

Clearly Defined Agency Goals and Expectations

Try to find out in the interview (or from counselors currently working in the agency) how clearly the goals and expectations of the agency are spelled out to counselors. If guidelines and policies are unclear or if they change from week to week, the danger of job burnout increases.

Compatible Outlook and Beliefs

Try to establish whether the agency and the people working in it have beliefs and an outlook on life that are compatible with your own. Differences in outlook and beliefs are major sources of dissension in social care agencies. An awareness of these issues will give you a chance to ask questions about all of the above areas of concern. Finally, you should establish the job's time demands. You must also ask yourself whether these time demands are consistent with your life roles. If you are married, with heavy family responsibilities, 15-hour days may not be appropriate for you. In conjunction with this question, you should try to ascertain whether the agency has realistic expectations and goals. Sometimes chemical dependency agencies expect staff to work extremely long days because the agency is unrealistic about the goals it is attempting to accomplish. One final comment is in order: It is unrealistic for applicant counselors to believe that they can come into an agency and bring about dramatic change. That is why it is so important to know the agency as well as possible before becoming a part of it: To not be fully aware of the agency eventually leads to lowered morale, frustration, and fatigue (i.e., burnout), and the counselor is unlikely to stay.

This chapter has outlined some of the problems that are faced by chemical dependency counselors in working with clients and the agencies that employ the counselor. As we have seen, chemical dependency counselors are faced with heavy—sometimes unreasonable—demands from the clients that they have in treatment. These demands are exacerbated by the fact that the treatment of those with substance abuse requires a counselor's strong, caring commitment in order to be effective. This situation places the chemical dependency counselor at risk for burnout. Stress on the counselor increases when emotional energy is directed toward dealing with communication problems within and among agencies. These intra-agency staff struggles (e.g., between lay and professional counselors) rob counselors of emotional energy and negatively affect the clients under their care. It has been pointed out here that there are actions that alcohol counselors can take to ensure their survival as viable, helping therapists throughout their employment in the chemical dependency field. Factors to consider when choosing a job (such as matching oneself with the appropriate agency depending on one's own needs and the agency's expectations of counselors) have been noted. It has also been pointed out that chemical dependency counselors should be aware of some of the possible adjustments they may need to make over time in their role in an agency. Finally, an attempt has been made to illuminate some of the issues that counselors will face in the chemical dependency field and how they can often effectively prevent or reduce problems that could affect their emotional and vocational survival.

This chapter has focused on issues of survival for the chemical dependency counselor working in a substance abuse agency. Adjustments that a chemical dependency counselor might have to make in other agencies (e.g., a correctional facility, the general hospital, industry, and the many other settings where the counselor could be employed) have not been dealt with specifically. It is hoped that chemical dependency counselors working in these settings will find many of the things discussed here useful to them. As chemical dependency caregivers become involved in new agencies, there will doubtless be workplace adjustments that differ somewhat across all settings.

At the present time, the number of personnel in the chemical dependency field has increased markedly. While some of this increase is no doubt tied to increased funding in the substance abuse area, it is also due partly to the discovery, by many people, that working with chemically dependent people is highly rewarding. While this chapter has focused on managing some of the difficulties of working as a chemical dependency counselor, it should be noted that most chemical dependency counselors find the work exciting and gratifying. There are few places in the human caregiving system where a remarkable turnaround in a person's life can be accomplished as dramatically and as rapidly. It is hoped that the issues covered in this chapter will help counselors maintain the enthusiasm and excitement with which they initially entered the field. In our opinion, their excitement is justified.

Addendum

When the material in this chapter was first written, in the early 1980s, much of the direct work with clients and patients in the field was done by alcohol and drug counselors. While that is still true in many states, there have been some significant changes in the type of personnel used in many agencies. According to the Institute of Medicine (1990), there was

> a reinfusion of psychologists and psychiatrists in the treatment
> force in the late 1970s after the development of a network of

nonmedical programs in the 1960s and early 1970s. . . . Today, given the need to develop programs that could receive third party health insurance funding, program accreditation standards often require that physicians take on supervisory and administrative responsibility for clinical operations and that treatment be carried out only by primary therapists who meet specific educational or licensing standards. (p. 125)

These shifts in who is ultimately responsible for treatment have been accompanied by professionals' more reasonable perceptions of those with alcoholism. In a survey of 100 mental health professionals working in a Veterans Administration Hospital, the majority were found to be open to diagnosing and referring for treatment people who had alcohol problems. For example, 96% of the sample reported that they would refer a client with alcoholism to Alcoholics Anonymous even though many of them did not know what the Big Book was. These researchers conclude that there has been "a marked improvement noted in professional attitudes toward alcoholic patients" (Schwartz & Taylor, 1989, p. 322).

These shifts in attitudes may explain part of the reason why there is an increasing involvement of professionals in the substance abuse field. Of course, these changes in attitudes are also related to the fact that there has been an increasing demand by third-party payers that the services they pay for be done by licensed professionals.

These shifts during the 1980s, 1990s, and 2000s in what and whom third-party payers will fund have had a tremendous impact on the alcohol and drug field in general and on the alcohol and drug counselor in particular. With the recent diagnostic changes contained within the DSM-5 (American Psychiatric Association, 2013), there is concern that insurance reimbursement may only be provided for those who meet the criteria for a "severe" diagnosis, thus leaving out a large percentage of folks needing treatment whose diagnoses are "mild" or "moderate" (Straussner, 2014b). Many programs have had to find new funding, and many counselors have found that they no longer fulfill the requirements such programs must meet in order to be reimbursed for evaluation and treatment.

In addition, many programs have gone out of business or downsized because the previous funding from insurance companies no longer will support inpatient treatment programs. This closing of programs and downsizing means that there are many more drug and alcohol counselors who have had to find new employment with another alcohol or drug agency or else leave the field entirely.

This shift has led to a transitional period in which many of the personnel working in the field are identified as "alcoholism counselors" regardless of their original discipline and training, and in which the non-degreed, recovering person who has become a counselor or administrator is feeling shunted aside by the professionals and the funding agencies (Institute of Medicine, 1990, p. 125).

This change in how the field is manned is still in flux. For the purposes of this addendum, the possible changes that the drug and alcohol counselor must adjust to will be discussed. In addition, some ideas will be explored as to how current counselors who find themselves deficient in credentials might approach retraining. Finally, the possible impact of increased training on the alcohol and drug treatment field will be examined.

There are several possible ways in which drug and alcohol counselors may be asked to change. There may be more emphasis on a multicausal approach to substance abuse. This will mean that drug and alcohol counselors must become aware of how a combination of factors can contribute to a person's becoming a substance abuser. Knowledge of the differential effects of family history, genetic factors, and personality factors on substance abuse must be understood. In addition, social and economic contextual issues will have to be factored in as possible concerns that could have elicited the problem. While these issues are often currently asked about in chemical dependency agencies, it is rare to see a selective, differential treatment plan that is based on that information.

To be able to establish differential treatment plans, the drug and alcohol counselor of the future must have a background that includes both general information about the precursors and associated problem areas *and* specific technologies that can be used to intervene. This future counselor must be educated in multiple areas, including psychology, sociology, social work, health education, and intervention technologies. It seems increasingly probable that this type of sophisticated training will require someone who is educated at the master's degree level or beyond.

Many of today's counselors would probably agree that training to this new level is either beyond them or of little interest to them. They would like to continue the role they have had over the past several decades, a role that has placed an emphasis on a close personal relationship with the person trying to recover from substance abuse. Some will resist any retraining and may be lost to the field as it moves beyond the disease model or the Minnesota Model approach.

Others will be quick to understand that the substance abuse field has always been one that "uses what works" and that the focus of concern should be helping the client. Many of today's drug and alcohol counselors may play important roles at what Rosenberg (1974) calls "paraprofessionals" and that future labelers might call "addiction technicians." That is, they will be individuals who carry out treatment plans established by the "drug and alcohol counselor" or master's-degree-level supervisor.

Of course, the new roles will carry with them not only differing levels of responsibility, but also differing levels of pay. While alcohol and drug counselors have never been paid salaries appropriate to their work demands and dedication, these lower-level jobs may be reduced in pay scale in order to hire the more advanced, better trained, and more credentialed "alcohol counselor" of the future. Whether this change results in better treatment is debatable:

> [Is it] possible that after years of developing a specialized discipline of "substance abuse" or "addiction," the new "behavioral health" field resulting from the combination of mental health and substance abuse . . . may move us back instead of forward in helping individuals with substance use problems? (Straussner, 2014b, p. 540)

However, no one can predict the future. As this is being written, health coverage continues to be debated in Congress and by the public. It may well be that little will change in the substance abuse field and things will return to their previous form if the national health debate is resolved. It may be that there will be a mandate for 30-day inpatient treatment as the treatment of choice. However, that seems unlikely. Whatever the choice of care, the issue of accountability and the need to demonstrate positive outcome for treatment that is economically viable will be an important treatment demand. Program evaluation and outside monitoring is likely to be required in any federal- and state-funded programs of the future. Similar and perhaps even more demanding proof of effectiveness may be asked of those agencies who are funded primarily by third-party payers.

One of the reasons that there is so much pressure on the alcohol and drug field is that several studies have demonstrated that there is little difference between relatively longer term inpatient treatment and lower cost outpatient therapy (Jung, 1994). In brief, this finding has forced a re-evaluation of alcohol and drug treatment by those who pay (i.e., the insurance companies).

Since the longer-term disease-based inpatient programs have not been demonstrated through rigorous research to be more effective than shorter and less expensive outpatient programs for the majority of those with addictions, insurance companies have been given the data to challenge these inpatient programs. At the same time, the concept of managed care has been developed to reduce costs. For example, if a person in treatment, say a person with alcoholism, is suicidal when first admitted, just as soon as he is detoxed enough and his depression has lifted, he will be declared as not needing inpatient treatment because he is no longer depressed and thus is no longer suicidal.

The fact that third-party payers may not as readily fund inpatient programs is not the only change. At the heart of this change has been the change in the way alcohol and drug problems are perceived. An emphasis on viewing substance abuse as a multifactorial problem has been established and accepted (Lewis, 2014; Miller, Forcehimes, & Zweben, 2011; Straussner, 2014a). There has also been an increasing emphasis on outcome-related research to demonstrate which types of programs and treatments work best for which types of patients. In the main, much of this outcome research has come out of behavioral and family therapy approaches because these approaches have had more of a research focus than have programs with an A.A. or Minnesota Model orientation. Many texts argue the position that addiction should be viewed as a multicausal problem. Thus, the field sees alcohol and drug problems as more complex disorders and as needing more varied approaches to treatment. For example, Witters, Venturelli, and Hanson (1992) have indicated that "drug use and misuse . . . go beyond body and mind reactions. Drug problems involve families, places of employment, neighborhoods, communities, educational and religious institutions, local, regional, national and even international social, political, and economic boundaries" (p. xii).

This increasing complexity has led to the notion that patients should be matched with programs and services. This has become important because it has been found that patient involvement in treatment is, at least in some studies, dependent on whether their perception of what is needed for them to get better is consistent with the philosophy of the treatment program. Marlatt (1988) put it this way:

> In our own laboratory, my colleagues and I have found that personal beliefs about the nature of the addiction problem and associated approaches to treatment are important determinants of treatment compliance. [In a study on smoking . . . it was found that subjects mismatched in treatment assignment (based on their underlying beliefs about the etiology of the problem) were significantly more likely to discontinue treatment than subjects who received a treatment program that was matched with their personal belief system. (p. 478)

The idea that patients can be matched with the treatment philosophy that they are most in agreement with is certainly not new. However, while the Minnesota Model has been the one often applied to treatment in the past two decades, the increase in knowledge about new treatment approaches means that more individualized treatment for each client is now possible. Programs that previously emphasized a single approach to treatment (or offered an unmatched "cafeteria plan," where all patients were exposed to several types of treatment programs, e.g., from individual to group therapy to "rapping with the chaplain") must now demonstrate that they are effective with a wide range of patients. They must also show that they can match treatment to patient needs.

There will be a new need for retraining many of the counselors so that they can effectively use the new treatment technologies. While some people might feel that it would be better to start from scratch and train a new cadre of treatment agents for alcohol and drug abusers, the "old" counselors (and especially the recovering ones) bring a commitment of care and concern for their patients that is rarely seen in the caregiving systems of this country.

In order to profit from retraining, these counselors must be open to new ways of getting their job done. For example, they may have to try techniques not usually included in 12-step treatment programs. This will require some dramatic changes in how counselors approach treatment. Change is never easy. It is even more difficult when one is asked to even slightly deemphasize a method that has been self-validated. This is very likely the case with the 12-step model in so many recovering counselors' lives. If, however, these newer technologies, including motivational counseling (Miller & Rollnick, 2013), brief interventions including SBIRT for those working in medical settings (Marlatt & Witkiewitz, 2010), and other more recent specific approaches to treating problem drinking and alcohol use problems can be utilized by these dedicated counselors, then both clients and the alcohol and drug treatment field will profit.

Learning these new skills will not be easy. But there is excitement in change. And the alcohol and drug counselor who has been in the field for as long as a decade or more can look back at the many changes he or she has faced and dealt with already. So the best way to deal with future change is to view it as an opportunity that can reinvigorate the field and the counselor. And, more importantly, it can provide better care for clients, which is the bottom line for all caregivers in the alcohol and drug field. Such change should be faced with some comfort since almost all alcohol and drug counselors have survived major changes in the field in the past and, for the recovering counselors, major changes in their lives!

References

American Psychiatric Association. (2013). *Diagnostic and statistical manual of mental disorders* (5th ed.). Arlington, VA: Author.

Cherniss, C. (1980). *Professional burnout in human service organization.* New York: Praeger Publishers.

Institute of Medicine. (1990). *Broadening the treatment for alcohol problems.* Washington, DC: National Academy Press.

Jellinek, E. M. (2012). *The disease concept of alcoholism.* New Brunswick, NJ: Hillhouse Press. (Original work published 1960)

Jung, J. (1994). *Under the influence: Alcohol and human behavior.* Pacific Grove, CA: Brooks/ Cole.

Kalb, M., & Propper, M. S. (1976). The future of alcohology: Craft or science? *American Journal of Psychiatry, 133,* 641–645.

Knauert, A., & Davidson, S. (1979). Maintaining the sanity of alcoholism counselors. *Family and Community Health,* 65–70.

Lewis, T. F. (2014). *Substance abuse and addiction treatment: Practical application of counseling theory.* Upper Saddle River, NJ: Pearson Education.

Marlatt, G. A. (1988). Matching clients to treatment: Treatment models and stages of change. In D. Donovan, & G. A. Marlatt (Eds.), *Assessment of addictive behaviors* (pp. 474–483). New York: Guilford Press.

Marlatt, G. A., & Witkiewitz, K. (2010). Update on harm-reduction policy and intervention research. *Annual Review of Clinical Psychology, 6,* 591–606.

Miller, W. R., Forcehimes, A. A., & Zweben, A. (2011). *Treating addiction: A guide for professionals.* New York: Guilford Press.

Miller, W. R., & Rollnick, S. (2013). *Motivational interviewing: Helping people change* (3rd ed.). New York: Guilford Press.

Oser, C. B., Biebel, E. P., Pullen, E., & Harp, K. L. H. (2013). Causes, consequences, and prevention of burnout among substance abuse treatment counselors: A rural versus urban comparison. *Journal of Psychoactive Drugs, 45*(1), 17–27.

Rivers, P. C., Sarata, P. B. V., & Book, T. (1974). The effect of an alcoholism workshop on attitudes, job satisfaction, and job performance of secretaries. *Quarterly Journal of Studies on Alcohol, 35,* 1832–1888.

Rosenberg, C. M. (Spring, 1974). The responsibility of direct treatment. *Alcohol, Health and Research World,* 3–5.

Sarata, P. B. V. (1979). Beginning employment as a child care worker: An examination of work experiences. *Child Care Quarterly, 8,* 295–302.

Sarata, P. B. V. (1982). *Burnout workshops for alcoholism counselors.* Unpublished paper. Lincoln: University of Nebraska. (A later edition of this paper, with the same title, is currently in press in *The Journal of Alcohol and Drug Education.*)

Schwartz, L. S., & Taylor, J. R. (1989). Attitudes of mental health professionals toward alcoholism recognition and treatment. *American Journal of Drug and Alcohol Abuse, 15,* 321–327.

Strausnner, S. L. A. (2014a). Assessment and treatment of clients with substance use disorders: An overview. In S. L. A. Straussner (Ed.), *Clinical work with substance-abusing clients* (pp. 3–38). New York: Guilford Press.

Strausnner, S. L. A. (2014b). Practice and policy issues: The changing landscape. In S. L. A. Straussner (Ed.), *Clinical work with substance-abusing clients* (pp. 539–542). New York: Guilford Press.

Wegscheider, S. (1981). *Hope and health for the alcoholic family.* Palo Alto, CA: Science & Behavior Books.

Witters, W., Venturelli, P., & Hanson, G. (1992). *Drugs and society* (3rd ed.). Boston: Jones & Bartlett.

Index

About the Authors

Gary W. Lawson, PhD, is a professor in the Department of Psychology and Family Studies at the United States International University in San Diego, California. He is a licensed psychologist in California, doing consulting and private practice. Dr. Lawson has 30 years' experience in the field of chemical dependency, including directing both inpatient and outpatient chemical dependency treatment programs. He has published numerous articles and presented related materials both nationally and internationally. His books include *Alcoholism and the Family: A Guide to Treatment and Prevention, Psychopharmacology for Nonmedical Psychotherapists, Alcoholism and Substance Abuse in Special Populations,* and *Adolescent Substance Abuse: Etiology, Treatment and Prevention.*

Ann W. Lawson, PhD, is a professor of marriage and family therapy in the United States International University in San Diego, California, and a licensed marriage and family therapist in private practice. She has worked in the addictions field for 23 years, including developing and directing the Children From Alcoholic Families Program at Lincoln-Lancaster Child Guidance Center in Lincoln, Nebraska. She was the clinical supervisor for an adolescent shelter in San Diego for 8 years. She has conducted national and international training, is a clinical member of the American Association of Marriage and Family Therapists, and is an approved supervisor. Her books include *Alcoholism and the Family: A Guide to Treatment and Prevention, Alcoholism and Substance Abuse in Special Populations, Adolescent Substance Abuse: Etiology, Treatment and Prevention,* and *Kids and Gangs and Essentials of Chemical Dependency Counseling* (2nd ed.).

Erik Schoen has been a professional counselor since receiving his master's degree in counseling from Arizona State University in 1993. He received the Carl Perkins National Advocacy award in 2008 from the American Counseling Association in recognition of his statewide leadership in establishing licensure for professional counselors in Nevada. Since 2009, Erik has been an instructor with the Center for the Application of Substance Abuse Technologies at the University of Nevada, Reno, where he received the "Senior Scholar Mentor" distinction for being chosen as the most influential faculty member for the top graduate from the largest college at the university. Mr. Schoen is currently the Deputy Director at Community Chest, where he has worked for over 18 years. In this capacity, Mr. Schoen works within communities to help develop positive, strengths-based, and collaborative approaches to addressing myriad issues that face communities so that all have what they need not only to survive but also to thrive.